Religion and Culture:
Essays in Honor of
Bernard Lonergan, S.J.

Bernard Lonergan, S.J.

Religion and Culture: Essays in Honor of Bernard Lonergan, S.J.

Edited by

Timothy P. Fallon, S.J.
Associate Professor of Philosophy
University of Santa Clara

and

Philip Boo Riley
Associate Professor of Religious Studies
University of Santa Clara

State University of New York Press   *Albany*

BL
65
C8
. R43
1987

Published by
State University of New York Press, Albany

© 1987 State University of New York

For information, address State University of New York
Press, State University Plaza, Albany, N.Y., 12246

Library of Congress Cataloging-in-Publication Data

Religion and culture.

   Papers from the International Lonergan Symposium on
Religion and Culture, held in March, 1984, at the
University of Santa Clara.
   Bibliography: p.
   Includes index.
   1. Religion and culture—Congresses. 2. Lonergan,
Bernard J. F.—Congresses. I. Lonergan, Bernard J. F.
II. Fallon, Timothy P., 1922-   . III. Riley, Philip
Boo, 1951-   . IV. International Lonergan Symposium on
Religion and Culture (1984: University of Santa Clara)
BL65.C8R43 1987   291.1'7.   86-30153
ISBN 0-88706-289-X

Contents

Orientations in the Human Sciences

Orientations in Economics

Foreword

Through four days in March of 1984 over one-hundred scholars from around the world gathered on the campus of the University of Santa Clara. The occasion was a symposium on the theme of Religion and Culture in honor of Bernard Lonergan, S.J. Discussions ranged over a number of topics and questions in each of four areas: Philosophy, Theology and Religious Studies, Human Sciences, and Economics. Comprised of papers by many of the symposium participants, the present volume represents both the fruit of those discussions and an effort to carry their spirit and goals forward. By way of an introduction we would like to convey something of the background and purpose of the symposium.

Bernard Lonergan, S.J. died on November 26, 1984, three weeks before his eightieth birthday. With the passing of one of our century's more distinguished contributors to philosophy and theology, the question of his intentions and significance arises anew. A helpful starting point for this assessment may be to distinguish what David Tracy documented as the "achievement" of Bernard Lonergan from what Frederick E. Crowe has described as the "enterprise" Bernard Lonergan initiated.[1] The former, surely, constitutes no small feat. Through his lectures, courses, papers, and books like *Insight* and *Method in Theology*, Lonergan's influence has been monumental and far-reaching. This achievement surely is worthy of celebration and study, as the pages of this volume illustrate. But a key to that achievement is the way it points beyond itself to a more significant future endeavor. For—to paraphrase his own description in *Method in Theology*—Lonergan's work consists not in a set of unrevisable static principles to be blindly followed and applied; rather, it consists in the call to a creative framework for collaboration among an intelligent, responsible and honest community of inquirers. It is this dimension of the enterprise that our symposium built on and sought to promote; and it is this legacy of Lonergan that we intend these pages to celebrate and study.

Lonergan has clearly made original and significant contributions to the established disciplines of philosophy and theology. But throughout he has stressed that his primary intention was neither philosophical nor theological nor, more recently, economic, but *methodological;* that his contribution lay less in particular areas of those disciplines than in radical methodological proposals cutting across and expanding the boundaries of many disciplines. The implementation of this method requires not only the self-appropriation essayed in Lonergan's work but also familiarity with the questions, techniques, and data of many specialized fields. The implemention requires, furthermore, not a solitary individual working in a single area on one project, but the ongoing and dialectical cooperation of many individuals involved in different fields, diverse projects, and various types and stages of work. The collaboration evidenced in the symposium and the papers collected in this volume, then, should serve to provide some indications for present and future communities of the scope and significance of Lonergan's proposals.

The theme contained in our title, Religion and Culture, suggested itself on two accounts. First, it best captures the intent and many facets of Lonergan's work over the years. The context for his efforts was the epochal shift from the normative universality of classical culture to the rootlessness of modern historical-mindedness. For him philosophy's role as a critic of cultural ideals and assumptions complemented that of theology as the mediator of religion in a culture. His work in both disciplines gave new meaning and life to the traditional maxim, *vetera novis augere et perficere,* to enlarge and enrich the old with the new.[2] As his labors testify, such transposition is no easy task, requiring a mind and vision "... big enough to be at home in both the old and the new, painstaking enough to work out one by one the transitions to be made, strong enough to refuse half-measures and insist on complete solutions even though it has to wait."[3]

Second, Lonergan's preoccupation with the relation of religion to culture places his work at the heart of modernity. Religion's encounter with modern culture has been a complicated and somewhat difficult course. Far from being immune, religious traditions have been dramatically beset by the myriad changes in human and cultural self-understanding over the past 300 years. How best preserve the inherited wisdom and values of these traditions in the context of a complex and varied civilization? Can their visions and insights withstand the relativizing and secularizing force of modern society? Can religion again be seen to contribute to cultural healing and progress so crucial in a conflict-ridden world? In ways that complement and extend the insights of the many modern thinkers he cited in his later works—Kierkegaard, Blondel, Dilthey, Nietzsche, Voegelin, Newman, and others—Lonergan began the formation of a new foundation, a new mediation of meaning and value, on which to address such questions. In ways not unlike Aquinas's efforts in the thirteenth century, Lonergan articulated and responded to the twentieth century mandate that modern culture, "... in many ways more stupendous than any that ever existed. ..., be known, assimilated, transformed."[4] His contribution was to propose a profound reorientation and renewal of the basic notions and ideals operative in the scientific, humanist and social-scientific methods of inquiry. As the papers in this volume illustrate, it is this proposal that allows the study of religion, joined through inter-disciplinary collaboration with philosophy, the human sciences, and economics, to take a decisive and transformative role in the life of a culture caught in the throes of change.

The essays presented here, then, are united by both a common spirit and theme. But uniform they are not. Each of the volume's four parts addresses the relation of religion to culture in light of a distinct discipline. The majority of our contributions are in the more traditional disciplines of philosophy and theology. But there the reader will find diversity and innovation: Lonergan's work is related to various other philosophic traditions (for example, the two quite different papers relating to Process thought) and the questions are many: soteriology, rhetoric, history, truth, pluralism, scripture, etc. Together these first two parts indicate the extent and complexity of the challenge the shift from a classical to a thoroughly historically-minded control of meaning poses to contemporary philosophers and theologians. The human sciences section was built around the issue of normativity, in something of the spirit of Lonergan's statement regarding their role in cultural progress: ''. . .human science cannot be merely empirical; it has to be critical; to reach a critical standpoint, it has to be normative. This is a tall order for human science as hitherto it has existed.''[5] Issues discussed in this section include values, affectivity, and war and peace in the nuclear age. The last part of the volume is designed to investigate—via comparison, contrast, exposition, and development—a facet of Lonergan's work that is only lately receiving sustained attention, economics. The papers identify the distinctiveness of Lonergan's approach—e.g. his demand for explanatory method—as well as the significance of this concern with economics for assessing his overall project.

As they served to set the tone for the symposium, the three keynote addresses have been placed in a separate section at the begining of our volume. Frederick E. Crowe, S.J. provides an account of ''what needs to be done'' from the perspective of one well-versed in the intricacies and subtleties of Lonergan's thought. Professor Stephen Toulmin relates and compares Lonergan's reflections on the problems of pluralism and relativism to parallel efforts in the fields of Jurisprudence, Jewish Studies, and Philosophy of Science. And William Johnston, S.J. draws on his studies in comparative mysticism to show ways in which Lonergan's transcendental method provides a basis for a renewed and contemporary mystical theology.

A project that took over three years involves indebtedness to a great number of individuals, groups and institutions. We would like to here extend our gratitude to all of them, mentioning only the few names that space allows. Frederick Crowe, S.J. should be credited not only for prompting the original ''bright idea'' of the symposium but also for his assistance in the planning and funding stages of our work; he has been a capable advisor and patient friend. A number of individuals in the ''Lonergan Enterprise'' deserve special mention: Fred and Sue Lawrence for their help through the Lonergan Workshop; Dave Oyler, Mike Rende, and Paul Marcoux for their energetic contribution to the initial plans; Joe Flanagan, S.J., Sean McEvenue, Bill Matthews, S.J., and Michael O'Callaghan for helping to develop and lead our four symposium panels; Terry Tekippe for assisting us through the *Lonergan Studies Newsletter,* and Mark Morelli and Tom McPartland for their considerable donations of insight, labor, and encouragement from start to finish. The University of Santa Clara was a gracious and capable host, especially through the help we received from the Philosophy and Religious Studies Departments and their respective secretaries, Sheila Speciale and Ethel Johnston; they gave long hours with considerable skill and understanding. Our manuscripts were most capably typed and revised by Mary Hull and Cindy LeFevre, whose patient work was most appreciated. The myriad details of the symposium were ably handled by an energetic group of volunteers: Dennis Roselli (who generously gave us much of a sabbatical), Louise Dillon, Art and Lorraine Bennet, Kevin St. George, Dan Rivers, Maurus Straumanis, and Megan Mulvehill. Finally, we acknowledge the generous financial support of the following: the Lonergan Trust Fund; the Method Institute sustained by the Jesuits of Upper Canada; the Loyola Jesuits (Montreal) University Fund; the Bannan Foundation, Jesuit Community, and Rev. William Rewak, S.J.'s President's Fund at the University of Santa Clara; Mr. James McGuire and Mr. Guy Giuffre; and the National Endowment for the Humanities. For both the funding they provided and their commitment to the merits of our endeavor, we are most grateful.

Philip Boo Riley

Timothy P. Fallon, S.J.

Summer, 1985

NOTES

1   David Tracy, *The Achievement of Bernard Lonergan* (New York: Herder and Herder, 1970) and Frederick E. Crowe, S.J., *The Lonergan Enterprise* (Cambridge: Cowley Publications, 1980).

2   Bernard Lonergan, S.J., *Insight: A Study of Human Understanding* (New York: Philosophical Library, 1958) p. 747.

3   Bernard Lonergan, S.J., "Dimensions of Meaning" in *Collection: Papers by Bernard Lonergan, S.J.,* ed. by F.E. Crowe, S.J. (Montreal: Palm Publishers, 1967), p. 267.

4   Bernard Lonergan, S.J., "Belief: Today's Issue" in *A Second Collection: Papers by Bernard Lonergan, S.J.,* ed. by W. Ryan, S.J. and B. Tyrrell, S.J. (London: Darton, Longman and Todd, 1974), p. 99.

5   *Insight,* p. 236.

Keynote Addresses

I

The Task of Interpreting Lonergan: A Preliminary to the Symposium

FREDERICK E. CROWE, S.J.

I am grateful for the privilege of introducing this symposium, so generously organized by the University of Santa Clara, on the significance for religion and culture of the work of Bernard Lonergan. With all of you here, I recognize the seminal promise and potential of that work, I am aware of the problems that crowd the field of religion and culture, and I hope for a creative discussion among us that will bring the power of the ideas to bear on the obstinacy of the problems. Such creative thinking is not only the permanent ulterior motive we all have for the study of Bernard Lonergan; it is also the best way by far to fulfill our immediate objective, to honor, in this his eightieth year, a teacher and friend who has labored unremittingly in the field of religion and culture, who early in life committed his whole talent and energy to the problems they raise, but has worked always on the most remote and fundamental level, and has thereby laid on us the responsibility of developing and implementing his ideas.

With that introductory platitude—for platitude it is, even though I utter it with all sincerity—I get down to business with a thesis that on first hearing will sound simply subversive. The thesis is: we are not yet ready to begin this symposium. We are not yet ready, because the long and difficult preliminary task is still unfinished, the task of interpreting Lonergan. Let me explain. The symposium would study the significance of certain ideas for certain contemporary problems. It would engage in what *Method in Theology* calls second-phase theology and what we by extension can call the second phase in general of methodical specialization. Such a purpose may be included by some thinkers

3

under a broader view of interpretation that would include application, but in my stricter use of the term, interpretation belongs to the first phase as one of its four functional specialties.[1] Its specific aim then is understanding. My thesis says we do not yet understand Lonergan, and so we are not yet ready for the work of application that the symposium proposes to undertake. My basic thesis could be divided, if you wish, into two parts: I personally do not understand him after thirty-seven years of study, and I have not found anyone who so excels in understanding him as to claim my discipleship.

The conclusion is not, however, that we should all go home and study Lonergan for another thirty-seven years, and then come together again to resume our interrupted discussion. Quite the contrary. The fact is, we never will be ready for such a symposium as this till we have held a score of them. It is the nature of seminal thinking to become clarified only in the harvest, and the harvest will raise as many questions as it solves. The process, then, is a to and fro movement in which we bring our limited understanding to bear on a problem area, discover in that effort our need for a deeper understanding, return with more specific questions to our seminal source, and so advance through lesser and lesser measures of failure to greater and greater measures of success. My conclusion, therefore, is that, because we are not yet ready for this symposium, we are obliged to hold it.

My own task in this introductory talk may be seen as the "to" in the "to and fro" swing of the pendulum of interpretation and application: that is, back to Lonergan for an interpretation that may orient us a little better in the work of application, and then forward in the discussions of the next three days of the symposium. But within the task I set for myself, there is a secondary to and fro movement, the familiar hermeneutic circle:

> The meaning of a text . . . is a unity that is unfolded through parts. . . . We can grasp the unity, the whole, only through the parts. At the same time the parts are determined in their meaning by the whole which each part partially reveals.[2]

The parts in question are, of course, an uncountable multitude, the several million words of Lonergan's lifetime production. Yet I propose to deal with them, as well as with the unity, at least to the extent of underlining the need we have for ongoing research into the details, in all their uncountable multitude, of Lonergan's thinking. Veterans in this field, I suspect, will await with more interest my treatment of the unity, to see whether I have anything helpful to contribute under that heading; may I say, without offense, that it is to them especially that I direct the first part of my talk; they are the very ones who need to return over and over to detailed study of their one-time teacher.

I

I am to talk, then, of the details, without understanding of which we will never fully understand the unity. I am limited to samples only, and I will take three: one from non-academic life, one that regards the sources of Lonergan's thinking, and one from the rich history of his own ideas. I deliberately choose three areas that are quite disparate; that very disparity will help the samples to function better as samples.

My sample from non-academic life has to do with music, and I introduce it with a minor bit of history. A few years ago, I was attending a congress in which discussion of Lonergan's ideas played some part, and a critic, not really an unfriendly one, told me, more or less in these words: The trouble with Lonergan is that he never listened to music; if he had done so, he would have written far better theology. The remark left me speechless—almost. We have recent documenting of Lonergan's boyhood love of music, but even years ago the general lines were familiar to anyone who knew him at all. We know, for example, that during his first Toronto period, a friend gave him season tickets to the Toronto Symphony Orchestra's performances, that he went year after year to hear them, that in fact he attributed to this musical experience the capacity to undertake and complete the labor of writing *Insight*. When his health deteriorated last year, and I had the job of packing and storing his possessions, I discovered on his desk a neatly typed set of cards listing his collection of music-recordings—there was no list of his books—and a set covering several years of the music magazine, *Ovation*. I will return in a moment to the intrinsic bearing all this may have on his thinking and theology; it is enough now to say that, if we base our interpretation of Lonergan on his supposed ignorance of music, we are moving about as directly as we can from the true course.[3]

My next sample is quite different. Last year I was browsing in the Regis College copy of Husserl's *Ideas: General Introduction to Pure Phenomenology* and discovered there a piece of paper, a mere scrap, with scribbling that is quite unmistakably Lonergan's and comments on Husserl that are quite distinctively Lonerganian. I would tentatively date this scrap and this scribbling in the period 1947-1953, but I do not recall a single reference to this particular work of Husserl's in any of Lonergan's writings or lectures. Now what is the point of this second bit of history, or non-history? The point is that we deceive ourselves if we think we have easy access to Lonergan's reading and all the ideas that went into the hopper of his thinking; even those interviews in which he was extensively questioned under this very heading, give us mere glimpses of his reading background. We have hardly begun even to list his sources, much less to evaluate their role in his formation.[4]

My third sample is the curious history in Lonergan of the notion of wisdom. During the years of his research into St. Thomas, wisdom was a fundamental intellectual virtue, the dominant one in the hierarchic trio that began with understanding, developed into science, and culminated in wisdom. It underwent some evolution at the time of *Insight*, but continued to play a major role well into the Roman period of 1953-65. Then, very suddenly, it drops out of the foreground and almost out of the picture.[5] Is this not a matter for curiosity, calling for research and interpretation? And might we not expect study of this detail to give us new insight into the ideas of the *Method* period from 1965 on?

I have given three samples of the need for ongoing research in our preliminary task of interpreting Lonergan. In a sense they are mere samples, that is, they stand for the three hundred, or the three thousand, points of detail that call for study. But my own view is that, in such a comprehensive and systematic thinker as Lonergan is, no sample is likely to be merely a sample. Nor are they mere straws in the wind, indicating a trend whose source and power must be investigated elsewhere. Each sample has its significance for the whole picture. Take, for instance, the case of music. Lonergan once drew an extended analogy between human consciousness and "a concerto that blends many themes in endless ways."[6] Now this is remarkably similar to what he found in the *Contra Gentiles* of St. Thomas: "the same arguments recurring over and over in ever slightly different forms . . . the differentiation of operations and their conjunction in ever fresh combinations."[7] It is remarkably similar to what we may find in Lonergan himself. Did his love of music perhaps affect his thinking in a more intrinsic way than we have yet realized? Or take Lonergan's relation to Husserl. The latter does not figure prominently in *Insight*, but some twenty years later Lonergan distinguished three meanings of the term, transcendental: the Scholastic, the Kantian, and one (obviously Lonergan's own) deriving from Husserl's intentionality analysis, in which *noêsis* and *noêma* are correlative.[8] If we recall how pervasive that pair of correlatives is in *Insight*, we might find this detail quite illuminating. My third sample was the role of wisdom in Lonergan's early "system" and its strange disappearance later. We know that his notion of theology went through a profound transformation around 1965, and that one factor in this complex question was the displacement of intellectual habits in the individual thinker by the new role given the community of collaborating specialists. Are these two bits of history not related, and must we not think of wisdom as resident now in the community, with dialectic as its guide and interdisciplinary collaboration as its expression?

I have been dealing with matters of detail, and have stated my view of their importance for the task of interpreting Lonergan. You may not agree with that view. But you cannot ignore the fact that on what is not a matter of detail, on what is so central a concern as transcendental method itself, there are diametrically opposed opinions in the interpretation of what Lonergan says, and this among those who have been long-time students of his thought. You may think, of course, that the remedy lies in dialectic and so take flight at once to that level, arguing that what one or the other side needs is a profound horizon change. And you may be right; no one regrets more than I do our failure to engage in real dialectic, as that term is understood in Chapter 10 of *Method*. But I have a more modest proposal for a starting point. I remind you of a simple statement: "Not all opposition is dialectical. There are differences that will be eliminated by uncovering fresh data."[9] My starting point, then, would be to collect, in extensive and thorough research, what Lonergan has said on the matter; I wonder how many differences would be eliminated by this simple procedure on the very first level of functional specialization.[10] In any case I am convinced, and that is the gist of this first section, that in the task of interpreting Lonergan far more attention must be paid to simple research.

II

We must understand the parts in order to understand the unitary whole, but the meaning of the parts is determined by the meaning of the whole. So we come to an overall interpretation of Lonergan, a unitary view of what he has done with his life and expressed in his work in academe. The various influences, ideas, bits of personal history—the three hundred or three thousand items that cannot even be listed here—they must yield now to some comprehensive pattern, some general view, some total framework. Since Lonergan himself, so far as I know, has never given more than stray hints for constructing such a totality, we have to supply our own, and so I am going to offer you mine.

We need, of course, some means of comprehensive classification, some device, be it only a set of pegs on which to hang our ideas. When Lonergan had set forth his eight functional specialties, to take us beyond field and subject specialization, he proceeded to demonstrate their unity. Something analogous might very well be possible here, but I have a simpler suggestion: a simple set of pegs provided by a simple logical device. I'm sure Father Lonergan would bristle, were he present to hear me invoking logic, as it may seem, to explain his life and work, just as I suspect he was not altogether happy five years ago with my comparison of his work with the Aristotelian *organon* and the *novum organum* of Bacon.[11] You too may be apprehensive. But, audience, be not affrighted; I use logic only as an external device to classify my findings, not as a principle to derive sterile conclusions from unverified premises.

My logical device is an imitation of the Porphyrean tree.[12] I will divide Lonergan according to an existential and cognitive duality. I will divide the latter aspect into learning and teaching phases, a *discens* Lonergan and a *docens*. I will subdivide the teaching phase according to work that is realized and work that is only programmatic. I will subdivide the programmatic into the structural and the historical. And lastly I will divide the historical into the two ways of achievement and heritage. The divisions are imperfect, overlapping one another. The dividing principle may be hazy. So I add my own transcendental precept to the four you know so well: besides being attentive, intelligent, reasonable and responsible, be patient too.

My first division corresponds to the familiar distinction between the fourth level of consciousness and the third. But while the third is readily understood as the cognitive, it is not so easy to find a single label for the fourth. This is the level of conscience, of responsibility, of decision, of action. It is also the level on which we decide not only what to do with the next moment but what to do with our very lives, so maybe "existential" will best serve to characterize this aspect of the whole Lonergan.

It seems important for at least two reasons to put this matter up front in our study. There is an intrinsic reason. For the fourth level is that of the grounding horizon whence are determined the meanings of all our statements, the values of all our choices, the purposes of all our actions. To miss this orienting factor is to overlook what is most fundamental and thereby to distort the whole picture. There is more: fourth-level activity is not just a bringing forth of an external product, be it ever so sublime; more importantly, it is a bringing forth of oneself. It is not only a making but a doing, not only a *poiêsis* but a *praxis*, by which doing and *praxis* we make ourselves what we are to be, and thereby—since no one is an island—contribute most significantly to the universe.

My second reason is more extrinsic to the logic of my presentation: it regards the complaint that Lonergan lacks concern for common people, does not involve himself in the effort to better their conditions of life. It seems an easy way for his critics to gain an advantage, for one has only to read him to discover how difficult and demanding his thought is. Then the argument is clear: he is an intellectual, therefore he is cerebral, therefore he lacks existential involvement. *Ecco*, a sorites of sorts, very satisfying if you don't much care about either *consequens* or *consequentia*.

We have here a question of fact, to which the simple but extensive answer would be a biography; I have not the space for that now. In any case, I suspect that the chief difficulty is one of principle. Those with an activist bent simply cannot see how there can be a "preferential option for the poor," in such a lifework as that to which Lonergan dedicated himself for half a century in unremitting labor. The question of principle is one, then, of understanding, and dealing directly with it requires a Socratic art that will vary from instance to instance. But there is an indirect way that has a common appeal and is recommended by the highest authority: the way of the parable.

My parable, which I have used elsewhere for the same purpose, is of two people who went out to a third-world country to work for the poor. One went at once into the streets of a large city to search out the hungry, the sick, the homeless, and respond to the need by providing food and building hospitals and shelters; relief then was immediate and the benefits reached hundreds or thousands according to the resources at hand. The other had studied the agronomy and economy of the country, knew that the land could produce twice what it currently yielded and that better methods of distribution could bring food to millions not then being fed, so responded to the need by setting up schools for young workers on the land and forming cooperatives for a more efficient economy; benefits then were not immediate but there was a well-founded hope that in the long run the effect might be felt not just by thousands of the hungry but by millions.

Which of these two showed the greater concern for the poor? We recognize at once that the question itself is faulty. There is a valid comparison, but not in terms of greater or less concern—rather in terms of ways and means, and indeed ways and means that are complementary to, not exclusive of, one another. Not then either/or, but both/and. For in fact both people in our parable were concerned, and deeply concerned, for the poor, but they had different vocations to respond in different ways, both ways good, both ways necessary. This, I submit, is the kind of understanding we must bring to Lonergan's vocation, and I allow myself one additional note in explanation. Namely, the more fundamental the level on which we approach a problem, the less relevant is our contribution going to seem to the casual eye, but the more widespread and efficacious is the real impact going to be in the long run. Lonergan's cognitional theory, epistemology, metaphysics, transcendental method are fundamental indeed; they belong to the first moment in the rhythm of a massive withdrawal and return, but we must not expect the return to take place overnight.

Let us turn to the cognitive half of our first division. The subdivision here corresponds to the familiar two phases of theology: receiving and handing on. "If one assimilates tradition, one learns that one should pass it on. If one encounters the past, one also has to take one's stand toward the future."[13] It corresponds also to an old pair familiar from our catechetics: the *Ecclesia discens* and *docens*, the learning and the teaching church. But that latter pair has come into some disfavor in our time, so I should explain my use of it here. There is nothing wrong, there never has been anything wrong, it seems to me, with the *discens-docens* pair as functions in the church. The trouble occurs when we apply them, not to different functions but to different people, when we divide the people of God into two camps, and call one the learning church and the other the teaching church. If, however, we understand the pair to refer primarily to functions, we will understand also that the whole church is a learning church and the whole church is in some sense a teaching church. Then, secondarily, we may ordain, empower, delegate, certain members of the church to speak for the whole; but on that secondary level the concept gives much less trouble.

In any case, to return to my topic, the learning I have in mind is not the learning of church doctrine. Since the days of Henry Denzinger we have had easy access to what the church teaches. What I have in mind is what the world teaches. Not the world simply in the scriptural sense of the enemy or even in the likewise scriptural sense of the world to be saved, though we may include both, but the world in its great enterprise of becoming human, the world in the sense of restless humanity seething with ideas and causes, advancing with incredible energy in arts and technology, developing scholarship and science, philosophies and cultures, with attention, intelligence, reasonableness, and responsibility, and just as often going astray through inattentive, obtuse, unreasonable and irresponsible conduct. It is a world from whose progress we must learn, as well as a world we must teach and redeem in its decline, but my topic now is learning, and I submit that seven centuries ago, in the person at least of Thomas Aquinas, the church ran neck and neck with the world in the vanguard of progress, of modernity, of the level of the times. I further submit that for a hundred years now we have been waking up as a church—waking up reluctantly, like Augustine's sluggish sleeper—waking up to find ourselves seven centuries behind the world, "in the unenviable position," to change the metaphor, "of always arriving on the scene a little breathlessly and a little late."[14]

I have said that the whole church is a learning church and so the whole church must wake up and rise to the level of the times. Still, some areas and some members seem to do so faster than others—here is a context where people, and not just functions, are divided—so we have to ask what particular significance Lonergan's work of self-education has for the church's *aggiornamento*. Possibly he has worked in some especially backward areas; possibly he has had considerable influence on others, dragging them kicking and struggling into the twentieth century. But such matters are not of world-historical significance. A full study of this question is needed, but meanwhile I would locate his importance for the church's *aggiornamento* in the comprehensive view he has attained of modernity. We may recall his keen analyses of modern scholarship, modern science, and modern philosophy, all to be laid "under tribute" to a renewed theology.[15] We are all familiar with his campaign to liberate us from a classicist world view into historical mindedness.[16] Some of us will remember his summation of five areas of modern influence on theology: "history, philosophy, religious studies, method, and communications."[17] We have read his extended study of history (the history that happens) in Chapter VII of *Insight,* and pondered his briefer but profound analysis of that history into its three moments of progress, decline, and redemption.[18] On the basis of these hints, perhaps I may say of him, due proportion being maintained, what he said of St. Thomas: "Even in this brief and rough delineation, one can perceive the magnificent sweep of genius."[19]

You realize, of course, that without giving notice of the move, I have already taken us over to the other half of our present division. Our Lonergan *discens* is already, through the power of his reflections on modernity, through the scope, the depth, the comprehensiveness of his analyses, already a Lonergan *docens*. So let us turn openly to that other half, which was subdivided, you remember, into the realized and the programmatic. Metaphorically, it is the difference between pointing the way and taking the road. More literally, it is the difference between an elaborated theology, philosophy, scholarship, science, the difference between all this on one side, and on the other the instrument of mind and heart, the organon of the incarnate subject, that he has created for our use.

It seems more natural to begin with the former, the realized work, for surely the programmatic is based on the realized as method follows achievement or procedural rules follow procedures in use. The matter, however, is not so simple. True, we have the monumental *Insight* for a sketch of a philosophy, while in theology we have some quite elaborate work on divine grace, the incarnate Word, and the Trinity, not to mention recent assaults on the economics establishment. But the philosophy has to be enlarged and completed by the work of the later Lonergan. As for his theology, we still need more study of the relation between his method and his material theology. The material theology was certainly the arena in which he worked out his method. But the method reached its term in a kind of quantum leap, and we still have to ask how a return to the theology would affect those early treatises, and what new form they would take in that total restructuring of theology his method calls for.[20]

Nevertheless, we have a number of hints and some fairly firm guidelines for that renewed theology (I will not venture to speak for the philosophy and economics). For divine grace, *Method* itself indicates the way the new theology would be structured.[21] For Christology we have such papers as "Christology Today: Methodological Reflections,"[22] too cryptic, it seems, to have received much attention from other theologians, but by the same token—in my view at least—as rich in promise as anything we have since *Method*. For the Trinity, there are scattered clues in the discussions of various workshops, with some published indications as well. And we have even a new and very important area of theology in the inner and outer word of *Method*, and the relation of this pair to the missions of Son and Spirit.[23]

That reference reminds us, of course, that we are not dealing merely with the material content of these various treatises. There are more general and formal elements which are not so likely to be affected by the quantum leap of method, elements indeed which helped greatly to ground and structure that method. I think of the place of truth in the many glories of the word of God, the notion of truth as meaning rather than formula, the transposition of meaning from context to context, the specification of contexts by differentiations of consciousness rather than by objective systems, the complementing of all this with the inner word and the eye of love, and the whole pouring into method and the functional specialties of theology. It is here, I think, that the realized work of Lonergan will have its most enduring impact. But content and program overlap in what I have been saying, and once again the first half of our division has led us inexorably into the other half—a witness to the intricate unity of the whole Lonergan we are trying to study.

So we come to the programmatic side of Lonergan's work. It was the focus of his thinking for most of his life. It is symbolized, though not exhausted, by his *Method in Theology*. It is the best known, the most distinctive, and probably the most important feature of his work. It deserves more of our time than the few minutes I can give it this evening, but some years ago I had the opportunity to devote three whole lectures to setting it forth, so I am able to refer you for a fuller account to those St. Michael's Lectures.[24] For a one-line statement I can do no better than quote Francis Bacon, whose stated purpose it was "to commence a total reconstruction of sciences, arts, and all human knowledge, raised upon the proper foundations."[25] Bacon proposed a *novum organum*, understood as replacing the Aristotelian *organon*, and I think we may call Lonergan's contribution an *organum novissimum*. I am not suggesting now, nor did I suggest it five years ago, that Bacon's plan for a *"Magna Instauratio"* of knowledge came anywhere near Lonergan's, but he did conceive with great clarity the difference between creating an instrument of mind and reconstructing on proper foundations the whole of human knowledge, and I find that illuminating for what Lonergan has been about. His precise focus may seem to limit the field, as when he speaks of "a total transformation of dogmatic theology,"[26] or again of "a complete restructuring of Catholic theology,"[27] but, if we remove the lens that served to focus his thought, we would find his instrument of mind broaden out to become a general instrument of mind and heart, of the incarnate subject; and his functional specialties would become, in his own words, "relevant to any human studies that investigated a cultural past to guide its future."[28] Such, in brief, is the programmatic side of Lonergan's work. It is programmatic, but it does not include a program. The creation of an organon does not by itself constitute a detailed plan for the new theology, the new philosophy, the new sciences and human studies. But it is a first great step; indeed, a giant step for mankind. In such matters we must say with Browning, "a man's reach should exceed his grasp."

I have been speaking in general, and all too briefly, of the programmatic work of Lonergan, but there is some compensation for the brevity in our present section. For we have now to make a further division, and can continue the same topic under two subheadings. I therefore divide the programmatic into a structural aspect and an historical, not wholly happy with those two terms, but not having a better pair at hand. By the structural I mean the invariant features of human consciousness, the levels, the framework. By the historical I mean what happens on the four levels, the various ways of filling in the framework, the differentiations of pattern and the forms of conversion that consciousness undergoes as it follows its historical course of progress, decline, redemption.

The structural is by far the more familiar aspect of consciousness for students of Lonergan, so much so that the pervasive but often unthematized historical treatment is regularly overlooked. That is perhaps inevitable, given that Lonergan himself focused for years on the structural levels and struggled unremittingly to distinguish and relate and exploit them.[29] There is no need then to linger on this half of the dichotomy; it is enough to say that the structural is utterly fundamental, for in all we do we exercise our experience, understanding, reflection, and responsibility, and that it is in the highest degree relevant to the programmatic, for it issues in the transcendental precepts that govern all human activity: be attentive, be intelligent, be reasonable, be responsible.[30]

Let us turn to the historical. I am referring here to the history that happens, as opposed to the history that records the happenings. I am not, however, referring to objective events in the sweep of history from Adam and Eve to the Apocalypse, but to what happens in human consciousness. It is of great importance, for a grasp of Lonergan, to conceive this historical aspect in its full generality and set it off against the structural, but all I can do here is list some of the headings. First, then, there are the patterns of experience that later became the differentiations of consciousness: the differentiations that make some of us artists, others mathematicians, still others philosophers or theologians, while we all remain subject to the transcendental precepts. Derivatively, there are the realms of meaning that correspond to the differentiations. Secondly, there are the stages of meaning, which we can relate by a political analogy to the realms: the historically evolving nations of England, France, and Germany would correspond somewhat to the realms of meaning, while the various measures of democracy achieved in those nations at any given time would have some analogy to the stages of meaning. Thirdly, there are the various conversions that, through their presence or absence in different combinations, differentiate us radically from one another, and indeed differentiate my former self from the person I now fancy myself to be or hope to become.[31]

Now this historical side of consciousness is subject in its own way to law and order. For example, insofar as the stages of meaning follow something like law we have Lonergan's three plateaus for the classification of meaningful activity: the practical concerned with doing, the logical concerned with speaking, and the interiorly based and methodical, concerned with understanding.[32] We can go even further. The law discernible in historically developing consciousness grounds specific precepts of method as well as classifications. If you go back to *Insight* and examine Chapter III, "The Canons of Empirical Method," from the present viewpoint, you will make a most interesting discovery: the first, third, and fourth canons correspond closely to the levels of experience, understanding, and judgment, and so relate directly to the structural. But the second and fifth canons relate directly to the historical side of consciousness. That is, the canon of operations, the second in Lonergan's list, has to do with the accumulation of insights, or the ongoing history of one's development; and the canon of complete explanation, the fifth in the list, has to do with perseverance toward the goal of empirical method, and not accepting to explain some data while excluding part of what is empirically given.[33]

We need one more division to complete our set: the historical side of consciousness is to be divided into two ways that we may call the way of achievement and the way of heritage. They refer to the opposite directions development may take within the framework of the structural levels. There is the development that Lonergan sees as moving from below upward, from experience, through understanding and judgment, to the formation of values—the way I label achievement. And there is development, he argues, from above downward, from values and beliefs received in trust, through critical understanding of the tradition, to more perceptive experience—the way I call that of heritage.[34] This very fundamental division, I would say, was one of the last of his great general ideas before he turned, in the final years of his active life, to the specific field of economics, and it remains, a decade later, largely unexploited. You have noticed, no doubt, that it has a link with an earlier pair in our study: the learning-teaching, the *discens-docens* division. Only now, instead of using these ideas to guide our analysis of Lonergan's life and work, we turn them on ourselves and use them to chart our own course, whether in the great plan of a life and career, or in the particular little detail of this weekend symposium.

III

My topic has been the task of interpreting Lonergan. I have gone round the hermeneutic circle from parts to whole, and will presently point to the follow-up from whole to parts. The parts, one grants, are an unmanageable multitude, but I hope my three sample details have at least shown the need for patient attention to the multitude, one by one, in ongoing research. The major difficulty is in achieving a total view, but some such view we must sooner or later adopt. We need it to research Lonergan's work as well as to interpret it; we need it to locate him in history as well as to allow him to challenge us personally. We need it too in the second-phase work of a personal stand—whatever our attitude, be it the negative one of opposing this nonsense and putting an end to this cult of method, or (an attitude some of us find more intelligent and reasonable, not to say responsible) the positive one of expanding and carrying forward his ideas, and applying his method to the problems that beset the church on every side. So I have given you my sketch of a total view. With some such sketch of the whole one can assign the intelligibility of the parts and eliminate the misunderstanding that inevitably results from their omission or from confusing them.

One cannot insist too strongly on the importance for correct interpretation of that follow-up from whole to parts, but I can only point, and then only negatively, to the follow-up as it might regard each of the six divisions of my second section. In general, then, to overlook the existential element is to miss what has been determining for Lonergan through half a century of dedication to a distinctly conceived purpose, and thus to misread all the work of those years. The field marshal surveying an old-style battle and the recluse in an ivory tower are both high above the hurly-burly, but there is all the difference between them of involvement and non-involvement. Again, to overlook his massive engagement with modernity, with the learning process that brings one to the level of the times, is inevitably to see him as unduly concerned with documents from the past, indeed the distant past, to the neglect of present experience. In fact, that massive involvement *is* concern with present experience; only it is concern with its fundamental features, rather than with the latest Gallup poll or charismatic congress. Again, to overlook his forty-year immersion in the deepest theological problems, is inevitably to see him as working out his method in a totally *a priori* manner, decreeing from some abstract command post what theologians must do when they engage in theology. In fact, from his doctoral dissertation to his last pre-*Method* lectures of 1965—I do not recall a single exception to this—he was wrestling at one and the same time with current questions of theology and with a method that might handle them more effectively. Fourthly, to overlook the programmatic character of his work, is inevitably to find him inarticulate, when we want answers, and already out-of-date on the contemporary scene; whereas, to discover his distinctive *apport,* the cutting edge of method, might alert us to the possibility that he is a generation ahead of his time, and for that reason incomprehensible to his contemporaries. Fifthly, to attend only to the structural side of consciousness and overlook the historical would be to find the programmatic devoid of the richness of life, even rigid and confining, despite its dynamism. But the historical restores the immense variety, the enormous wealth and versatility, the unlimited range of incarnate spirit. Finally, to overlook the two ways of human development is to come to confused conclusions, with regard to the church in general and Lonergan in particular, on such stock dichotomies as those labeled the liberal-conservative and the community-individual. In fact, this pair of concepts (the two ways) enables us to see liberal and conservative, not as epithets to divide people but as functions to control heritage and achievement. Similarly, we will see the way of achievement as appealing to the individual dynamism of human consciousness, but in a community setting; and we will see the way of heritage as appealing to the community setting of love and trust, for the benefit of the individual person and individual achievement.

* * * * * *

When Lonergan wrote *Insight* he subtitled it *A Study of Human Understanding.* It turned out that a good part of the philosophical world was not ready to acknowledge even the existence of a distinct activity of consciousness to be named understanding. But as long as we disregard that activity we are bound to be less sensitive to the need for understanding an author, most especially an author who talks a good deal about understanding. That, I think, will give a clue to the distance that separates much of academe from the very real task of interpreting Lonergan. May this essay do something to shorten the distance.

NOTES

1   Bernard J. F. Lonergan, S. J., *Method in Theology* (London: Darton, Longman & Todd, 1972). Ch. 5 outlines the two phases of theology, each with its four functional specialties.

2   Ibid., p. 159.

3   For some information on Lonergan's love of music, see Pierrot Lambert et al., eds., *Caring about Meaning: Patterns in the Life of Bernard Lonergan* (Montreal: Thomas More Institute, 1982), pp. 28, 194, 195, 236, 258.

4   There are references to Husserl in the Halifax lectures of 1958, but the only work mentioned is *The Crisis of European Sciences and Transcendental Phenomenology;* see Bernard Lonergan, *Understanding and Being: An Introduction and Companion to* Insight, eds. Elizabeth A. Morelli and Mark D. Morelli (New York and Toronto: The Edwin Mellen Press, 1980), pp. 45, 238. In *Caring about Meaning* (note 3, above), the most persistent effort we have had to draw Lonergan out on his readings, no work of Husserl is mentioned.

5 Three soundings will show the trend: Lonergan's *Verbum: Word and Idea in Aquinas,* ed. David B. Burrell, C.S.C. (Notre Dame: University of Notre Dame Press, 1967), indicates the early importance of the term; see the Index, *s. v.,* Wisdom. His *Insight: A Study of Human Understanding* (London: Longmans, Green and Co., 1957) would develop Thomist wisdom by adding a new form of it, p. 407. The Index of *Method in Theology* shows only one entry, and that to the Wisdom literature of the Bible.

6 "Religious Experience," in Thomas A. Dunne and Jean-Marc Laporte, eds., *Trinification of the World: A Festschrift in Honour of Frederick E. Crowe* (Toronto: Regis College Press, 1978), pp. 71–83; see p. 81. (This paper is now included in *A Third Collection: Papers by Bernard J. F. Lonergan, S.J.,* ed. Frederick E. Crowe, S. J. [Ramsey, N. J.: Paulist Press, 1985].)

7 *Method in Theology,* p. 30.

8 Religious Studies and/or Theology: The Donald Mathers Memorial Lectures for 1976, Queen's University, Kingston, Ontario; the passage occurs on p. 45 of the typescript, in note 8 to the second lecture. (These lectures are now published in *A Third Collection;* see p. 145, note 8, for the passage in question.)

9 *Method in Theology,* p. 235.

10 The investigation should take account, not merely of more formal statements on what method is, but of the use of words like "recipe," of repeated references to the New Method Laundry, of contrasts with scientific method, of the transition Lonergan calls for from logic to method, etc.—As I like to insist, we need to study the details if we are to be accurate on the whole.

11 Frederick E. Crowe, S.J., *The Lonergan Enterprise* (Cambridge, Mass.: Cowley Publications, 1980); see especially Ch. 1, Lonergan's Work as an Organon for Our Time.

12 It has been remarked to me that this approach is too static to convey the wealth and dynamism of Lonergan's thinking; I quite agree, and caution my readers against taking this logical device as anything more than a means for organizing conceptually ideas that depend on a far more fertile source. Incidentally, the device was used by Lonergan himself in his lectures, *De intellectu et methodo* (Gregorian University, Rome, 1959), where he says in effect: When you would get a handle on the universe of being, and lack the idea of being, then proceed by the Porphyrean either-or dichotomies within the notion of being; see pp. 19ff. of the student notes on those lectures, Lonergan Research Institute, Toronto.

13 Lonergan, *Method in Theology,* p. 133.

14 Lonergan, *Insight,* p. 733.

15 A reference to Lonergan's remark in his *Grace and Freedom: Operative Grace in the Thought of St. Thomas Aquinas,* ed. J. Patout Burns, S.J. (London: Darton, Longman & Todd, 1971), p. 139: the program of Aquinas "was to lay under tribute Greek and Arab, Jew and Christian, in an ever renewed effort to obtain for Catholic culture that (most fruitful understanding) which is the goal of theological speculation."

16 An early thematic statement is "The Transition from a Classicist World-View to Historical-Mindedness," in *A Second Collection: Papers by Bernard J. F. Lonergan, S.J.,* eds. William F. J. Ryan, S.J., and Bernard J. Tyrrell, S.J. (London: Darton, Longman & Todd, 1974), pp. 1–9; further references passim in that volume and in *Method in Theology* (consult the indices).

17 *A Second Collection,* p. 135, in the paper, "Theology and Man's Future," pp. 135–148.

18 Ibid., pp. 271–272, in the paper, *"Insight* Revisited," pp. 263–278.

19 *Verbum,* p. 24.

20 References below, notes 26–27.

21   *Method in Theology*, pp. 288–289.

22   In Raymond Laflamme and Michel Gervais, eds., *Le Christ: Hier, Aujourd'hui et Demain* (Québec: Les Presses de l'Université Laval, 1976), pp. 45–65 (appears also in *A Third Collection*).

23   On the Trinity: ibid., pp. 63–65, for one example. On the inner and outer word, with a hint of their relation to Son and Spirit, see *Method in Theology*, pp. 112–115, and *A Second Collection*, pp. 170–175, in the paper, "The Response of the Jesuit as Priest and Apostle in the Modern World," pp. 165–187; I myself have developed this relation a little in my "Son and Spirit: Tension in the Divine Missions?", *Science et Esprit* 35 (1983) 153–169 and *Lonergan Workshop* 5 (1983) 1–21.

24   Crowe, *The Lonergan Enterprise*, note 11 above.

25   Ibid., p. 11, from Bacon's *Essays, Advancement of Learning, New Atlantis, and Other Pieces*, ed. R. F. Jones (New York: The Odyssey Press, 1937), pp. 239–240.

26   *A Second Collection*, p. 67, in the paper, "Theology in Its New Context," pp. 55–67.

27   Ibid., p. 161, in the paper, "The Future of Christianity," pp. 149–163.

28   Philip McShane, ed., *Foundations of Theology* (Dublin: Gill and Macmillan, 1971), p. 233, in "Bernard Lonergan Responds," pp. 223–234.

29   One result of Lonergan's long struggle with the structural aspect is that the rest of us can now in five minutes learn to use the words: experience, understanding, reflection, value; maybe in five years we could learn to identify and locate in our consciousness the corresponding activities, and relate them to one another; when that is done we would be ready to investigate the implications of those activities for the objects they intend in the universe. If we have not taken those three steps, we can at least conceive them with something like a notional apprehension (Newman). But we have hardly even conceived the historical side as such, in its totality and in its relation to the structural, though good work has been done on some of its elements (conversion, etc.).

30   *Method in Theology*, p. 20 and passim; see the Index, *s. v.*, Transcendental.

31   The most succinct table I know, of categories pertaining to the structural and historical aspects of consciousness, is found in *Method in Theology*, pp. 286–287.

32   "Natural Right and Historical Mindedness," *Proceedings of The American Catholic Philosophical Association* 51 (1977) 132–143; see pp. 138–140 (this paper too appears in *A Third Collection*). —The three plateaus correspond to the stages of meaning in *Method in Theology*, pp. 85–99.

33   *Insight*, Ch. III. The sixth canon (of statistical residues) pertains also to the historical, but in a more complex way; I have discussed this in "Transcendental Deduction: A Lonerganian Meaning and Use," *Method: Journal of Lonergan Studies* 2,1 (1984) 21–40—see pp. 27–29.

34   Lonergan returned over and over to this pair of complementary notions in his papers from 1974 to 1977. Two of the more accessible loca are in papers already cited, "Natural Right and Historical Mindedness" (note 32 above), at pp. 141–142, and "Theology and Praxis" (note 23 above), at p. 15.

II

Pluralism and Authority

STEPHEN TOULMIN

IF asked to identify the focal problem of twentieth century intellectual life—the crucial *scandalon* that affects thinkers and writers in all fields of learning and culture—we need look no further than the problems of Pluralism and Relativism, to which David Tracy, who is one of Bernard Lonergan's more distinguished students, had given so much attention.[1] In a dozen fields, twentieth-century scholars have been obliged to acknowledge the facts of historical mutability and cultural diversity; and, in response, they have repeatedly been tempted into adopting a philosophy of relativism, assuming that no way exists of mediating and transcending that diversity and mutability. It is one of Lonergan's more striking virtues that he has always been committed to finding a language in which to keep a constructive discussion going, across all the boundaries between different historical epochs and different contemporary cultures.

As my main task here, I shall try to throw light on this project of Lonergan's with the help of some comparisons. I shall remind readers of Lonergan of some other people who have tackled the same project from within the context of other disciplines, since I believe that people working on both sides have something to learn from these similarities. While Lonergan may be one of the most lucid analysts of the problems of pluralism and relativism, as these arise in the field of theology—notably though not exclusively Catholic theology—many of the patterns of argument to be found in Lonergan's writings, far from being unique, have counterparts in the trains of reasoning pursued by leading writers in several other fields of inquiry.

This is not in any way to argue that Lonergan is *unoriginal.* On the contrary, it is to say that the ways in which Lonergan's theological formulations have proved to be crucially original starting points for further progress in theology are similar to those in which, for example, Karl Popper's formulations have been crucial for progress in the philosophy of science, or those of H.L.A. Hart and Edward Levi for jurisprudence and the philosophy of law. If I can show you how the problematic of recent debate in those other fields bears comparison with what has happened in twentieth century theology, my efforts will have been well spent.

Take, for instance, the Philosophy of Science. In the last 20 or 25 years, the scandal of relativism has been most notoriously associated with the writings, and even more the public reputation of Thomas Kuhn. Now, I would never claim that Kuhn ever set out to become what he has in fact become: the symbolic figure of modern historical relativism and revolutionary irrationalism. To the contrary, he is personally a very conservative man; and, coming from the stockbroking family of Kuhn, Loeb, he has (as Churchill might have put it) plenty to be conservative about. When the rebellious students at Columbia University in the 1960's took over Kuhn's terminology and declared, "What we need is a new paradigm of Society!," Kuhn himself was reportedly horrified: that was not at all what he had had in mind. For him, *normal* science was "normal" not just in the sense of *usual* or *average:* it was also supposed to set the *norm.* Even where "scientific revolutions" could not actually be prevented, they were things to get over with as soon as possible, certainly not to be encouraged or regarded with favor![2]

Yet, despite all the misunderstanding involved, Kuhn's use of the term "paradigm" has been made an excuse for all kinds of sloppy thinking, and also a license for arguing in just the kinds of relativistic ways that Lonergan rightly opposes, and has done his best to transcend. This is especially the case in the social sciences. I had numerous conversations with my late lamented anthropologist friend, Victor Turner; and, just at the moment when we were approaching the most crucially interesting points, Victor repeatedly sidetracked them, by saying, "Well, Stephen, you've got *your* paradigm, and I've got *my* paradigm . . .;" which was supposed to bring matters to an end. This typically happened when we reached a point at which there was the real prospect of achieving some transcendence of intercultural boundaries or historical gulfs. This was no accident; for that transcendence is just what the fashionable appeals to "paradigm differences" and "paradigm shifts" are repeatedly used to forestall.

If Lonerganians share any commitment with non-Lonerganians who value rationality in all aspects of intellectual life, it is the desire to stop people getting away with this move: to stop them using the appeal to "paradigms" and "paradigm differences" as a reason for ending conversations just at the point where they begin to be serious. If we are to escape from relativism, our central question must be, "How can *I,* who am arguing out of one tradition and cultural milieu, establish intellectual contact with what is at stake for *you,* who are arguing out of your own, different tradition and milieu?" Far from helping us to answer that thorny question, the appeal to "paradigm differences" is a way of turning one's back on it.

In a more special and particular sense, of course, that question is one that faces me in contributing to a symposium dealing with Lonergan's work. The fact that I am ready to address a group of Lonerganians demonstrates my confidence that our "paradigms" (like our "concepts") are not traps, in which we are inevitably snared. Rather, they are intellectual instruments *(topoi),* which we put to use for our own purposes: instruments from whose use we can stand back, understand, and exchange notes and opinions about, in the hope of arriving at well-founded comparative opinions.

I. POPPER AND THE PHILOSOPHY OF SCIENCE

First, let me remind you how Karl Popper responds to this kind of relativism, as it appears in the philosophy of science. He replies to it as follows:

> Certainly, in point of historical fact, the scientists working at any given place and time can only say *for sure* which human theories, hypotheses and/or conjectures about the real character of the natural world have not *yet* been discredited. So, scientists can only say "the best that can now be said" about nature, on the basis of the beliefs that have not yet been falsified, refuted, discredited.
>
> However, in presenting hypotheses about the world of nature, scientists themselves never talk only about how the physical world appears to them, *here and now,* at their own place and time. That would reduce the content of science to the "First World": the world of brute physical objects, things that are always changing, i.e. the Heraclitean flux. Nor, for that matter, do they consider only what ideas, beliefs, paradigms and so on human thinkers, *here and now,* happen to operate with, in interpreting how the world appears to them at that place and time. That would confine the subject matter of Science to the "Second World": the world of human thoughts, feelings and other mental objects.
>
> No, we must assume that there exists a "Third World", comprising all those enduring entities, relationships and truths that constitute the permanent structure of nature, quite apart from the scientists' own thoughts about it, and form the true objects of scientific inquiry, as scientists move ever closer to a true knowledge of nature.[3]

There is an interesting duality in Popper's view of Science, and that is my main concern here. He acknowledges that the time-bound situation in which any human scientist works (what a theologian might call the *finitude* of the scientist's position) implies that the best beliefs he can put forward in his own time are always "fallible" or "corrigible": as seen from a later standpoint, they may well prove to have been quite off the mark. Yet, at the same time, he insists that the proper *subject matter* of Science is itself permanent and unchanging. As Popper would say:

> Nature is as Nature is, and the Laws of Nature are what they are: Namely, enduring features of the Third World. Ideally, scientists may succeed in discovering what those Laws in fact are; but they can never claim that their knowledge of Nature is beyond possibility of correction. Pragmatically, the best available understanding of Nature thus rests on (and is constituted by) the authority of the best informed current members

of the relevant scientific community; but it is corrigible for the very reason that it speaks about a Nature that goes beyond it.[4]

On this account, the only Nature we can know and deal with, here and now, is the Nature we are told about by scientists who are, here and now, in a position to speak authoritatively about the relevant aspects of Nature; and their position of authority is always subject to revision in the light of new information and reflection. The theoretical language of Science may speak of the unchanging, unitary order of the Third World, the permanent, orderly realm whose laws are changeless and determinate, i.e. the unchanging *ordo essentiarum;* in the actual practice of Science, however, scientists deal directly not with eternalities and truths, but with the current ideas and beliefs of qualified members of the intellectual community of, e.g., biochemists. Seen realistically, therefore, the content of this pragmatic "Science" forms part not of Popper's Third World, but of his *Second* World, composed of "mental" objects: i.e. the historically variable and culturally plural *ordo cognitionis.*

In this way, Popper's philosophy of science reproduces the traditional contrast between the *ratio cognoscendi* and the *ratio essendi* in a new context. Scientists may *talk about* an order of "permanently existing things," but all they have to work with in practice is the "best established beliefs" about that eternal order, and those beliefs are historically mutable and culturally variable. (That is what creates the tension in Popper's view.) For better or for worse, Popper is right to react as he does to the threat of relativism. The trouble is that he counters it by insisting on an equal exaggeration: viz. that, however mutable and variable human beliefs about Nature may be, the underlying truth about Nature cannot itself be mutable and variable *at all.* The permanent reality of Nature is what scientists inquire about, and toward which they continually work their way, even though they never know for sure whether they have actually made it to their longed for destination.

II. TORAH IN RABBINICAL DEBATE

At this point, let me change the terrain of the discussion. The problem of pluralism has played a lively part also in the twentieth-century rabbinical debate about the status of Torah. With the splitting of Judaism into Orthodox, Conservative and Reform strands, a novel diversity and multiplicity has entered Judaism, and this fact has been a source of serious intellectual problems. If we look at the form the recent debate about Torah has taken, we find that the issues arising are strikingly similar to those we have already looked at in Popper's case.

On the one hand, the growth of understanding of Judaic Law involved the development of a method for mediating between the multiplicity of rabbinical opinions. That is an old, old story: historically, Jewish scholars dealt with it in the same way that Catholic casuists did with the multiplicity of opinions about moral cases, by distinguishing between laxists and rigorists, probabilists and probabiliorists: i.e. they developed ways of judging the *degrees of authoritativeness* of different opinions. So long as there was a single coherent, authoritative body of Rabbis and tradition of interpretation, all was well; but, with the multiple strands of modern Judaism, the question *who,* or *which tradition,* to take most seriously becomes more difficult. (Only within Orthodox Judaism, which retains its old confidence, is there still general agreement about the locus of "authority.") Meanwhile, on the other hand, as situations have turned up that are historically and culturally quite novel, new problems have arisen. The rise of novel medical technologies (for instance, sex change surgery and amniocentesis) presents moral problems that were not, and could not have been, explicitly covered by the earlier debate about the traditional Torah.[5]

Current rabbinical opinion divides along much the same lines ("historicist" *vs.* "conservative") that we found in philosophy of science. In the U.S., the conservative view is best represented by Rabbi J. David Bleich.[6] He holds that Torah was given to the Jewish people as a set of permanent truths whose form and meaning hold good as they stand, at all times and places equally. It is not liable to revision or reinterpretation, still less to rival interpretations at a given time. Authoritative Rabbis may differ about how its truths are best paraphrased into modern colloquial vernaculars, but these differences do not touch the actual truths themselves, nor do they touch the general meaning of the truths. Likewise, Rabbis may initially disagree about the implications of those truths for the novel situations that arise out of (say) the use of new medical technology; but, on the conservative view, the resulting discussions only show *what Torah already says* about cases of the kind in question. They do not extend or reinterpret the provisions of Torah in ways that were not (implicitly, at least) covered by the classical formulations.

What Lonergan says about Dogma in *Doctrinal Pluralism* may be seen as what conservative Rabbis say about Torah. The central issue arises from the contrast between a realm of permanently existing "realities" (Popper's "Third World," the conservative Rabbis' "true meaning of Torah," or Lonergan's "Dogma") with the realm of human knowledge, in which human perception of those realities is liable to variation, deepening and refinement. Can we, that is, identify an unchanging "order of essences" which is the object of human reflection in the Law, as in Nature, but which escapes the cultural plurality and historical variability of the "order of human knowledge"?

III. JURISPRUDENCE AND COMMON LAW

Let us change the terrain of discussion again. What we find in Rabbinics applies also to jurisprudence in the Anglo-American common law tradition. As epitomized in Sir William Blackstone's *Commentaries,* the conservative 18th century British view closely resembled the conservative rabbinical view of Torah.[7] The general maxims of the common law were "immemorial" in their origins, and were capable of covering all human situations. In that respect, they were permanent, even timeless. To those who know about the reactions of 16th and 17th century working lawyers to ,e.g., the colonial expansion of Europe, and to the rise of mercantilism and capitalism, Blackstone's account might well appear historically questionable, for the actual permanence and continuity of common law was somewhat less complete than he would have had us believe. But the rival doctrine, which treats the development of common law in explicitly historical terms, came on the scene only after the middle or late 19th century.

Where before *tort* was presented in straightforward terms, as *willful harm*, rooted in human nature and common experience, lawyers and judges now modified that doctrine for practical purposes, by adopting the supplementary theories, first of "negligence," and later of "strict liability." On the new view, people were in certain cases legally liable to provide remedy, even for harms they did not wilfully inflict: firstly, where those injuries resulted from failure to exercise proper skill or attention, e.g. when driving a car carelessly, and secondly, where there was no practicable way for an injured person to have protected himself from harm caused by a defective product (e.g. a motor car) whose manufacturer should have checked its construction before sale. Reflecting on these changes in legal practice, leading writers on common law jurisprudence, especially in the United States, came to view the common law as a variable product of historically evolving social demands. Hence arose the new school of historical and sociological jurisprudence associated with the names of scholars like Roscoe Pound, Oliver Wendell Holmes, and more recently Edward Levi.[8]

In the consequent standoff, we find the same division of opinions. The greater the diversity in actual judicial practice the historians and anthropologists bring to light, the more the arguments of sociologically-minded legal scholars evoke in reply the contrary *topoi* of permanence and plenitude. On the one hand, most working judges reject the suggestion that their decisions *alter*, rather than merely *apply*, existing law—to say nothing of their *creating* novel, "judge-made" law. This reaction is especially typical in England, where the general attitude to the law has always been more conservative than it is in the United States. The only task of the Courts (it is said) is to discover what the established state of the law implies about the present case. The law, as it already stands, it a *plenum:* i.e., it is free from gaps of kinds that will need to be filled in the future, through "creative" judicial decision.

On the other hand, the substance of judicial pronouncements gives historians and sociologists more grist for their mills. Just because the original maxims of the common law are shrouded in their immemorial past, they are inaccessible to our twentieth century scholars. So, the appeal to "immemoriality," which was originally relied on to guarantee the authority of the common law, turns back on itself, and becomes an epistemological obstacle. Previously, people assumed that anything as longstanding as the common law must be "a good thing." But now that same fact makes the common law appear, rather, an *uncertain* thing, about whose rational basis we no longer have confidence: certainly not confidence that it is truly *permanent.*

IV. THE RELEVANCE TO LONERGAN ON DOGMA

If I have come to see a common pattern in current disputes in philosophy of science, Rabbinics and jurisprudence, that was not least as a result of reflecting on what Bernard Lonergan wrote about historical and cultural diversity in the human understanding of

Christian doctrine in the last part of *Insight* and in his 1971 Marquette Lecture, *Doctrinal Pluralism.*[9]

For reasons explained in section 9 of Lonergan's Marquette Lecture, the ultimate ontological status of dogma is, no doubt, very different from that of the "original" common law. The hypothetical primitive common law is simply "lost in the mists of time"; but the basis of dogma is inaccessible to direct human perception for deeper reasons, because it presents the mystery of "God's understanding of Himself in his transcendence."[10] From an epistemological point of view, however, thought of in terms of human *rationes cognoscendi,* the differences among the quandaries involved in the four cases are much less significant. In the natural sciences, for instance, the more we come to understand and accept the inescapable historical variability and cultural plurality in human ideas about nature, the further we move away from the intellectual parochialism of both Newtonian and Positivist orthodoxy.

We can put the point in Lonergan's terms: "The more that classicist culture yields place to modern culture, with its historical dynamism and worldwide pluralism, the less certain we can be that any particular statement about the laws of Nature or about the principles of Science are absolutely unique, correct and unrevisable for all places and for all times."

In this way, an epistemic gap opens up in all four fields of human experience. For a start, it separates the idealized canon of Popper's Third World, i.e. the true meaning of any statement that correctly captures some enduring feature of that World, from any current and variable human (or Second World) understanding of the physical and natural (or First) World. As the gaps between Popper's three Worlds widen, the true content of the Third World becomes as mysterious as the true content of "God's understanding of Himself in his transcendence." So, the Third World itself becomes part of the *transcendent* real. In the legal examples, similarly, the real meaning of Torah and the original common law are not as clearly "transcendent" as God's self-understanding, or even the Third World: ontologically, the four cases are problematic in different ways. Yet the same epistemological gap exists, between the ideal content of Judaic or Anglo-American Law and its actual, historically and culturally diverse formulations, as it speaks to the conditions of different communities and peoples in particular situations.

For those of us who are concerned about historical change and cultural diversity, accordingly, the crucial task remains the same in each case: to find ways of understanding and arbitrating the differences between all these diverse formulations, given the specific characters of the problems at issue, in one community and situation or another.

V. Reconsidering the Problem of Authority

Going beyond the provisional and tentative parallels between Lonergan's discussion of doctrinal pluralism and the current debates in other fields of scholarship, we are now in a position to take up one particularly vexed question: "How are the traditional ways of justifying intellectual and spiritual authority to be sustained, in an historically and anthropologically-minded, 'post-classicist' age?'' Let us approach this problem by considering two preliminary questions first: viz., i) In what kinds of argumentative forums, and why, is it indispensable to invoke "absolute," i.e. permanent and idealized, rather than "relative," i.e. historically and culturally diverse formulations?; and ii) What determines the relevant kind of authority (and/or learning) appropriate to argumentative forums and issues of each kind?

To start with the common law: these two questions are faced explicitly in Herbert Hart's book, *the Concept of Law*.[11] Hart draws a helpful distinction between two ways in which "rules" are objects of thought or action by judges, lawyers and scholars. As a result, the concept of a legal rule plays quite a different part in the discussions of historians and sociologists of law, or in the deliberations and opinions of working judges.

Historians and sociologists look at the judicial process *from outside:* for them the activities of judges, including the "rules" they invoke, define certain of the explanatory factors that are operative in any judicial situation. But these are only some factors, among others; and the historian or sociologist is free to report on, and speculate about them as he pleases, thus turning the "rules" that are appealed to in different cases into intellectual "objects of thought."

Working judges are in a very different position. If a judge pronounces on some case over which he has authority *ex officio,* from the bench of justice, he is no longer free to behave like an onlooker, who speculates about the legal process from outside. On the contrary, he is involved in that process *as agent,* and his words carry a force that an onlooker's words never could. So it is essential for working judges to see the particular aspects of the law relevant to the case under their present consideration as requiring to be *discovered,* not as something that they *invent,* or otherwise *think up.* As a result, judges are generally unhappy about treating the rules by which their decisions are guided as mere "objects of thought," and find it natural to attribute to those rules a kind of independent reality which some onlookers find excessive, or even naive.

Likewise in the natural sciences: a scientist who commits himself to finding ways of explaining the aspects of Nature that engage his personal interest is involved *within* a set of rational activities which he cannot, at the same time, study and speculate about *from outside,* as an historian or sociologist of science is free to do. For the working scientist, it goes without saying that the World of Nature is more than an "object of thought," and that Nature exists in its own right. So working scientists, once again, naturally view Nature in "absolute" terms, and treat the relationships that hold within the world of Nature as something that it is their task to *unveil,* not to *invent.* By contrast, the sociologist or historian of science looks on at Science and the scientist's work from outside, and is free to adopt a "relative" point of view. For working scientist, the diversity of views about Nature, as between different cultures or periods, is irrelevant for scientific purposes; but for historians and sociologists, who are concerned to understand how scientific ways of thinking are influenced by the human situations out of which they arise, this pluralism is "of the essence."

Readiness to accept the reality of Nature, in its own right, is thus *constitutive of* the scientist's professional role, in the same way that a readiness to treat the law as an independently existing *plenum* is constitutive of the judge's role. For the scientist as for the judge, the *topoi* of permanence and plenitude have indispensable parts to play in his professional discourse and modes of argumentation. Those who act as "learned doctors," with the task of pronouncing with authority on doctrinal issues, are thus in much the same position, whether the field in question is dogmatic theology or natural philosophy (basic science) or law. It is never permissible for them to adopt, *at the same time,* the critical or skeptical posture that is implicit in any historical or sociological investigation. The learned doctor has to say "the best that can be said" about the questions at issue *here and now,* i.e. lend his credit to the most up-to-date and authoritative account he can give of those issues, while speaking here and now: any implication that his is only "one possible account among others" will undercut his authority.

In this task, he may treat as "discovering the truth" decisions that onlookers might see as plugging gaps in existing ideas, or even as determining public policy. For instance, a judge may face a case of "wrongful harm" by a physician to a patient which raises questions of law that are, at least for the present, quite problematic; and he may have to choose between dealing with it in either of two alternative ways, which rest on quite different precedents and analogies. In doing so, he may either extend beyond its previous application the scope of some existing category, such an "negligence"; or else he may bring some quite other legal theory to bear, by construing the injury, instead, as, for example the "breach" of terms in an implicit "contract."

Will such a decision then be an exercise of a judge's legal perception, or of his creative imagination? The answer to that question is to pose another question: viz., "Who is to reply?" If the answer is given by an onlooker, it may appear as though the decision turns on a *policy choice:* i.e. whether, in this case, a contract theory or a tort theory best preserves the continuity and determinacy of the law. If the answer is given from inside the judicial process, the decision will be seen as a genuine "finding" or "discovery" about what the existing state of the law *requires* the judge to decide.

A physical scientist may find himself facing a situation requiring a comparable decision. As happens once in a while in physics, a phenomenon under investigation may resist explanation in terms of (say) the Principle of the Conservation of Energy, as hitherto understood; and the physicist has to decide whether to challenge that principle, with all the long-term and far-reaching consequences this would have for physics, chemistry and the rest, or whether to posit some new, previously unidentified variety of "energy" which may, if interpreted aright, allow him to balance the books, and so enable the broader principle to be maintained.

At this point, the same questions arise as in the law: "Which should he decide to do? And what kind of choice is involved in that decision?" To an historian or sociologist, the question, "Can we find a way of keeping the Conservation of Energy Principle on its feet?", may look like a policy question. Yet, if a physicist succeeds in balancing the books by invoking some new form of energy, he will surely claim to have "discovered" a kind of energy that *always existed.* He will not concede that he "invented" or "created" it: it was always there, but nothing drew our attention to it before. Likewise, he will not claim to have "changed the meaning of" the Conservation Principle. Rather, he will respond to the situation by saying that we have now come to understand better what that Conservation

Principle *really meant* all along. So, what Lonergan says about the First Vatican Council Canon on *dogma* is also true of the basic doctrines of both jurisprudence and natural philosophy: viz., that the permanence attaches to the meaning and not to the formula: to retain the same formula while giving it a new meaning is excluded.

In choosing to put the point in these terms, of course, Lonergan speaks in the capacity of a "learned doctor" pronouncing a doctrine; and the topical considerations appropriate to that role debar him, as they would debar a working judge or scientist, from treating the *act* of presenting this doctrine as some kind of "socio-historical event." Meanwhile historians and sociologists, *qua* historians or sociologists, are subject to very different topical demands. These permit them to say (for instance) that, when Heinrich von Helmholtz and James Clark Maxwell introduced the new ideas of thermal and electromagnetic energy, they thereby "extended the scope" and "modified the meaning" of the Energy Principle, which was previously understood as concerned with mechanical relationships and energy alone.

The same is true of theological novelties as well. From the First Vatican Council's decree on Papal Infallibility, down to the most pedestrian statement of doctrine, sociologists and historians can ask many questions that would be unacceptable, if they came from the mouth of an authoritative "doctor." Just because historians, for example, are *not* expounding the principle or dogma in question with the authority of the Church, but speaking in their own roles as commentators on the historical or social changes with which doctrines are associated, their reasoning is subject to different patterns of argumentation from those that apply to the pronouncements of "learned doctors" who speak authoritatively and *ex officio.*

VI. CONCLUDING REMARKS

Let me round off this presentation by commenting briefly on two last points.

(1) I have had only one serious conversation with Lonergan, and I regret not being able to carry our exchange further. For I did not understand then, and do not fully even now, his reply to the question I raised on that occasion. It is my sense that any appeal to the "permanence" of dogma (or of the *meaning* of dogma) leaves open an issue that any person as historically-minded as Bernard Lonergan must be prepared to deal with: "In the light of what considerations can we say that, in the *current human understanding* of the meaning of a dogma, our 'best' ideas (our 'best formulated' ideas, or the best that we can say, here and now) represent a real *advance* on earlier ideas and understandings?"

The advances referred to in this question need not be viewed (so to speak) as advances out of the Second World, and into the Third. It is not a question about how we can reach the point at which we finally and definitively master, e.g., the "true nature" of Grace, let alone come to share "God's understanding of Himself in His transcendence": that option is not open to us. No, the problems I had in mind were ones that Lonergan is surely ready to accept as legitimate: namely, how we can recognize when a *better* way has been found of relating a dogma to the experience of a particular culture, and stating it in the local vernacular in a way that conveys its permanent meaning *better*. In this context, what force and sense can we give to the word "better"? Suppose that, after reflecting on psychoanalytic ideas about the "self," a serious theologian were to argue (say) that these ideas open up illuminating ways of rethinking the doctrine of Grace: how would we then decide whether this rethinking produced fruitful results, or whether it proved only a dead end?

That problem is a counterpart of the problem I tackled in Part I of *Human Understanding: sc.* the problem of describing the historical evolution of the central *topoi* of scientific thought.[12] There I tried to show how, within the processes of theoretical change in science itself, we may find criteria for deciding what does, or does not, count as movement in the directions that constitute "scientific progress": e.g., those that *approximate* to Popper's philosophical ideal of the Third World. True: on account of our finite, time-bound, culture-bound human situation, both "God's self understanding" and the definitive content of the "Third World" are unknowable with any human certainty. Yet, despite that finitude, it should be possible for us to ask which novel ways of formulating Dogma (or the Laws of Nature) serve as arrows pointing in promising directions: which of them, that is, show promise of *improving* our human, and so finite and variable understanding of their permanent, transcendent content.

In theology as much as in science, that is to say, we should be ready and able to discuss the question, how we can tell which of those arrows to follow, and which to ignore.

(2) Finally, let me close by restating the deepest and most provoking of the questions I have touched on here: "By what tests, then, are we to decide, not *what novel ideas* are to be taken seriously, but *which scholars and teachers* in an intellectual or spiritual community are to be taken as speaking with authority?"

In Lonergan's Marquette Lecture, he very subtly distinguishes the "continuity or permanence" of a doctrine from its "immutability."[13] He himself opts for permanence rather than for immutability, and so places himself philosophically alongside Popper, and against Descartes. For the term "immutable" carries implications that Lonergan clearly wishes to avoid: e.g., that *incorrigibility* can be claimed for at least *some* human statements.

The great subtlety and importance of this distinction becomes evident, when Lonergan uses it to make a crucial point about the infallibility of any doctrinal pronouncement. This infallibility (he argues) is limited to the meaning which the doctrine had *in the historical context of* its pronouncement. Any later human reading or understanding of the doctrine is a fresh historical event, about which scholars are entitled to ask, "How far did it really capture the doctrine's *original and infallible* meaning?" So, even on this basic level, the duties of historical and linguistic analysis are not be evaded.

That brings us to the central question: viz. the nature and basis of the authority that is claimed on behalf of the doctors of the Church, in their current interpretations of doctrine. I am here speaking of "authority," not so much in the *institutional* sense, in which hierarchical superiority confers authority and so commands obedience, as in the *rational* sense, in which we set hierarchical considerations aside, and commune within our own consciences about whose judgement we can best trust. In this as in all other fields of discussion, we must surely be permitted to exercise some selectivity. Even the most sympathetic onlooker will find it hard to concede to the pronouncements of a Simoniac medieval Pope, merely on hierarchical grounds, the same authority over his conscience today that he might grant to the arguments of some contemporary theologian in whose integrity and perception he had first-hand confidence.

In Science and Rabbinics and Common Law, as we saw earlier, the best we can humanly and rationally do is to concede authority over any issue to the wisest and most reflective, most widely, deeply and relevantly experienced of those who pronounce on it, as they address our local, contemporary conditions and problems. Not being a Catholic myself, I would not hesitate to employ the same discrimination in a theological context as in a legal or scientific one.

It was perhaps a price that Bernard Lonergan has had to pay, in virtue of his loyalty to the Church to which he gave a lifetime of service, that he did not address explicitly and openly before the gaze of a possibly sceptical readership, the question how he himself decides just which of his theological colleagues he regards as speaking with greater or lesser wisdom, reflectiveness, experience, and hence *rational* authority.

This is not to be understood as a snide anti-Catholic remark, for the same thing is equally true among scientists and lawyers. They too take care to speak only behind closed doors about the "rational authority" of their colleagues, and they regard it as unprofessional to discuss such matters before the great unwashed public. So, when Jim Watson wrote his popular account of the decipherment of the genetic code, The Double Helix[14], there was a hissing and a scandal in the Land of Science. The governing board of Harvard University Press reportedly declined the manuscript, since some members saw it as outrageous for Watson to flaunt before the general public the fact that not all scientists are embodiments of rationality, and feared that the book would help to bring the whole profession of Science into hatred, ridicule and contempt. (Needless to say, it would be easy to find a dozen illustrations of the point.)

In conclusion, then, let me leave you to consider those two most vexing questions in the *epistemology* of theology:

(1) In any theological discussion, how do we know which "arrows of change" point in the most fruitful directions?

(2) When our colleagues discuss theological issues, how do we know which of them have the wisdom, experience and reflectiveness that should be listened to with respect, as carrying intrinsic rational authority? If I have succeeded in showing you the force of these questions, these remarks have accomplished what I set out to do.

NOTES

1 See *Blessed Rage for Order: The New Pluralism in Theology* (New York: The Seabury Press, 1975) and *The Analogical Imagination: Christian Theology and the Culture of Pluralism* (New York: Crossroad, 1981).

2 See T. S. Kuhn, *The Structure of Scientific Revolutions*, 2nd Edition (Chicago: University of Chicago Press, 1970); and his "Reflections on My Critics" in I. Lakatos and A. Musgrave, eds., *Criticism and the Growth of Knowledge* (Cambridge: University Press, 1970).

3 See Karl Popper, *Conjectures and Refutations: The Growth of Scientific Knowledge,* 2nd ed. (New York: Basic Books, 1965), *passim.* These are my words, but I take them to represent the heart of Popper's argument.

4 Popper: Ibid.

5 See Jacob Neusner, ed., *Understanding Rabbinic Judaism: From Talmudic to Modern Times* (New York: KTAV Publishing House, Inc., 1974).

6 See J. David Bleich, *Contemporary Halakhic Problems, Volume II,* The Library of Jewish Law and Ethics, Volume X (New York: KTAV Publishing House, 1983).

7 Sir William Blackstone, *Commentaries on the Laws of England,* Volumes I and II, ed., William C. Jones (San Francisco: Bancroft-Whitney Company, 1916).

8 Roscoe Pound, *The Spirit of the Common Law* (Boston: Marshall Jones Co., 1921); *Interpretations of Legal History* (Cambridge: Harvard University Press, 1946); *Contemporary Juristic Theory* (Claremont Colleges, 1926); and compiler, *Readings on the History and System of the Common Law,* 2nd ed. (Boston: The Chipman Law Publishing Company, 1925); Oliver Wendell Holmes, *The Common Law* (Boston: Little, Brown and Company, [1881] 1951); and Max Lerner, ed., *The Mind and Faith of Justice Holmes: His Speeches, Essays, Letters and Juridical Opinions* (Boston: Little, Brown and Co., 1943); and Edward Levi, *An Introduction to Legal Reasoning* (Chicago: University of Chicago Press, 1949).

9 *Insight: A Study of Human Understanding* (New York: Philosophical Library, 1958), "Epilogue" and *Doctrinal Pluralism,* The 1971 Pere Marquette Theology Lecture (Milwaukee: Marquette University Press, 1971).

10 *Doctrinal Pluralism,* p. 54.

11 H.L.A. Hart, *The Concept of Law* (Oxford: Claredon Press, 1963).

12 Stephen Toulmin, *Human Understanding,* Volume I (Princeton: Princeton University Press, 1972).

13 *Doctrinal Pluralism,* p. 46.

14 James Watson, *The Double Helix: A Personal Account of the Discovery of the Structure of DNA* (New York: Atheneum, 1969).

III

Renewal in Mystical Theology

WILLIAM JOHNSTON, S.J.

IN seminaries before the Second Vatican Council there was a branch of theology known as *Ascetical and Mystical Theology*. Or it was called *Spiritual Theology* or *The Theology of the Spiritual Life* or just *Mystical Theology*. It was associated with the names of Adolphe Tanquerey, the Dominican Reginald Garrigou-Lagrange, the Jesuit Joseph de Guibert and many others who, following the great teachers of the Christian tradition, insisted that the life of prayer, and particularly the life of mystical prayer, should be guided and protected by sound theology. Furthermore, these theologians knew that the dogmatic and moral theologies of that time were not helpful in leading would-be mystics to the summit of Mount Carmel. Hence their efforts to elaborate a special branch of theology.

It should be noted that the ascetical and mystical theology about which I here speak is different from what we call *spirituality*. Books of spirituality (and in these I include such great classics as *The Confessions* of St. Augustine and *The Interior Castle* of St. Teresa of Avila) are written in literary language or in the common sense language of their day. Ascetical and mystical theology, on the other hand, is rigorously systematic; it has its own mode of apprehension; it is written in a technical language which is baffling, even unintelligible, to the uninitiated. To understand it one must have what Bernard Lonergan calls a new "differentiation of consciousness."

Let me first speak about the background to this branch of theology.

I. Mystical Theology in Historical Perspective

Probably the most influential treatise on this subject in the ancient world was the *Theologia Mystica* of the so-called Dionysius the Areopagite. Written by a Syrian monk in the sixth century this treatise was greatly influenced by Gregory of Nyssa, Origen and the Christian tradition. But it was written in a neoplatonic framework and used neoplatonic language. In reading this treatise one should recall that the words "mystical theology" had a different meaning for the author than for us. For him mystical theology approximated to what we call mystical experience where the word "mystical" means "pertaining to the mystery." The treatise contains a lot of spiritual direction and begins with practical advice on how to enter the mystical path:

> As for thee, O well beloved Timothy, in thy desire to reach mystical contemplation strive without wearying to detach thyself both from the senses and from the operations of the understanding, from all that is sensible and intellectual, and from all that is or is not, in order to raise thyself by unknowing, as much as it is possible to do so, to union with Him, who is above all being and all knowledge; that is to say, to raise thyself by detachment from self and from all things, stripped of all and untrammelled, to the supernatural, transluminous way of divine darkness (C.1,1)[1]

Dionysius is here describing an experience that is found in the mystical prayer of all the great religions; namely, the experience of going beyond all words, all reasoning, all thinking to enter the realm of silence in what we now call an altered state of consciousness. In doing so, however, he uses not biblical language but the neoplatonic language of his day, speaking of sense and intellect, of the One who is above knowledge, of knowing and unknowing, of the divine darkness. He puts heavy emphasis on detachment. Later in his treatise he will speak of *kataphatic theology* or the theology of affirmation and *apophatic theology* or the theology of negation. Elsewhere he refers to the purgative, illuminative and unitive ways. And all this Dionysian language, as well as the Dionysian approach to mystical prayer, was to exercise the greatest influence on subsequent mystical theology. Much of this influence, it is true, stems from the fact that the medievals believed that this author was the disciple of Paul mentioned in the *Acts of the Apostles*. Consequently, he had quasi-apostolic authority. Be that as it may, with Dionysius we find the first glimmerings of a systematic approach to the life of prayer and, in particular, to the life of mystical prayer.

I have said that in its beginnings mystical theology was greatly influenced by the way of thinking and the language of neoplatonism. Much more decisive and important, however, was the impact of mainstream scholasticism about which a word may now be appropriate.

While the church fathers and early Christian writers composed classics of spirituality and penetrated profoundly into the mystery of Christ, their language, as I have already indicated, was commonsensical or literary. It was only in the middle ages that theology became systematic in the strict sense of the word with its own distinctive mode of apprehension, its own technical language, its own differentiation of consciousness, its own professional group. For a substructure the medievals turned to Greek and Arabic thinkers of whom the most influential turned out to be Aristotle. And so we find the schoolmen speaking their own language—about essence and existence, act and potency, matter and form, substance and accidents, about the efficient, final and exemplary causes, about the Unmoved Mover and so on. Bernard Lonergan can speak of "the total rethinking of Christian doctrine in systematic terms by medieval theologians."[2]

And this scholasticism transformed mystical theology. St. John of the Cross, educated by the Dominicans at the University of Salamanca, was a dyed-in-the-wool Thomist who, in his most systematic work, *The Ascent of Mount Carmel,* united the Dionysian tradition of divine darkness to a thorough-going scholasticism. And through St. John of the Cross scholasticism shaped the many Latin manuals of *Ascetical and Mystical Theology* used in seminaries prior to the Second Vatican Council. And it also shaped Tanquerey and the authors I have already mentioned. Garrigou-Lagrange, for example, constantly appeals to St. Thomas Aquinas and St. John of the Cross as the pillars of his mystical theology.

And so mystical theology used scholastic terminology and looked at the life of prayer through scholastic spectacles. It spoke of a discursive prayer according to the three powers of the soul: the memory, the understanding and the will. Following St. John of the Cross, it spoke of a twofold purification found in the night of the senses and the night of the spirit. In this second night the three powers of the soul were transformed in such wise that there was faith in the intellect, hope in the memory and love in the will.

But most important in this theology was the distinction between ordinary and extra-ordinary prayer or between acquired and infused contemplation. Acquired contemplation was attained by one's own efforts with the help of ordinary grace. The knowledge thus obtained came through the senses according to the scholastic dictum that there is nothing in the intellect that was not previously in the senses. More concretely, the active intellect or *intellectus agens* dematerialized the phantasm and the passive intellect or *intellectus possibilis* acquired the species, now called *species acquisitae* or acquired species. Hence the term "acquired contemplation."

Infused contemplation, on the other hand, which was the technical name for mysticism, did not come through the senses but was immediately given by God when He communicated Himself to chosen people by pure spirit or by *species infusae*. Hence the term "infused contemplation." Within infused contemplation there were degrees of intensity. To describe these, mystical theologians side-stepped Aristotle and generally appealed to St. Teresa of Avila. Joseph de Guibert reduces St. Teresa's mansions to three main categories. First is the prayer of quiet. Second, the prayer of full union or simple union. Third, is the prayer of transforming union.[3] I cannot here describe these states in detail. Only let me say that while they are difficult to explain through a faculty psychology that speaks of memory, understanding and will, they fit rather easily into a more modern psychology that speaks in terms of layers of consciousness or altered states of consciousness.

The ascetical and mystical theology that flourished from the seventeenth century until the Second Vatican Council dealt not only with prayer but also with discernment of spirits, the acquisition of virtues, spiritual direction, examination of conscience and every facet of the spiritual life. Garrigou-Lagrange distinguishes between the ascetical and mystical dimensions in the following words: "Ascetical theology treats especially of the mortification of vices or defects and of the practice of virtues. Mystical theology treats primarily of docility to the Holy Spirit, of the infused contemplation of the mysteries of faith, of the union with God which precedes it, and also of extraordinary graces, such as visions and revelations which sometimes accompany infused contemplation."[4]

> In its methodology this theology was highly deductive. Let me quote Tanquerey in the preface to his famous treatise on ascetical and mystical theology:
> It is the writer's conviction that Dogma is the foundation of Ascetical Theology and that an exposition of what God has done and still does for us is the most efficacious motive of true devotion. Hence, care has been taken to recall briefly the truths of faith on which the spiritual life rests. This treatise then is first of all doctrinal in character and aims at bringing out the fact that Christian perfection is the logical outcome of dogma, especially of the central dogma of the Incarnation.[5]

Tanquerey is clear: Christian perfection is the logical outcome of dogma; it is the living out of dogma, and dogma guides us in the way of prayer. Other authors (notably Auguste Poulain), however, were more empirical and set great store by the experience of the mystics through the centuries.

II. THE CONTEXT FOR MYSTICAL THEOLOGY TODAY

I have said that mystical theology took scholasticism as its substructure. But now (and here I quote Bernard Lonergan) "the era dominated by scholasticism has ended. Catholic theology is being reconstructed."[6] Let me quote Lonergan more at length:

> There can be little doubt that it was necessary for medieval thinkers to turn to some outside source to obtain a systematic structure. There is little doubt that they could not do better than turn to Aristotle. But today it is very evident that Aristotle has been superseded. Magnificently he represented an early stage of human development—the emergence of systematic meaning. But he did not anticipate the later emergence of a method that envisaged an ongoing succession of systems. He did not envisage the later emergence of a *Philologie* that made its aim the historical reconstruction of the constructions of mankind. He did not formulate the later ideal of a philosophy that was at once critical and historically-minded, that would cut to the roots of philosophic disputes, and that would ground a view that embraced the differentiations of human consciousness and the epochs of human history.
> Not only has Aristotle been superseded, but also certain defects have become manifest. His ideal of science in terms of necessity has been set aside not only by modern empirical science but also by modern mathematics.[7]

"The era dominated by scholasticism has ended. Catholic theology is being reconstructed." And mystical theology also must be reconstructed. This is not to deny that in its scholastic form it did a great service to the Church and helped many people in the paths of prayer. It is simply to say that we live in a world that is different from the world of Aristotle or of St. Thomas or of Adolphe Tanquerey or of Garrigou-Lagrange. We live in a different culture with a different horizon and a different consciousness. The human race has undergone a series of revolutions which have profoundly changed our way of thinking, our way of praying, our way of looking at the world and even our way of thinking about God. Let me briefly mention some of these revolutions.

One revolution has been caused by the Christian encounter with Asian religions. It is precisely mystical dimension in these religions that has appealed to thousands of men and women in Europe and America. Moreover their approach is empirical, practical, "from below." With specific teaching on breathing and posture they promise to lead to profound religious experience those who are committed—not to their theory but to their practice. By comparison the Christian emphasis on dogma and our talk about acquired and infused contemplation are unintelligible to the ordinary person who dismisses the whole thing as an irrelevant "head-trip."

Our Christian theology, particularly our mystical theology, can no longer ignore these religions, nor can we deny that the Holy Spirit is at work in them. We see in them a pattern of religious and mystical experience which is very similar to ours. Moreover we find in South-East Asia people who enter into trance and altered states of consciousness with the greatest facility. Indeed the state they enter closely resembles Christian contemplative states and makes us ask if we can still talk of an "infused contemplation" wherein God intervenes and communicates himself "by pure spirit."

Again (and I continue with the revolutions) modern psychology has opened new vistas in the human mind. It has discovered the personal unconscious, the collective unconscious, the world of the archetypes, the world of symbols and the world of dreams. It has found new significance in human feelings and human sexuality. Faced with this new view of the human psyche can we continue to speak of the three powers of the soul? Can we continue to speak of the *intellectus agens* and the infused species?

Nor is it only modern psychology that has caused a revolution. Modern science has caused an even greater revolution by reason of its dynamic and ongoing methodology. And now, confronted with the subatomic world, many scientists find themselves drawn to mysticism. *The Tao of Physics* by Fritjof Capra was a best-seller. And when scientists look for a language and a system in which to express their experience, they do not turn to Aristotle nor to St. Thomas nor to scholasticism. They are attracted more by the way of thinking and speaking of the great Asian religions.

Yet another revolution was caused on August 6, 1945, when the first atomic bomb exploded over Hiroshima. And again on August 9, 1945, when a second atomic bomb exploded over Nagasaki. Since then, human consciousness has not been the same. Now we are aware of the horrendous power for destruction that lies within the grasp of men and women everywhere. We find ourselves surrounded by an atmosphere of collective fear of nuclear war together with a collective longing for peace. A mystical prayer which simply ignored our modern predicament could not be called Christian. Neither could a mystical theology be called Christian, or even human, if it ignored problems of world hunger, oppression of the poor, political torture, international terrorism, racial discrimination, exploitation of the weak and the like.

All this means that mystical theology has to be reconstructed. To reconstruct, however, does not mean to reject. It means to discard what is outmoded and retain what is of permanent value.

III. METHOD AND MYSTICAL THEOLOGY

I have spoken about reconstructing our mystical theology. What, then, will be the nature of this new construct?

In the old classical days the ideal was to create a system that would endure forever and to express it in doctrines that would not change: in other words, to create a static and unshakable pyramid of truth. Today, however, we know that we are on safer ground if we propose a methodology, humbly confessing that our theological doctrines will grow and develop as future generations ask new questions and obtain new insights, as future generations obtain new enlightenments and new mystical experience.

As a methodology I propose fidelity to what Bernard Lonergan's identifies as the five transcendental precepts: Be attentive, be intelligent, be reasonable, be responsible, be in love. Fidelity to these precepts is fidelity to one's truest self; it is fidelity to the most basic law of human mind and heart. To be obedient to these precepts is to walk the path whereby one becomes fully human and authentic. It is to walk the path whereby we undergo intellectual, ethical and religious conversion. "The three-fold conversion" writes Bernard Lonergan, "is not a set of propositions that a theologian utters but a fundamental and momentous change in the human reality that a theologian is."[8] So far are we from the purely academic approach or from the proverbial head-trip.

And obviously this is a very demanding path. Which of us is constantly attentive, intelligent, responsible and loving? We all have our dark areas wherein we are inattentive, stupid, unreasonable, irresponsible and hateful. But the struggle for authenticity goes on both in individuals and in cultures. And it goes on in the heart of the theologian as he does theology.

Now if we are to apply this methodology to mystical theology we must first ask about sources. What are the sources of an authentic mystical theology?

From the earliest period of Christianity the word "mystical" was associated with the mystery. This is the mystery of the New Testament, the mystery "which was kept secret for long ages but now is disclosed and through the prophetic writings is made known to all nations" (Rm 16:26). It is found in *Ephesians* where the author, writing of how the mystery was made known to him by revelation, goes on:

> To me, though I am the very least of all the saints, this grace was given, to preach to the Gentiles the unsearchable riches of Christ, and to make all men and women see what is the plan of the mystery hidden for ages in God who created all things. . . . (Eph 3:8)

This mystery is the very core of Christian revelation. It is the mystery of Jesus himself, the mystery of his incarnation, the mystery of his death and resurrection. It is the mystery of our redemption. It is the mystery of the Trinity. It includes all those mysteries of Jesus Christ that have been celebrated by millions of Christians as they have offered the eucharistic sacrifice (the *mysterium fidei* par excellence) as they have read the scriptures, and as they have prayed in their churches and in their families.

And so a mystical theology finds its sources in the scriptures and in the eucharist. It finds its sources in the words and writings and lives of the great mystics who have experienced this mystery in the depths of their being in states of heightened consciousness. It finds its source in the masses of the people who pray—the *ecclesia orans*—and who touch this mystery in their own ineffable way through their popular devotions and through their recital of the mysteries of the rosary. It finds its source above all in the cross of Jesus—not only that cross from which Jesus cried out: *Lama Sabacthani* but also the cross of Jesus in the modern world. For the *Lama Sabacthani* rises from the lips of millions who suffer from hunger and oppression and violence. The *Lama Sabacthani* rings out as a result of war and terrorism and sin. All this pertains to the mystery of the cross of Jesus which is the center and core of mystical theology.

Now a mystical theology will approach the mystery from two standpoints: a scientific standpoint and a religious standpoint. By the scientific standpoint I mean fidelity to the first three precepts: Be attentive, be intelligent, be reasonable. And it is obvious that to be attentive, intelligent and reasonable towards the sources I have described is an immense work of scholarship which ordinarily will be shared out amongst many scholars. I cannot speak about it in detail here.

Here I prefer to speak about the religious approach enshrined in the fifth trancendental precept: Be in love. Concretely I mean that the mystical theologian must be in love with the mystery. And from this love will come knowledge (or should I say wisdom?) which will be the very basis of his or her theology. To compare this wisdom with the knowledge that comes from research is to compare the light of the sun with the light of a candle.

Let me here add that this fifth transcendental precept of love is part of the life of scientists insofar as they strive to be human, to be authentic, to be truly themselves. But it is not part of their science—it is not part of the mathematics or physics or whatever. On the other hand it *is* part of theology. And this makes theology quite different from any other science. Theologians who lack the wisdom that comes from love, theologians who are religiously unconverted—such theologians, even if they have a wealth of scholarly knowledge, will be working with a candle, totally ignorant of the wonderful wisdom to be found when one works by the light of the sun.

Let me say a further word about this love.

IV. THE PLACE OF LOVE IN MYSTICAL THEOLOGY

The unrestricted love of the fifth transcendental precept is the unconditional, unrestricted love that goes on and on. It is the love of the covenant, the love inculcated by the sixth chapter of *Deuteronomy* which says: "Hear, O Israel: The Lord our God is one Lord; and you shall love the Lord our God with all your heart, and with all your soul, and with all your might" (Dt 6:4). It is a love which is an answer to the prior love of God: "In this is love, not that we loved God but that he loved us..." (1 Jn 4:10). It is a love that leads to *metanoia* or conversion of heart.

Now as I have already said, this love leads to knowledge. And the knowledge that stems from religious love can be called wisdom or *sapientia*, the first gift of the Holy Spirit or (if one uses the terminology of St. John of the Cross and of Bernard Lonergan) it can be called faith. In either case it is dark, obscure, supraconceptual knowledge of the mystery. This is the wisdom that forms the very core of contemplative prayer when one sits or stands silently before the mystery—without thinking, without reasoning. This wisdom St. John of the Cross calls "loving knowledge" or "loving awareness." It is the wisdom of the cloud of unknowing and the dark night.

I have said that this wisdom (which in the terminology of St. John of the Cross, and of Bernard Lonergan is faith) is part of theology. I believe that this is the faith of which Anselm spoke when he said: *Crede ut intelligas*". On this saying Lonergan comments:

> *"Crede ut intelligas."* It does not mean, Believe that you may judge, for belief is already a judgment. It does not mean, Believe that you may demonstrate, for the truths of faith do not admit of human demonstration. But very luminously it does mean, Believe that you may understand, for the truths of faith make sense to a believer and they seem to be nonsense to an unbeliever.[9]

Believe that you may understand! Love that you may understand! For if you love in obedience to the fifth transcendental precept, then what seems like nonsense to the unbelieving mind will make sense to you.

Concretely, if by faith we mean the knowledge that comes from religious love, then faith will play a role, a key role, in the life of the theologian who reads the scriptures and attends to the other sources. For he will come to an understanding of the scriptures not only through exegesis but also through love—love for the scriptures themselves and for God who he believes to be the ultimate author of the scriptures.

And so there will be times when the authentic theologian puts aside books and typewriter because she is drawn beyond the words of scripture to that mystery, to that reality, towards which the words of scripture point. And now the theologian is engaged in contemplative prayer. She is silent and wordless in the cloud of unknowing. But in this cloud she is imbibing the highest wisdom, which is like the light of the sun. This is the wisdom which Thomas himself imbibed at the end of his life. Now it became so powerful that the angelic doctor could say that all his writings were like straw. He did not say they were false. He said they were like straw. He meant that they were totally inadequate to express the mystery he had experienced in the cloud of unknowing.

I have said that fidelity to the transcendental precepts means that one is attentive to the mystery, and this leads to understanding; and it means that one loves the mystery and this leads to wisdom. Now let me mention a further dimension of these precepts.

One who is faithful to them is not only attentive to the mystery of God. He or she is also attentive to the mystery of self. One not only gets insight into the mystery, one also gets insight into one's self. One not only loves the mystery, one also loves one's self. And this knowledge of self and love of self is a vital aspect of the path to knowledge and wisdom. Hence the importance of what Bernard Lonergan calls "the shift to interiority."

In short, the theologian's understanding of self and love of self is crucial. His or her prayer, his or her examination of consciousness, his or her journal or mandala, his or her spiritual direction. "One's interpretation of others," writes Bernard Lonergan, "is affected by one's understanding of oneself."[10] And to this I would add that one's love of others is affected by one's love of oneself. And I would go further and say that one's understanding of, and love for, the Father, for Jesus, for the mystery, is affected by one's understanding and love of oneself.

And let me add a corollary. When one is lovingly attentive to the mystery and lovingly attentive to oneself, one comes to understand one's inner processes and one's inner movements. One comes to understand one's understanding and to know one's knowing. But above all one comes to know what loving is. And when one comes to know what loving is, when one comes to recognize the presence or absence of love within oneself, then one is capable of discernment. For discernment is precisely this: the sorting out of positive and negative movements within oneself, the sorting out of love and hate within oneself, so as to follow the love and avoid the hate. And all this is part of the contemplative experience.

And so I am saying that if one is faithful to the method in theology of Bernard Lonergan one will find that theology and religion come together. In this way theology is not just academic, not just a "head-trip." It is indeed academic; but it is also a religious experience and even a mystical experience. "Be intelligent" leads to intellectual conversion: "Be in love" leads to religious conversion. And so the age-old split between theology and prayer, lamented by holy men like a Kempis, is healed.

V. CONCLUSIONS

Let me now draw some conclusions and bring my paper to an end. I have already said that to reconstruct mystical theology is not to reject but simply to discard what is outmoded and to retain what is of permanent value. Now in the methodology I have suggested, pride of place in the mystical life and in mystical theology is given to the fifth transcendental precept: Be in love. And this is very traditional teaching. While the medievals took their framework or substructure from Aristotle they knew that the center of Christian holiness and of Christian mysticism was found not in Aristotle but in the New Testament. And so the primacy of the greatest commandment is enshrined in the teaching of mystical theologians from Dionysius to Tanquerey. Let me quote the great Spanish doctor. Speaking of the central thrust of his whole doctrine, St. John of the Cross writes:

> . . . I find no more fitting authority than that written in the sixth chapter of *Deuteronomy* where Moses says: "Thou shalt love the Lord thy God with thy whole heart and with thy whole soul and with thy whole strength". Herein is contained all that spiritual persons ought to do, and all that I have to teach them, so that they may truly attain to God, through union of the will, by means of charity.[11]

Now St. John of the Cross writes these words in a scholastic framework. He is speaking of the purification of the three powers of the soul: the memory, the understanding and the will. And he stresses that this third power, the will, is purified and transformed through charity.

I have tried to express this basic doctrine of the love of God, not in terms of the three powers of the soul, but in terms of levels of consciousness. In this way the dynamic dimension of charity comes to the fore. Moreover I have tried to say that fidelity to this precept of ongoing, developing love is not only the center of mystical experience but is also the center of mystical theology. Just as the theologian who asks new questions will get new insights, so the theologian whose love is unrestricted will get new enlightenments, new illuminations—until finally, like Thomas, his illumination is so powerful that he wants to be silent and say nothing. In this way, mystical theology will make progress along two paths: the scientific and the religious. Progress along the scientific path will come from questions; progress in the religious path will come from love and from the knowledge born of love.

Again, the methodology I have suggested is not one that takes us out of the world into a mysterious realm above the clouds. It is very much in touch with the modern world with its enormous social and cosmic problems. For the theologian who follows this methodology is attentive to the cross of Jesus not only as it is described in the New Testament but as it appears in the world of today. He or she is attentive to the mystery of evil not only as it exists in the New Testament but as it exists in the world around us.

Again, this methodology is ecumenical in its approach to Asian religions. If the Christian is present to the mystery hidden from all ages, so also is the non-Christian mystic. When the Second Vatican Council wanted to speak about a religious experience that is common to all religions it spoke of presence to mystery. Here are the words of the Council:

> From ancient times down to the present, there has existed among diverse peoples a
> certain perception of that hidden power which hovers over the course of things and over
> the events of human life. . . .[12]

This hidden power is indeed the mystery. Who can doubt that mystics of the great Asian religions are faced with the same mystery as we? And we can join hands with them, learning from their ways of prayer, from their illuminations, from their insights, from their way of life. In this way we will make progress. And one thing is sure: Asia will never listen to our mystical theology unless it is closely linked with mystical experience.

Again, in this approach, mystical theology becomes the center of all theology. For what could be more central to theology than presence to, and experience of, the mystery of God? Bernard Lonergan has spoken of conversion of heart as the foundation of theology. And experience of the mystery is a deep form of conversion of heart. Mystical theology is no longer a minor branch of theology as it was in the 1940s but the queen of theology, the lady wisdom herself.

Finally, let me anticipate one objection. Someone may say that I have not sufficiently distinguished between theology and religion. Someone may say that religion is prayer, faith, conversion of heart, mystical experience and so on, while theology is reflection on religion and the objectification of religion. I recognize the distinction between theology and religion. But my contention is that in fidelity to the transcendental precepts theology and religion converge. The theologian without faith and without religion is working in the dark with a candle: whereas the theologian with living faith is working by the light of the sun. Yet he never throws away the candle of reason. In a paradoxical way the theologian working in the brilliant light of the noonday sun still needs that little candle.

NOTES

1 *Theologia Mystica* 1,1.

2 Bernard Lonergan, S.J., *Method in Theology* (London: Darton, Longman and Todd, 1972), p. 345.

3 Joseph de Guibert, *The Theology of the Spiritual Life* (New York: Sheed and Ward, 1953), p. 332.

4 Reginald Garrigou-Lagrange, *The Three Ages of the Interior Life* (St. Louis: Herder Book Co., 1946), Vol. 1, p. 10.

5 Adolphe Tanquerey, *The Spiritual Life: A Treatise on Ascetical and Mystical Theology* (Tournai: Desclee and Co., Tournai, 1930), Preface.

6 *Method,* p. 281.

7 Ibid, p. 310.

8 Ibid, p. 270.

9 Ibid, p. 336.

10 Ibid, p. 271.

11 "The Ascent of Mount Carmel" in *The Collected Works of St. John of the Cross,* trans. K. Kavanaugh and O. Rodriguez (Washington, D.C.: ICS Publications, 1979), Bk III, Ch. 16.

12 *Declaration of the Relationship of the Church to Non-Christian Religions (Nostra Aetate),* in *The Documents of Vatican II,* Walter M. Abbott, S.J., gen. ed. (New York: America Press, 1966), art. 2 (p. 661).

Orientations
in Philosophy

IV

Is God In Process?

MICHAEL VERTIN

I. INTRODUCTION

SURELY one of the more distinctive and influential perspectives in North American theological reflection during the last few decades has been provided by what most commonly is called "process theology."[1] Drawing heavily on the philosophical work of Alfred North Whitehead and Charles Hartshorne, process theologians have elaborated a notion of God, and correlative notions of the world in general and humankind in particular, that allegedly do far better justice both to the central features of religious experience and to the perduring claims of religious traditions than previous notions did.[2] Though initially a primarily Protestant phenomenon,[3] process theology has increasingly found favor of late among Roman Catholic[4] and Jewish[5] thinkers as well; and its frequency as the topic of recent theological books, articles, and symposia testifies to the interest and enthusiasm that it generates today in many quarters.[6]

It remains that process theology is not without its detractors, not least of all among those present-day scholars standing in some way within the broad intellectual tradition that stems from Thomas Aquinas. For this latter group, the process thinkers' specifically theological contentions regarding God are seriously flawed because their underlying philosophical suppositions about God are gravely defective; and their philosophical suppositions about God are defective, in turn, because in important ways the process thinkers' more general philosophical suppositions are mistaken.[7]

My aim in the present essay is to contribute to a further clarification of the philosophical differences underlying the theological disagreements between the present-day process and Thomist thinkers.[8] Taking Charles Hartshorne as a representative of the former[9] and Bernard Lonergan as a representative of the latter,[10] I will proceed in two main steps. First, I will sketch Hartshorne's philosophical claims regarding (a) God and, then more generally, (b) actuality, (c) the fundamental criterion of meaningfulness and truth, and (d) the features of cognitional performance. Secondly, I will reconstruct something of Lonergan's stances on the same issues, along with the criticisms of Hartshorne's claims that Lonergan's stances imply.[11] Insofar as this effort to clarify is successful, it may be expected to facilitate the reader's assessment of the opposed process and Thomist philosophical claims, and thus at least indirectly to help that reader in her attempt to reach a conclusion about the ultimate tenability of process theology.

II. Hartshorne: Four Philosophical Claims

a) God is the "relatively-supremely intelligent, wise, and loving lure and result of worldly reality."[12]

One of the hallmarks of process philosophizing about God is that, historically speaking, it typically conceives itself as developing in reaction to so-called "classical"—Greek and Medieval, and paradigmatically Thomist—philosophizing about God.[13] It sees the latter as underlying religious and theological notions of God that, although common, are finally quite unacceptable. Consequently, process philosophical discussions of God usually include a negative critique of classical claims, as a preliminary to the elaboration of positive process claims; and Hartshorne's work illustrates this approach.

In Hartshorne's view, the crucial supposition undergirding the classical metaphysics of God is the identification of perfection with unity, simplicity, self-identity. Since God is supremely perfect, on this supposition he therefore must be "monopolar" in nature: utterly unitary, simple, and self-identical. In more detail, God is totally non-spatial and eternal, diversified neither spatially nor temporally. He is completely necessary, immutable, changeless, without any novelty. And he is wholly absolute and independent: he is not "really related" to the world, in no way dependent upon it in his reality, knowledge, or affectivity; rather, he is its totally self-sufficient efficient cause.

In short, when the implications of identifying perfection with unity are made explicit, to say that God is "perfect" is to say that he is "unsurpassible in every respect"; and this in turn supplies the specific meanings of other terms commonly applied to him. Thus God is "intelligent" in the sense of "omniscient": he knows utterly all that could be. God is "wise" in the sense of "omnisapient": he knows utterly all that was, is, and will be. And God is "loving" in the sense of "omnipotently, or irresistibly, directing all things to what he judges to be their best ends."

For Hartshorne, however, such a notion of God is philosophically well nigh unintelligible, to say nothing of its lack of congruence with religious experience and tradition. A being who in total autonomy both knows and controls everything about everything is hardly a being who takes others very seriously, who is respectful of others and responsive to to them, who displays the openness and, indeed, the vulnerability that invariably we count as essential marks of genuine love. God thus conceived would be not the supreme lover but the supreme dictator. And since this conception is obviously problematic, the basic supposition from which it flows—the identification of perfection with unity—is problematic as well.[14]

Not surprisingly, then, a rather different supposition undergirds Hartshorne's's own metaphysics of God: the identification of perfection not with *one* line of ultimately-contrasting traits but with *both* lines. That is to say, Hartshorne conceives perfection as unity *and multiplicity*, simplicity *and complexity*, self-identity *and self-diversity*. Thus God, as supremely perfect, is supremely both one, simple, self-identical, and many, complex, self-diverse. More exactly, God is not "monopolar" but "dipolar" in nature: in his "abstract essence" or "totality of possibilities" he possesses more or less the traits that classical thinkers ascribed to him; while in his "concrete actuality" he possesses traits that are more or less their opposites. Hence in his concrete actuality God is concretely both spatially and temporally diversified. He is the most contingent, mutable, developing, and ever-novel of all individuals,[15] unequalled in the extent to which in any given moment he transcends what he was in the prior moment. And he is utterly relative and dependent: he is "really related" to the world, radically conditioned by it in his reality, knowledge, and feelings.

In brief, when the implications of identifying perfection with both unity and multiplicity are made explicit, to say that God is "perfect" is to say that he is "surpassable by none save himself"; and this in turn provides the specific meanings of other terms commonly applied to him. Thus, God as "intelligent" knows relatively more than anyone else of what could be, but he is not omnniscient. God as "wise" knows relatively more than anyone else of what was, is, and will be, but he is not omnisapient.[16] And, similarly, God as "loving" is by no means omnipotent: he sympathetically delights with the world in its joys and suffers with it in its sorrows; he influences worldly realities not by coercively "moving" them as their efficient cause but only by persuasively "luring" them as their final cause; and in part he is immanently constituted by the particular character of the world's response. Hartshorne argues that only by conceiving divinity in this way can we employ such expressions as "God is love" without compromising our basic philosophical insights regarding genuine love—or, for that matter, compromising our common religious experience and doctrines.[17]

In sum, to the question, "Is God in process?", Hartshorne (and, more broadly, the process tradition) responds, "In his abstract essence, no; in his concrete actuality, yes."[18]

b) The actual is whatever is "concretely spatiotemporal" and "creative."[19]

Hartshorne's metaphysics of God presupposes, of course, a more general metaphysical perspective. We can indicate something of that perspective by specifying more exactly what Hartshorne means by "actuality" and then noting that, for him, "concrete spatiotemporality" and "creativity" are, in effect, its "transcendental features."

In the first place, then, according to Hartshorne the reality of any entity at any moment includes both what the entity up to that moment has become and what henceforth it might become. The first is the entity's "actuality"; the second, its "possibility." The actuality, as the culmination of the entity's past, is now closed, relatively limited or finite, determinate in this or that particular way: it is "concrete." The possibility, as the totality of real alternatives in the entity's future, is still open, relatively unlimited or infinite, indeterminate, universal: it is "abstract." In the concrete actuality and the abstract possibility of any entity, then, the first and the second members respectively of such logical polarities as "actual/possible," "concrete/abstract," "closed/open," "finite/infinite," "determinate/indeterminate," and "particular/universal" coalesce and achieve ontological status.

Secondly, the actual, in Hartshorne's view, invariably is concretely spatiotemporal. Indeed, it is fair to say that for Hartshorne "to be actual" means, in part, "to be concretely spatiotemporal." Actual entities, the fundamental instances of actuality, are not enduring substances of any kind; rather, they are spatially and temporally discrete events, occurrences, happenings. And what we ordinarily call "things" in fact are nothing other than limited sets of events that are spatially proximate and temporally sequential; while God in his actuality is uniquely the total, unlimited set of events.

Thirdly, within the Hartshornian framework "to be actual" also means, in part, "to be creative." In its actuality each and every entity without exception possesses awareness; each and every entity is a subject, a "drop of experience."[20] The precise content of this awareness is shaped partly by prior events that the event intuits, feels, prehends, and partly by the event's own self-constituting synthesis of what it intuits.[21] In the first respect the event is passive, receptive, and determined; while in the second respect it is active, spontaneous, free. This state or condition, in which an event constitutes itself under the influence of the antecedent events that it intuits but without being completely determined by them, and in which it can influence subsequent events in turn by serving as a datum for their intuition, is what Hartshorne labels "creativity."[22] The creativity of individual events, or even of the limited sets of events that we ordinarily call "things," is severely restricted in its spatial and temporal scope. The creativity of God, on the other hand, is uniquely characterized by its lack of any restriction in this regard.

c) My fundamental criterion of the meaningfulness and truth of any assertion is "concrete experience."[23]

Two especially important philosophical questions can be raised regarding the manifold claims that persons may make about ordinary matters, scientific matters, ethical matters, religious matters, etc. First, what in general is the basic measure of the meaningfulness of these claims? I.e., precisely what is it that comprises the primary touchstone of their intelligibility? Second, what in general is the final gauge of their truth? I.e., what is the ultimate standard in light of which one deems them correct?

What are Hartshorne's answers to these questions, answers indicating the tests to which presumably he subjects, e.g., the metaphysical claims that he himself makes?

In fact, Hartshorne's responses to the first and second questions are the same: "concrete experience." In the context of the present issues he intends this expression to underline the importance of a certain kind of development on the part of anyone who would be a genuinely critical thinker, a development that we might call both a "turn to the actual" and a "turn to the subject." Uncritical thinkers are those who tend to focus attention chiefly on the possible, the universal, the non-spatial and non-temporal, the abstract. The critical thinker, by contrast, has recognized that these are real only in function of the actual, the particular, the spatial and temporal, the concrete. Again, uncritical thinkers allow themselves to be entranced by past and therefore static objectivity, mere givenness. The critical thinker, on the other hand, discerns that this is secondary in comparison with present and therefore creative subjectivity, experience.[24]

In brief, the critical thinker sees that it is the realm of present spatiotemporal entities, particular creative occurrences, actual subjective events—in a word, the realm of concrete experience—against which the supposed meaningfulness of any claim is ultimately to be tested and through reference to which the purported truth of any claim is finally to be substantiated. She sees, moreover, that the difference between "empirical" and "metaphysical" claims—and, more broadly, between "empirical" disciplines and "metaphysics"—eventually is nothing other than a difference in the *scope* of the respective claims' reference to concrete experience. "Empirical" claims are more or less particular, concrete, and hence contingent. Some experience may illustrate them but some other experience may contradict them (e.g., "This table is red," "The recent weather will result in a small wheat crop"). But "metaphysical" claims are utterly universal, abstract, and hence necessary. Every conceivable experience must illustrate them and no conceivable experience can contradict them (e.g., "Something exists," "The present is always influenced by the past").

d) My cognitional activity is my "experiencing," in its aspect of "unmediated conscious-intentional awareness."[25]

I have suggested that the question of the fundamental criterion of the meaningfulness of the claims that persons may make about various matters and, as well, the question of the fundamental criterion of their truth are issues of considerable philosophical importance; and I have indicated something of Hartshorne's stance on them. I now draw attention to a further significant philosophical question: What in general are the mental steps, procedures, operations, that a person goes through in arriving at the claims that he makes? I.e., what are the recurrent characteristics of a person's cognitional performance, the invariant features of a person's knowing activity?[26]

What is Hartshorne's response to this question, a response presumably covering his own cognitional practice in, e.g., coming to the metaphysical claims that we have seen him make?

As far as I have been able to determine, Hartshorne never addresses this question explicitly. He devotes a good deal of effort to developing a "metaphysics" of knowing, a "third-person" elucidation of the general traits of cognitional activity that treats that activity simply as an element or feature alongside other elements or features in the cosmic inventory. But he makes no sustained effort to elaborate a "phenomenology" of knowing, a "first-person" account of the general traits of cognitional activity that recognizes that activity as performatively presupposed by each and every express claim that one makes, whether metaphysical or other. Indeed, Hartshorne regularly stresses that by "experience"—including "knowing" as one of its key aspects—he almost always means the "creative synthesizing" that, on his metaphysical scheme, is constitutive of every actual entity whatsoever, from least to greatest.[27] In other words, his account of cognitional activity is virtually never an account of distinctively *human* cognitional activity, much less an account of *his own* cognitional activity as such; and since an elucidation of recurrent features of one's own subjectivity is what finally underpins any phenomenology, Hartshorne's account of knowing is surely not explicitly phenomenological.

It remains that Hartshorne's metaphysical claims, taken as a group, provide three kinds of clues to the *implicit* Hartshornian phenomenology of cognitional activity, clues from which the latter can be reconstructed at least in outline. Specifically, there are some phenomenological claims that, on the assumption of consistency, necessarily are presupposed by the metaphysical claims; there are others that are directly manifest in the metaphysical claims; and there are still others that are indirectly manifest in the metaphysical claims.[28]

I would argue, then, that "my knowing activity" for Hartshorne is nothing other than the direct and unmediated awareness that is one aspect of "my experiencing." This awareness has two distinct "dimensions," as it were. First, there is the "intentional" dimension, the dimension in which, as object, the "other" is present to me (Hartshorne's "perception") or I am reflexively present to myself (Hartshorne's "memory"). Secondly, there is the "conscious" dimension, the dimension in which, as subject, I am non-reflexively present to myself—and, moreover, not merely self-present but also self-constituting (Hartshorne's "self-determination").[29] In the fundamental instances of cognitional awareness, the object or subject is present as concretely spatiotemporal; in the less fundamental instances, as abstractly spatiotemporal.[30] And thus a partial connection stands forth between Hartshorne's (implicit) phenomenological stance on cognitional activity and his metaphysical claim, discussed previously, about actuality. For on the phenomenological stance that I am imputing to him, that toward which my cognitional awareness is fundamentally oriented, and which thus at least performatively is defined as the actual, is concretely spatiotemporal.

III. LONERGAN: FOUR PHILOSOPHICAL CLAIMS

d') My cognitional activity is my successfully answering sequential "what," "is," and "ought" questions.[31]

Positive. Apologizing in advance for the oversimplification, I would like to summarize in six points the explicit and detailed cognitional phenomenology that Lonergan proposes. First, "for me to know," in Lonergan's view, is "for me successfully to answer questions." Presupposing some data in the dimension of intentional presence ("data of sense") or of conscious presence ("data of consciousness"), these questions successively intend the intelligible unity or similarity of the data ("What is it?"), and the affirmability ("Is it so?") and evaluability ("Ought it be so?") of the intelligible unity ("thing") or similarity ("property").[32]

Secondly, the questions (and their answers) may be subdistinguished into "concrete," insofar as they regard the things or properties in the fulness of their individuality and the totality of their aspects (including particular spatiotemporal location, if any), and "abstract," insofar as they regard them to some extent in precision from the latter. Again, the questions (and their answers) may also be subdistinguished into "descriptive," insofar as they regard the things or properties explicitly in relation to me as a concrete sensing/ imagining subject, and "explanatory," insofar as they regard them explicitly in relation to one another (and thus only implicitly in relation to me as a concrete sensing/imagining subject).

Thirdly, there are two main kinds of activity in each of the three successive lines of questioning: initially, my developmental inquiry or reflection or deliberation, where I am on the way to an intended cognitional achievement; subsequently, insofar as I achieve the goal, my active but nondevelopmental complacency in that achievement.

Fourthly, my "successful" answering of the questions is in important part a function of the skill with which I constitute myself as intelligent in my inquiry, reasonable in my reflection, and responsible in my deliberation. And the very possibility of such self-constituting, in turn, underlines the non-reflexive character of my primitive self-presence or consciousness. For there could be no cognitional self-constituting where there was not even cognitional self-presence; but if I became self-present only through reflection, then I would lack self-presence in the moment of my original, pre-reflexive, constitution.

Fifthly, the general "four-levelled" pattern of my cognitional activity, a level of data plus three successive levels of questioning and answering, is *a priori*. That is to say, it is a pattern that, although manifested in all instances of my knowing and capable of being objectified only after some instances have occurred, nonetheless is given in advance of all those instances and thus is dependent upon none of them. It is a pattern that is part of the very structure of my dynamic conscious intentionality.

Sixthly, although in its actual direct achievements my structured questioning is restricted to whatever intrinsically is intelligently understandable (and reasonably affirmable and responsibly evaluable) *in relation to me as a concrete sensing/imagining subject,*[33] in its objective or goal it is not so restricted. On the contrary, in its objective or goal my structured questioning is altogether unrestricted, oriented toward simply whatever intrinsically is intelligently understandable (and reasonably affirmable and responsibly evaluable).

Critical. In the perspective of the Lonerganian phenomenology of knowing, Hartshorne's (implicit) cognitional phenomenology has at least one major strength; but it also has a very significant weakness, a weakness from which further important defects flow.[34]

The major strength is the recognition that as a subject one is primitively present to oneself *non-reflexively* and, moreover, *as self-constituting.* The notion of one's primitive self-presence as non-reflexive is uniquely adequate to the latter as genuine *self*-presence; and the notion of that self-presence as self-constituting is uniquely consistent with the fact that as a knower—and, more generally, as an actor—one is capable of proceeding intelligently, reasonably, and responsibly, rather than invariably functioning just mechanically, blindly, unwittingly, as purely other-determined.

While Hartshorne's cognitional phenomenology is astute in its retrieval of consciousness, however, it is seriously flawed in its retrieval of intentionality. For Hartshorne overlooks the fact that one grasps a full cognitional term not immediately, in direct and unmediated awareness, but rather through the mediation of questions and answers—and, furthermore, that once one has grasped that term one's activity, though continuing, is no longer a "movement" in any sense but rather "activity beyond movement."

This oversight of the constitutive role of questions and answers in the knowing process gives rise, in turn, to two further grave faults. First, the distinctions among data (whether "data of sense" or "data of consciousness"), descriptive intelligibility, and explanatory intelligibility are blurred, so that a thing or property merely as given, as understood in relation to me as a concrete sensing/imagining subject, and as understood in relation to other things or properties unfortunately all tend to be conflated. Second, the distinction between intelligibility, on the one hand, and affirmability (and evaluability), on the other, is identified with the distinction between the abstract and the concrete, so that the difference between a thing or property merely as hypothetical and as verified is mistakenly reduced to the difference between the thing or property as taken apart from any particular spatiotemporal location and as taken here/there and now/then.[35] And these two deficiencies, finally, are what undergird Hartshorne's erroneous (albeit largely just implicit) phenomenological supposition that that toward which one's cognitional awareness is fundamentally oriented, and which thus at least performatively is defined as the actual, is concretely spatiotemporal.[36]

c') My fundamental criterion of the meaningfulness and truth of any assertion is "the constitutive structural aspect of my concrete cognitional praxis."[37]

Positive. A level of data of sense or of consciousness, followed by three successive levels of questioning and answering, with the orientation of the latter three levels not restricted to *descriptive* intelligibility (and affirmability and evaluability), and with the entire four-levelled pattern given *a priori*, as reflecting in part the intrinsic character of my dynamic conscious intentionality—this is what a Lonerganian means by "the constitutive structural aspect of my concrete cognitional praxis."[38] On the Lonerganian approach, this given pattern of my cognitional activity is my fundamental, though not necessarily my only, measure of the meaningfulness of any claim. For unless I understood in advance at least something of what I wonder about, I wouldn't be able to recognize it if I found it; but it is just this "something" that is given *a priori* in my dynamic structural orientation to intelligibility, an orientation expressed in my "what" questions. And similarly for the ultimate criterion of truth: the final, though not necessarily the only, measure of the truth of any claim is that I cannot deny the claim without at least implicitly denying "something" of myself, namely, what is given *a priori* in my dynamic structural orientations to affirmability and evaluability, orientations expressed in my "is" and "ought" questions respectively.

Furthermore, just as the *a priori* features of my cognitional activity and its terms necessarily prefigure in a general way their *a posteriori* features, so explicit philosophy (as the articulation of the former) in a general way necessarily relates and distinguishes the various empirical disciplines (as articulations of the latter). Again, just as the *a priori* features of my cognitional activity necessarily prefigure the *a priori* features of its terms, so, within explicit philosophy, cognitional phenomenology (as the articulation of the former) underpins metaphysics (as the articulation of the latter). Consequently, just as the *a priori* features of my cognitional activity necessarily either directly or indirectly prefigure in a general way the *a posteriori* features of my cognitional activity and its terms, so explicit cognitional phenomenology necessarily either directly or indirectly relates and distinguishes the various empirical disciplines.[39]

Critical. From the Lonerganian viewpoint, Hartshorne is to be commended for recognizing that the ultimate standard of the meaningfulness and truth of any claim must lie in the line of what is actual rather than merely possible, and in the line of subject rather than mere objects. Nonetheless Hartshorne does not go far enough in this "twofold turn," for he fails to turn explicitly to *his own* concrete cognitional subjectivity. Specifically, his retrieval of himself as a knower is insufficient to manifest that the intelligibility, affirmability, and evaluability of his own cognitional terms, and thus of the meaning and truth of the claims that would express those terms, are determined in their *a priori* features by the *a priori* features of the cognitional activity that intends them.[40] And thus overlooking the foundational character of his own cognitional subjectivity, he cannot discuss criteria of meaningfulness and truth in any more basic way than in terms of cognitional objects, albeit objects that he conceives as themselves being subjects. That is to say, he can do no more than give metaphysical answers to questions that fundamentally are phenomenological, answers that thus miss the basic thrust of the questions and to that extent are non-answers.

Moreover, Hartshorne's neglect of himself as a knower has three further negative consequences for his scholarly enterprise. First, he is misled into conceiving the difference between explicit philosophy and the various empirical disciplines as the difference between utterly abstract claims and those which are less abstract, rather than as the difference between claims expressing the *a priori* features of one's own cognitional subjectivity and what it prefigures and claims expressing something else.[41] Second, he remains quite unaware of the foundational role of cognitional phenomenology in relation to metaphysics within philosophy. Third, feeling no philosophical pressure to develop a really detailed and thoroughgoing explicit cognitional phenomenology, he fails to do so.

b') The actual is whatever intrinsically is "intelligently understandable," "reasonably affirmable," and "responsibly evaluable."[42]

Positive. On the Lonerganian approach, intelligibility, affirmability, and evaluability are "transcendental features" of actuality. This follows from the prior claim about the given character of knowing: that toward which my questioning is oriented, and which thus performatively (if not always explicitly) is defined as the actual, is whatever intrinsically is intelligently understandable, reasonably affirmable, and responsibly evaluable.

In addition, since my *a priori* wonder about intelligibility, affirmability, and evaluability is without restriction, I cannot—without operational self-contradiction—deny that actuality is more than just what is concretely spatiotemporal, more than just what I can grasp in relation to myself as a concrete sensing/imagining subject.[43] That is to say, I cannot consistently deny that actuality has a non-spatiotemporal, immaterial, strictly spiritual dimension as well.

Again, in my dynamic orientation toward intelligibility, affirmability, and evaluability I am self-present in a non-reflexive way, though only primitively. I am self-constituting, though only partly. And I do on occasion succeed in achieving incremental cognitional terms in which I am actively complacent, though often I am merely in process toward such achievements. Given these features of my own subjectivity, I cannot exclude, at least in advance, the possibility of a subject that, not suffering such limitations as mine, would be fully self-present in a non-reflexive way, would be totally self-constituting, and would never be in process because it would already possess the fulness of all that it could possess, a subject simply perduring in utterly unlimited activity altogether beyond "movement" in any sense.

Critical. From the Lonerganian standpoint, just as Hartshorne's philosophical claims regarding cognitional activity and the fundamental criterion of meaningfulness and truth are defective, so also is his philosophical claim—shaped to some extent by the foregoing— regarding the actual. More exactly, since I have no performatively incontrovertible grounds for asserting that my grasp of things or properties *in relation to me as a concrete sensing/imagining subject* is characteristic of my knowing as such (rather than of merely one kind of knowing), neither does it follow philosophically that concrete spatiotemporality is characteristic of actuality as such (rather than of merely one kind of actuality). And, again, since I have no performatively incontrovertible warrant for asserting that creative self-determination is intrinsically characteristic of whatever I desire to know (rather than of merely one kind of knowable), neither does it follow philosophically that every element in the concrete actual universe is creatively self-determining. The claim of universal creativity is either an utterly uncritical—i.e., dogmatic—philosophical assertion, or else it is a mere empirical hypothesis, to be established, if at all, through the usual procedures of empirical verification.

a') God is the "unrestrictedly intelligent, wise, and loving ground and goal of all that is."[44]

Positive. On Lonergan's philosophical argumentation, the notion of God, the supremely perfect one, is identically the notion of the ultimate objective of one's dynamic cognitional orientation toward actuality. It is the notion of that which in function of itself intrinsically is intelligently understandable, reasonably affirmable, and responsibly evaluable, and in function of which everything else intrinsically is intelligently understandable, reasonably affirmable, and responsibly evaluable. It is the notion of that which, if known exhaustively, would allow all of one's questioning to cease.

Working out the implications of this notion brings one at length to conceive of God as an unrestricted act of understanding, an act that is identically an unrestricted act of affirming and of loving.[45] This act is fully self-present in a non-reflexive way and, moreover, it is totally self-constituting. It is completely one, simple, self-identical in nature. It is purely immaterial, strictly spiritual, diversified neither spatially nor temporally. It is totally necessary. And it is wholly immutable and changeless—not, however, as though suffering under some constraint but rather as free from any need, already possessing the fulness of all that it could possess.

The primary content of this unrestricted act is the act itself: God is unlimited self-understanding, self-affirmation, self-love. There is, however, a secondary content: in and through the act whereby without limitation he understands, affirms, and loves himself, God understands, affirms, and loves everything else. And thus, although in one sense God is utterly transcendent to the world, not "really related" to it, not ontologically dependent upon it, in another sense God is utterly immanent in the world, "intentionally related" to it, totally attuned to it in exhaustive knowledge and effective love. God is "more intimate to me than myself."

In this context, of course, the notion of God as unrestricted act of understanding, affirming, and loving also eventually determines the specific senses of words commonly applied to God. Thus, as "intelligent," God is omniscient, knowing perfectly all that could be. As "wise," God is omnisapient, knowing perfectly all that was, is, and will be. In addition, God is omnipotent: as "loving," he wishes everything well with a constancy and efficacy of which we have only a hint in our human relationships; he undergirds all things and calls all things to himself, but in a way that respects each thing's characteristic nature—the spontaneity of evolving beings, the freedom of human beings, etc.[46]

In sum, to the question, "Is God in process?", Lonergan (and, more broadly, the Thomist tradition) responds, "No, God is activity altogether beyond process."[47]

Critical. On the Lonerganian view, Hartshorne is to be applauded for his effort to eliminate the inadequacies in a certain popular religious and even theological notion of God by eliminating the inadequacies in the philosophical notion of God that underlies it. For one cannot deny that the idea of God as an irresistible cosmic controller, such that creaturely spontaneity and freedom are ultimately just illusions, is an idea that, though not uncommon, is religiously and theologically at least somewhat problematic. Nor can one deny that this idea, whatever its strictly religious origins, has on occasion found explicit confirmation in a certain philosophical account of divine omnipotence, an account that in any event it systematically presupposes.[48]

Furthermore, Hartshorne is undoubtedly correct in attempting to emend this philosophical account of God by emending the more general philosophical account from which it follows. For just as religious and theological suppositions about God necessarily reflect underlying (though not always explicit) philosophical suppositions about God, so the latter necessarily reflect underlying (though not always explicit) general philosophical suppositions. Hence, just as a thorough revision of the first requires a thorough revision of the second, so the latter requires a thorough revision of the third.

Unfortunately, however, Hartshorne's general philosophical revision is seriously defective, defective precisely because it is insufficiently radical. For if Hartshorne is keenly aware that the metaphysics of God systematically presupposes a general metaphysics, he appears to be almost completely unaware that a general metaphysics in turn, insofar as it is not simply dogmatic, methodologically presupposes a cognitional phenomenology—in the limit, a phenomenology of the cognitional activity of the very person asserting the metaphysics. This oversight of the foundational role of cognitional phenomenology in relation to general metaphysics within philosophy detrimentally affects Hartshorne's revised general metaphysics in two ways. First, since he neglects to develop a careful explicit cognitional phenomenology, certain assertions that are critically metaphysical in the sense that they do indeed flow from his implicit cognitional phenomenology are nonetheless as truncated and unrefined as the latter. Notable among these is his identification of *the actual* with *the concretely spatiotemporal.* Second, certain other assertions that Hartshorne takes to be somehow "critically" metaphysical in character are in fact either dogmatically metaphysical or else just empirical. And notable among these is his identification of *the actual* with *the creative, the self-determining.*

Now, Hartshorne's revised metaphysics of God follows with perfect consistency from his revised general metaphysics.[49] In particular, the account of divine actuality as supremely extended spatiotemporally, supremely contingent and developing, supremely dependent and vulnerable, is very much of a piece with the general account of actuality as concretely spatio-temporal and self-constituting. But what follows consistently from a flawed principle shares the flaws of that principle. Hence in the final analysis Hartshorne's notion of God is philosophically—and thus, on that ground, as well as perhaps on other grounds, also religiously and theologically—at least as problematic as the notion he would reject.

IV. CONCLUSION

Is divine actuality in process, or is it activity altogether beyond process? Specifically, in the terms of the present essay, is the Hartshornian (and, more broadly, the process) notion of God philosophically superior to the Lonerganian (and, more broadly, the Thomist) notion, or just the reverse?

Furthermore, exactly how does one decide that question? What in this case is the criterion to which, as a philosopher, one makes appeal?

Let me conclude this essay by briefly indicating my own stances on these two issues, beginning with the latter.

It strikes me that among the most important contributions of modern and post-modern philosophy to the scholarly enterprise in general must be counted their elucidation of the fact that one's fundamental, though not necessarily only, criterion of the meaningfulness and truth of any statement whatsoever is concrete rather than abstract, *a priori* rather than *a posteriori*, and personal rather than impersonal.[50] Although it is not always appreciated sufficiently in principle or remembered sufficiently in practice even by professional philosophers, let alone others, post-medieval philosophical discussions taken collectively show rather clearly, I would suggest, that one's basic gauge of meaningfulness and truth is necessarily a function of the actual rather than the merely possible, of invariant structures rather than variable complements, and of cognitional activity (and, in the limit, one's own) rather than cognitional terms. Or, again, objectifying one's primary cognitional standard is a matter of appropriating the "lived" rather than developing a theory, of engaging in explicit philosophy rather than empirics, and of doing (ultimately personal) cognitional phenomenology rather than metaphysics.

In relation to the issue at hand, I would amplify this point as follows. First, empirical claims are those whose criteria of meaningfulness and truth include both *a posteriori* and *a priori* elements, while philosophical claims are those whose criteria are entirely *a priori*. More exactly, metaphysical claims are those whose proximate criterion is the *a priori* structure of one's own concrete cognitional terms. Cognitional-phenomenological claims, on the other hand, are those whose proximate criterion is the *a priori* structure of one's own concrete cognitional activities. And just as the *a priori* structure of one's own concrete cognitional activities necessarily prefigures the *a priori* structure of one's own concrete cognitional terms, so the proximate criterion of cognitional-phenomenological claims is identically the remote criterion of metaphysical claims.

Secondly, to grasp any claim as meaningful and true is to grasp that claim as satisfying the relevant criteria of meaningfulness and truth. But since the criteria for the meaningfulness and truth of any philosophical claim are entirely *a priori*, to grasp any philosophical claim as meaningful and true is to grasp that claim as satisfying criteria that are entirely *a priori*.

Thirdly, to grasp a claim as satisfying criteria that are entirely *a priori* is nothing other than to grasp that claim as expressing, at least partially, precisely those criteria.[51] Hence, to grasp a cognitional-phenomenological claim as meaningful and true is to grasp it as immediately expressing, at least partially, the *a priori* structure of one's own concrete cognitional activity. And to grasp a metaphysical claim as meaningful and true is to grasp it as both *immediately* expressing at least something of the *a priori* structure of one's own concrete cognitional terms and *ultimately* expressing at least something of the *a priori* structure of one's own concrete cognitional activity.

Fourthly, as we have been interpreting them, the two diametrically opposed claims about God that we are presently considering are philosophical claims—and, more narrowly, metaphysical claims. Therefore, to grasp either of them as meaningful and true is to grasp either of them as both *immediately* expressing at least something of the *a priori* structure of one's own concrete cognitional terms and *ultimately* expressing at least something of the *a priori* structure of one's own concrete cognitional activity. Or, summarily, one can properly resolve the metaphysical question about God only in function of resolving the cognitional-phenomenological question about oneself.

If the reader interprets what I have just said as intimating my total endorsement of what I have sketched earlier as the Lonerganian stance on the character of one's fundamental criterion of meaningfulness and truth, and my corresponding rejection of the Hartshornian stance on the same issue, she is quite correct. It is important to note, however, that this endorsement does not necessarily imply my preference of the Lonerganian over the Hartshornian stances on the other three philosophical issues that I have raised—the character of the invariant structure of one's concrete cognitional activity, the character of actuality in general, and the nature of God. For a given thinker's failure to recognize explicitly the foundational character of his own cognitional subjectivity need not prevent him from maintaining a correct cognitional phenomenology in implicit fashion, and thus being impelled, despite his oversight, toward a correct general metaphysics and, in turn, a correct metaphysics of God.

Nonetheless, I should say that I completely endorse the Lonerganian stances on those three remaining issues as well, and I reject the Hartshornian stances insofar as they are at odds with them. I find Lonergan's cognitional phenomenology to provide an account of me as a knower that is both incontrovertibly correct and astonishingly complete. And I find his general metaphysics to follow consistently from this cognitional phenomenology, and his metaphysics of God to follow consistently in turn from this general metaphysics. On the other hand, I find Hartshorne's (implicit) cognitional phenomenology, though not without its strengths, especially in regard to my cognitional consciousness, to be grossly underdeveloped and at least to that extent highly misleading, especially in regard to my cognitional intentionality. I find his general metaphysics similarly crude and inadequate insofar as it follows consistently from this cognitional phenomenology, and simply unacceptable as metaphysics insofar as it does not follow consistently from any cognitional phenomenology. Finally, I find Hartshorne's metaphysics of God to be quite consistent with his general metaphysics and thus radically invalidated by the flaws of the latter. In function of her grasp of her own concrete cognitional subjectivity, does the reader of this essay find otherwise?

NOTES

1 Besides "process theology," this position also is sometimes called "neo-classical theism," "dipolar theism," and "panentheism." For a bit of background on the matter of the labels, see John Cobb & David Griffin, *Process Theology: An Introductory Exposition* (Philadelphia: Westminster, 1976), pp. 7–8.

2 For a clear and concise account of the process theologians' principal claims and arguments, see Cobb & Griffin, esp. pp. 13–94.

3 For an excellent and detailed summary of the history of process theology after Whitehead, see Delwin Brown, Ralph James & Gene Reeves, *Process Theology and Christian Thought* (Indianapolis: Bobbs-Merrill, 1971), pp. 21–64. A list of the most influential figures surely would include Henry Nelson Wieman, Bernard Loomer, Daniel Day Williams, Bernard Meland, Schubert Ogden, John Cobb, William Beardslee, and Norman Pittenger. Among more recent writers of note are Richard Overman, Don Browning, Eugene Peters, William Dean, and David Griffin.

4 See, e.g., Ewert Cousins, "Process Models in Culture, Philosophy, and Theology," in Cousins, ed., *Process Theology: Basic Writings* (New York: Paulist Press, 1971), pp. 3–20; Bernard Lee, *The Becoming of the Church* (New York: Paulist Press, 1974); "The Two Process Theologies," *Theological Studies*, 45 (1984), 307–319; David Tracy, *Blessed Rage for Order* (New York: Seabury, 1975), esp. pp. 122–203; Robert Mellert, *What is Process Theology?* (New York: Paulist Press, 1975); Joseph Bracken, "Process Philosophy and Trinitarian Theology," *Process Studies*, 8 (1978), 213–30; "Ecclesiology and the Problem of the One and the Many," *Theological Studies*, 43 (1982), 298–311; John Stacer, "Divine Reverence for Us: God's Being Present, Cherishing, and Persuading," *Theological Studies*, 44 (1983), 438–55; and J.J. Mueller, "Appreciative Awareness: The Feeling-Dimension in Religious Experience," *Theological Studies*, 45 (1984), 57–79.

5 See, e.g., Harold Kushner, *When Bad things Happen to Good People* (New York: Schocken, 1981).

6 See, e.g., the works listed in Cobb & Griffin, pp. 180–85. And of course many more writings on process theology have appeared since the publication of this list in 1976.

7 See, e.g., E.L. Mascall, *He Who Is* (London: Longmans, Green, 1943), pp. 150–60; W. Norris Clarke, "A New Look at the Immutability of God," in Robert Roth, ed., *God Knowable and Unknowable* (New York: Fordham Univ. Press, 1973), pp. 43–72; *The Philosophical Approach to God* (Winston-Salem, N.C.: Wake Forest Univ. Press, 1979); William Hill, "Does the World Make a Difference to God?" *The Thomist*, 38 (1974), 146–64; "Does God Know the Future? Aquinas and Some Moderns," *Theological Studies*, 36 (1975), 3–18; "In What Sense is God Infinite? A Thomistic View," *The Thomist*, 42 (1978), 14–27; "The Historicity of God," *Theological Studies*, 45 (1984), 320–33; John Wright, "Divine Knowledge and Human Freedom: The God Who Dialogues," *Theological Studies*, 38 (1977), 450–77; and David Burrell, *Aquinas: God and Action* (London: Routledge

& Kegal Paul, 1979), pp. 78–89; "Does Process Theology Rest on a Mistake?" *Theological Studies,* 43 (1982), 125–35.

8   Although various works undertake comparisons of process and Thomist thinkers on this or that philosophical issue or restricted set of such issues, to date I have not found any work that undertakes a comparison across what I would judge to be the full range of distinct philosophical issues over which the two groups disagree. I intend this essay, then, as a contribution, however small, to a philosophical comparison of the two groups that would be truly comprehensive.

9   Although there are some very significant and well-recognized differences between the philosophical views of Hartshorne and those of certain other seminal process thinkers, notably Whitehead, the similarities are surely far more massive and significant; and thus for the broad comparative purposes of the present essay I feel quite justified in selecting Hartshorne as representative of the group as a whole. On Hartshorne's historical and systematic relations to Whitehead, see Cobb & Griffin, pp. 167–69, and Lewis Ford, ed., *Two Process Philosophers: Hartshorne's Encounter with Whitehead* (Tallahassee: American Academy of Religion, 1973).

10   Just as Hartshorne differs in important ways from other process thinkers, so Lonergan differs in important ways from others in the modern Thomist tradition. Nonetheless, in the latter case as in the former the underlying similarities are far more numerous and important; and thus for present purposes I deem it fully legitimate to propose Lonergan as a representative Thomist (albeit a highly original one). For more on this issue, see Joseph Donceel, "Introduction," in Emerich Coreth, *Metaphysics* (New York: Herder & Herder, 1968); and Michael Vertin, "Marechal, Lonergan, and the Phenomenology of Knowing," in Matthew Lamb, ed., *Creativity and Method* (Milwaukee: Marquette Univ. Press, 1981), pp. 411–22.

11   In terms familiar to those persons acquainted with Lonergan's later writings, I should say that I conceive this essay as an exercise chiefly in the functional specialty, "Dialectic." But it necessarily also reflects something of my personal efforts in the functional specialty, "Foundations"—implicitly in the two expository sections, and explicitly in the concluding section.

12   To facilitate a wide-range comparison of Hartshorne and Lonergan within the confines of a relatively short paper, I shall provide neither many quotations nor exhaustive page-references. Rather I shall proceed by expounding a series of philosophical claims that, although formulated by me, are faithful reflections, I believe, of the intentions of these two thinkers; and I shall provide representative page-references for each of these claims. For Hartshorne on what I am here formulating as his characteristic philosophical claim regarding God, see, e.g., *The Logic of Perfection* (La Salle, Illinois: Open Court, 1962), pp. 3–27, 133–47, 191–215, 245–62; *A Natural Theology for Our Time* (La Salle, Illinois: Open Court, 1967), pp. 1–28, 29–65; and *Creative Synthesis and Philosophical Method* (London: SCM, 1970), pp. 1–18, 227–44, 261–74.

13   On the accuracy of the process tradition's account of the history of explicit philosophy, see below, n. 48.

14   A further difficulty with this notion of God, in Hartshorne's judgment, is that it forces one either to impute evil to God or else to make light of it. See, e.g., *Logic,* pp. 12–14, 143–44, 203–207; and *Natural Theology,* pp. 80–82, 116–28.

15   Hartshorne's God is not, of course, an individual in the ordinary sense. While ordinary individuals are particular, God is uniquely the "universal" individual. See, e.g., *Natural Theology,* pp. 24–43; and *Logic,* pp. 92, 158, 262.

16   More exactly, while Hartshorne's God does not know what will be but as yet is not, he never ceases to know even the slightest detail of what once was. See, e.g., *Logic,* 245–62.

17   Hartshorne also proposes that this notion of God uniquely allows us to take evil seriously without compromising the goodness of God. See, e.g., *Logic,* pp. 44, 203–207, 295, 310–15; and *Natural*

Theology, pp. 80–82, 116–28. Moreover, Hartshorne argues at some length that, by means of a suitably refined form of ontological argumentation, God conceived in this way can be proved to exist. See *Logic,* pp. 28–117; and *Natural Theology,* pp. 29–65.

18   To be precise, the Whiteheadian distinction between God's "primordial nature" and his "consequent nature" is similar to the Hartshornian distinction between God's "abstract essence" and his "concrete actuality"; but it is not identical with it in every respect. See, e.g., Cobb & Griffin, pp. 41–62.

19   See, e.g., *Logic,* pp. 118–32, 161–90, 191–215, 216–33; *Natural Theology,* pp. 66–89; and *Creative Synthesis,* pp. 19–42, 57–68, 99–130.

20   It is important to note that for Hartshorne, and for the process tradition generally, "experience" is a far broader notion than "consciousness." Experience is basic to every actual event. Consciousness, on the other hand, is a further development: it is the selective, structuring, and unifying "illumination" of experience. See, e.g., Cobb & Griffin, pp. 16–18, 33–35, 87–90.

21   This intuiting, feeling, prehending, is radically affective, by no means just "neutral." See, e.g., *Creative Synthesis,* pp. 76, 91–92, 109, 241.

22   On the process approach, "creativity" thus replaces "causality" as traditionally understood. Here, the effect intuits its causes and thus is superior to them.

23   See, e.g., *Logic,* pp. 191–215, 216–33, 280–97; *Natural Theology,* pp. 90–125; and *Creative Synthesis,* pp. 69–98, 99–130.

24   Note that for Hartshorne "to be objective" means "to be a datum for intuition," and "to be subjective" means "to intuit a datum." I.e., by contrast with an interpretation often appropriate in other philosophical contexts, these expressions in Hartshorne's writings do *not* mean "to possess epistemological validity" and "to lack epistemological validity" respectively.

25   See, e.g., *Logic,* pp. 191–215, 216–33, 280–97; *Natural Theology,* pp. 90–125; and *Creative Synthesis,* pp. 57–68, 99–130, 205–226.

26   This question is the one that Lonergan will label "the question of cognitional theory." For references, see below, n. 31.

27   See, e.g., *Creative Synthesis,* pp. 6, 31–33, 112, 164. Cf. *Logic,* pp. 118–32, 216–33.

28   It is one thing to interpret an author on the basis of what he says; it is quite another to interpret him on the basis of what one judges to be implied by what he says. The first demands care and sensitivity; the second, even more care and sensitivity. Nevertheless, it remains that the second, and not just the first, surely is both legitimate in principle and well established in scholarly practice.

29   Used in this way, "intentional" and "conscious" are my terms, not Hartshorne's.

30   More fully, in the fundamental instances of cognitional awareness, the object is present as constituted by concrete spatiotemporality; the subject, as conditioned by it. In the less fundamental instances, the object is present as constituted by abstract spatiotemporality; the subject, as conditioned by it. Also see below, n. 36.

31   As a way of reflecting something of the different sequences in which Hartshorne and Lonergan elaborate their respective overall philosophical perspectives, the order in which I present the Lonerganian stances on the four key issues that we are considering is the inverse of the order in which I present the Hartshornian stances. To facilitate comparison of correlative claims, however, I denote them by the same letter, with a distinguishing "prime" mark for the Lonerganian claims. For Lonergan on what I am here formulating as his characteristic philosophical claim regarding one's cognitional activity, see, e.g., *Insight: A Study of Human Understanding* (New York: Philosophical Library, 1957), pp. 271–347; *Collection: Papers by Bernard Lonergan* (New York: Herder & Herder, 1967), pp. 152–63, 173–92, 202–220, 221–39; and *Method in Theology* (New York: Herder & Herder, 1972), pp. 3–25.

32   For the sake of restricting the focus to the most important points on which to compare Lonergan with Hartshorne, in the present essay I wish to prescind largely from the "later" Lonergan's contention that the human intention of "value," "the positively evaluable," is a distinct intention beyond that of "the real," "the actual," "the affirmable." At the same time, however, I wish both to underline Lonergan's constant contention that *all* full-fledged human knowing is ultimately a matter of successfully answering questions and, as well, to point toward the later development in his thought. Therefore I regularly speak here of the human intentions of "intelligibility," "affirmability," *and* "(mere) evaluability": in this formulation, "(mere) evaluability" is "convertible" (in the scholastic sense) with "affirmability."

33   On the need for descriptions even in the development and verification of explanations, see *Insight,* pp. 247, 291–99, etc.

34   Lest any errors in this critique of Hartshorne or any of the three other critiques to follow be wrongly imputed, I should stress that all four critiques, though intended to reflect Lonergan's perspective in an authentic way, are my own extrapolations from his work.

35   This twofold criticism may be expressed in another way by saying that Hartshorne (1) confuses the psychological distinctions among sensation/consciousness, description, and explanation, and (2) wrongly identifies the metaphysical distinction between potency/form and act with the logical distinction between universal and particular.

36   Within the Lonerganian framework one may distinguish among (1) contents of sensing, as wholly constituted by the concretely spatiotemporal; (2) acts of sensing, as wholly conditioned intrinsically by the concretely spatiotemporal; (3) contents of concrete descriptive understanding, etc., as partly constituted by the concretely spatiotemporal; (4) acts of concrete descriptive understanding, etc., as partly conditioned intrinsically by the concretely spatiotemporal; (5) contents of abstract descriptive understanding, etc., as partly constituted by the abstractly spatiotemporal; (6) acts of abstract descriptive understanding, etc., as partly conditioned intrinsically by the abstractly spatiotemporal; (7) contents of explanatory understanding, etc., as in no way constituted by either the concretely or the abstractly spatiotemporal; and (8) acts of explanatory understanding, etc., as in no way conditioned intrinsically by either the concretely or the abstractly spatiotemporal. On my interpretation, Hartshorne identifies actuality with the first four members of this sequence, without however always distinguishing them clearly.

37   See, e.g., *Insight,* pp. 348–84; *Collection,* pp. 152–63, 202–220, 221–39; and *Method,* pp. 3–25.

38   The term "praxis" is used here as a way of specifying not just any cognitional practice but rather cognitional practice at its best, cognitional practice that is wholly intelligent, entirely reasonable, and thoroughly responsible.

39   For more detail on philosophy as relating and distinguishing the empirical disciplines, see, e.g., *Insight,* pp. 398–401, 483–87, 497–98, 513, 521–29, 743–47.

40   It may not be untimely to recall that "cognitional terms" for Lonergan are not of course "*merely* cognitional"—i.e., as opposed to "ontological." On the contrary, Lonergan regularly argues that what one at least implicitly means by "cognitional term" is inevitably the basic component of what one means by "ontological term." See, e.g., *Insight,* pp. 497–502.

41   Note that abstract notions and *a priori* notions both are sometimes called "general" notions (and similarly for the claims expressing them). In such cases, however, the word "general" then has two very different senses. For abstract notions are "precisively" general. They arise through one's prescinding from certain features of a concrete thing, and their genesis presupposes at least some progress of one's actual cognitional process. *A priori* notions, by contrast, are "heuristically" general. They arise through one's anticipating the features of a concrete thing, and they antecede actual knowing as question antecedes answer.

42   See, e.g., *Insight*, pp. 385–529; *Collection*, pp. 152–63, 202–220, 221–39; and *Method*, pp. 3–25.

43   See above, n. 36.

44   See, e.g., *Insight*, pp. 634–86; *Collection*, pp. 54–67, 84–95; and *Method*, pp. 100–118.

45   For our present purposes, the most important point about this conclusion regarding God is not the precise details of the lengthy argument through which Lonergan arrives at it but rather the fact that he views it as following inexorably from what I have formulated above as his characteristic claim regarding actuality in general. For the details of Lonergan's argument, see *Insight*, pp. 641–65.

46   Lonergan also carefully distinguishes what commonly is labelled "evil" into "basic sin," "moral evils," and "physical evils," and then goes on to argue that none of these necessarily contradicts the nature of God as he portrays it. See, e.g., *Insight*, pp. 666–68. Moreover, by means of what we might call a "transcendental" argument, Lonergan claims to vindicate the existence of God as thus portrayed. See *Insight*, pp. 669–77; cf. pp. 651–57.

47   It remains, of course, that both Lonergan and other Christian thinkers in the Thomist tradition, while denying that God in any way "becomes," nevertheless assert two intra-Trinitarian "processions." "Process" in this latter sense, however, totally excludes the "becoming" that gives the sense of the word as used throughout the present essay. See, e.g., Lonergan, *Verbum: Word and Idea in Aquinas* (Notre Dame: Univ. of Notre Dame Press, 1967), pp. 183–220.

48   Thinkers of a Lonerganian bent, and by no means only these, nonetheless have deep reservations about the accuracy of the Hartshornian—and, more broadly, the typical process—account of the history of explicit philosophy. In their judgment, the historiographical sensitivity of the process tradition is greatly diminished by that tradition's close adherence, even in the doing of historiography, to systematic suppositions that themselves are highly inadequate. Thus, to take but one example, process thinkers regularly fail to recognize that what Aquinas means by such words as *"esse"* and *"operatio"* is something utterly different from either potency or form or passage from potency to form. And, failing in this recognition, they wrongly assimilate the philosophy of Aquinas to that of Greek or modern thinkers who, whatever their merits, do not envisage the range of metaphysical elements that Aquinas does. Nor is Aquinas' metaphysics of God therefore necessarily vulnerable to criticisms that may, perhaps, justly be levelled against the metaphysical claims of these other thinkers. For criticisms such as these, see, e.g., the authors cited in n. 7, above.

49   To put the point in a way that is more faithful to Hartshorne's own view of their relationship, I might say that his metaphysics of God, as the crowning principle of his general metaphysics, is perfectly consistent with the other principles within the latter. See, e.g., *Logic*, pp. 3–27.

50   It would, however, be quite mistaken to think that this fact went totally unrecognized before the advent of modern philosophy. On the history of the inchoate recognition of this fact in Greek and medieval philosophy, especially in the work of Aristotle and Aquinas, see Joseph Marechal, *Le point de depart de la metaphysique*, I (Bruxelles: L'Edition Universelle, 1944), pp. 21–56, 254–55. Cf. Joseph Michael Vertin, *The Transcendental Vindication of the First Step in Realist Metaphysics, according to Joseph Marechal* (Ann Arbor: University Microfilms International, 1982), pp. 160–80.

51   To put the point in another way, any *a priori* claim is "analytic." I.e., either it is "formally" analytic, or else it is "formally" synthetic but "transcendentally" analytic. See. e.g., Marechal, *Le point de depart de la metaphysique*, III (Bruxelles: L'Edition Universelle, 1944), pp. 122–24, n. 1.

V

Lonergan and a Process
Understanding of God

Thomas Hosinski, C.S.C.

To speak of Lonergan and process theology in the same breath usually signals a debate. The discussion, we suspect beforehand, will compare, evaluate, judge and finally side with one against the other. Certainly almost all philosophers and theologians who have addressed this topic have understood Lonergan's philosophy of God to be at odds with the interpretation of God presented by Alfred North Whitehead or Charles Hartshorne. It is difficult to disagree with this stance—and difficult to envision any other type of discussion—so long as we confine ourselves to Lonergan's conscious intention, his stated philosophy of God in *Insight*, and his own judgment: in Lonergan's own mind, his philosophy of God *is* at odds with a process understanding of God.[1]

Despite this state of affairs, I intend to address this topic in a most unexpected way. I will not directly compare Lonergan's philosophy of God to Whitehead's,[2] nor will I debate their relative merits. Instead, my concern will be entirely with the inner dynamic and the implications of Lonergan's own thought. In my estimation, the implications of the important developments in Lonergan's post-*Insight* thought ought to have an effect on Lonergan's philosophy of God. Although they have been applied to the context in which the philosophy of God is done, they have yet to be applied fully to the understanding of God that results from the inquiry. Reflection on this will lead me to advance the novel and unexpected thesis that Lonergan's thought can be a resource for a process understanding of God.

Although this thesis certainly goes beyond what Lonergan himself intended and is even in opposition to his own stated judgment, I hope to show that the dynamic of his thought and the pursuit of his insights can lead legitimately in this direction. Moreover, such an approach might help to persuade both those influenced by Lonergan's thought and those influenced by process thought that it is actually possible for them to have collaborative discussions.

Since the thesis that Lonergan's thought can give rise to a process understanding of God is novel and unexpected, I must begin by discussing the grounds which support such an approach to Lonergan's thought.

I. THE GROUNDS FOR RETHINKING THE IDEA OF GOD

The tasks of the philosophy of God and the functional specialty of systematics are distinct but, as Lonergan has argued persuasively, this does not mean that they ought to be separated.[3] In fact, as Lonergan points out, the philosophical and the religious questions of God are related fundamentally in several ways. Stemming from a common root in what, on a theological analysis, can be called "religious experience," all the questions of God are trying to discover the ultimate ground and final end of our experience as subjects.[4] The questions are distinct because of the contexts in which the inquiry is pursued, but even so they are cumulative and the strictly philosophical questions lead into the strictly religious questions of God.[5]

The strictly philosophical questions of God ask about the ultimate ground of our experience. They arise when we reflect on the implications of our subjective experience as it has been philosophically analyzed and understood. They are "wondering" questions, which begin with the structures of experience and ask what makes our experience, so understood, possible. Thus reflecting on the implications of the human subject's cognitional experience, Lonergan raises the questions concerning the ultimate ground of the intelligibility and the contingency of the universe.[6] Reflecting on the existential subject's moral intentionality, Lonergan raises the question concerning the ultimate ground of value.[7] But the philosophical questions of God do not end here. As is implicit especially in the moral question of God, the philosopher can also ask about the final meaning of human experience and the universe. In this form the question becomes more "anxious" than "wondering," more existentially acute. It is moved by craving for importance, for meaning, for purpose, for fulfillment. The "anxious" question is distinct from the "wondering" questions, yet they are related since both ask about the ultimate ground of the universe in different ways. Whereas the wondering questions ask about the ultimate ground in the sense of wanting to know what makes experience *possible*, the anxious question asks what experience *means* relative to that ultimate ground; it asks about the *character* of that ground.

Here the final philosophical question of God merges with the strictly *religious* question of God, which always asks about meaning and fulfillment. In the anxious, unfulfilled form, the strictly religious question asks, "Is there anyone or anything I can love without restriction?" And when we examine religious experience, we find religion preoccupied with discovering the divine *character* and the consequent meaning of our experience. As Lonergan expresses it, the strictly religious question of God (in the fulfilled form) emerges from the experience of being in love without restriction and asks, "with whom am I in love?"[8] Thus the questions of God are cumulative; the philosophical questions are drawn to and merge with the strictly religious questions of God.

Furthermore, Lonergan has argued that the ground of the *answers* to all these questions is to be found in religious experience.[9] Faith, the knowledge born of religious love, answers our anxious questions in *experience* because in faith we apprehend a boundless love poured into our hearts; we experience the character of the God we seek. But religious experience also discovers in itself the answers to the "wondering" questions raised by reflection on our cognitional and moral intentionality. This may be a "clouded revelation"[10] (because the subject lacks the proper differentiation of consciousness), but religious experience brings with it a conviction regarding the ground of the universe, so that even if we do not know how, cognitively and reflectively, nevertheless we know with our hearts that God is the answer to all questions for intelligence, reflection, and deliberation concerning the ultimate ground of our experience. Thus, Lonergan can argue, in actuality the God of the philosophers and the God of Abraham, Isaac, and Jacob are one and the same, and so the philosophy of God and the functional specialty of systematics, though distinct, ought not to be separated.[11]

Now if all of this is the case, then it seems to me that it ought to have some effect on the idea of God. If the ground of the answers to the cognitional and moral questions of God is to be found in religious experience, then certainly it seems reasonable to hold that the testimony of religious experience ought to have an important role in the understanding of God that emerges from those inquiries. If the *questions* of God are related, then it would seem that the *answers* to those questions, as expressed in ideas, would also be related. Moreover, if the questions of God are *cumulative*, then it would seem that any answers proposed to the "wondering" philosophical questions are in an important way incomplete until they have been united with and complemented by the understanding of God derived from religious experience. The very idea of God *itself* ought to reflect the fact that the God of the philosophers and the God of Abraham, Isaac, Jacob and Jesus are one and the same.

Lonergan, I believe, has pointed in this direction. In a brief but rich and tantalizing set of remarks, he has shown how the testimony of religious experience transforms the idea of God as it emerges from reflection on our moral intentionality. "Without faith the originating value is man and the terminal value is the human good man brings about."[12] But when a subject has been transformed by religious experience, when the subject's values have been transvalued by the supreme value known in faith,

> originating value is divine light and love, while terminal value is the whole universe. So the human good becomes absorbed in an all-encompassing good. Where before an account of the human good related men to one another and to nature, now human concern reaches beyond man's world to God and God's world.[13]

In short, religious conversion leads to moral conversion and moral conversion reveals to us the supreme value in the God with whom we are in love. Cognitive reflection on this experience enables us to understand that God is the originating and supreme instance of moral consciousness and that we find value in the world and in our moral intentionality because both we and all our fellow creatures are God's terminal values. Conceiving of God and the world in this way, Lonergan states, has certain implications.

> To conceive of God as originating value and the world as terminal value implies that God too is self-transcending and that the world is the fruit of his self-transcendence, the expression and manifestation of his benevolence and beneficence, his glory. . . . To say that God created the world for his glory is to say that he created it not for his sake but for ours. He made us in his image, for our authenticity consists in being like him, in self-transcending, in being origins of value, in true love.[14]

In cognitive reflection on what we know in faith, we gradually come to understand that the self-transcending moral intentionality found in every human subject has its ground and fulfilment in the self-transcedence of God. Our subjectivity is in God's image.

Lonergan's analysis of God as the supreme self-transcending subject implies that the idea of God is to be conceived by analogy with the structure we discover in our own subjectivity as that structure is enlightened by the testimony of religious experience. I am in complete agreement with this approach, but when I turn to Lonergan's discussion of God in *Insight*, I do not find this approach exemplified there.

II. The Procedure of "Insight" and a Possible Alternative

Although he provided a new context, Lonergan never revised the content of the notion of God presented in *Insight*.[15] Yet Lonergan's brief discussion of God in *Method in Theology* leads me to believe that it is a fruitful line of inquiry to consider how the post-*Insight* developments in Lonergan's thought might affect not just the context for the philosophy of God but also the content of the notion of God itself. Such a development of Lonergan's thought can be faithful to his methodological insights and might bring greater coherence and unity to the idea of God as it emerges from Lonergan's philosophy. My reasons for suggesting this line of inquiry can be presented most easily by first directing attention to several methodological issues.

First, it is important to notice that when Lonergan discusses the question of God as it arises from an analysis of our moral intentionality he actually raises a double question, or a question with both objective and subjective sides. He asks for the ultimate ground of the value we feel in the world (the objective side) and for the ultimate ground of the subject's moral intentionality (the subjective side).[16] Because he asks the subjective side of the question, Lonergan comes to conceive of God by analogy with the structure of human moral self-transcendence: God is discovered to be the supreme self-transcending subject. But when discussing the question of God as it arises from the two cognitional questions, Lonergan raises only the objective side.[17] He asks for the ultimate ground of the intelligibility and the contingent existence of the universe.[18] But he does not ask for the ultimate ground of the subject's ability to understand the intelligible or to make virtually unconditioned judgments of fact. It is clear that the subjective sides of these questions are implicit in Lonergan's thought. But if we raise them explicitly, it might lead us to reflect on the ultimate implications of understanding God analogically by reference to our experience of ourselves as knowing subjects. I will pursue the importance of this point below.

Second, it is important to notice that the two cognitional questions of God are metaphysical in character. Lonergan explicitly asks for the ultimate ground of the intelligible, contingent universe. Yet the analysis designed to answer these questions is expressed only in cognitional terms (concluding to the existence of the unrestricted act of understanding). Lonergan does not express these questions or pursue his analysis in terms of his own metaphysical elements. It might prove interesting to consider what would result if this cognitional analysis were complemented by an expression and an analysis in Lonergan's metaphysical terms as well. Furthermore, since we are attempting to discover the metaphysical characteristics of God and God's relation to the world, it seems methodologically reasonable to ask that this be done.

A third methodological issue concerns Lonergan's procedure when, in *Insight*, he attempts to show that the unrestricted act of understanding is properly called "God." It may help to set this in context. If we carefully examine Lonergan's procedure in Chapter XIX, we find that in the first eight sections of the chapter[19] Lonergan prepares the ground, raises the questions, and performs the analysis which conceives of the transcendent and unrestricted act of understanding as the ultimate ground required by the intelligibility and contingent existence of the universe. Having established this, Lonergan attempts to show in section nine that the unrestricted act of understanding is properly called "God."[20] In light of Lonergan's later discussion of the philosophical and religious questions of God, let us ask what Lonergan is attempting to do methodologically at this point. It seems to me that he is no longer addressing the strictly philosophical questions of God; in the new context provided by his post-*Insight* thought, these questions are effectively met by the first eight sections of Chapter XIX.[21] Rather in section nine[22] Lonergan seems to be trying to answer the strictly *religious* question of God by deriving the character of God from the implications of the philosophical conceptualization of God as unrestricted act of understanding. Yet Lonergan's procedure in section nine seems to be at variance with his procedure in discussing God in *Method in Theology* and this suggests that a procedure different from the one Lonergan actually follows in *Insight* might be possible within the framework of Lonergan's thought.

In *Method in Theology* Lonergan reflects on the implications of religious experience in order to conceptualize the character of God in relation to moral intentionality. He develops an understanding that presents God as exhibiting or exemplifying the same structure found in human subjects. God, like human subjects, is originating value and the world and human subjects are God's terminal values. Certainly we could understand God to be transcendent in the perfection with which God illustrates this structure: God is perfectly related to all terminal values by means of divine feelings, whereas we are severely limited in this regard. Yet neither the perfection nor the transcendence of God prevents Lonergan from conceiving of God as exemplifying the basic structure of moral intentionality and self-transcendence.

Yet when we examine how Lonergan conceives of God in section nine of *Insight*, it is clear that his discussion immediately makes God a radical *exception* to structure of cognitional process. This is obvious in the first major implication Lonergan derives from the unrestricted act of understanding. He argues that since the unrestricted act of understanding must be invulnerable as understanding, it must also be unconditional knowing.[23] The observation I would make here is that this argument does not depend on Lonergan's own brilliant analysis of cognitional process, which has shown that knowing is always a complex process of distinct acts and operations. Understanding is not knowing but is always a grasping of potential or possible intelligibilities that may have relevance for knowledge. Knowing, in contrast, always requires a reflective grasp of the possible intelligibilities as given in experience. Knowing, in short, always requires judgment; and judgment rests on encounter in experience. But when he comes to God, Lonergan makes God the radical exception to this structure. Unlike all cognitional structure with which we are familiar, in God understanding and knowing are identical and occur in a simple act.

I would argue that instead of making God a radical exception to the affirmed structure of cognitional process, one could pursue an understanding of God and God's knowledge as supremely illustrating this structure, just as Lonergan did in the face of the moral question of God. Such an approach would have the merit of employing generalized empirical method, utilizing the affirmed structure of cognitional process, subjectivity, and being, and calling upon the testimony of religious experience just as Lonergan does in *Method in Theology*. Generalized empirical method would not allow us to invoke exceptions to what has been discovered in our previous inquiries. Rather, the starting point would be that we have no reason to think that God's knowledge and (God's being), transcendent and perfect though God may be, is ontologically different from the structure we find in our knowing. After all, the entire philosophical conception of God is based on the assumption that we may conceive of God by analogy with the structure we discover in human subjective experience. If God's transcendence is taken to mean that God must be an exception to the structure of human cognitional process and becoming, then how can we ever be sure at what point to invoke the exception? It seems far more reasonable to assume that God is not an exception to the structure—though God may very well be transcendent in the perfection of how God illustrates it—and to try to work out an understanding of God in these terms. Moreover, such an approach would allow us to unify Lonergan's understanding of God as derived (in *Method in Theology*) from reflection on moral experience with an understanding of God derived from reflection on cognitional experience. We could then understand how God is the supreme illustration of *all* levels of our subjective experience.

There is another feature of Lonergan's development of the notion of God that I must consider since it would seem to preclude any process conception of God. This has to do with the attribute of perfection and what is derived from it. After having shown that the unrestricted act of understanding can be understood to be the primary being, Lonergan goes on to argue that "the primary being would be without any defect or lack or imperfection."[24] But later in the analysis, when Lonergan turns to the relation between the primary and the secondary intelligibles (or the relation between God and the world), he argues that "the perfect primary being does not develop, for it is without defect or lack or imperfection."[25] The clear presupposition of this argument is that development is inherently a "defect or lack or imperfection." Yet I believe it is possible to argue that this presupposition can find no ground in Lonergan's own metaphysics.

In the climactic moment of Lonergan's metaphysics, there occurs the insight into the isomorphism of knowing and the known. The ontological structure of being is discovered to be isomorphic with the affirmed structure of cognitional process. This results in a metaphysics of being understood as a dynamic process of becoming.[26] The ontological elements conceive of each actuality as a process, an emerging act of form developing from potency.[27] Moreover, Lonergan's cosmology, the world view of emergent probability, envisions the universe as a whole as a process of self-transcendent development.[28] The affirmed structure of being in Lonergan's metaphysics is a dynamic process of becoming, a process of development. This metaphysics offers no ground that I can find for holding that development per se is inherently an imperfection. This presupposition of Aristotelian-Thomist metaphysics appears to be at odds with the implications of Lonergan's own metaphysics. Moreover, God's transcendence and perfection do not demand this presupposition; in the understanding of God Lonergan worked out in *Method in Theology*, God's transcendence and perfection are shown not by making God a radical exception to the self-transcending structure discovered in human subjectivity, but by having God supremely illustrate that structure.

Thus it seems to me that it is possible to develop an approach to the understanding of God that differs from the one Lonergan actually took in *Insight* but which is in accord with the implications of his later thought. Since I have argued, however, that the notion of God must also be expressed in terms of Lonergan's metaphysics, I must first outline a reformulation of Lonergan's ontology that includes the most important developments of his post-*Insight* thought. This will make it possible to outline a process understanding of God based solely on Lonergan's own thought.

III. A REFORMULATION OF LONERGAN'S PROCESS ONTOLOGY

One of the hallmarks of Lonergan's post-*Insight* thought is the attention he devoted to the fourth level of the human subject, the level of "rational self-consciousness," the level on which the human subject deliberates, evaluates, decides, and acts.[29] This fourth level, Lonergan argues, sublates the first three levels of empirical, intelligent, and rational consciousness. But even as Lonergan is speaking of this sublation and the emergence of the "existential subject" as "human consciousness at its fullest," he notes that this fourth level emerges and sublates the first three "when *the already acting subject* confronts his world and adverts to his own acting in it."[30] The importance of this remark for my present concern emerges when we consider Lonergan's discussion of feelings and value in *Method in Theology*.

Lonergan distinguishes between non-intentional states and trends ("feelings" such as fatigue or irritability for the former and hunger or thirst for the latter) and *intentional responses* ("feelings" such as joy, sorrow, love, hatred, tenderness, or veneration).[31] Intentional responses relate us to objects in terms of apprehended values. Such a response has two elements: the recognition of value (which is feeling's "absolute" element), and the preferential ranking and selection of values (which is feeling's "relative" element).[32] *Decision* is the making of a judgment of value, the selection of which value we shall attempt to actualize. From our decisions flows our conduct.[33]

It is important to note that this fourth level of human subjectivity is driven toward the actualization of value by the presence in the subject of the transcendental notion of value.[34] This notion is an orientation in the subject toward the good, and it is the urgency of this orientation that calls, leads, or draws the subject to self-transcendence. Thus just as the first three levels of human subjectivity are driven by the immanence in the subject of the notion of being, so is the fourth level driven by the immanence in the subject of the notion of value. Further, since the fourth level sublates and unifies the first three, so does the notion of value sublate the notion of being. If we consider this in light of Lonergan's ontological element of finality, we can say that the notion of being is the presence of finality in knowing, and the notion of value is the presence of finality in our deciding and acting.

Lonergan is clearly aware that he is presenting the *ideal* possibility of how our knowing and acting can be unified.[35] As I pointed out above, Lonergan recognizes that before ever the subject can attempt such rational self-consciousness, the subject is *already* acting in the world. If acting can only be understood as the result of a decision to pursue the actualization of some value selected on the basis of feelings, then clearly such a process goes on without benefit of *reflective* knowing in all of us much of the time. Lonergan himself notes that long before rational consciousness differentiated itself, feelings apprehended values and that feelings were expressed in and evoked by symbols.[36] This implies that in our actual experience the existential level of subjectivity is prior to the cognitional levels.[37]

My point in reviewing this is that it can be generalized and related to Lonergan's ontology. If the human subject acts on the basis of a decision to pursue some value, apprehended and selected by means of feelings, then we can argue that "decision" occurs very often without the benefit of judgment in the sense of *reflective* judgment. If we can further admit (as Lonergan does in *Insight*[38]) that animals exhibit emotion and conation, we have a basis for generalizing the notions of value, feelings, purpose, and decision beyond the specifically human case. If we were also convinced that this whole area of our experience is so important that it must be generalized and reflected in our ontology (because the notion of value sublates the notion of being), then we would try to connect it integrally with the ontological elements of potency, form, act, and finality. But first we would recognize that subjectivity itself must be generalized so that each ontological act is understood to be a subject. This is necessary because we can only understand feelings, responses based on the grasping of value, selection among values, and the formation of purpose as operations of a subject.

Lonergan affirms that the fundamental facts of the universe are "acts of form developed from potency." They present themselves as the result of a dynamic process of construction and there is a true sense in which each of these concrete actualities is unique (central act). But Lonergan's ontology does not suggest that one ought to conceive of these "acts" as subjects, as agents of their own construction. There are, however, at least two aspects of Lonergan's thought which seem to demand such an interpretation. Both concern the implications of the metaphysical insight into the isomorphism of knowing and becoming.

First, Lonergan's cognitional theory argues most persuasively that knowing does not occur in a vacuum, but within a *subject* as a complex functioning *of* that subject. When

Lonergan works out the implications of the insight into the isomorphism of knowing and becoming, he discovers in the structure of becoming a parallel to all the dynamic and functional elements of knowing except for this one: that knowing is always *by* a subject. It seems to me that the insight of isomorphism demands this further parallelism of knowing and becoming, that just as it is subjects who know, so it is subjects which become.

There is a further reason in Lonergan's ontology which seems to demand this interpretation. Lonergan draws his notion of "finality" in the dynamic structure of becoming from the correspondence to the notion of being as the unifying drive in knowing. Just as the notion of being drives and unifies the process of knowing, so does finality drive and unify becoming. But the notion of being is identical in his thought with the unrestricted desire to know being; it is the Eros which drives the subject through the cognitional process. Ontologically, finality must play the same function. It is the unconscious "heading for being" that develops form from potency and results in a unified concrete act of form. But unless we are to conceive of "dead matter" pushed and prodded by some unintelligible force, we must conceive of finality as an *experienced* drive. This seems to me to require the further notion of a subject as the developing center experiencing this unconscious "orientation" toward and "heading for" being.[39] Lonergan's notion of finality seems to demand that we postulate a subject experiencing the drive to actualize form from potency.

If we conceive of ontological act as a subject, we can then generalize the notions of value, feelings, purpose, and decision so as to connect them integrally with the ontological elements. We could do this not by postulating yet another "elemental" level of becoming, but by integrating value, feeling, purpose and decision with the functions and relations of potency, form, act, and finality. The grounds for doing this are in the structure of the *acting* subject (the "existential" subject). The intentionality of the acting subject sublates all other levels; the notion of value sublates the notion of being. This is the immanence of "finality" within the acting subject. If the insight of isomorphism grasped that the structure of knowing *and acting* must be isomorphic with the structure of becoming, that, indeed, our acting exhibits the ontological structure of all becoming, then the pursuit of value (and with it, feelings and decision) would be understood to be integral to becoming.[40]

If finality is immanent in the developing act and is experienced by the developing center of that act, then we could understand it as a purposive or intentional desire to actualize some form for itself. Finality, as experienced, constitutes the "subjective aim" of the developing ontological act.[41] In other words, finality inherently orients a subject toward the value of being; finality heads the subject for being. The developing subject is "attracted," so to speak, to being because of the values inherent in the potential or possible forms it finds given for it. The developing act is related to these forms by means of its "feelings." Thus one could speak of the developing act grasping "forms" in its potency by means of its "feelings." These feelings would be understood to be the subject's unconscious but intentional responses to its potential forms, valuations of them for the becoming of the subject (act). Recalling that there is both an absolute and a relative element to feeling, we can understand that such feelings would embody both the recognition of value and the preferential ranking of the values in the forms. The standard for the preferential ranking of the values is contained in the "subjective aim," the "pull" of finality as it is experienced by the developing act.

We could also distinguish between feelings that grasp and respond to the values inherent in possibilities or forms and feelings that grasp and respond to other actualities. The basis for such a distinction is in cognitional theory, for Lonergan has distinguished between two kinds of insights: the insight that grasps an intelligibility, which leads to understanding; and the reflective insight that grasps an intelligibility as virtually unconditioned, that is, as given in the facts of experience, which leads to knowledge. Thus we could speak of insights having to do with possible intelligibilities and insights having to do with encountered intelligible actualities. The ontological counterpart to this cognitional distinction would be what we might call "conceptual" and "physical" feelings.[42] The physical feelings orient the developing ontological act toward other actualities which form both the immediate ground of and the limit on the potency of the developing act. The conceptual feelings enable the developing act to grasp and respond to the values inherent in both potential forms and other ontological acts.

Ontological act, then, is the result of a process of becoming. Through its physical feelings the act has been oriented with regard to other actualities. Through its conceptual feelings the developing act grasps and responds to the values inherent both in actualities and in potential forms (which together constitute the potency of the developing act). Because of its subjective aim or finalistic drive, the developing act ranks all the values in its potential forms and selects the form it shall attempt to actualize. This selection is ontological "decision." Ontological act, in other words, emerges as the result of a process of "decision" among potential forms based on the "preference" of one form over others. Both the drive and the standard for such "selection" is inherent in the "subjective aim," the immanence of finality in the developing act.

It is no doubt evident to the reader familiar with Whitehead's philosophy that such a reformulation of Lonergan's ontology in light of his later thought bears a remarkable resemblance to Whitehead's ontology. While limitation of space prevents both a thorough expression and any defense of this reformulation, I hope that my brief remarks have at least illustrated both that such a reformulation of Lonergan's ontology is possible and that the grounds for it can be found in Lonergan's own thought. I will now try to show that the results of my analysis thus far make it possible to formulate a process understanding of God in dependence on Lonergan's own thought.

IV. A LONERGANIAN PROCESS THEOLOGY

I have argued above that it is important to raise the subjective sides of the cognitional questions of God and that both the questions and the analysis designed to answer them ought to be expressed in metaphysical terms. The two cognitional questions as Lonergan expresses them ask for the ultimate ground of the intelligibility and the contingent existence of the universe. Expressing the subjective sides of these questions, we would ask for the ultimate ground of the subject's ability to grasp intelligibilities and to make virtually unconditioned judgments. When these questions are expressed in terms of Lonergan's ontology as I have reformulated it, the result is *one* set of questions (since ontological act is understood as a subject). The questions would have the following form.

If ontological acts depend on intelligible forms and potency, then what is required to ground ultimately the dynamic universe of emergent probability? First, each developing act must be endowed with its potency, that is, the general, specific, and particular conditions that make that emergent act possible. But what is the ultimate ground of all these conditions? Second, each developing act requires its potential intelligible forms. These forms are really possible precisely because of all the conditions which constitute the potency of the act, but if they are merely potential and not actual, where do they come from? How is it possible for the developing act to grasp forms that are merely potential and not actual? Third, from among these possible intelligible forms the emergent act will select the one it shall attempt to actualize. But the ability to select and the drive to actualize some form depends on the presence of finality in the developing act. One could say that finality is the very dynamism of becoming, its very "life." But where does this dynamism come from? It cannot explain itself, and so it seems that the emergent act must derive the living dynamism of its own becoming—its ability to develop form from potency—from some ultimate ground. Taken together, these three questions outline all the conditions required for the occurrence of an ontological act.

The questions heuristically point to the required answer. The ultimate ground must be an *act*, but it cannot be a *temporal* act since every temporal ontological act requires all these conditions for its occurrence. As the required ground of these conditions, the required act must transcend temporality. Second, this act must somehow be the ultimate ground and source of all potency and all intelligible forms. Finally, the required act must be the source of the finality immanent in all temporal ontological acts. Employing generalized empirical method we can, as Lonergan has done, conceive of a transcendent and unrestricted act of understanding as the answer required by the questions. The unrestricted act of understanding is the transcendent, eternal, complete, and unrestricted grasp of all intelligible forms. It is unconditioned and not contingent in any way. In the unity of this unrestricted act of understanding we find established the relationships between all intelligible forms; these relationships constitute the ultimate ground of all the conditions which form the potency for the occurrence of temporal ontological acts. In the complete and unrestricted nature of this act of understanding we find the required source of all potential intelligible forms grasped by developing acts of form. In the creativity of this unrestricted act of understanding we find the dynamism which grounds the finality immanent in each ontological act. This is only a rough sketch, but it is enough to indicate that thus far the understanding of God retains almost every single attribute Lonergan works out for the unrestricted act of understanding as he addresses the cognitional questions.[43]

At this point, by philosophical reflection we have discovered the ultimate ground of the universe, the ultimate ground of all subjective experience. The "wondering" questions have been met; we know what makes our experience possible. But now the "anxious" questions arise. If the ultimate ground of the universe is God, what is God like? What is God's character? Generalized empirical method would require that we examine this notion of God in light of the already affirmed structures of subjectivity. We would not presume that the necessary transcendence of the unrestricted act of understanding means that it is a radical exception to the structure of cognitional process and being. Rather, we would attempt to work out an understanding of God by analogy with these structures. Moreover, since we are asking the final philosophical question which merges with the *religious* question of God, we will have to take into account the testimony of religious experience.

Doing this reveals that our notion of God is not yet complete. We have found thus far that God is the ultimate ground of the universe, that God gives the potency, the intelligible forms, and the finalistic drive to each ontological act. But reflecting on the implications of cognitional process and the structure of becoming, we would recognize that all of this has to do with *possibility*. The cognitional questions ask for the ultimate ground of all the conditions that make contingent existence both intelligible and possible. These questions can be met by conceiving of an unrestricted act of understanding. Thus far God has been understood to be the supreme illustration of understanding. But understanding has to do with possibility. In cognitional terms, understanding is the product of insights grasping possible intelligibilities. Thus metaphysically, our notion of an unrestricted act of understanding postulates that God as ultimate ground has infinite "conceptual" feelings grasping, evaluating and organizing all intelligible forms. But this in itself offers no ground for conceiving of God as *knowing* anything. Knowing, as we have affirmed in cognitional theory, is based on reflective insights into intelligibilities as *given* in the facts of *experience*. In both cognitional and metaphysical terms this means that knowing is always based on encounters in actuality. Understanding is accomplished through "conceptual" feelings, but knowing always requires "physical" feelings (since it is through physical feelings that the subject is related to other actualities). Thus to conceive of God as an unrestricted act of understanding does not in itself offer any basis for conceiving of God's knowledge. Note that it is the structure disclosed by *cognitional theory* that establishes this.[44]

This reveals to us that our notion of God is incomplete, that we have actually conceived of God as a *truncated* subject. As unrestricted act of understanding, God must enjoy infinite "conceptual" feelings; God's grasp of possible intelligible forms is complete, unrestricted, transcendent, unconditioned and perfect in every way. But subjectivity, as the structure disclosed by cognitional theory and metaphysics has shown us, involves more than "conceptual" feelings or insights into possible intelligible forms; it also involves "physical" feelings or reflective insights into intelligible forms as given in experience. It was not incorrect to have conceived of God as unrestricted act of understanding, for that is the answer required by the cognitional questions of God. Nor was it incorrect to conceive of God as transcendent and completely unconditioned in this respect, for in order to answer the questions we must hold to God's complete and unconditioned transcendence as ultimate ground of all potency, forms, and acts. But reflecting on this in light of the affirmed structure of subjectivity, we discover that this is not yet a complete notion of God, since we cannot yet conceive of God as a full subject, nor can we yet conceptualize either God's knowledge or God's love. Both knowing and loving are dependent on encounters in experience with the known or loved *actuality*. Neither are mere "conceptual" operations. Our notion of God thus far has conceptualized only God's understanding of possibilities. When we turn to religious experience, we find it testifying most forcefully that God both knows and loves the world. There must be, then, some way of conceptualizing God's knowledge and love.

On the strength of the testimony of religious experience and following generalized empirical method, we would employ the affirmed structure of subjectivity as our analogical guide. We could then conceive of God as supremely illustrating *every* level of the structure of subjectivity. Cognitionally, we would predict that God's knowing illustrates the same structure as all knowing exhibits: God knows by grasping together the intelligible possibility and the givenness of that intelligibility in the facts of actual experience. Metaphysically, this means that God, like all subjects, must have "physical" feelings which relate God to the actualities of the universe. God's knowing is then an integration of God's conceptual feelings of what is possible with God's physical feelings of what is in fact the case. Physical feelings, by their very nature, are dependent on their objects; they are thus necessarily conditioned and occur in dependence on actualities. This implies that God's physical experience and God's knowledge must have to do with an aspect of God distinct from God's function as ultimate ground of the universe, since in the latter function God must be completely unconditioned.

It is difficult for us to think of God in this fashion, especially if we are accustomed to thinking in the Thomist tradition. But this is the direction in which we are led when we conceive of God as a subject who supremely illustrates the structure of cognitional process and being. If we are patient and work out all the implications, the result is not incompatible either with reason or with Christian faith. For example, conceiving of God and God's relation to the world in this way immediately resolves the classical problem concerning the freedom of contingent events which are rooted in the necessary and efficacious *knowledge* of God.[45] Every ontological act enjoys a true, though limited, freedom as it develops itself. God creates by providing the potency, the intelligible forms, and the finalistic drive; but the developing ontological act is finally free to develop itself. Or, as Whitehead might say, God creates by providing all the necessary conditions for an actual occasion and "luring" the creature to create itself on this divinely-given ground. Once it has been endowed with the necessary conditions which make it possible, the self-formation of an ontological act is free. Ontological act, then, is not caused by *knowledge* of it as *actual*, but by *understanding* of it as *possible*. Finality, derived from God, includes the gift of freedom and is the world's share in God's own freedom. Once the developing act has become actual, once it has developed itself, God's physical feelings encounter it and know it for what it has made of itself. This divine response in knowledge and love makes possible the next moment in temporal becoming.

Thus by analogy with the structure of our own subjectivity and the structure we find in all becoming, Lonergan's thought could give rise to a process understanding of God and God's relation to the world. Instead of regarding God's knowing and being as an exception to the structure of cognitional process and becoming, we can understand them to be the supreme illustration of that structure. God develops the divine experience in an everlasting act of self-transcendence in relation to the world. God's perfection and transcendence are exhibited by the completeness of the divine conceptual and physical feelings and in the infinite wisdom and love involved in their integration. God is a trans-temporal act which develops as all self-transcending acts develop, but which infinitely transcends all the limitations of knowing and becoming by temporal acts in the world. If at first we find it incredible that God can be both absolutely unconditioned and also dependent, incredible that God is both necessary, infinite source of every ontological act and also dependent on the world for physical feelings, in the end we are able to understand how this incredible fact can be, and we understand it by conceiving of God as a subject with the same basic structure as all subjects, except that God is the everlasting and perfect subject who illustrates that structure in an infinite degree. Our subjectivity is truly in God's image.

It can be shown, I believe, that such an understanding of God allows us to include the testimony of religious experience *within* the philosophical understanding of God. Religious experience, as is clear in the biblical witness, testifies that God is affected by the world. But the Thomist understanding of God could not express this *within* the philosophical idea of God. I am not saying that it was not *expressed;* surely Aquinas expressed it if one takes his entire theological system into account. Yet it was difficult to reconcile the transcendent, completely unconditioned God to which the philosophical analysis concluded with the God of Scripture. This is precisely what gave rise to the observation that the God of the philosophers and the God of Abraham, Isaac, and Jacob were *not* the same. If we are to show that they *are* the same, we ought to try to exhibit this in the very *idea* of God. This is possible, I believe, if we are faithful to the implications of Lonergan's thought; and it would enable us to fashion an idea of God that is both intelligible to our culture and a service to our faith.

My proposal raises a multitude of questions, but I hope that my brief remarks have at least illustrated that such an approach to Lonergan's thought is both possible and in accord with the implications of his thought. In conclusion I would simply note that such a process understanding of God based on Lonergan's thought has much in common with Whitehead's philosophy and that to recognize this gives good reason for collaboration rather than contention between Lonerganians and process theologians.

NOTES

1   See Bernard J. F. Lonergan, *Philosophy of God, and Theology* (Philadelphia: Westminster Press, 1973), pp. 64–65. (Hereafter cited as *PGT.*)

2   I have elsewhere compared Lonergan and Whitehead at great length and defended the thesis that their philosophies are fundamentally compatible. See Thomas E. Hosinski, "Process, Insight, and Empirical Method," 2 vols., (Ph.D. Dissertation, The Divinity School, University of Chicago, 1983). (Hereafter cited as "Process".)

3   See Bernard Lonergan, *Method in Theology*, 2nd ed. (New York: Herder and Herder, 1973), pp. 337–344 (hereafter cited as *Method*): and *PGT,* pp.11–14, 33–35, 45–59.

4   See *PGT,* pp. 50–58.

5   See *PGT,* pp. 54–55, 58.

6   See *Method,* pp. 101–102; *PGT,* pp. 53–54.

7   See *Method,* pp. 102–103; *PGT,* p. 54.

8   See *Method,* pp. 105–107; *PGT,* p. 54. For the "anxious" form of the strictly religious question of God, see *PGT,* p. 55.

9 See *Method,* pp. 115–116.

10 See *Method,* p. 116.

11 See *PGT,* pp. 11, 14, 50–52; and Bernard J. F. Lonergan, *A Second Collection,* ed. William F. J. Ryan and Bernard J. Tyrrell (Philadelphia: Westminster Press, 1974), pp. 120–121, 131–132. (Hereafter cited as *Second Collection.*)

12 *Method,* p. 116. See *Ibid.,* pp. 47–52 for Lonergan's analysis of the structure of the human good which forms the background here.

13 *Method,* p. 116.

14 *Ibid.,* pp. 116–117.

15 Bernard Lonergan, *Insight: A Study in Human Understanding,* revised ed. (New York: Philosophical Library, 1958), "General Transcendent Knowledge," pp. 634–686. (Hereafter cited as *Insight .*)

16 See *PGT,* p. 54; *Method,* pp. 102–103.

17 This was first pointed out by Langdon Gilkey, "Empirical Science and Theological Knowing," in Philip McShane, ed., *Foundations of Theology* (Notre Dame: University of Notre Dame Press, 1972) pp. 76–101; see pp. 83–84, 94–97.

18 See *Insight,* pp. 641–657; *Method,* pp. 101–102; *PGT,* pp. 53–54.

19 *Insight,* pp. 634–657.

20 *Ibid.,* pp. 657–658.

21 I cannot take the space here to substantiate this at length; see Hosinski, "Process," 2: 587–594.

22 *Insight,* pp. 658–660.

23 *Ibid.,* p. 658.

24 *Ibid.,* p. 658.

25 *Ibid.,* p. 661.

26 I can find no place where Lonergan uses this exact expression, but this clearly represents his position. For example, see *Insight,* pp. 444–451.

27 See *Insight,* Chapters XV and XVI, pp. 431–529, esp. pp. 483–487, 497–509.

28 See *Insight,* pp. 115–139, 259–267, 451–483.

29 See especially "The Subject," *Second Collection,* pp. 79–84; also see *Method,* pp. 14–16, and Chapter 2, "The Human Good," pp. 27–55.

30 *Second Collection,* pp. 80, 81; my emphasis.

31 *Method,* pp. 30–34.

32 See *Ibid.,* pp. 30–32, 115:

33 See *Ibid.,* pp. 36–41.

34 See *Ibid.,* pp. 34–36.

35 See, e.g., *Ibid.,* pp. 39–40.

36 See *Ibid.,* pp. 64–69, esp. pp. 66–67.

37 Lonergan's analysis of religious experience supports this position; see *Ibid.,* pp. 104–107, 115–117, 120–123.

38 See *Insight,* p. 183.

39 It is interesting that Lonergan speaks of such unconscious "orientation" toward and "heading for" being, but never pursues what this implies ontologically. See *Insight,* p. 355.

40 There will no doubt be objections to extending the notions of feeling, value, purpose, and decision to the ontological structure of all becoming. However, some support for such an extension of these notions can be found in Lonergan's brilliant (and completely overlooked) discussion of explanatory genera and species; see *Insight,* pp. 259–265, and Hosinski, "Process," 1: 396–398, 450–452.

41   I have deliberately chosen one of Whitehead's technical terms ("subjective aim") because such a development of Lonergan's ontology corresponds quite closely to what Whitehead meant by this term. See Alfred North Whitehead, *Process and Reality: An Essay in Cosmology.* Corrected Edition, David Ray Griffin and Donald W. Sherburne, eds. (New York: The Free Press, 1978), pp. 19, 47, 87, and *passim* (see Index).

42   I have again deliberately chosen Whitehead's technical terms ("conceptual" and "physical" feelings) because such a development of Lonergan's ontology corresponds exactly with what Whitehead means by these terms. See *ibid.,* pp. 236-243 and *passim* (see Index).

43   I am referring here to what Lonergan discusses in sections five through eight of Chapter XIX, *Insight,* pp. 644-657.

44   In his presentation at the Lonergan Symposium held at the University of Santa Clara in March, 1984, Michael Vertin argued that Lonergan discusses God in cognitional terms in order to maintain critical control over the discussion. I would not disagree with this intention, but I would argue that by making God a radical exception to the structure affirmed by cognitional theory, Lonergan has inadvertently subverted what he hoped to achieve. If cognitional theory is to provide both the meanings and the relations for metaphysical terms and is to control critically the metaphysical discussion of God, then the metaphysical description of God and God's relation to the world cannot be based on a radical exception to the structure disclosed by cognitional theory; instead, it must be based on a faithful employment of that structure. Though Vertin and I will no doubt continue to disagree, I am grateful to him for a conversation in which he helped me to understand more clearly Lonergan's intention in this regard.

45   Even Bernard Tyrrell acknowledges that Lonergan's response to this problem does not establish or attempt to explain how it can be possible and true both that God necessarily and efficaceously knows from all eternity each contingent act and that contingent acts are truly free. See Tyrrell, *Bernard Lonergan's Philosophy of God* (Notre Dame: University of Notre Dame Press, 1974), p. 160.

VI

Viktor Frankl's Notion
of Intentionality

W. F. J. RYAN S.J.

VIKTOR Frankl distinguishes two aspects of his Logotherapy: (1) Logotherapy as a type of psychiatric treatment which presents meaning to patients in order to cure their psychological disorders; (2) Logotherapy as a philosophy with its taproot in the key phenomenological notion of intentionality.[1] This paper will occupy itself with Logotherapy as a philosophical method characterized by the capital role of the notion of intentionality. The aim of this paper, in keeping with the overall goal of the Lonergan Symposium to examine the themes of religion and culture, will be to show the bearing of Viktor Frankl's notion of intentionality on some of the foundational principles of religion and culture. To achieve its goal, this paper is divided into three parts: the first part concerns some essential elements of Frankl's phenomenological method; the second deals with two important results of this method; and the third examines the benefits and limitations of Frankl's conception of intentionality. This paper is written from the perspective of Bernard Lonergan's methodology. His philosophical method, then, will be called upon to elucidate topics of Frankl's philosophy, especially the will to meaning and its correlative, supra-meaning, or God.

I. VIKTOR FRANKL AND HIS PHENOMENOLOGICAL METHOD

Among phenomenologists Viktor Frankl cites three men whose specific influence he acknowledges in his philosophical thinking. These men are Edmund Husserl, Max Scheler, and Martin Heidegger. Phenomenology from its very beginning, as explicitly stated in a platform-declaration which these three phenomenologists endorse, was to be, not a "system," but a philosophical method.[2] Although Frankl employs the phenomenological method to establish certain basic principles for his Logotherapy, he never lays out in a detailed manner—as does Husserl—a listing of the phenomenological elements which he adopts. One must rather assemble these elements from Frankl's numerous writings in order to draw up a list. Some of these elements, then, of Frankl's phenomenology should be identified to serve as guidelines in an examination of his philosophy.

Frankl asserts—as do Husserl, Scheler, and Heidegger—the central importance of the notion of intentionality. Instead of the idea of intuition, which is too often employed to identify Husserlian phenomenology, the idea of intentionality is more basic since it offers the possibility of a more comprehensive explanation of the elements found in the three essential kinds of intentionality: knowing, feeling, and free choosing. The essential structure of a human being is intentionality. Or, one could say, the eidos (Husserl's term for the essential structure of something as known; in Lonergan's terminology, a higher viewpoint comprising a number of insights) of the person consists in an orientation to, and correlation with, transcendent reality. By the notion of intentionality, Frankl signifies, first of all, the fundamental ontological orientation of the person which continuously manifests itself in a diversity of acts. These diverse acts are the three general classes of intentional acts which may be designated as knowing, feeling, and the free choosing of values (named "meaning" by Frankl). There are, then, two aspects of intentionality in Frankl's phenomenology. First, the very structure of the human person in the orientation to a transcendent reality which is distinct from the subject's conscious states. Husserl would say that the noesis and the noema are distinct from the object, or referent. Secondly, this orientation ceaselessly appears in a diversity of particular intentional acts. To overlook the radical, ontological orientation of the person and to enumerate only the diverse acts is to lose sight of the intentional structure itself. This structure is the condition of possibility for either any generic type of intentional act or any individual act. Granted that there are eide encompassing the generic intentional types of knowing, feeling, and meaning, but there exists just as much the eidos of the premoral orientation of the person, or a priori structure, to the transcendent reality of any known, felt, or chosen object whatever. Types of intentional acts, then, are correlative to types of transcendent realities, or objects. Lonergan, for his part, would say that being is the objective of the primordial notion of being, whereas individual known, felt, or chosen objects are the objects of distinct intentional operations. One must grasp both these eide of intentionality—the orientation as well as the acts—to understand Frankl's thinking on intentionality.

The method which Edmund Husserl requires for uncovering the intentional structure of the person is the epoche, or transcendental reduction.[3] The epoche is a reflective act of analysis with two results: (1) The subject finds the grounds for determining what objective, transcendent reality is (2) by uncovering the eidos of the intending subject (the transcendental Ego). Husserl uses the term "eidos" to indicate either the act of understanding of the essential structure of something or this structure itself. Eidetic elements, then, are essential characteristics discovered in the correlation between the act of intending and its object.

Husserl insists that not only are the subject and object given in the epoche's inspection of an intentional act, but that the very *correlation* between the two of them is likewise given at the same time. And the correlation is given at the same time as belonging to the essential make-up of intentional acts and their intended objects. The object is given, the subject is given, and the correlation is given.

The phenomenon examined in phenomenology is a unified reality comprising not only an intending subject and an intended object, but also their correlation. One might, for example, think of the crowd of people pressing through O'Hare Airport's terminal. One pays little attention to the adult passengers and the adult employees. On the other hand, one would pay startled and close attention to a naked three-year old child wandering about. The adults, in a sense, are self-explanatory in their activities; they do not require some other person or thing to be along with them to account for what they are doing. The naked child, however, is not self-explanatory in his activity; his presence requires an explanation; his presence requires some other person or thing to account for his activity there, at O'Hare in the midst of thousands of people whose presence and activities are accounted for. The correlation to other persons and things which the adults have is not immediately necessary to explaining their presence at O'Hare. The correlation which the child has to an absent and necessary adult is essential for explaining the child's presence. The adults have an independence; the child has a dependence. The dependence of the child is the correlation of the child to someone else. In an analogous way for phenomenology, then, all intentional acts—those of knowing, feeling, and choosing—are correlative to their objects. One may examine either the object or the subject, although phenomenology prefers to examine the intending subject first since the objects are dependent upon the conscious constituting of the subject. This conscious correlating is what Husserl, and Frankl following him, judge to be the cachet of intentionality.

Frankl, openly invoking Husserl's epoche, makes use of some of its main features to delineate this conscious correlating between subject and object.[4] From Scheler he borrows the distinction between feelings as a response to values and nonspecific emotional states, such as fatigue and boredom.[5] From Heidegger he takes the ontological orientation that a person finds in himself by calling into question this orientation itself and its focal point, the world.[6] Further, Frankl seems to follow Heidegger in pointing out premoral and prelogical aspects in the person. These two aspects are not individual intentional acts but rather the prior grounds for any intentional act in the first place. Or put another way, they are the radical orientation of the person to know objective reality and to make free choices of meaning.[7] In Husserl's terminology, the prelogical and the premoral potentialities of the subject are eidetic characteristics of the subject. In Lonergan's terminology, they are the notion of being as it comprises the desire to know and the notion of value. They are the fundamental orientation of the subject towards these two kinds of intentional acts: knowing and choosing (meaning). They are the condition of possibility of the correlation between the intending subject and his intended objects. Frankl's chief interest is this premoral aspect of intentionality and then the intentional acts of free choosing it makes possible. This premoral aspect is what Frankl calls the "will to meaning." The will to meaning is not all of intentionality, then. It is that limited aspect of intentionality that makes possible free choosing (meaning).

In performing an eidetic analysis of the person, Frankl distinguishes three dimensions: the somatic, the psychological, and the spiritual (mental, nonempirical).[8] Frankl, in thus designating three distinct but interrelated aspects of the person, presents his conception, or eidos, of the person and the inherent mind-body relation. Though irreducible, these dimensions are functionally interrelated such that the one, unified intending of the person is achieved through the diverse intentional operations that are grounded in each dimension as in their source. Once Frankl has designated the threefold dimensional structure of the person, he can locate the will to meaning. This he locates in the spiritual, the nonempirical, core of the person. To take another tack, one can understand the essence of Frankl's phenomenology if one considers the simple diagrams which he introduces to represent the three cores of the person—somatic, psychological, and spiritual—as three concentric circles. One can grasp that his epoche is a higher viewpoint. In a word, the epoche enables Frankl to produce such drawings in the first place, especially drawings so simple and accurate.[9] As such, they are excellent heuristic diagrams.

Since Frankl holds that the will to meaning resides in the spiritual core of the person, he can swiftly point out that the will to meaning is nonempirical, not essentially physiological. In thus positing that the will to meaning is a nonempirical element of intentionality, Frankl is emphasizing the difference between the will to meaning and the instinctual desires of Freud's will to pleasure. Freud, in Frankl's judgment, is a reductionist. For reductionism is the oversimplified representation of a complex reality—for example, the human person—which compresses this reality into one of several key characteristics. So, Freud reduces the will to meaning to either the somatic or the psychological cores. Such reductionism is the inevitable oversimplifying program by a pscyhology and a philosophy innocent of the epoche. Any talk about a spiritual core which might constitute an essential trait of the human person Freud brushes aside as a neurotic hankering for interesting but unattainable fantasies.[10] Frankl often asserts that the reductionism of Freud as well as that of Jung and other deterministic psychologists can be encapsulated in the pat formula, "nothing but": The will to meaning is "nothing but . . ." a neurotic pining according to a Freudian, or "nothing but . . ." an urging from a collective unconscious according to a Jungian.

Frankl's epoche empowers him to grasp the person as a three-cored intentional structure and thereby to reach what Lonergan would call a higher viewpoint. Frankl's higher viewpoint for his inspection of intentionality has a negative and a positive function. The negative function of his epoche is to reject the reductionist mythological sloganeering which conceals all nonempirical elements of the person. To be exact, the negative function of the epoche occurs simultaneously with the positive function of the epoche. The positive function, for its part, is to uncover the eidetic structure of intentionality. Thus, to grasp the person as a three-cored structure is to be in a position to wave off the Freudian and Jungian myths according to which all apparently free choices are "nothing but" irresistible drives or urgings.

Having obtained the eidos of the person as intentional, Frankl concentrates on the premoral aspect of intentionality. This premoral aspect is like an a priori structure. That is to say, this structure is antecedent to any individual instance of moral evaluation and free choosing. As already remarked, this premoral orientation is the will to meaning. Frankl purposely uses the phrase, "will to meaning," to contrast his position with those of Freud and Adler. Frankl's phenomenology uncovers neither a will to pleasure nor a will to power. But its higher viewpoint does establish the existence of the will to meaning as a premoral orientation of the person to freely choose values.

Here one should note that Frankl distinguishes value and meaning. A value is anything that has worth. So, a value can be aesthetic, such as the architecture of the Cathedral of Amiens, or it can be moral, such as a marriage, or it can be religious, such as Catholicism. All values, however, are to a certain extent what Frankl calls "abstract," that is to say, accessible to anyone at all. But the mere accessibility of a value and someone's notice of it do not automatically suffice to move him to choose a value and thereby make it a meaning. A meaning is a freely chosen value. Consequently, Frankl's phenomenology speaks of the will to meaning rather than a will to value. For beyond the mere existence of values accessible to anyone at all, there must occur the individual person's weighing of the value and then the person's choice. Values are like books on the shelves of a vast library. The books are there for the choosing; as long as they remain upon the shelves they do neither good nor harm. Meanings, however, are like the actual choices to take down the books and read them. Further, meanings in Frankl's image are always something morally good. An evil free choice, then, is not a meaning. It is the absence of meaning; it is an instance of what Frankl calls the "existential vacuum." Nor does Frankl consider aesthetic and political values to be acts of meaning even though they, too, may be free choices.

Frankl, in the possession of his phenomenology's higher viewpoint, sorts out the essential traits of meaning insofar as meaning is the exercise of freedom. The premoral ground of choosing lies in the spiritual core of the person. The possibility of a free choice requires at least two options, neither of which determines the choice. But free choosing is nothing at all like an instinctual drive or a stimulus-response experience which determine a reaction, limiting it to just one specific type of act, like feeding or reproducing. Rather, the horizon of possibilities for a free choice exceeds the horizon open to instinctual drives. In order to show the spiritual core of the person as the source of all choosing with its open horizon, Frankl invokes his common manner of proof: he tells a story. The story concerns an exchange between Frankl and an interlocutor after a speech and presentation by Frankl:

> In the setting of a discussion a young man asked whether it was justified to speak of a soul if it cannot be seen. Even if we explore the brain tissue in a microscope, he said, we will never find anything such as a soul. Now the moderator asked me to handle the issue. And I started by asking the young man what motivated him in raising the question. "My intellectual honesty," he answered. "Well," I continued challenging him, "is it bodily? Is it tangible? Will it be visible in a microscope?" "Of course, it won't" he admitted, "because it is mental." "Aha," I said, "in other words, what you were searching for in vain in the microscope is a condition for your search, and presupposed by you all along, isn't it?"[11]

Frankl is claiming that not only is one, individual choice immaterial but that *a fortiori* the will to meaning itself is immaterial. At any time and any place, the will to meaning is a general orientation which can express itself in an act of meaning. The horizon of the will to meaning is as limitless as the number of values that can be chosen.

Values, however, present a range of validity, not a simple uniformity. Some values are of a higher rank than others and according to this rank are to be preferred. But where does this ranking come from? Why is the eminence and merit of values not simply uniform so that all values have the same worth? Frankl introduces an objective criterion of meaning. The person must observe this criterion to preserve the richness of values and to avoid the reductionist bias of someone like Protagoras who opines that all value is measured by whatever the individual wants; in the sense explained, however, Frankl's phenomenology does place the burden of choice upon the individual. Although there exists a manifold of values, some proffered to the person through a religious or ethical tradition, nonetheless the person alone must choose the meaning for himself.

Frankl's assertion that values are general but meanings unique has made him open to the suspicion that he might be like a new Protagoras with an old message of moral relativism.[12] Meanings are unique, not because the individual is the measure of all values to be chosen, but because some specific condition of a value moves one individual rather than another to make a choice. To be generous is a value many people may admire without actually choosing to be generous until a unique situation arises that summons forth a choice out of them. For example, what does a person do in the face of a direct request for financial help from someone in need?[13]

But the first question to be answered in examining Frankl's theory of value and meaning is: What is Frankl's objective criterion for achieving meaning? What is the standard that he employs to decide whether some free choices are evil and some are good, and thus are meanings? In answer to such possible queries, Frankl indicates that the end of man is the basis for setting up a specific criterion for judging values. Again, the epoche empowers Frankl to grasp the end of the person. One can clarify the end of the person and a concomitant criterion of morality by posing the following question: What is man for? Frankl's answer is that people must live in a friendship that is marked by justice and mercy. He asserts that there is one fundamental truth that governs all human values: "no one has the right to do wrong, not even if wrong has been done to him."[14] His approving citation of Albert Schweitzer in the midst of a discussion on happiness and the end of man can further enlighten his notion of this end as the objective criterion for all human values: "Only those of you will be happy who learn to serve others."[15]

Frankl can, therefore, set forth a hierarchy of values by setting forth the end of man. Frankl's higher viewpoint of the human person again enables him to set up a comprehensive criterion for human values. This criterion is always to be invoked to decide what is the ranking of values. This criterion disqualifies the insolent relativism of Gorgias and Protagoras, the "noble feelings" of John Stuart Mill, the pernicious biases which Lonergan enumerates, and the pervasive gnosticism which Voegelin unmasks. In brief, the *epoche* reveals the structure of the person and the end of the person, and thus it enables one to find an eidetic and objective criterion of morality.

Frankl is certain that his phenomenology uncovers a three-cored structure in the person. In Heideggerian terms, this is the ontological structure which Frankl discovers as he penetrates the ontic level of intentional acts as lived and experienced. But Frankl makes it abundantly clear—as does Husserl—that this eidetic structure of three cores is pregiven to the person. All that any epoche can achieve is to uncover the phenomenon, that which appears, and to uncover the phenomenon *as given prior to the analysis of the epoche.* The power to choose freely is granted to the person; with it the person makes free choices. It is obvious to Frankl that the person does not have the ultimate control over the orientation of his will to meaning. This orientation is pregiven; it is built-in by someone else whom Frankl will call supra-meaning. The person has not created himself in any way at all, least of all through the epoche. Any attempt on the part of an individual to pervert the will to meaning is doomed to failure. Although the will to meaning can be repressed, distracted by neurosis or psychosis, or confused by the existential vacuum, it can never be totally derailed from its orientation to search for meaning. The person can make free choices but the person cannot make the free choice to destroy his will to meaning. Its existence and structure lie beyond the person's tampering. In a striking fashion, to show the indestructible orientation of the will to meaning, Frankl declares that the will to meaning can never become ill.[16]

II. RESULTS OF VIKTOR FRANKL'S PHENOMENOLOGY

In following the summons of Husserl's epoche "Back to the things the way they are," Frankl has cast aside the slogan of empiricism "Back to 'nothing but' empirical things!" The results of Frankl's higher viewpoint achieved through the epoche can be summed up: the three-cored structure of the person; the existence of the will to meaning in the spiritual core; the free choices emanating from the will to meaning; and the distinction between value and meaning. In this portion of this paper, two elements will be examined which are intimately related to the results just mentioned. These elements are: (1) Frankl's presentation of the will to meaning as a type of questioning and answer; and (2) the notion of supra-meaning, the ultimate correlative of the will to meaning, that is to say, God.

First, then, one can study how Frankl presents the will to meaning in terms of questioning and answering. The will to meaning, taken as premoral, can be considered as the source of limitless questions about values that find their answers in meanings.[17] Frankl's conception of the will to meaning in terms of questioning-answer affords a powerful and comprehensive manner of viewing the will to meaning. Questioning occurs in the subject. Answers are obtained when the will to meaning, after weighing a value, issues in a free choice. The free choice is the answer to the questioning which may be thematized as: What should one do here and now? Questions and answers, then, are correlative; the will to meaning and the chosen meaning are correlative. Thus one may grasp how powerful and comprehensive Frankl's conception is. For Frankl's conception of the will to meaning as correlated questioning and answering allows one to perceive the two essential characteristics of the will to meaning as intentional: (1) The will to meaning is the basic orientation, similar to Lonergan's notion of value, to question any value (2) in order to reach individual meanings. When conceived in this manner the will to meaning can be said to set up a horizon of unlimited possible answers that can be intended by an unlimited number of questions. The free choices which a person makes from the manifold values encountered intend and therewith constitute the specific world of freedom of the person. Briefly, then, the premoral will to meaning projects a horizon of values against which the person constitutes his world of freedom. This world is correlative to the will to meaning; it is the set of free choices which the person has made.

One can perceive the power and comprehensiveness of Frankl's conception when one compares a wide-spread description of intentionality as "consciousness of an object." In such a descriptive phrase, consciousness all but loses any precise sense because so many meanings have been packed into the word. Consciousness can mean the whole mental life of the subject, or the knowing of the subject, or the intending of the subject, or the sense that Lonergan gives to it: the self-presence of the subject that is the necessary and sufficient condition for any intentional act. Husserl, too, in his *The Phenomenology of Inner Time-Consciousness* presents consciousness as a self-presence. To conceive intentionality in terms of questioning-answer is to conceive it in an explanatory manner. An explanatory manner of conceiving intentionality, however, focuses on the correlation of intending subject and intended object. The concept of correlation is best clarified by pinpointing the terms which constitute the correlation; these terms are the questioning and the answers. Thus, the subject as questioning about values is one term and the values being questioned to attain answers are the other term. The descriptive account of intentionality as "consciousness of" appeals for the most part to images and graphic examples, whereas the explanatory account appeals only to an understanding of the nonimaginable correlation with its two constitutive terms.

Now if there are questions about values in order to reach meanings, is there an order of questioning for Frankl, or does the questioning occur haphazardly? One might think from observing one's own questions about what is right and wrong that these questions occur almost unpredictably. Should one, however, use the epoche as Frankl does, one would see that there is an order in one's questioning. Such an order is a hierarchy. Such an order is teleological.[18] And though it may be unpredictable in the sense that no choice is predetermined, there is a goal towards which the will to meaning is pointed. Meanings for Frankl are morally good choices. But what makes them morally good? And what makes some of greater merit than others? Above we have stated that the criterion of morality according to Frankl is the end of the person by which the person can evaluate different meanings. And the end of the person can be discovered when one asks the epoche-type question: What are human beings for? To respond to this question, Frankl invokes Schweitzer to identify mutual service and love as the telos of the person. Such service and love ground human happiness. Thus love, service, and happiness only flourish together. Supra-meaning entails happiness inasmuch as one serves and loves supra-meaning. Frankl seems to be asserting that love and service bring a person into relationship with supra-meaning, God, because love and service are the manners in which supra-meaning as a person God deals with humans.

Frankl identifies supra-meaning with God, whether he is discussing the problem of evil and God, or whether he is talking about loving God. Although the term "supra-meaning" is somewhat impersonal and foreboding, God in Frankl's thinking is always the personal, ultimate Thou. Frankl shuns what he considers the unjustifiable claims of metaphysics; nonetheless he himself predicates some of the traditional properties of an almighty creator to supra-meaning. Nor should one be surprised. After all, two key sources for Frankl, the Hebrew Scriptures and Martin Buber, assert many things about God. And so does Frankl himself. He at least attributes meaning to God for he names God supra-meaning, borrowing much from the imagery and conceptual apparatus of the Hebrew Scriptures and Buber. These sources of his knowledge about God, however, are not so much a clearly differentiated metaphysics as rather the sometimes majestic, sometimes compact, imagery of the Old Testament, or the descriptive categories of Martin Buber's I-Thou philosophy. From reading Frankl and becoming acquainted with his philosophical and religious antecedents, one may gain some knowledge of the relation of meaning and supra-meaning. But one does not find in these sources the coherent explanation that one has anticipated when Frankl presented the will to meaning as a questioning-answer structure. The notion of questioning-answer takes one beyond the compact thinking of the Bible and Martin Buber to the differentiated notion of not only individual intentional acts of meaning and their correlative object but also the very will to meaning and its correlative object.

Nevertheless, by means of the epoche, Frankl does distinguish individual intentional acts and their ground, the will to meaning. He grasps well the interlinkings of an order where one thing is set in a rank because of its relation to something else. He understands the necessity of an objective criterion of meaning that lines up the values which instincts or free choices intend. The criterion of meaning—the end of the human person—determines a hierarchy of values to be decided upon and then freely chosen. Indeed, Frankl keenly appreciates the fact that without a criterion there simply does not exist an order where one choice is related to another and the whole is determined by its relation to supra-meaning. But what is lacking in Frankl is the same phenomenological analysis by which he retails both general types and individual acts of intentionality. He does not distinguish carefully enough between the nature of an individual free choice with its content that determines it from other free choices. (For example, Frankl's free choice "not to run against the wire" in the concentration camp, or his free choice to speak to a man on death row at San Quentin are different choices because they have different specifying contents from the nature of the will to meaning itself.)

For the will to meaning has no particularized content in the way that an individual free choice does. The will to meaning is the recurrent pattern of questioning-answer which the person can summon up and implement in innumerable particular situations. The will to meaning is like Lonergan's notion of value. Lonergan's notion does not determine what any individual act of evaluation will be; this notion does determine that any individual act of evaluation can only occur because the notion of being is its ground. The notion of value is the condition of possibility for any individual act of free choosing.

Lonergan distinguishes precisely between what he would call acts of valuing and the notion of value, and what Frankl would call acts of meaning and the will to meaning. The individual acts have specific contents, specific objects, specific circumstances. The notion of value has no specific content, no specific object, no specific circumstances. It is an a priori scheme for doing certain things. The notion of value is the capacity of the subject to operate in a certain fashion and consciously make choices. Further, the notion of value erects the horizon within which any choice is to be made. That horizon is identified with reality inasmuch as reality is designated as that which has been valued, or is being valued, or can be valued. Lonergan's methodology does not in any way contradict Frankl's conception of intentionality but rather expands it to afford a more differentiated account.

One may go further. Both Frankl's will to meaning and Lonergan's notion of value are pre-given heuristic orientations. Both are accurately portrayed as questioning-answer patterns that occur in several stages. But what Lonergan's account adds to that of Frankl is the realization that just as one can reach an understanding of the individual free choices and their correlated objects so equally can one reach an understanding of the will to meaning and the notion of value with their correlated objectives. Frankl thinks that the human mind can only know the properties of individual free choices but not those of supra-meaning, or God. Lonergan, on the other hand, thinks that not only can the human mind know the properties of individual free choices but that it knows them as contingent. Since the human mind, then, knows them as individual contingent acts, it can come to know the relation that they have to a necessary and transcendent God.[19] The crux of Lonergan's argument is clearly that, although individual acts of free choosing can be understood piecemeal, they are understood ultimately only insofar as one understands them in their relationship to God. Furthermore, the individual acts are intelligible because God is intelligible.

But some questions interpose. Is it germane to an analysis of Frankl's will to meaning to introduce epistemological and metaphysical considerations? Is it not enough to simply align individual meanings with the will to meaning without speculating on the attributes of a personal but transcendent supra-meaning? Perhaps one could do a phenomenological study of meaning and the will to meaning without delving into metaphysical theorizing about the supra-meaning. Perhaps in all fairness to Frankl one must cast out such speculations. However, Frankl himself is the person who has raised the problem of what and who supra-meaning is. Frankl himself is the person who denies the possibility of making valid attributions about God that disclose real aspects of God. In denying the possibility of knowing some real aspects of God and not just some nouns and adjectives, Frankl has himself adopted a metaphysics of sorts. He denies that one may examine the correlatives supra-meaning and meanings in order to affirm valid knowledge about supra-meaning. He appears to be denying what his own epoche has wrought. So, one is not at all out of order to discuss Frankl's notion of the "unknowable" relation between God and contingent realities, such as humans with their choices and their will to meaning.

Lonergan's method of intentionality analysis allows the epoche more scope than does Frankl's; Lonergan's method goes beyond the compact philosophizing of Frankl about meaning to an examination of the notion of value and its relation to God. When Frankl turns his attention to supra-meaning, he makes some uneasy concessions to the necessity of having some language for talking about God. Nevertheless, Frankl's justification of human language for attributing properties to God totters on the edge of nominalism. Frankl's difficulty seems to be that his compact philosophizing cannot distinguish the reality of individual free choices from the reality intended by the questioning-answer of the will to meaning. Frankl does not seem to understand that the reality correlative to an individual free choice is not the same as the reality correlative to the possibility of any free choice whatsoever, to the reality which is intended by the will to meaning. There are two spheres of reality. In order to understand that there are different spheres of reality and that there is a criterion to distinguish them, Frankl needs the analogy of being. The complete epoche could have brought him to the analogy of being, for one of the compelling motives of the epoche from the time of Husserl's *Ideas I* of 1913 is to discover and name distinct regions of being, or reality. Lonergan, for his part, avows the necessity of the analogy of being to understand the interrelationship of the will to meaning, meaning, and God. Frankl asserts only a *via negativa* that halts abruptly before a phenomenological study of God. Lonergan, however, asserts both a *via negativa* and a *via analogiae.*

III. The Way of Analogy

Frankl, in discussing the knowledge which the person can have of God, uses the consecrated term, "analogy."[20] He draws upon the conceptions of the Old Testament to establish his prime model for explaining the knowledge that a human can attain of God. The Old Testament source which Frankl cites is the Hebrew usage of the word "know," signifying "to know sexually." For Frankl, the love of a man and woman for each other is the acme of all possible human love which we can experience in this life. In it one finds mutual dedication and the ever-present possibility of intensification. Such love accepts the other as a person, not as a thing to be confronted. Frankl, by employing this model, wishes to assert that genuine knowledge of God must be conjoined with love. Having designated this type of love-knowledge as his paradigm for all knowledge of God, he then dismisses all other claims to knowledge of God as misleading inasmuch as they ignore or inadequately follow his paradigm.

This notion of the term analogy seems to be the only one that Frankl will permit. In his book, *The Unconscious God,* Frankl openly repudiates the Freudian misconception of God as the neurotic objective that is "nothing but" the future of an illusion. The person's unconscious, according to Frankl, is oriented to a personal God; the person's unconscious is an a priori structure which is to discover meaning and supra-meaning. But having admirably assembled the elements for establishing a differentiated account of the intentional relation of the human person and God, Frankl reverts to compact thinking, to that of his childhood, for which he declares a privileged status. He affirms that his notion of God is one which he formulated as a boy. Although he speaks of God as "meta-meaning," nevertheless he immediately lapses into his compact mode of thinking:

> The concept of such a *meta-meaning* is not necessarily theistic. Even the concept of God need not necessarily be theistic. When I was fifteen years old or so I came up with a definition of God to which, in my old age, I come back to more and more. I would call it an operational definition. It reads as follows: God is the partner of your intimate soliloquies. Whenever you are talking to yourself in utmost sincerity and ultimate solitude—he to whom you are addressing yourself may justifiably be God.

But then one may inquire: Just what does Frankl mean when he speaks of communicating in oneself "in utmost sincerity and ultimate solitude?" Just what do sincerity and solitude have to do with knowing anything about a lovable God? Does one really learn something about God such that one could attribute mercy, providence, love, and personhood to him, and such that sincerity and solitude are the ways of dealing with him? These questions are perfectly legitimate since—once again—it is Frankl who speaks of God as a certain type of person. Frankl would probably answer that the only valid attribution one could make of God is that he is a person who loves us and whom we can love. Such a conception of God on Frankl's part is almost entirely limited to a representation of God as vaguely personal. In sum, then, Frankl's conception of God is almost entirely limited to a compact representation of God as a person of totally ineffable greatness which sincerity and solitude do little to render intelligible.

But if Frankl can speak of God as the partner of his soliloquies in isolated sincerity and solitude, then it seems that he has indeed set foot on the way of analogy. For whence does he derive his notion of God as a person? Whence his notion of God as supra-meaning, or meta-meaning? May one not assert that Frankl is arguing from the attributes of certain realities in this world to certain attributes in God who is transcendent to this world? Broad is the road of analogy and it seems as though Frankl has entered upon it no matter how vigorously he disavows any real knowledge about God based on this world. For he has taken one of the first steps on the way of analogy: Frankl calls God a person who is present to our inmost selves, and in doing so, Frankl leaves himself open to the charge that he at least knows this much about God: God is supra-meaning with all the intelligible content and significance of that notion for Frankl.

The situation is confusing, for to put the question baldly, is Frankl coherent or not in his notion of our knowledge of God? In his work, *The Will to Meaning*, he clarifies his position on human knowledge of God but at the same time exacerbates the incoherence we have just cited. In *The Will to Meaning* he seems to eliminate any possibility of a knowledge of God from this contingent world. On the basis of what he declares in this book—as elsewhere—in order to be coherent, he would have to admit that one may not know God, not even when speaking in solitude and sincerity with God and with himself. However, Frankl goes on. There is an human world and a divine world. Argumentation on the "logical," or rational grounds is not possible from the human world to the divine world:

> From petrified footprints you may infer that dinosaurs have existed. But from natural
> things you cannot infer that a supra-natural being exists. God is no petrification.
> Teleology is not a reliable bridge between anthropology and theology.[22]

Such argumentation recalls Kant (and perhaps Heidegger?). One may not infer a transcendent cause of the existing effects of this world or even of the very existence of this world as a reality. Teleology is not the orientation of supra-meaning and meanings to a knowable God; it is merely the acknowledged admission of the dualism in human living, the world of the knowable phenomenon and the world of the inaccessible noumena, like God. The rationalism of Kant is the elaborately constructed irrationalism based upon the empiricism of David Hume. In spite of manifesting some of the family traits of Kantian and Humean empiricism, Frankl explicitly rejects Kant's epistemology.[23] Nonetheless, Frankl asserts that there is a rupture between the reality of this world and the reality of God which human knowledge cannot bridge. Such an assertion is the total acceptance of only the *via negativa*. Such an assertion is also the negation of the analogy of being. Although Frankl is not strictly speaking a disciple of Kant in his epistemology, the results of his thinking about God are roughly the same. One finds himself in a strange situation now because Frankl finds himself in a strange situation. On the one hand, Frankl affirms the correlation of the will to meaning and supra-meaning but denies that humans can know anything real about this supra-meaning who is designated as supra-meaning, or meta-meaning. On the other hand, one would expect that God designated as the correlative of the will to meaning and called supra-meaning would be knowable at least as some sort of meaning on the analogy of what human intelligence already knows about meaning. But, according to Frankl, though one may know that there is a supra-meaning, one can know nothing about it. This is the strange situation of Frankl. This is the strange situation of his incoherence. In a word, one cannot know what the will to meaning, meaning, and supra-meaning are and that God is supra-meaning, and not at the same time know some minimum content about God. This incoherence is the result of Frankl's rejection of the analogy of being.

Really, there is no reason why there should be incoherence in Frankl's thinking about the knowledge of God from this world, since he understands so well the structure of intentionality which the epoche has disclosed. However, Frankl does not recognize the exigences of the analogy of being already inherent to his phenomenological conception of intentionality. The eidos of intentionality, as already explained, discloses the correlation of the intending subject *and* the intended object. Frankl's insistent use of the modes of compact thinking when he should shift to differentiated modes of thinking about the will to meaning and meaning on the one hand, and supra-meaning on the other, does not determine his refusal of the way of analogy. This tenacious use of compact thinking, though constantly wandering into areas that only differentiated thinking can handle, does not account for the absence of the analogy of being in Frankl.

The reason that Frankl cannot rise from the world of contingent meanings to the knowledge of the supra-meaning of the transcendent world is that he does not distinguish the spheres (regions, as Husserl would say) of being: one sphere is correlative to the will to meaning and another is correlative to the individual acts of meaning. These spheres are distinct but analogous. Frankl has not perceived that the objective of the will to meaning is a very different kind of reality from the particular reality which a person might intend in his particular choice. If reality is—as it seems to be for Frankl—contingent and univocal, then there is no validity in predicating certain types of attributes of God that are likewise predicated of this contingent world. What Frankl needs is to distinguish the different types of attributes which one may predicate of God and contingent reality. Some attributes qualify the reality as limited and assert that it is somewhere, that the reality is angry or happy (recall the limiting notions of the Bible in speaking of God); some attributes do not qualify the reality as limited but rather, assert that it simply exists, without any reference to a time or a place, that the reality is simply benevolent, provident, and merciful. One is not dealing here with merely a pure language game, a set of rules telling one how to use language, independently of the exigences of intentionality. Reality, then, seems to be for Frankl that which signifies what is contingent and univocal, not what is possibly transcendent and certainly analogous.

The mingling of compact and differentiated thinking in Frankl has rendered hazy the correlation of human intentionality and the knowledge of supra-meaning. One must recall that it is Frankl who denies the inference of valid knowledge about supra-meaning from the contingent world. And so, there are in fact two difficulties with his position: (1) the collision of compact thinking and differentiated thinking, and (2) the rejection of the analogy of being by which one could know something real and revealing about supra-meaning. The second of Frankl's difficulties constitutes the aporia in which the claims for a valid human knowledge about God become an "unheard cry for meaning." There is the step which one may take to follow the broad road of the analogy of being, namely intentionality, but Frankl seems to have hesitated to follow it systematically. And so, one finds in Frankl a "forgetfulness of being," or at least a forgetfulness of the personal being of supra-meaning. One might summarize Frankl's thinking about God in two theses; according to Lonergan they are clearly two counterpositions:

1. The real is not completely intelligible.

2. The world of contingent reality does not offer the use of the way of analogy to infer the existence of the world of the divine.

Summary

In the introductory remarks we mentioned that this paper is divided into three parts: the first concerns Frankl's (and Lonergan's) phenomenological method; the second, the will to meaning conceived in the differentiated and explanatory fashion of questioning-answers, and supra-meaning as the ultimate correlative of the will to meaning; and the third, some serious problems in Frankl's inadequate and even incoherent use of the notion of intentionality when he encounters the different spheres of reality but lacks the *via analogiae*. In the body of this paper, we allowed Frankl to have the last word, but here in the summary we will grant Lonergan (as well as the author of this paper) the final statement, expressed in two theses:

1. The real is completely intelligible.

2. The world of contingent reality does offer the use of the way of analogy to infer the existence of the world of the divine.

Notes

1   See, for example, (in the order of their publication in German) Viktor Frankl, *The Doctor and the Soul*, trans. by Richard and Clara Winston (New York: Bantam Books, 1969), Introduction; *The*

Unconscious God (New York: Simon and Schuster, 1975), Preface and Ch. 1; *The Will to Meaning* (New York: New American Library, 1969), Preface and Part One.

2   See Herbert Spiegelberg, *The Phenomenological Movement,* 2nd ed., Vol. I (The Hague: Martinus Nijhoff, 1965), p. 5.

3   See, for example, Edmund Husserl, *The Idea of Phenomenology,* trans. by William P. Alston and George Hakhnkian (The Hague: Martinus Nijhoff, 1964), Lecture II; *Ideas,* 3rd impression, trans. by W. R. Boyce Gibson (London: George Allen & Unwin, Ltd., 1958), #56–62. See further Rudolf Boehm, "Basic Reflections on Husserl's Phenomenological Reduction," *International Philosophical Quarterly,* 5 (1965), 183–202; W. F. J. Ryan, S.J., "Intentionality in Edmund Husserl and Bernard Lonergan," *International Philosophical Quarterly,* 13 (1973), 173–90.

4   See, for example, *The Unconscious God,* p. 14; *Anthropologische Grundlagen der Psychotherapie* (Bern: Hans Huber, 1975), pp. 109–28.

5   See, for example, *The Unconscious God,* p. 39.

6   See, for example, *The Unconscious God,* pp. 26–27, 30–31.

7   See, for example, *The Will to Meaning,* pp. 16, 48–49, 57–58.

8   See, for example, *The Unconscious God,* Ch. II; *The Will to Meaning,* pp. 23–30.; *Anthropologische Grundlagen,* pp. 109–25.

9   See, for example, *The Unconscious God,* p. 29; *The Will to Meaning,* 23–24, 147–148.

10   See, for example, *The Unconscious God,* Ch. 6.

11   *The Will to Meaning,* p. 151.

12   See, for example, *The Will to Meaning,* pp. 54–58.

13   See, for example, *The Doctor and the Soul,* p. 34 and *The Will to Meaning,* p. 54.

14   Viktor Frankl, *Man's Search for Meaning,* 16th printing, trans. by Ilse Lasch (New York: Washington Square Press, 1969), p. 144.

15   *The Unconscious God,* p. 85, n. 1.

16   See, for example, *Man's Search for Meaning,* p. 211 and *The Unconscious God,* pp. 10–11. Cf. Karl Jaspers, *General Psychopathology,* trans. by J. Hoenig and Marian W. Hamilton, fourth impression (Chicago: The University of Chicago Press, 1972), p. 839, where the Doctor in *Macbeth* is quoted approvingly: "Therein the patient/Must cure himself."

17   See, for example, *Man's Search for Meaning,* p. 122; *The Will to Meaning,* pp. 61 and 95; Viktor Frankl, *Pscyhotherapy and Existentialism* (New York: Simon and Schuster, 1967), pp. 17, 20, 104, 107, 110–11.

18   See, for example, *The Unconscious God,* Preface; *Anthropologische Grundlagen,* pp. 18–19, 53, 178–179. Cf. Alasdair MacIntyre, *After Virtue* (Notre Dame: Notre Dame University Press, 1981), Chs. 12–18.

19   See Bernard Lonergan, *Insight,* rev. ed. (New York: Philosophical Library, 1958), Chs. XII, XIV, and XIX.

20   *Anthropologische Grundlagen,* p. 126, n. 25.

21   Viktor Frankl, *The Unheard Cry for Meaning* (New York: Simon and Schuster, 1978), p. 63.

22   *The Will to Meaning,* p. 148.

23   See *Anthropologische Grundlagen,* pp. 110–17.

VII

The Feeling of Freedom

Elizabeth A. Morelli

THE essential freedom of the human subject has an emotional dimension as well as rational, volitional, practical, and theological dimensions. There is the range of intentional feelings through which we are made aware of the values, which can precipitate and steer deliberation, help to determine moral judgment, and carry us to action. There is, in addition, one specific feeling commonly associated with that critical moment of moral consciousness, the act of decision. It is called variously 'angst,' 'dread,' 'anguish,' and the term I wish to use, 'anxiety.' The question to be pursued here is what kind of feeling or affect is anxiety? This is not a question regarding the pathological conditions which so often share the appelation 'anxiety.' I am not concerned here with the soma-pathological condition of debilitating stress, the psychopathological condition of neurotic phobia, or the pneumopathological condition of despair; but rather with the general affective form of the act of decision, with the nature of the feeling of freedom.

Turning our attention to the heart may seem like turning an untrained eye on the starry sky; yet, as the celestial reaches have been mapped so has the field of affectivity. Not merely gross constellations, but rather intricate systems have been discerned. What at first glance may appear to be a random, however fascinating, array of feelings, upon further analysis is seen to be a structure of distinct yet related elements. And kinds of affects, from sensations and impulses to emotions and passions, can be as different from one another as comets are from suns.

Despite rationalist and positivist aversion to the serious investigation of the emotional life,[1] significant advances in this area have been made in this century. In the works of three

95

phenomenologists in particular one can trace the emergence of a metaphysics of feelings or a typology of affectivity. Max Scheler presents a stratification of the emotional life in *Der Formalismus in der Ethik und die materiale Wertethik* (1913–16).[2] D. von Hildebrand, advancing Scheler's thought in some areas, contributes a classification of intentional responses in his *Ethics* (1953).[3] And Stephan Strasser, building on the works of both Scheler and von Hildebrand among many others, develops an outline of the levels of the heart in his *Das Gemut* (1956).[4]

I. FEELING ACTS AND FEELING STATES

The most fundamental means of differentiating affects, employed commonly in the works of Scheler, von Hildebrand, and Strasser, is the structure of conscious-intentionality and the corresponding metaphysical strata of subject/object or self/world. A related distinction operative to varying degrees in their typologies is that between feeling acts and feeling states. This distinction cuts across the various emotional strata they have isolated, so that we can ask of a feeling on any level whether it is act-like or state-like. Scheler and von Hildebrand distinguish act-like and state-like feelings on the basis of the presence or absence of intentionality. In von Hildebrand's account, which recognizes only two main categories or levels of affects, this way of distinguishing act-like and state-like feelings relegates all affective states to the lower level, the non-intentional level. Although Scheler bases the distinction on the same grounds, he allows that between the state-like, non-intentional, sensible feelings and the act-like, intentional, spiritual feelings there are mid-range vital and psychic feelings, which can be either state-like or act-like. Since vital feelings and psychic feelings are relations to vital and psychic values, this suggests that perhaps there are feelings which have objects and are, nevertheless, state-like. The mere suggestion of intentional states in Scheler's work is followed by an explicit account of spiritual dispositions in Strasser's work. Contrary to both Scheler and von Hildebrand, Strasser bypasses the intentional/ nonintentional basis for distinguishing feeling acts and feeling states, and describes the dispositional (thymic) core of affectivity as penetrating all the levels of the heart. Either Strasser is mistaken when he characterizes certain spiritual or intentional affects as disposi- tional, or there must be some other basis for distinguishing operational and dispositional feelings.

'Intentional' and 'non-intentional' are contradictory attributes. One and the same phenomenon cannot be both intentional and non-intentional at the same time, but it is not the case that act and state stand in the same relation to one another. 'State', from the Latin *status* (a standing), means a condition or a manner of existing, and it has the special meaning of a mental or an emotional condition in which a person finds himself at a particular time. 'Act', from the Latin *actus* (a doing), means the process of doing, operating, performing of an intelligent being. The manner of one's existing, the condition one finds oneself in, might very well be that of doing, operating, or performing. An active state is not a contradiction in terms. So Lonergan, for instance, writes of "the *dynamic state* of being in love" (italics added), the supreme example of those feelings that are "so deep and strong, especially when deliberately reinforced, that they channel attention, shape one's horizon, direct one's life."[5]

The terms 'active'/'passive' and 'dynamic'/'static' are descriptive. Perhaps, it would be better to approach the task of distinguishing feeling acts and feeling states explanatorily. Scheler dismisses the possibility of state-like spiritual feelings, because, as spiritual, feelings are the person himself as existing, as acting. They do not, therefore, presuppose any substratum. But, if spiritual feelings cannot be states, then states must presuppose substrata; states must be qualities or functions of something underlying. If state is defined as a quality of an act, then we can account for the state-like affects described in all three typologies. Different kinds of states qualify different kinds of acts. The sensory states described by Scheler, the non-intentional states described by von Hildebrand, and the pre-intentional dispositions described by Strasser are all qualities of biological or neurological acts. The vital and psychic states described by Scheler are qualities of perceptual and to some extent intellectual acts. And the spiritual dispositions described by Strasser are qualities of rational and moral acts.

This last instance of states as qualities of acts may seem to be at odds with Strasser's account of spiritual dispositions. He describes modes of comportment, particularly basic modes, as underpinning and organizing one's cognitive and feeling acts. This suggests that on the spiritual level acts are a function of one's basic disposition rather than this disposition being a quality of an act. Yet, spiritual acts can be functions of an underlying disposition and that disposition remain a quality of an act, if a basic or transcendental act (intention) is seen as serving as substratum for the disposition. This basic act is the very dynamism of conscious intentionality. So, for example, on the level of intelligence, the fundamental dynamism is the intention of intelligibility, and this basic intention is qualified by the affective state of wonder. And wonder is a state within which distinct cognitional and affective acts, such as bewilderment, frustration, delight, etc., occur and of which these acts could be said to be functions.

The identification of affective states with qualities of acts raises another difficulty, however. Lonergan defines consciousness as "a quality immanent in acts of certain kinds."[6] How is consciousness as a quality of acts to be distinguished from affective states? By 'consciousness' Lonergan further means self-presence, the awareness of oneself that is immanent in all intentional operations.[7] While he writes of different degrees of consciousness corresponding to different kinds of acts, there is a limited number of kinds of consciousness, namely, empirical, intellectual, rational, responsible, and the consciousness of the fifth level of love. If one is on the intellectual level, for example, one is intellectually conscious as performing various operations, such as inquiring and having insights. But while one's degree of consciousness, in this case intellectual, does not change as one moves from asking a question to understanding, one's affective state can change. As faced with a problem while questioning one may feel perplexed, and this perplexity may be replaced by a feeling of relief when one finally catches on. While the affective quality of different acts on the same level may vary, the type of consciousness remains the same. Furthermore, one and the same operation can be qualified by different affective states at different times, but it will invariably be qualified by some one degree of consciousness. In acting intentionally one is made present to oneself. One cannot have an intentional operation that is not qualified by some degree of self-presence, some degree of consciousness; however, one can óperate intentionally without any noticeable affective state.[8] The key difference, then, between the affective and the conscious qualification of intentional acts lies in the fact that consciousness is a quality immanent in acts, while affective states are generally extrinsic qualities of acts.

Feeling acts, then, are distinguished from feeling states insofar as the former are operations of the subject presupposing no other substratum, and the latter are qualities of underlying acts. While the active/passive distinction can be discounted as an adequate means of distinguishing feeling acts and feeling states, it remains that feeling acts and feeling states have distinctive descriptive characteristics. Feeling acts, as processes, are transitional and tend to be transitory; feeling states tend to have more permanence. Feeling acts are definite or limited and feeling states are generalized or pervasive. An intentional response to value (a feeling act), for example, the admiration one feels for a person who has truly mastered an art or discipline, has the threefold structure of the human act: a definite beginning with the initial apprehension of the personal value; an intermediary phase, which may involve deepening appreciation; and a termination, when one ceases to attend to that value.[9] On the other hand, an intentional feeling state, for example, a haughty attitude, which is a function of an inflated estimation of one's own worth as compared to that of others, pervades one's consciousness. It is a lasting, generalized feeling that can interfere with any number of cognitive acts and intentional responses (such as admiration), which would possibly alter the attitude. Feeling states and feeling acts, then, can be distinguished on the basis of whether a feeling is an indefinite, pervasive, lasting quality or function, or a definite, focused, transitory process. And, with this means of distinguishing feeling states and feeling acts, instead of the intentional/non-intentional distinction, it is consistent to speak of intentional (specifically spiritual) affective states.

II. AN ILLUSTRATION: THE EXPERIENCE OF VERTIGO

It is not necessary "to visit Paris and London" or to peruse and recount the wealth of clinical material available in order to observe the phenomenon which I wish to study. "If an observer will only pay attention to himself, he will have enough with five men, five women, and ten children for the discovery of all possible states of the human soul."[10] As it is the general form of anxiety which we wish to grasp, any instance of anxiety will be sufficient for our purpose. But because of its starkness and a certain symbolic value, the experience of vertigo provides a particularly useful illustration of anxiety. Kierkegaard employs dizziness before the abyss as an analogy for subjective anxiety in general, for the experience of spirit facing its freedom:

> Anxiety may be compared with dizziness. He whose eye happens to look down into the yawning abyss becomes dizzy. But what is the reason for this? It is just as much in his own eye as in the abyss, for suppose he had not looked down. Hence anxiety is the dizziness of freedom, which emerges when the spirit wants to posit the synthesis and freedom looks down into its own possibility, laying hold of finiteness to support itself.[11]

Sartre, too, employs vertigo to illustrate anxiety. His purpose in phenomenologically describing vertigo is to reveal anxiety in the face of one's future, in the face of the nothing that lies between what I am presently and what I am to be.[12] Let us review Sartre's account of the anxiety involved in vertigo, for our purpose of determining the general affective form of anxiety.

"Vertigo is anguish to the extent that I am afraid not of falling over the precipice, but of throwing myself over."[13] Vertigo is not a fear of heights, but an experience of a threat to me that comes from myself. Nevertheless, I first experience vertigo as a fear of falling, as a horror of the prospect of hurtling over the edge to my death. I react to this fear with reflective vigilance, taking special pains to watch my step, to avoid the edge, to locate secure handholds, to steady my balance. But "at the very moment when I apprehend my being as *horror* of the precipice, I am conscious of that horror as *not determinant* in relation to my possible conduct."[14] This awareness of the fact that my caution is not *caused* by my fear of falling, that I need not protect myself, that I could just as well run recklessly or even throw myself over the side, is not an afterthought. It does not occur to me in the moment after I feel the horror; rather, it is realized concomitantly with the horror, and is constitutive of the horror. Still, contemplation of my contradictory possibilities serves as a reflective refuge from the fearful prospect of the fall. In this reflection, I find that my future course of action is completely undetermined. My safe conduct depends upon how I will act, but because my actions are undetermined, even by my horror and my concern for my safety, I cannot rely on myself in the next instant. Yet, now I desperately cling to this self which I am not yet. In the experience of vertigo I apprehend that the self that I am now depends on the self that I am to be, but that the self that I am to be does not depend on anything—not on what I am presently, not on any horror I feel.[15] As I survey my possibilities—the possibility of securing my safe conduct and the possibility of suicide—I discover that as nothing necessitates my caution, so nothing necessitates my suicide. This realization of the indeterminateness of the negative possibility momentarily lightens the weight of its pull. Suspended now between equally powerful yet powerless possibilities, I can take hold of the moment and put an end to my vertigo by deciding, and resuming my way.

The symbolic value of using vertigo as an example of anxiety resides in the analogy between a leap over the edge of a cliff and a free act of decision. In stepping or jumping over the edge, one leaves the safety of the ground behind, one is supported by nothing, one is left totally and irrevocably to oneself. So too, in an act of decision, one moves beyond all antecedent conditions or determinants; nothing necessitates the act but oneself. A disanalogy lies in the fact that as a body one is unable to support oneself in mid-air, but as spirit one is able to support oneself in freedom. Thus, the outcome of a leap over the edge is most likely physical destruction, but the outcome of an act of decision is unknown—it may be personal destruction or salvation, or, at least, renewed equilibrium. In his repeated use of the term 'qualitative leap' of spirit or of freedom, Kierkegaard draws on this analogy but largely overlooks the disanalogy, for the leap he focuses on in *The Concept of Anxiety* is the leap into sin, which like the physical leap has a sure, destructive outcome.

The question of the general affective form of anxiety is the question of whether anxiety is an act-like affect or a state-like affect. We find, in the description of vertigo, that anxiety is distinguished from other components of the experience. It is related to and yet distinct from my fear of an external threat to my well-being, from my feeling of horror at the prospect of suicide by falling, from my comtemplation of or reflection on my possibilities, from my discovery or realization of the radical indeterminateness of the possibilities, and, finally, from my decision and subsequent action. Anxiety pervades the entire experience of vertigo, giving rise to the other distinct components as its concomitants. It perdures as the other components begin, proceed, and end. In addition to its pervasiveness and its perdurance, anxiety is distinguished from the cognitive and the other affective elements of the experience of vertigo by reason of its indefiniteness. The cognitive acts of contemplation, reflection, discovery, and realization have definite possibilities as their respective objects. So too, the feeling acts of fear and horror are responses to specific possibilities. The fear is felt in the face of the external threat posed by the precipice; the horror is felt in the face of the internal threat posed by the possibility of suicide. The anxiety, on the other hand, is in response to both (yet neither) the external and the internal threats. In Heidegger's words, "That in the face of which one has anxiety is characterized by the fact that what threatens is *nowhere*. Anxiety 'does not know' what that in the face of which it is anxious is."[16] While, in this case, horror is closer to anxiety than fear, because a threat from within, from oneself, is more oppressive and ineluctable than any external threat, it remains that the horror is felt in response to a specific possibility, suicide. But in the case of anxiety, "That which anxiety is profoundly anxious about is not a *definite* kind of Being for Dasein or a *definite* possibility for it. Indeed the threat itself is indefinite. . . ."[17]

Anxiety as illustrated in the experience of vertigo has the marks of a feeling state. It is distinguished from cognitive and affective acts, operations, or processes by its pervasiveness, perdurance, and indefiniteness. The remaining, and most essential, characteristic of a feeling state is that it is a quality or a function of an underlying act, operation, or process.

III. ANXIETY AS A BASIC AFFECTIVE STATE

Having determined that anxiety bears the descriptive characteristics of an affective state, it remains to be seen how anxiety is a quality or a function. In our account of the experience of vertigo, we found that one feels anxious in the face of the equally undetermined possibilities of leaping to one's death or of securing one's safe conduct. In vertigo one is not merely contending with the threat of external forces, but with one's freedom. The experience of vertigo, as a whole, is an experience of freedom. This is manifested in the acts of practical reflection, deliberation, evaluation (drawing on the horror, which is a response to the disvalue of self-destruction), and eventual decision and subsequent action, which together constitute the experience. These rational and affective acts are characteristic of the fourth level of conscious intentionality, the level of rational self-consciousness, of responsibility, of conscience, of freedom. Anxiety, then is a quality or a function of the level of freedom.

In our account of vertigo, we further determined that anxiety is not a function of any *one* of the acts constitutive of moral consciousness. One does not feel anxious because one is deliberating; one deliberates because one feels anxious. Anxiety underlies and permeates the various acts of this level; they arise as functions of the basic state of anxiety. Yet, anxiety, insofar as it is a state rather than an act, cannot be the ultimate substratum of the acts of this level of conscious intentionality. That which functions as the basic *dynamism* of moral consciousness is the pure intention of value.

The transcendental dynamism of moral consciousness is not another act distinct from the acts constitutive of moral consciousness, but rather that drive which gives rise to and informs each of these acts. It promotes one from the level of rational consciousness to the level of moral, free, existential consciousness. The notion of value is a demand for what is truly good, not in the abstract, but as achieved concretely in freedom, in moral self-transcendence. It not only drives one to achieve the good, but it also provides the criteria for determining whether or not one is meeting the demand.[18] In its normative force this transcendental dynamism or intention is what I mean by the term "conscience." Lonergan writes that on the fourth level, consciousness becomes conscience.[19] I understand him to mean by "consciousness" here conscious intentionality as a whole, not specifically the self-awareness immanent in the intentionality. Conscience or the normativity of the intention of the fourth level is experienced either as the peace of a satisfied moral demand or as the unrest, even torment, of an unmet moral demand. It is the further questions and second thoughts which continue to plague us as long as the demand is unmet.[20]

Inasmuch as anxiety is an affective state rather than an affective act, it is a quality or a function of some substratum. The substratum presupposed by anxiety is the transcendental dynamism of the fourth level of conscious intentionality. As qualifying this intention of value, anxiety is analogous to the affective states of wonder and doubt. Wonder qualifies the intention of intelligibility on the second level of conscious intentionality, and doubt qualifies the intention of the true and the real on the third level. These three affective states are basic or fundamental because they underlie and permeate the particular cognitive and affective acts of their respective levels. As wonder gives rise to inquiry and understanding and to such affects as perplexity and relief, and as doubt gives rise to reflection and judgment and to such affects as wariness and confidence, so anxiety gives rise to deliberation and decision and to such affects as boredom and excitement.

Anxiety is the basic affective state qualifying the intention of the fourth level of conscious intentionality. And inasmuch as we identify conscience with the normativity of this intention, anxiety is a quality of conscience.[21] The question that now arises is what kind of quality anxiety is. Intrinsic and extrinsic qualities of intentional acts have been distinguished, and consciousness, that is, one's self-awareness or self-presence, has been characterized as an intrinsic quality of intentional acts. An alternative formulation for our question is, What is the relationship of anxiety to the consciousness immanent in the intention of value? Is anxiety an extrinsic quality of one's moral self-presence? Does anxiety accompany consciousness as another immanent quality of moral intentionality? Or is Sartre correct in indentifying anxiety with moral consciousness?

> We wished only to show that there exists a specific consciousness of freedom, and we wished to show that this consciousness is anguish. This means that we wished to establish anguish in its essential structure as consciousness of freedom.[22]

Let us tackle these questions by examining Sartre's contention that anxiety is moral consciousness or what he calls consciousness of freedom.

Consciousness, for Sartre, following Husserl, is invariably "consciousness of," that is, it is essentially intentional or "positional."[23] Sartre also admits another dimension of consciousness, its reflexivity. Consciousness, in positing or intending an object, is always simultaneously aware of itself: "The type of existence of consciousness is to be consciousness of itself. And consciousness is aware of itself insofar as it is conscious of a transcedent object."[24] This immediate self-awareness is not knowledge of the self. One's intention is completely taken up with the object. Sartre distinguishes a pre-reflective and a reflective consciousness. Both are intentional and self-aware. The self-awareness of pre-reflective consciousness is non-positional; consciousness does not become an object for itself. It is merely self-aware while intending some (other) object. In reflective consciousness, consciousness does become an object for itself, but not in the manner of a "transcendent object": "It is necessary that the reflective simultaneously be and not be the reflected-on."[25] Reflective consciousness is positional insofar as consciousness as reflected-on becomes its object, and it is concomitantly self-aware insofar as it is immediately present to itself as reflective in a non-positional manner.

This non-positional relation of consciousness to itself, the self-awareness of both pre-reflective and reflective consciousness, is what I mean here by the term "consciousness".[26] We have found consciousness to be the self-awareness or self-presence that is distinguished from and yet inseparable from the intentionality of acts. It is distinguished as a quality of the intentionality; and it is inseparable not because consciousness is itself intentional, as Sartre contends, but because intentionality is essentially conscious. Consciousness, while an immanent quality of intentional acts, is not itself an intentional act. It does not give us an object. Sartre, on the other hand, means by "consciousness" the whole complex, conscious intentionality.

While consciousness is an intrinsic quality of intentional acts, affective states are extrinsic qualities of acts. In the performance of an intentional act one is necessarily present to oneself, and this self-present intending may be further qualified by some feeling. For Sartre, however, consciousness does not admit of qualification. Inasmuch as consciousness is pure spontaneity, absolute translucence, it lacks the interiority, the constituent, the qualifications found in transcendent objects.[27] States, such as hatred and love, are transcendent objects characteristic, not of consciousness but of the ego which is a transcendent object as well, an object in the world beyond consciousness.[28]

Since, for Sartre, consciousness as spontaneity or intentionality cannot be qualified by any state, and yet man invariably is conscious of freedom in anxiety, anxiety must be identical with the consciousness of freedom. On the other hand, I understand anxiety to be an affective state. Yet I can agree that anxiety is identical with moral *consciousness,* because I mean by consciousness the quality of self-presence immanent in the intention of freedom. In other words, the "pure spontaneity" of the fourth level is qualified essentially by consciousness and this consciousness is anxious. Thus, we find that anxiety as an affective state, is basic or fundamental, not only because it underlies the various acts emergent on this level, but also because it is an *intrinsic* quality of intentionality and not merely an extrinsic quality as are other possible affective states. For this reason, anxiety as well as wonder and doubt are special affective states. One is present to oneself on the second level as wondering, on the third level as doubting, and on the fourth level as anxious.

In describing anxiety as invariably present when one confronts the possibility of freedom, Sartre echoes his predecessors' accounts of anxiety. For Kierkegaard man as qualified by spirit is never without anxiety. Although anxiety is defined as "freedom's disclosure of itself in possibility,"[29] the actual qualitative leap does not terminate the anxiety. Having actualized one's freedom in a decision, one faces the possibilities of freedom anew. Thus there is anxiety prior to and subsequent to the leap. "To the extent that in every state possibility is present, anxiety is also present."[30] For Heidegger, too, the basic state of anxiety, as an existential structure of Dasein, is ever present: ". . . anxiety, as a basic state-of-mind, belongs to Dasein's essential state of Being-in-the-world."[31] I must also agree that one can never face one's freedom without anxiety because anxiety is an intrinsic quality of the intention of the fourth level of conscious intentionality.

However, this claim seems to contradict our everyday experience. It seems that while occasions of making decisions and of acting freely are frequent, experiences of anxiety are rare. Can it be true that every choice one makes is made in anxiety? More radically, if man as spirit is essentially faced with possibility, can it be true that he is always anxious? Sartre states the difficulty in the following way: "Someone will say, freedom has just been described as a permanent structure of the human being; if anguish manifests it, then anguish ought to be a permanent state of my affectivity. But, on the contrary, it is completely exceptional. How can we explain the rarity of the phenomenon of anguish?"[32] This question can be answered in three parts. First of all, although man is essentially free, essentially qualified by spirit, he is not always rationally self-conscious. Man, who leads a checkered existence of wakefulness and sleep, cannot possibly maintain rational self-consciousness uninterruptedly. One may be asleep, or as just arising in the morning merely empirically conscious, or as engrossed in a theoretical problem merely intellectually conscious. Secondly, as actually conscious on the fourth level, as consciously intending one's possibility in freedom, one may very well not attend to the anxious intending itself. As we have seen, consciousness is mere self-presence or self-awareness, and this self-presence for both Sartre and Lonergan is non-positional or non-cognitive. To be conscious, in this case to be anxious, is not to know that one is conscious or anxious. That which is anxiously intended may be so engrossing that one is, in a sense, oblivious to one's current state. And thirdly, the experience of anxiety is usually so unpleasant in its dizziness, its uncanniness, and in the enervating effect of its instability; and, further, the implications of the freedom it reveals are so threatening, that anxiety is positively fled. "Everything takes place, in fact, as if our essential and immediate behavior with respect to anguish is flight."[33]

We have established, then, that the general form of anxiety is that of a feeling state. It bears the descriptive characteristics of pervasiveness, perdurance, and indefiniteness, and it functions as a quality of an underlying intention. It is one of three basic or fundamental states in that it is an intrinsic or essential qualification of the transcendental dynamism of conscious intentionality. As such, it is an immanent quality of conscience, and it is identical with the consciousness of the fourth level of conscious intentionality—the level of freedom.

At least two further questions, far-reaching in their implications, arise at this point: Is anxiety ineluctable? and How ought one relate genuinely to one's anxiety? Rather than pursue these questions here, I will instead merely point in the direction of their answers. Analysis of the *intentional* nature of anxiety reveals this affect to be the experience of the subject drawn by the possibility of real self-transcendence and simultaneously checked by the inertia of his present horizon. In anxiety one experiences what Voegelin calls the pull and counterpull of human existence.[34] One experiences, in other words, the *tension* of limitation and transcendence on the fourth level of conscious intentionality.[35] If anxiety is this basic tension, and the tension of human existence is ineluctable,[36] then it seems that anxiety is ineluctable.

On the other hand, can religious conversion working from above downwards eliminate or transform our anxiety? Is it possible to face one's freedom in the basic state of joy or hope instead of anxiety?[37] Does the complacency which can issue from intellectual conversion cast out anxiety?[38] Can conversion of any type eliminate, mitigate or transform anxiety, or does it rather transform our relation to this fundamental condition of human freedom? And, finally, if there is a "converted," an authentic, way to deal with one's anxiety, what is it? While these and further questions remain, it is hoped that some light has been shed on the nature of this fundamental disposition—this feeling of freedom.

NOTES

1   Max Scheler understands reluctance on the part of some thinkers to deal with the affective life to be but a symptom of a general malady: "If not only this or that individual man but whole generations have forgotten how to see this, if entire generations see the whole emotional life as a dumb, *subjectively* human matter of fact, without a meaning on which objective necessity can be based, without sense and direction, this is not something engineered by nature but is the responsibility of men and ages. It comes from the *general slovenliness in matters of feeling*, in matters of love and hate, from the lack of seriousness for all the depths of things and for life itself, and, by way of contrast, from the ridiculous ultraseriousness and comical busyness over those things which our wits can technically master." See "Ordo Amoris," in *Max Scheler: Selected Philosophical Essays*, trans. David R. Lachteman (Evanston: Northwestern University Press, 1973), p. 118.

   J. Habermas, too, describes the toxic effect of rationalist bias: "From the mainstream of rationality the pollutants, the sewage of emotionality, are filtered off and locked away hygenically in a storage basin—an imposing mass of subjective value qualities" (*Theory and Practice*, trans. John Viertel [Boston: Beacon Press, 1973], p. 265).

2   Max Scheler, *Formalism in Ethics and Non-Formal Ethics of Values*, trans. by Manfred S. Frings and Roger L. Funk (Evanston: Northwestern University Press, 1973).

3   Dietrich von Hildebrand, *Ethics* (Chicago: Franciscan Herald Press, 1953).

4   Stephan Strasser, *Phenomenology of Feelings: An Essay on the Phenomena of the Heart*, trans. by Robert E. Wood (Pittsburgh: Duquesne University Press, 1977).

5   Bernard Lonergan, S.J., *Method in Theology* (New York: Herder and Herder, 1972), pp. 115, 32.

6   Lonergan, *Insight: A Study of Human Understanding* (New York: Philosophical Library; London: Longmans, Green & Co., Ltd., 1957), p. 321.

7   Lonergan, *Collection: Papers by Bernard Lonergan, S. J.* ed. by F. E. Crowe, S. J. (New York: Herder and Herder, 1967), pp. 225–27.

8   It has been argued, however, that although one may not be aware of having any particular feeling, the dispositional ground of intentional activity is both ever-present and all-pervasive. The detachment of the intellectual pattern of experience, for example, presupposes a certain disposition, a "neutral" affective state free from rapid and exaggerated emotional swings. This calm, enabling disposition, which is deliberately fostered in the pursuit of science, also functions spontaneously, if unevenly, in everyday commerce. The vacuity experienced by clerks in a bureaucratic setting and by customers waiting in line is not a total absence of affects, but rather the presence of a certain "practical" mood. One may transcend or abandon determinate feelings in the pursuit of truth or the exercise of duty, but one is never free of some disposition. See Strasser, *Phenomenology of Feeling*, pp. 180–200.

In his diatribe against the ascetic ideal, Nietzsche describes the attempt to overcome the influence of the will and the emotions, and its ultimate futility: "Henceforth, my dear philosophers, let us be on guard against the dangerous old conceptual fiction that posited a 'pure, will-less, painless, timeless knowing subject;' . . . But to eliminate the will altogether, to suspend each and every affect, supposing we were capable of this—what would that mean but to *castrate* the intellect?'' (*On the Genealogy of Morals*, trans. by Walter Kaufman and R. J. Hollingdale New York: Random House, 1967), p. 119.

9   Strasser, *Phenomenology of Feeling*, p. 215.

10   Soren Kierkegaard, *The Concept of Anxiety*, trans. by Reidar Thomte (Princeton, NJ: Princeton University Press, 1980), p. 126.

11   Ibid., p. 61.

12   Jean-Paul Sartre, *Being and Nothingness*, trans. by Hazel E. Barnes (New York: Washington Square Press, 1966), pp. 66–69.

13   Ibid., p. 65.

14   Ibid., p. 68.

15   Ibid., p. 69.

16   Martin Heidegger, *Being and Time*, trans. by John Macquarrie and Edward Robinson (New York and Evanston: Harper & Row, 1962), p. 231.

17   Ibid., p. 232.

18   Lonergan, *Method in Theology*, pp. 34–36.

19   Ibid., pp. 268–69.

20   The term "conscience" traditionally has been used either in a broad sense to mean man's capacity for moral knowledge or in a narrower sense to mean the particular application of moral knowledge to what we are to do. I am using it in a refined sense of the latter usage to mean the normative exigence of the fourth level of conscious intentionality.

21   This view is in conformity with Heidegger's view of the relation of anxiety and conscience. In his analysis of conscience, Heidegger refers to this exigence in its capacity as discourse, as the call or summons to return to one's authentic potentiality-for-Being; and anxiety is designated as the basic disposition of the call of conscience. See *Being and Time*, pp. 342 ff.

22   Sartre, *Being and Nothingness*, pp. 70–71.

23   Ibid., p. 11.

24   Sartre, *The Transcendence of the Ego*, trans. by Forrest Williams and Robert Kirtepatrick (New York: Farrar, Straus and Cadahy, The Noonday Press, 1957), p. 40.

25 Sartre, *Being and Nothingness,* pp. 213–14.

26 Kierkegaard "describes" this non-positional self-presence when he writes: "The most concrete content that consciousness can have is consciousness of itself, of the individual himself—not the pure self-consciousness, but the self-consciousness that is so concrete that no author, not even the one with the greatest power of description, has ever been able to describe a single such self-consciousness, although every single human being is such a one" (*The Concept of Anxiety,* p. 143).

27 Sartre, *The Transcendence of the Ego,* pp. 40–41.

28 Ibid., pp. 61–68.

29 Kierkegaard, *The Concept of Anxiety,* p. 111.

30 Ibid., p. 113.

31 Heidegger, *Being and Time,* p. 234.

32 Sartre, *Being and Nothingness,* p. 73.

33 Ibid.

34 Eric Voegelin, "Reason: The Classic Experience," *The Southern Review* (July 1974), pp. 237–264.

35 Lonergan, *Insight,* pp. 472 ff.; *Understanding and Being,* ed. by Elizabeth A. Morelli and Mark D. Morelli (New York and Toronto: The Edwin Mellen Press, 1980), p. 235.

36 Lonergan, *Insight,* p. 474.

37 Heidegger mentions joy as another basic mood which can qualify the confrontation with one's own potentiality-for-Being, with one's freedom (358).

38 Frederick E. Crowe, S. J., "Complacency and Concern in the Thought of St. Thomas," *Theological Studies* 20 (September 1959), p. 381.

VIII

Historicity and Philosophy: The Existential Dimension

Thomas J. McPartland

THE triumph of historical consciousness in the past two centuries has hurled an acute, even seemingly insuperable, challenge to the ideal of objective philosophical truth—and perforce has rendered problematic the relationship of philosophy to culture and to religion.[1] Even Kant's modest claims for critical philosophy have been overthrown by the dominant currents of logical positivism, linguistic analysis, and Sartrean existentialism, each in its own right, among other imperatives, attempting to salvage some residue of philosophy from the ravages of historical consciousness. One of the burning questions that most agitated Descartes and Kant, namely, how to surmount the plurality of antagonistic philosophical schools, has apparently now begun to consume philosophy itself in the flames of relativism. Hegel's dazzling gnostic speculation of the meaning of history notwithstanding, more characteristic of the spirit of the age has been the tortured ambivalence of Dilthey's critique of historical reason, simultaneously displaying a kind of pantheistic enthusiasm and then a deeply felt frustration and foreboding over the restriction of philosophy to an aesthetic contemplation of the diversity of irreconcilable philosophical worldviews.[2] The contemporary assault on philosophy, however, has had as a fomenter not so much historical consciousness per se as the strident pronouncements of historicism, an inchoate philosophy that would consign truth solely to the cultural context, if not the vagaries, of a certain point in time and of the social and technological setting in which the context is embedded: thus human nature, according to historicism, varies from historical age to historical age much as philosophical—and presumably religious—truth varies from one *Weltanschauung* to another.[3] Historicism, not surprisingly, is one of the more conspicuous perpetrators of the cultural crisis of the twentieth century, a crisis in which the decisive issue is ultimately the nature, value, and integrity of higher intellectual culture itself, which is to say, of philosophy in its more generic sense. Hence the dubious relation of philosophy to culture and to religion in the climate of opinion of the twentieth century simply reflects the dubious status of philosophy—along with the dubious status of culture itself and of religion.

Historical consciousness has unquestionably dislodged from its previous position of ascendancy the kind of culture that viewed itself as a set of universal and permanent standards. In the bosom of this "classicist culture," to use Bernard Lonergan's term, philosophy, no matter how debatable might be its other attributes, would inevitably aspire to be a perennial philosophy; moreover, by supplying rudimentary metaphysical principles this perennial philosophy would prepare the ground for theological reflection on the timeless truths of religion.[4]

But when classicist culture has been jettisoned can it be supplanted? Can philosophy arise again like the phoenix from the ashes of the cultural crisis? Can philosophy once again speak to religion of the concerns of epistemology and metaphysics?

I. LONERGAN AND HISTORICAL CONSCIOUSNESS

No one has been more resolute in responding to this challenge than Bernard Lonergan, although he has not been alone in this endeavor. There has indeed been at work in the twentieth century a creative minority of philosophers, theologians, social theorists, and historians—such thinkers as Martin Heidegger, Michael Polanyi, Hans Georg Gadamer, Jurgen Habermas, and Eric Voegelin, earlier preceded by such nineteenth-century precursors as Kierkegaard and Newman[5]—all of whom, with varying degrees of intensity and exactness, have been breaking away from the intellectual horizon reigning ever since the late Middle Ages, the hallmark of which has been the confrontation theory of truth. With an arc of influence, immediate or indirect, extending from conceptualist metaphysics to nominalism, from rationalism to empiricism, from Kantianism to positivism, from idealism to historism, the confrontation theory of truth has asserted, as its fundamental premise, that knowing must involve, at least in some analogous sense, an unimpaired vision of reality, whether the emphasis be given to looking at sense data, concepts, or ideas. The historicist position, for example, depicts historical objectivity as an empathetic entry by an historian divested of any personal evaluation into the horizon under investigation; while some of the more sophisticated historicists, such as Dilthey, have advocated re-experiencing the creative moments beneath the tangible expressions of the horizon, still such a creative process is a subjective process, and it offers no objective criteria by which to discriminate among the myriad expressions of meaning and value.

Lonergan provides what is arguably the most comprehensive alternative to the confrontation theory of truth. He suggests that we probe beneath the oftentimes bewildering heterogeneity of ideas, concepts, and values found in historical horizons as finished products to the conscious activities that constitute them. He would have us ask whether waging the struggle for philosophical foundations principally in the arena of theories and concepts has been, in fact, a strategy of capitulation to the confrontation theory of truth, leading inexorably to the battle fatigue and exhaustion of the present cultural crisis. Lonergan insists that contemporary philosophical culture retrace the journey in search of foundations along the path from medieval essentialism to Descartes' thinking substance, to Kant's transcendental ego, to Hegel's subject, to Kierkegaard's *this* subject: from object as object, to subject as object, to the subject as subject.[6] The venture of cultural reconstruction must take the road of, in his unique phrase, "self-appropriation."[7] By this Lonergan means that epistemology, metaphysics, and all other branches of systematic philosophy, including the philosophy of religion, must rest on an existential underpinning; they must be founded on an explication of the conscious activities of the self as knower.[8] Through a studied application of the old Socratic injunction "know thyself," issuing in what Lonergan styles "cognitional theory," we can, he claims, fashion a basic philosophical semantics.[9] Truth, objectivity, and reality now assume meaning in terms of the norms ingredient in the very process of inquiry with its directional tendency.[10] The knower, then, rather than being a self-contained *cogito* "in here" confronting a world "out there," is a self-transcending subject dwelling in the luminous openness of the horizon of being, and knowing is precisely fidelity to the project of questioning through its recurrent cognitive structure of experiencing, understanding, and judging. Fundamental differences in metaphysics, ethics, and epistemology can usually be reduced, explicitly or implicitly, to differences in cognitional theory, and those differences can be resolved, and only be resolved, by an appeal to the data of consciousness.[11] Such is Lonergan's tack. His focus on self-appropriation and the systematic expansion of the positions of cognitional theory into all domains of philosophy stands as his most original achievement and perhaps as an enduring legacy to the history of philosophy. For he allows philosophy, with its refurbished critical apparatus, once again to address itself to the normative concerns of culture and to the vital issues of religious truth. Furthermore, by keeping in full perspective in his philosophy both the subjective pole of self-appropriation and the objective pole of cognitional theory Lonergan strives to avoid the twin dangers of either subjectivism, irrationalism, and romanticism, on the one hand, or objectivism, essentialism, and conceptualism, on the other hand. And by discovery of a normative and transcultural pattern in subjective operations he empowers philosophy to outflank historicism in the very territory of historical consciousness itself.

Increasingly throughout his work Lonergan has sought to exploit the riches of historical consciousness in order to erect what he calls a basic science of human living.[12] Cognitive life, integral as it is to human living, is not the totality of the human existential situation. Indeed, Lonergan remarks, "a life of pure intellect or pure reason without the control of deliberation, evaluation, responsible choice is something less than the life of a psychopath."[13] Thus he emphasizes how the intention of the good is the fuller flowering of the desire to know, the animating principle of cognitive operations;[14] how cognitive self-appropriation, or intellectual conversion, has, as existential conditions, a conversion to values and a conversion to the sacred;[15] how, conversely, moral conversion and religious conversion preserve, enrich, and carry forward the essential features and properties of intellectual conversion;[16] how the life of inquiry—cognitive, moral and spiritual—is that of an incarnate subject whose knowing and deciding are driven by the power of feeling, image, and symbol, releasing the energy of the *elan vital* with its teleological momentum;[17] how the incarnate inquirer undergoes "a development that is social and historical, that stamps the stages of scientific and philosophic progress with dates . . . .;"[18] how at the core of historical process is the ongoing project of self-interpretation;[19] and how human self-interpretation—and with it the entire panoply of institutions and cultural forms—can become distorted, in desperate need of critique.[20]

All these elements point in one direction—to the historicity of man. While Lonergan has more outlined than systematically explored the region thus opened up, the implications of his approach are clear. We might say that, for Lonergan, human existence is an odyssey: a search for meaning and a quest for value. It is constituted by a process of inquiry one can flee but not escape. The search and the quest are tasks never finished. The meaning and value sought are elusive, never fully grasped. The interpretation of what it means to be human is always ongoing, where past performance becomes data for present interpretation and present interpretation informs future performance. This holds for individual biography as well as for communal destiny, in which the participants interact and live with each other, are nurtured by a common past named tradition, and are called to collective responsibility. The search and the quest are a search and a quest for "something," a "something" which gives a sense and direction to inquiry, and simultaneously a "something" which remains the mysterious object of the question. What it means for man to be is known in the sense that it is the "ideal" of historical action; it is the object of the question. What it means for man to be is unknown in the sense that it is revealed only in the performance of seeking the goal, performance that never (authentically) ceases; it is a question, and no answers are so complete as to end the seeking. The tension of knowledge and ignorance, of knowing ignorance and the mystery of the known unknown, pervades the field of history. Neither knowledge nor ignorance is total, absolute. Understanding can be both gained and lost, self-understanding both advanced and distorted. The gaining and the losing, the questioning direction, the striving and fleeing, all suggest a normative dimension to historical life. (Does not the normative dimension of history, surrounded by the aura of tension and mystery, capture the old root meaning of "culture"—stemming from the Latin *cultus*—namely, "to cultivate and to educate?")[21] Excellence, taste, style, are the emblems of true culture, true *paideia*, but not as frozen in the immobile standards of classicist culture; rather they properly adorn the heuristic ideals of the process of inquiry; the norms of culture are immanent in the search for meaning and the quest for value and in the story which necessarily emerges from that perilous journey. Thus the odyssey of history bears with it existential overtones of a drama. Like any drama, this "primordial drama that the theatre only imitates"[22] is essentially a matter of movement and countermovement, a primal battle of striving and fleeing, gaining and losing. And if inquiry is an infinite striving, an unrestricted openness to what is experienced as a sacred pull then the movement and countermovement of the drama of history is fundamentally that of sacred presence and human response. The unity and the diversity in the drama of history stem from the same dynamic source: the search and the quest, as forging the continuity of questioning, and as impelling diversity through the challenge of every particular formulation, every limited viewpoint, every given horizon.

The tenor of Lonergan's reflections, then, attests to the intimate relation of culture and religion to historicity. This immediately becomes an avenue to our major theme. For central to our purpose in this essay is the question: where does philosophy fit into the portrait sketched above? If the odyssey of historical existence is indeed the odyssey of everyman, how is the journey of the philosopher different? If Lonergan, as we have earlier remarked, sees cognitive self-appropriation, or intellectual conversion, as presupposing moral conversion and religious conversion, does this observation pertain to philosophy at its core? If he views moral conversion and religious conversion as sublating cognitive self-appropriation, does this likewise apply to the essence of philosophy?

Lonergan, as we have maintained, more than any other contemporary philosopher, emphasizes both the existential and the systematic character of philosophy; to ignore either would be to distort philosophy, heading for either subjectivism or objectivism. His philosophical perspective includes more than the systematic positions derived from cognitional theory. Yet Lonergan, for all the wealth of his existential analysis, tends to accord the systematic dimension of philosophy more treatment. And when he makes his most penetrating statements about existential issues, he addresses them more to the topic of human living in general, and of religious and cultural communities in particular, than to the topic of philosophy per se.

Our main goal here must be to place in some higher unity Lonergan's ideas about the subjective pole of philosophy. That higher unity is captured in the notion of historicity. This is by no means to downgrade the significance of systematic philosophy or the perpetual relevance of metaphysics. For the existential nature of philosophy itself demands metaphysics. It is by no means to divorce philosophy from the exigency of cognitive self-appropriation. It is rather to supplement, not replace, cognitive self-appropriation with the category of historicity.

II. Philosophy and Existence

If we are to develop adequately the train of Lonergan's thought on the existential nature of philosophy, we must eventually arrive at a startling conclusion, which goes to the very heart of philosophy, its origin, destiny, and historicity: philosophy is a variety of religious experience. It is precisely the religious essence of philosophy that defines its unique cultural mission and, as we must presently explore, links together the two poles of philosophy. We must first examine carefully these two poles.

The Subjective Pole of Philosophy

Philosophy, to repeat a leitmotif of this essay, has an existential aspect and a systematic aspect; both are intrinsically related to each other as subjective and objective poles of the horizon of philosophy. The existential pole is the experience of the philosopher as a lover of wisdom, an incarnation of the desire to know with its cognitive structure of experiencing, understanding, and judging. But because philosophy is a search for complete intelligibility, the systematic imperative emerges. Thus systems, expositions, treatises, arise ever anew to do homage to the desire to know. The subjective pole therefore specifies the objective pole. The philosopher does not look at an objective pole of essences, of systems, of being; the philosopher is immediately related to being in the philosopher's questioning unrest.

We must not, however, confuse the existential pole—the philosopher as subject, the concrete philosopher as consciously engaged in the pursuit of wisdom—with objectifications of that activity in the objective pole. Indeed, if we follow Lonergan's revolutionary stress on cognitional theory, we must distinguish within the objective pole itself a subjective dimension and an objective dimension. In the latter case (object as object) we have metaphysics and allied fields, fundamental positions about the structure of reality, the ultimate ground of being, and the relationship among the various sectors of being investigated by the several intellectual disciplines. In the former case (subject as object) we have cognitional theory, an explanatory account of the process and structure of knowing present in consciousness. Now, for Lonergan, metaphysics must be critically grounded in cognitional theory; metaphysical positions on reality must be consonant with basic positions on knowing, truth, and objectivity derived from cognitional theory; erroneous metaphysical statements are those, explicitly or implicitly, tied to a faulty cognitional theory, usually some variation of the confrontation theory of truth; correct metaphysical statements are those, explicitly or implicitly, joined to a cognitional theory in which the process and structure of questioning is given full play. The sense and meaning of reality, the metaphysical status of what is known, is determined by the orientation, pattern, and norms of inquiry.[23] Hence within the objective pole metaphysics is conditioned by cognitional theory.

But the objective pole itself is conditioned by the subjective pole. Another way of putting this is to say that metaphysics is conditioned by methodology and methodology by method. Lonergan has proclaimed that one of the most profound transformations in modern philosophy is the transition from logic to method.[24] We may judge that Lonergan is speaking in two senses here. In the first place, metaphysics rather than simply founding itself upon the logical ordering of propositions must assume the exigency of method, namely, one in which its conclusions would be verified by an appeal to cognitional theory and the conclusions of cognitional theory, in turn, would be verified by an appeal to cognitional fact. In the second place, cognitional theory is nothing but methodology, where methodology is a systematic reflection upon method, an objectification of method. Cognitional theory, then, is a reflection on the basic method of questioning, not on any given science or academic discipline or field of inquiry as such, but on the basic, or transcendental, structure of cognitional operations. This structure with its immanent norms embraces not only purely intellectual endeavors but also practical reason, the self-correcting process of moral learning, the subtle path of spiritual inquiry, and the creative project of the aesthetic imagination. Lonergan defines method as "a normative pattern of recurrent and related operations yielding cumulative and progressive results."[25] While perhaps Lonergan has principally in view the procedures of the sciences, the spirit, and probably the letter, of his definition, we believe, can legitimately be extended to include the orientations and structures mentioned above.

Now if method is restricted in meaning to the mere following of rules or to the interpretation accorded it by positivists and neo-Kantians, then, of course, Lonergan would join those, such as Gadamer, who attack the modern preoccupation with "method" as technique.[26] If, however, "method" is taken in its etymological sense as "way" (*methodos*) and is seen as referring to the numerous ways of apprehending and communicating meaning, then the proper existential contours of method can be illuminated. Basic method is a way of apprehending and communicating meaning that is structured by sets of operations, and structured only because it is oriented to a *goal;* which is to say that it is underpinned by an intentional and existential orientation: the desire to know, the intention of the good, and unrestricted loving. This orientation of the pure question specifies a basic horizon that bears a normative relation to all concrete, historically relative horizons. The method of basic horizon is a road toward fuller and deeper understanding, a creative journey towards its goal. At the same time, method is both a way of knowing and a way of being. An horizon, according to Lonergan in his celebrated lectures on existentialism, is a "concrete synthesis of conscious living."[27] Basic horizon has its intellectual openness to a reality correlative to the pure desire to know, its unlimited moral concern, its affective power and drive toward being and the good, and its undertow of religious consciousness. It is the concrete integration of cognitive, moral, affective, and religious facets of existence. It is, moreover, the concrete integration of the concrete living of a concrete person. Herein we encounter a distinctly hermeneutical factor. For when an individual faithfully pursues the goal of inquiry—thereby actualizing the basic method of inquiry—this performance becomes data for self-interpretation, for self-knowledge of who the person is and can be. It likewise evokes some notion of reality, typically a common-sense interpretation, and, as such, one often inchoate and liable to confusion by the potent, omnipresent extroversion of biological consciousness, which generates the confrontation theory of truth. The quality of performance within basic horizon, its sophistication and authenticity, together with the ongoing dialectic of performance and interpretation, each decisively influencing the substance of the other, reveal the unmistakable traits of historicity. We must conclude that if we are not to reify method, we must always connect it with horizon, hermeneutics, and historicity.

Philosophy therefore is clearly an interpretation of basic horizon. It is equally self-interpretation. It has this irreducibly personal dimension because the experiential foundation of philosophy is the performance of the person and the creative and responsible effort of the person is the sine qua non of philosophizing. In this vein, Lonergan can contrast the self-appropriating philosopher with the "plaster cast" philosopher, the one whose philosophy Kant described as relying exclusively on outside authority.[28] As thematic self-interpretation, philosophy is the objectification of interiority, and this interiority is a luminous performance in the drama of living, a performance structured by a basic method, a basic orientation, a basic horizon. Given the dialectical interplay of performance and interpretation at the core of personal existence, philosophy must be intimately tied to the horizon it objectifies; philosophy is not a matter of a look at a distant interiority; indeed, because an horizon is a concrete synthesis of conscious living, philosophy is a way of life, a kind of conscious living. It is conscious living ordered by inquiry, by the search for meaning and the quest for the good.

Philosophy and Religious Experience

What, then, to return to a question posed earlier, distinguishes the philosopher from everyman, for everyman's existence, too, is bound up with the imperatives of inquiry, which he follows or flees? Insofar as the philosopher is an inquirer (or at least called to inquiry) he is the *same* as everyman. But insofar as the philosopher raises inquiry to a thematic focus, identifies and names the authentic performance of everyman as inquiry, inquires about inquiry itself (and inquires about the metaphysical objective of inquiry), then the philosopher is *different*. Nevertheless, as implied above, this difference does not mean that the philosopher is just like everyman except that he takes a closer look at everyman's conscious performance. The personal horizon of the philosopher differs in two crucial respects.

In the first place, the philosopher is unlike everyman in that his performance must be a *sufficient* incarnation of the spirit of inquiry to be adequate datum for interpretation of basic horizon. Furthermore, if fidelity to the norms of inquiry carries with it attunement or correspondence or participation between the being of the inquirer and the being intended in the search and the quest, because there is an immediate relation between inquiry and its objective, then the philosopher as an incarnation of inquiry is also an incarnation of being. While sufficient incarnation is not the same as perfect incarnation, we might reasonably expect that the representative philosopher (a Socrates) would likewise be a representative to mankind of genuine human possibility. But, we must ask, what is it about the horizon of the philosopher that leads him to inquire about inquiry itself?

In the second place, then, the existential disposition of the philosopher has a certain distinct quality and definition, his orientation of consciousness a certain focus and clarity, and his experience a certain range of intensity—all of which nourish and sustain the particular devotion of the philosopher to the pursuit of the true and the good. The specifically philosophical differentiation of consciousness, as it was articulated by the ancient Greeks, was experienced as a response to a call, a pull, a transcendent sacred presence. Plato, for example, depicted his prisoner as leaving the cave because he had been drawn out.[29] Voegelin perceptively describes the Greek philosopher's search for meaning as an inner trial of the soul whose victory is the saving of his life in response to the divine pull; the symbols of the philosopher, according to Voegelin, originate in the engendering experience of mutual participation of human and divine.[30] Moreover, to sustain the activity of philosophical inquiry requires a continuing openness to reality that so far transcends human moral impotence as to be termed, in Lonergan's language, "openness as a gift," again the experience of a sacred presence.[31] Finally, the philosopher, literally the "lover of wisdom," experiences and embodies an unrestricted love of the true and the good, a generic wonder, an unqualified openness to reality. Now these elements of call, gift, and unrestricted love, at the heart of the existential dimension of philosophy, constitute an experiential unity that displays unmistakable traits of religious experience.

What is the core of this experience? What distinguishes it from other varieties of, or even what we might ordinarily mean by, religious experience? Of the three elements of the religious experience of the philosopher—the call, the gift, and the unrestricted love—the unrestricted love seems to be the key to understanding the philosophical nature and unity of the experience, since the call is precisely the unrestricted attraction to inquiry and the gift of openness sustains the unrestricted desire to know.[32] The experience of unrestricted love, of course, would not be externally observable sense experience; it would be the self-presence of one with a certain orientation of consciousness and mode of life, a *bios,* as the Greeks styled it. The experience of the love of wisdom would likewise carry with it an interpretation, what Lonergan calls an "elemental meaning," a meaning whose understanding is intimately and necessarily bound up with a set of acts of experiencing.[33] Philosophical inquiry would be grounded in a heuristic insight, a knowing ignorance, a knowledge rooted in religious love. The experience of the love of wisdom would be an understanding born of unrestricted love and the discernment of value; the philosopher's unrestricted love would thus give rise to a "faith," in the sense of the term employed by Lonergan to refer to the "knowledge born of religious love."[34] But faith in what? The generic wonder, the unqualified attraction, the pure openness of the gift would be unrestricted because they would be correlative to an unrestricted goal, and the unrestricted goal would be precisely the goal of the philosopher because it would be a goal of unrestricted or complete or intrinsic intelligibility.[35] So the distinguishing stamp of philosophy as a variety of religious experience would seem to be the experience of, and the faith in, the intrinsic intelligibility of being and the intrinsic intelligibility of the good. Is this not also to say that philosophy is an experience of participation in unrestricted love—with this specific difference, which marks it off from other varieties of religious experience—that the experience is of the divine as intrinsically intelligible? The love of wisdom is a participation in the same divine reality sought as the objective of questioning. Aquinas, accordingly, views the human intellect as the created participation in the uncreated light of divine understanding.[36] Lonergan, following Aquinas, describes divine reality as "the unrestricted act of understanding, the eternal rapture glimpsed in every Archimedean cry of Eureka."[37] The experience of the participation of human reason in, as the Greeks speak of it, the divine Nous or the divine Logos grounds an unrestricted *love* of truth, a *faith* in the intelligibility of reality, a *hope* in gaining insight and knowledge about reality (without ending the mystery of the divine beyond). The Greek philosopher, Heraclitus, who perhaps first called philosophy by name, attested to an existential disposition of faith, hope, and love as the infrastructure of the search and the quest of the philosopher.[38] Perhaps it is no coincidence that such philosophers in antiquity as Xenophanes, Parmenides, Heraclitus, Plato, Aristotle, and Plotinus were mystic philosophers or that such medieval philosophers as Augustine, Anselm, Albert, Bonaventura, and Aquinas were recognized as saints by their tradition. Is the shift to interiority in modern philosophy, for the most part, only an incipient attempt to recollect the true experiential heart of philosophy?

To summarize the relation between philosophy in its existential sense and philosophy in its systematic sense—or, we might say, the relation between the philosopher and philosophy—we must avoid any trace of a radical subject-object dichotomy, where the philosopher is a subject confronting philosophy as an object, a system "out there." On the one hand, the philosopher is the foundation of philosophy. Philosophy is an interpretation of basic horizon, and this interpretation is self-interpretation. On the other hand, the philosopher intends philosophy; that is, the unrestricted desire to know opposes all obscurantism, for the search for intelligibility and truth demands the continuing development of conceptual formulations, theoretical tools, and systematic accounts ever adequate to the exigencies of the search. Similarly, we must not postulate any false dichotomy between faith and reason. The philosopher, while participating in the drama of history as a fellow inquirer with everyman, is different not only by his more thematic interpretation but also by his more intense—religious—experience of the intrinsic intelligibility of being, which gives philosophy its mass and momentum and direction. Indeed it is the religious experience of the philosopher that impels him on the path toward explicit intellectual conversion. The "noble piety" of the philosopher, according to Kierkegaard, or, as he phrased it, of the "simple wise man," must be to acknowledge that all persons are equal under God but that he is different.[40]

Noetic Consciousness and History

The religious dimension of philosophy is historical. It happened first in Hellas among mystic philosophers. We must, of course, consider the possibility that something parallel was happening in China and India. But in these two civilizations the outburst of philosophy seems incomplete, with different religious overtones. Chinese civilization has boasted its countless schools of philosophy, but, if we are to accept Voegelin's careful asessment, its mode of differentiation was subdued and muted; neither the Confucian nor the Taoist sage was able to break away completely from the older, more compact cosmological order since both sought, in their different ways, attunement with (relatively) undifferentiated cosmic order.[41] "Philosophy" in Indian civilization, in spite of its obviously penetrating insights in logic, psychology, metaphysics, and other fields, is possibly a misnomer because the animating force of Indian higher culture has been the desire for *moksha*, spiritual liberation, rather than the Hellenic love of wisdom.

Philosophy attained full stature and identity in Hellas. The Ionians saw the divine in *physis*, the ground of cosmic order;[42] the social philosopher, Solon, wrote in his lyric poetry of the divine "unseen measure" of human conduct;[43] the Pythagoreans and Empedocles were deeply influenced by the Orphic tale of the purification of the soul;[44] Xenophanes proclaimed his *arete* (excellence) as noble wisdom, which enabled him to critique unseemingly, anthropomorphic images of the divine;[45] Parmenides, perhaps influenced by the Greek notion of "like to like," posited some kind of identity between thinking and being, between human *nous* and ultimate divine being;[46] Heraclitus, unlike the sleepwalkers, who live in their private worlds, was open through his discourse (*logos*) to the common world (*koine cosmos*) of the divine Logos, the "Alone Wise";[47] Anaxagoras pictured the divine Nous as the ordering principle of the cosmos;[48] Socrates faithfully obeyed the divine command emanating from his *daimon* to seek wisdom;[49] Plato, who coined the term "theology," spoke of the philosopher as the "son of Zeus," an incarnation of the divine Nous;[50] Aristotle categorized human reason (*nous*) as being either "divine or only the most divine element in us."[51]

Most revelatory of the sacred character of Greek philosophy were the origins of two dominant terms in the Greek philosophical vocabulary, *nous* and *theoros*. As Douglas Frame has demonstrated, the root of *nous* was tied to myths of the sacred cycle of the sun god, who sojourned and struggled in the dark underworld each night; it originally conveyed the idea of a return home from death and darkness to light and consciousness.[52] The dramatic imagery of *nous* pervaded the story of Odysseus, "the wanderer," who "saw the townlands and learned the minds of many distant men."[53] Odysseus in his return home to Ithaca had to contend with the forces of darkness: the cave of the infamous Cyclops (from which his *nous* extricated him); the cave of the seductive Calypso; the cavernous bay of the Laistrygones, where "the course of night and day lie close together"; and the region of the fog-bound Kimmerians, over whom "a glum night is spread."[54] He had to encounter fabulous creatures whose very names echoed the myth of the cycle of the sun: the Cyclops, Circe, and Calypso. These themes were conspicuously present at the opening of Parmenides' great poem: he was carried on the renowned road of the goddess "who leads the man who knows through every town"; there, leaving the "abode of night" and far "from the beaten track of men," he was granted the vision of being through the exercise of his *nous*.[55] We should also recall the most famous allusion to the original meaning of *nous* in Plato's allegory of the cave.[56]

We likewise find the theme of a sacred journey—the search for meaning and the quest for value—in the word *theoros*. The original Greek meaning of theorist referred to a person sent on a sacred mission to oracles or to religious festivals, such as the Olympic games.[57] The theorist was to question and to transmit faithfully a divine message; he had to venture forth, searching along the road, in order to hear the voice of God. The *theorion*, according to the poet, Pindar, was the place where theorists competed in the games as official participating delegates; they were simultaneously spectators and participants on their journey, not disengaged Cartesian observers.[58] Thus the theorists traversed beyond the pale of the everyday to the "festive and awesome realm of the divine," guarding, along the way, against uncritical acceptance of the dominant values of their native surroundings, but eventually to return, transformed, to the home country, where the journey began.[59] For Plato in his *Laws*, the *theoroi* were to embark upon a course of inquiry to inspect the doings of the outside world, most especially to visit divinely inspired men, only to come back to the native *polis* to share the spectacle.[60] Out of this religious background emerged the Greek idea of reason; gradually *theoria* came to be associated with travel inspired by the desire to know, as in the visits of Solon; and eventually it referred to the experience and knowledge acquired while travelling.[61]

We can postulate that behind the statements of major Greek philosophers and behind the use of the terms *nous* and *theoria* was an eruption of divine reality. This was not an event extrinsically imposed upon history, conceived as a closed world-immanent process, for, as we have argued above, the divine-human encounter is at the center of historical existence itself, whose focus is the tension of "time" and "eternity." The enduring of the physical universe may be called "time" in its elementary sense; to order totalities of such durations we employ frames of reference, whether the explanatory theories of physical science, the personal descriptive language of such terms as "soon," "recently," "long ago," or such public measurements as clocks and calendars.[62] And if by "eternity" is meant the lastingness intimated in the experience of openness to the transcendent beyond (and hence not the enduring proper to a thing in the world), then man, as an historical creature, is at the intersection of "time" and "eternity."[63] In addition to the time of the physical universe and the lasting of transcendence is the existential experience of time, the *duree* described by Bergson, in which the "now" is not a mathematical point but a psychological present, a time span of overlapping moments.[64] This psychological dimension of time, we would suggest, is grounded in the conscious intentionality of the human subject: the subject, an identity of conscious acts, by his intentionality reaches into a past through memories and into a future through anticipations; this experience of time is an experience of historicity, first, since the field of memory is present interpretation of past performance informed by past interpretations and, secondly, since the field of anticipations, with which it is fused, is comprehended by the generic openness of the pure question oriented to the beyond. To cut off the experience of transcendence is to cut off the openness of questioning. A purely world-immanent history is the equivalent of the closed horizon of Heraclitus' sleepwalking idiots.

Philosophy, then, is a constitutive event of history, a discovery of human participation in the divine Nous on the road of inquiry. We can detect this sense of historical epoch in Plato's myth of the age of the great god, Nous, replacing the previous ages of Cronos and Zeus.[65] We can speculate with Voegelin about the actual impact of philosophy on Greek historiography. He suggests that historiography arose in Hellas in a fashion similar to its birth in Israel and China, when a carrier of spiritual meaning came into conflict with, or was threatened to be absorbed by, an empire with universal aspirations; in the case of Hellenic civilization it was the carrier of the spiritual outburst of philosophy, the cutting edge of the culture of the *polis*, and the clash with the Persian empire made the struggle worthy of historical memory.[66] We can further note that Herodotus, the "father of history," was probably influenced by the ideas of Anaximander and the Greek faith in the intelligibility of cosmic order; the Herodotean law of compensation, the inevitable fall of great empires and of great men, seems to be an expression of Anaximander's dictum that all things come out of and return to the *apeiron* (the "boundless") paying their penalty according to the assessment of time.[67]

Now if the event of philosophy was born in particular and irreducible circumstances, is it forever limited to the spiritual and political context of its origins? Is it inextricably bound to what Voegelin has characterized as the "burden of the polis," the wedding of philosophy to the abiding sense of political community present in the classical *polis?*[68] Is the essence of philosophy, as a variety of religious experience, restricted completely to the compactness of, to use Voegelin's words, the "Dionysiac soul"?[69] Granted that the contemplative vision of the philosopher is neither the Christian beatific vision, nor the Hindu *moksha*, nor the Buddhist *nirvana*, still must it remain entirely circumscribed by the Greek experience of the cosmos?[70] Needless to say, even to begin to broach these issues would require the most intricate of historical investigations and of theological reflections; this essay has the more modest endeavor of posing the questions in their most striking terms. But this much we can hazard to state: surely the very nature of philosophy as an unrestricted love of wisdom points to something universally human, transcending, though not leaving behind, the peculiar religious tradition of Hellas. The spirit of philosophy is open to communion with other varieties of religious experience, especially when the misleading duality of "faith" and "reason" is dissolved. Nevertheless genuine interaction can happen only as a dialogue with the tradition of Hellenic philosophy in which the cardinal goal is authentic appropriation of the love of wisdom, albeit under different historical and religious conditions than obtained in Hellas. To argue thus for the integrity—the *sui generis* character—of philosophy as a variety of religious experience is not to argue that it is the only variety of religious experience or that its universality renders it the supreme form of religious experience.

Historical diffusion has, in fact, spread philosophy to the religious traditions of Judaism, Christianity, and Islam. While the usual treatment of "Jewish philosophy," "Christian philosophy," and "Islamic philosophy" tends to place a premium almost solely on the level of doctrine, the more profound and substantive approach would be to stress the existential pole. What specific religious experience will be that of a philosopher who is a Christian? Will such a philosopher, for example, express his radical philosophical experience in terms of the central Christian experience of the trinity, equating the love of truth with the spirit of truth, hearkening to Plato's language of the son of god in describing the fidelity of the philosopher, and identifying the objective of the desire to know with the father? What will be the unique fusion of religious horizons of a Jewish philosophy? Of a Muslim philosopher? Of a Confucian or a Hindu or a Buddhist lover of wisdom?

We can conclude that once the spiritual breakthrough of the love of wisdom has burst forth on the stage of history a twofold imperative emerges to continue it: first to engage and appropriate the meaning of the original tradition; and, secondly, to cultivate the inner life of the unrestricted love of wisdom, which initially spawned the tradition. These two imperatives are allied and necessarily reinforce each other. They entail that the event of philosophy bears an integral and dynamic relation to past, present, and future. Herein we can observe the intrinsically historical nature of philosophy. Historical relativism is thus buried in the ongoing fidelity to the norms of philosophical inquiry.[71]

NOTES

1 For general discussion, see Franklin L. Baumer, *Modern European Thought: Continuity and Change in Ideas, 1600-1111* (New York: Macmillan Publishing Co., 1977), pt. 5.

2 Wilhelm Dilthey, *Pattern and Meaning in History*, ed. and trans. H. P. Rickman (New York: Harper and Row, 1962), chaps. 5-6; D. E. Linge, "Historicity and Hermeneutic: A Study of Contemporary Hermeneutic Theory" (Ph.D. Dissertation, Vanderbilt University, 1969,) pt. 1, esp. pp. 252-53, n. 271.

3 On historicism, see Maurice Mandelbaum, *The Encyclopedia of Philosophy*, s.v. "historicism; idem., *History, Man, and Reason: A Study in Nineteenth-Century Thought* (Baltimore: Johns Hopkins Press, 1971) pt. 2; Emil L. Fackenheim, *Metaphysics and Historicity* (Milwaukee: Marquette University Press, 1961).

4 Bernard J. F. Lonergan, *A Second Collection*, ed. William F. J. Ryan and Bernard J. Tyrrell (Philadelphia: Westminister Press, 1974), pp. 101, 182.

5 Among the key works: Martin Heidegger, *Being and Time*, trans. John Macquarrie and Edward Robinson (New York: Harper and Row, 1962); Michael Polanyi, *Personal Knowledge: Toward a Post-

Critical Philosophy (New York: Harper and Row, 1958); Hans Georg Gadamer, *Truth and Method* (New York: Seabury Press, 1975); Jürgen Habermas, *Knowledge and Human Interests*, trans. Jeremy Shapiro (Boston: Beacon Press, 1971); Eric Voegelin, *Order and History*, 4 vols. (Baton Rouge: Louisiana State University Press, 1956–74); Soren Kierkegaard, *Concluding Unscientific Postscript*, trans. David F. Swenson and Walter Lowrie (Princeton: Princeton University Press, 1941); John Henry Newman, *An Essay in Aid of a Grammar of Assent* (Garden City, N.Y.: Doubleday and Co., 1955).

6 Bernard J. F. Lonergan, *Method in Theology* (New York: Herder and Herder, 1972), p. 316; idem., "Horizon as a Problem of Philosophy," *Notes on Existentialism* (author's notes for lectures given at Boston College, Summer 1957, reprinted by Thomas More Institute, Montreal), pp. 14–15.

7 Bernard J. F. Lonergan, *Insight: A Study of Human Understanding*, rev. ed. (New York: Philosophical Library, 1958), pp. xviii–xxiii, xxviii.

8 Ibid., pp. xviii–xix, 319–39, 396–401, 602–04 , 636–38.

9 See Ibid., pt. 1; *Method*, chap. 1; Bernard J. F. Lonergan, *Collection: Papers by Bernard Lonergan*, ed. Frederick E. Crowe (Montreal: Palm Publishers, 1967), chap. 14.

10 *Insight*, pp. xxviii–xxix, 348–50, 357–59, 375–84, 388, 390–96, 549–62.

11 Ibid., pp. xi–xii, xxix, 387–88, 602–04, 623–30, 677–86.

12 Bernard Lonergan, "Questionnaire on Philosophy," *Method: Journal of Lonergan Studies* 2 (1984), p. 8.

13 *Method*, p. 122.

14 See *Collection*, p. 82.

15 Bernard Lonergan, "Bernard Lonergan Responds," in *Foundations of Theology: Papers from the International Lonergan Conference, 1970*, ed. Philip McShane (Notre Dame: University of Notre Dame Press, 1972), pp. 233–34.

16 *Method*, pp. 241–42.

17 *Collection*, p. 219; *Method*, pp. 30–31, 66; Bernard Lonergan, "Reality, Myth, Symbol," in *Myth, Symbol, and Reality*, ed. Alan M. Olson (Notre Dame: University of Notre Dame Press, 1980), pp. 33, 37.

18 *Collection*, p. 219.

19 *Method*, p. 212; Bernard Lonergan, "Notes from the Introductory Lecture in the Philosophy of History" (Mimeographed copy of lecture given at Thomas More Institute, Montreal, 23 September 1960), p. 12.

20 *Collection*, p. 219.

21 See Charlton T. Lewis and Charles Short, *A Latin Dictionary*, s.v. "cultus"; for the ancient Greek interpretation of culture, see Werner Jaeger, *Paideia: The Ideals of Greek Culture*, trans. Gilbert Highet, 3 vols. (New York: Oxford University Press, 1943–45).

22 *Insight*, p. 188.

23 *Collection*, pp. 227–31; *Second Collection*, pp. 40–41; Bernard Lonergan, *Understanding and Being: An Introduction and Companion to "Insight"*, ed. Elizabeth A. Morelli and Mark D. Morelli (New York: Edwin Mellen Press, 1980), pp. 184–91, 193–210; idem., *Verbum: Word and Idea in Aquinas*, ed. David B. Burrell (Notre Dame: University of Notre Dame Press, 1967), p. 7; *Insight*, p. xxviii.

24 *Method*, pp. 94, 305.

25 Ibid., p. 4.

26 See ibid., pp. 5–6, 157–58, 169, 223–24.

27 "Horizon and Dread," *Notes on Existentialism*, p. 10; *Collection*, p. 158.

28 *Understanding and Being*, pp. 38–39; Immanuel Kant, *Critique of Pure Reason*, trans. Norman Kemp Smith (New York: St. Martin's Press, 1965), A385–86, B863–64.

29 Plato, *Republic*, 515e.

30 Eric Voegelin, "The Gospel and Culture," in *Jesus and Man's Hope*, ed. D. G. Miller and D. Hadidian (Pittsburg: Pittsburg Theological Seminary, 1971), pp. 59–101; idem., *Order and History*, IV, 183–92, 214–18; idem., *Anamnesis*, trans. Gerhard Niemeyer (Notre Dame: University of Notre Dame Press, 1978), pp. 91–97. For Lonergan's favorable comments, see Bernard Lonergan, *Third Collection: Papers by Bernard Lonergan, S. J.*, ed. Frederick E. Crowe (Ramsey, NJ: Paulist Press, 1985), pp. 189–91, 194–96, 219–21.

31 *Collection*, pp. 200–01.

32 Being in love in an unrestricted fashion Lonergan regards as the essence of religious experience. *Method*, pp. 105–07.

33 Ibid., pp. 67, 75; *Insight*, p. 569.

34 *Method*, pp. 115 ff.

35 *Insight*, pp. 499–502, 552–53, 596, 604–07, 652–53, 672.

36 *Verbum*, pp. 78, 80–84, 87, 89–93.

37 *Insight*, p. 684.

38 Heraclitus B18, B35, B86; for trans. of these and fragments cited in ns. 45–48, see Kathleen Freeman, *Ancilla to the Pre-Socratic Philosophers* (Cambridge, Mass.: Harvard University Press, 1957).

39 See n. 30 above.

40 Kierkegaard, *Concluding Unscientific Postscript*, p. 205.

41 Voegelin, *Order and History*, I, 62; IV, Chap. 6; Voegelin refers to Peter Weber-Schaefer, *Oikumene und Imperium: Studien zur Ziviltheologie des chineischen Kaiserreichts* (Munich, 1968).

42 Werner Jaeger, *The Theology of the Early Greek Philosophers* (New York: Oxford University Press, 1947), chap. 2.

43 See Voegelin, *Order and History*, II, 194–99.

44 See F. M. Cornford, *From Religion to Philosophy: A Study in the Origins of Western Speculation* (New York: Harper and Row, 1957), pp. 194–214, 224–42.

45 Xenophanes, B2, B11–12, B14–16, B23–26; Voegelin, *Order and History*, II, 171–80.

46 Parmenides, B3; Voegelin, *Order and History*, II, chap. 8; Jaeger, *Theology of the Early Greek Phisolophers*, chap. 6.

47 Heraclitus, B1–2, B32, B89, B114; Voegelin, *Order and History*, II, chap. 9.

48 Anaxagoras, B12–14.

49 Plato, *Apology*, 28e, 30a, 31d, 33c.

50 Plato, *Phaedrus*, 252–56.

51 Aristotle, *Nicomachean Ethics*, 1177b30 ff.

52 Douglass Frame, *The Myth of Return in Early Greek Epic* (New Haven: Yale University Press, 1978).

53 Trans. Robert Fitzgerald, *The Odyssey of Homer* (Garden City, N.Y.: Doubleday and Co., 1961).

54 Trans. Richmond Lattitmore, *The Odyssey of Homer* (New York: Harper and Row, 1961).

55 Paramenides, B1; trans. G. S. Kirk and J. E. Raven, *The Presocratic Philosophers* (Cambridge: At the University Press, 1971), p. 266.

56 Plato, *Republic*, 514–517d.

57 Gadamer, *Truth and Method*, p. 111; Bernd Jager, "Theorizing, Journeying, Dwelling," in *Duquesne Studies in Phenomenological Psychology: Volume II*, ed. Amedeo Giorgi, Constance Fisher, and Edward L. Murray (Pittsburg: Duquesne University Press, 1975), pp. 235–60; John Navone, *The Jesus Story: Our Life as Story in Christ* (Collegeville, Minn.: Liturgical Press, 1979), pp. 103–09; H. Koller, "Theoros und Theoria," in *Glotta Zeitschrift fur Griechische und Lateinische Sprache* 36 (1958).

58 Gadamer, *Truth and Method*, p. 111; Koller, "Theoros und Theoria," cited by Jager, "Theorizing," p. 236. Jager, ibid., p. 235, following Koller, "Theoros und Theoria," p. 284,

suggests that the origin of *theoros* may "echo" a combination of *theo* and *eros*. One of the roots of *theorion* and *theoros* is *theaomai,* meaning "to look on, gaze at, view behold"; a second root, more specific to the motif of religious ambassador, is a combination of *theos* and *ora* (care); see Henry George Liddel and Robert Scott, *An Intermediate Greek-English Lexicon,* s.v. "theaomai" and "theoros"; idem., *A Greek-English Lexicon,* 9th ed., rev., s.v. "theaomai" and "theoros."

59 Jager, "Theorizing," pp. 239–40; Navone, *The Jesus Story,* p. 105.

60 Jager, "Theorizing," pp. 237–38.

61 Ibid., p. 237; Navone, *The Jesus Story,* p. 104.

62 *Insight,* p. 144.

63 Voegelin seems to express a similar idea in his formulation of the "flux of presence in the Metaxy." Voegelin, *Order and History,* IV, 331, 333–35.

64 Henri Bergson, *Time and Free Will,* trans. F. L. Pogson (New York: Harper and Row, 1960); *Method,* p. 177.

65 Plato, *Laws,* 713c–714b; see Voegelin, *Order and History,* IV, 226–27.

66. Voegelin, *Anamnesis, pp. 122–23;* see also idem., *Order and History,* I, 6. Israel, with its spiritual outburst in the person of the prophets, went on a collision course with the major empires of Babylon, Persia, and the Seleucids, thus occasioning the writing of the history of the conflict; in the case of China, sages witnessed the absorption of classical Chinese society by imperial dynasties. Idem., *Anamnesis,* pp. 122–23.

67 Anaximander, B1; see Kirk and Raven, *Presocratic Philosophers,* pp. 105–07.

68 Voegelin, *Order and History,* II, 169–70.

69 Ibid., III, 62, 70, 92, 115–16.

70 At the same time, can we simply bypass the Greek idea of the divine depths of the cosmos and of the philosophical relevance of myth, as formulated, for example, in Plato's *Timaios* ? Must not these insights be reappropriated?

71 For a further exploration of these themes, see Thomas J. McPartland, "Historicity and Philosophy: The Event of Philosophy, Past, Present, and Future."

Orientations in
Theology and
Religious Studies

IX

On Not Neglecting the Self in the Structure of Theological Revolutions

Quentin Quesnell

I. Two Senses of Paradigm; Two Kinds of Revolution

IN Kuhn's refined definitions of paradigm (see the Postscript to the second edition of *Structure*), he distinguishes two senses of the word, which were not distinguished in the original text. The first sense is "the entire constellation of beliefs, values, techniques and so on shared by the members of a given community."[1] Applying this sense of paradigm to theology, one sees in the history of dogma a long series of changes in paradigms as old doctrines are changed or abandoned and new ones are formulated within ongoing or newly sprouting historical communities calling themselves "Christian." Such changes in commonly accepted theological doctrines can be revolutionary, affecting the life and thought of succeeding generations. When they are, I suggest they deserve the name of "minor revolutions."

The second sense of paradigm noted by Kuhn refers to the "shared examples" of a science. It is above all the reality and importance of this second sense of paradigm which Kuhn had most at heart when he wrote his book. "It is the central element of what I now take to be the most novel and least understood aspect of this book."[2] "Philosophically at least this second sense of paradigm is the deeper of the two, and the claims I have made in its name are the chief sources for the controversies and misunderstandings that the book has evoked. . . ."[3]

This second sense of paradigm is described in terms of "exemplary past achievements"; or "the concrete puzzle-solutions which, employed as models or examples, can replace explicit rules as a basis for the solution of the remaining puzzles of normal science." Applied to theology, it would refer to the exemplary work of the outstanding theologians from whom each age derives its notion of what it is to produce an adequate theological demonstration. These paradigm-changes amount to changes in the very idea of what it is to do theology. Such changes, when they occur, deserve, I would say, to be called "major revolutions."

Kuhn's Postscript does not explain why these two senses of paradigm were not distinguished in the original book, but he hardly had to; the reason is so obvious. For ordinarily the two kinds of paradigm occur together. Revolutionary developments in scientific knowledge commonly are themselves the introduction of "new beliefs, values, techniques" and at the same time themselves become "the exemplary past achievements" which will provide the "shared examples" for succeeding generations.

When Kuhn wrote about paradigm in the *second* sense, he inevitably illustrated his point with historical instances which were simultaneously instances of paradigm in the *first* sense. Readers did not always get his point. They were more struck with the achievements noted than with how they were achieved.

The two kinds of paradigm frequently occur together in theology as well. The new formulations of doctrine which in fact meet the great crises of Christian thought also themselves become to the next generation the exemplary past achievements which set everyone's idea of how theology ought to be done. The open disputes at the time of major theological revolutions are about doctrines; but the doctrinal issues are in fact comparatively superficial. At a deeper level what is really in question is, What is a satisfactory theological demonstration? What does it mean to verify something theologically? How does one embody a new religious insight in a manner which will convince the religious community? The fight, while it lasts, seems to be about a point of doctrine; but after the fight is over, one finds that the real change which has taken place is a change in the way of doing theology.

II. THEOLOGICAL EXAMPLES OF THE SECOND SENSE

For example, the doctrinal dispute at Nicaea was over the relative status of the Word and the Father. Solving that dispute by the definition of "homoousion" was revolutionary, and the textbooks of the history of dogma dutifully record it as such. But that advance in insight was a minor revolution compared to the profound change of tacitly admitting that not all issues in theology could be solved on the basis of biblical words and concepts. "Homoousion" was a non-biblical word; and after the Arian dispute was settled, that non-biblical word was a part of the Church's creed. Suddenly there opened for theology a whole new world of possible developments; developments which in fact occurred as the following Christological councils went on to define such non-biblical concepts as nature and person and *communicatio idiomatum;* while later councils could add circumincession, procession as from a single principle, and transsubstantiation.

Most writing about the history of theology tends to record and explain the first type of revolutions—the doctrinal changes themselves, for those are the changes most laypeople are aware of and interested in. This is an exact parallel to the way Kuhn says most textbooks in the physical sciences record and explain the steady, single-line progress from one new theory to another. But, just as in the physical sciences the deeper and more significant changes were not the new theories but the changes in the way of doing science which followed when new syntheses became exemplary models for subsequent "normal science," so in theology other and deeper revolutions were occurring than the shift from one doctrinal formulation to another. But this second and deeper kind of revolution is one that only theologians themselves are likely to appreciate, and not all of them; namely, that changes in method through the centuries have been changes in the very conception of what it is to do theology.

This was the real point of the frequent five-minute summaries of the history of theology which Bernard Lonergan loved to slip into his lectures and articles. Let me try to illustrate the point again here.

In a first stage, the ideal of theology was to appeal directly to the ancient Scriptures in support of the new revelation and to make the Christian revelation come to life by means of application and exhortation. Soon began the larger projects of comparing one part of the Scriptures to another, where the theological ideal was to find analogies, types, which illuminated one another and could at the same time be models for life. After Justin, theologians feel called to establish Christian superiority and manifest destiny by exploiting the pagan classics and philosophy, at first with a hermeneutics of suspicion, later in an effort to coopt them. After Origen follow centuries of attempts to work the whole of Christian life and doctrine into a line-by-line commentary on the Scriptures, thus making the ancient records of a foreign people a matter of vital, consuming interest, while at the same time directly touching every moment and aspect of life with divine revelation. With Origen also begins perception of the need for critical philological reflection on the Scriptures themselves as theology's presumed foundation.

Since Augustine's conflict with the Donatists, the ideal theological argument involves some demonstration of universality, a principle soon summed up in the *"quod semper, quod ubique, quod ab omnibus"* of Vincent of Lerins. Abelard's *Sic et Non* created a passion for systematically lining up the authorities *pro* and *con* each position, and the excellence of a theological exposition soon became judged in terms of its ability to reconcile or at least account for the differences. This procedure became the standard school exercise for centuries, as each degree candidate faithfully produced his own commentary on the *Sentences* of Peter Lombard. Such theology, centered on the individual *question*, becomes in the hands of Master Thomas only the instrument of something further; the ordering of thousands of questions into a single architectonic structure of wisdom. Writing his own *Summa* becomes each theologian's aspiration.

The Protestant reformers hoped to restore a bible-dominated theology, but events required them to devote much of their writing to controversy. Their example was imitated rather than their aims fulfilled, and theologians busied themselves not in asking new questions nor in trying to understand, but in proving through isolated biblical texts the rightness of their fellow-believers and the errors of their adversaries. This method was soon extended to range over the works of the Fathers for the same purpose, and the essence of good theology became to refute your adversary by binding him in endless chains of individual texts from the collected works of antiquity.

The new scholasticism which followed in the exhausted aftermath of the wars of religion made theology largely a training program for aspiring clergy. That which had once been life-centered, then bible-centered, then problem and question-centered now retreated to the seminary and labored only to achieve a safe, mechanical encapsulating of its own glorious past into easily memorizable discrete units: the seminary thesis method. Theologians indeed supposed that those units could later be applied to life by pastors and to controversy by apologetes and to understanding by contemplatives; but neither life nor controversy nor understanding were their own direct concern.

Since Schleiermacher, theologians—especially Protestants—have tried more and more in a variety of ways to render religion plausible in the eyes of "its cultured despisers," to "meet the needs of modern man," practice "correlation" of Christian doctrines and natural aspirations, through all the varieties of liberal theology down to our own day. During the same period, the most influential school of Catholic theologians, impressed by the definitions of the Immaculate Conception (1854) and papal Infallibility (1870), began to look on the goal of theology as the steady promotion of favored theses up the ladder from "communis et certa" to "de fide definita." But then Vatican II, while refusing to define anything at all, unleashed a new image of theology. Intending nothing more than pastoral concern over the needs of the poor, the sick, the disadvantaged of every kind, the Council in fact implied the possibility of "liberation theology," which began to measure the success of theology by the degree to which it rises out of the situation of the oppressed and is able to help relieve that situation.

All or most of these steps were major revolutions in theology, for they were the revolutions which created revolutions. When such major revolutions succeed they cast entire worlds of previous research into the dull limbo of uninteresting antiquities. Nobody asks the old questions any more; nobody cares about the old answers. Once the revolution succeeds, the generations of those in its wake take it for granted that the right way to do theology is the way their successful predecessor did it. Everyone in training in the schools reads Lombard or Aquinas or Cajetan or Suarez; and tends either to write theology in the same way or at least to judge the success of what others are writing by how close they come to achieving what Aquinas or Suarez achieved.

III. TRANSITIONS AND GAPS

But the revolutions do not come about suddenly. As in the physical sciences, there are always still earlier predecessors who made tentative advances in the same direction, but whose work did not happen to catch on. And there is always a long period of opposition to the new way, an opposition which history normally tries to minimize after the event. And so there is always a period of gap, an interval between the old way and the new, during which—as in the physical sciences—one waits more or less patiently for the retirement of certain key figures from their professional chairs.

But there is another kind of gap as well, and it may last even beyond the time that a new generation consciously pledges allegiance to the new model. It takes time for a major change in the conception of a science to reach to all the practitioners of the science, not just because of an age-gap, but because the implications of a new method are not immediately apparent. Scientists must learn by practice how far-reaching a revolution really is.

IV. The Shift Toward the Subject in Modern Theology
According to Hans Kung and Bernard Lonergan

Thus, for instance, in modern theology there has been a gradual shift to the subject; a growing appreciation of the fact that the *self* is included in any and every judgment of truth; a spreading awareness that every serious, considered affirmation is to some extent a free commitment of one's *self*. Hans Küng, in "Paradigm Change in Theology"[4] stresses the importance of this trend. He rightly observes that, with advances in modern hermeneutics and theory of knowledge, "Nowhere—not even in the natural sciences—can absolute objectivity be sought by excluding the human subject, the researcher himself." Even "in the experiments of physics, the method changes the object—what it reveals is always only one perspective and only one aspect."

Küng's paper not only states this in general, but tries boldly to apply it in the concrete by summing up five parallels between shifts of paradigm in theology and in physical science. He sums up the whole modern direction in a call for a theology which will be completely *truthful, free, critical* and *ecumenical.*

This is indeed a summary of the shift to the subject, characteristic of the modern age. *Truthful* replaces "true," because the subject can always be the one, but can only aspire to the other. It is *free,* because theology in its mediating phase is assimilated from the past according to the capacity of the thinking subject theologian, but can pass to the future in its mediated phase only through the free decision of the theologian subject, responding to what Lonergan identifies as the central question of all self-aware theology; "In what manner or measure am I to carry the burden of continuity, or risk the initiative of change?"[5]

Subject-centered theology is *critical,* because that central question can be answered in a responsible way only by one who has tried to be open to all the data, understand all the evidence, and make a personal judgment as to the correctness of the synthesis inherited from the past. Subject-centered theology must be *ecumenical* because the decision about continuity or change can be made responsibly only when it is made in awareness that other traditions exist beside that which one has personally happened to inherit; that there are sets of data one has oneself never experienced; and there are other traditions of understanding and accounting for the evidence. These must be faced before one can responsibly decide "In what manner or measure am I to carry the burden of continuity or risk the initiative of change?" In other words, a subject-centered, self-aware theology understands itself as a process, and recognizes the large part that fallible human observation, understanding and judgment play in that process.

V. THE REMAINING GAP EXEMPLIFIED IN HANS KÜNG'S ACCOUNT OF CONTINUITY: "THE CHRISTIAN MESSAGE" CANNOT FUNCTION AS "NORMA NORMANS" OF A FREE, CRITICAL AND ECUMENICAL THEOLOGY

But we are in an in-between period, as Küng says. The new paradigm of a subject-centered theology has been perceived in outline, but if it has already been somewhere masterfully implemented, that instance of implementation has not yet caught on and been recognized as a satisfactory model for future researchers. In this in-between period, it is not only possible but likely that attempts to explain and practice the new will waver, and sometimes even those most committed to the new will discuss significant minor revolutions in terms which on the major-revolutionary scale are pre-revolutionary or even counter-revolutionary.

This, it seems to me, is what has happened in the latter part of Küng's paper. There he takes up the question of continuity, wanting to avoid "the choice between an absolutist and relativist view."[6] To do this, he feels bound to list "the differences between natural science and theology" and set down as a principle that for Christian theology "its presupposition and its object is the Christian message, as attested originally in Scripture as it was transmitted through the centuries . . ."[7] Again, "the original testimony of faith of this Christ Jesus forms the basis of Christian theology." Theology is "in a wholly specific sense related to the origins." "For theology, the primordial event . . . and consequently the primordial testimony, the original record of the Old and New Testament, remains not only the historical origin of the Christian faith, but also the point to which it must constantly return."[8] Throughout this section of his paper, Küng seems to me repeatedly to lose sight of his own new paradigm, the subject-centered theology toward which he desperately wants us to move.

He wants to subject "all theological authorities" to "the primary norm, the *norma normans*, that decides all other norms—the primordial biblical testimony."[9] "The same primordial Christian testimony is also the permanent basic testimony for theology and the Church."[10] "A revolution in Christian theology—if it is to be and remain Christian—can never take place except on the basis of and ultimately because of the gospel and never against the gospel."[11]

The second of two "constants" of the new theological paradigm is to be "the Christian message as standard"; "its primary norm cannot be anything except the Christian message, on which this tradition is constructed as on its ultimate ground."[12]

None of these statements is possible in a self-aware, subject-conscious theology. Though it is obvious that these statements meet the criterion of being *truthful,* fully expressing Küng's love for Scripture and his personal Christian commitment, they cannot begin to meet the criteria of *critical, free* or *ecumenical.* Why is the norm itself not subjected to criticism? How is theology free, if there is a "point to which it must constantly return"? How can it be ecumenical, open to all traditions, if "its primary norm cannot be anything except the Christian message, on which *this* tradition is constructed?" The reason for these contradictions is that Küng's stipulations about "the Christian message" do not belong to the new paradigm of a theology aware of the role of the self. They belong to the old paradigm, which always imagined it could proceed objectively on the basis of a "norm," a "standard," an "ultimate ground," which it always imagined as somehow lying there open to the eyes of all, and which each one was simply invited to recognize and accept.

Of course Christian theologians think they are doing theology on the basis of the Christian message; but that tells us only that what any person or group conceives to be the Christian message is always correlative to what the same person or group will admit to be truly Christian theology. It gives no criterion for judging which person or group is right, and so it gives no criterion, norm or standard by which to measure and affirm continuity.

One's particular judgment of the Christian message, whether held by utterly private interpretation or in conjunction with millions of others in one of the recognized Christian sects or Churches—is always only a paradigm in sense 1. It is itself, in other words, always only a doctrine. It can never be the real *foundation* of doctrine.

Even one's conviction that the Scriptures are the word of God is itself only a doctrine, one interpretation of what is essential to the Christian message. (Compare it to the positions of those who affirm instead that the Scriptures only "*contain* the word of God," or again "*witness* to the word of God," or "contain ancient records of *how people confronted* the word of God," or "represent a primitive stage in the evolution of the divine indwelling in humankind," etc.)

Scripture is not a given. It must be constituted. There is no intrinsic reason for the canon having the precise shape it has for each theologian, whether that is the Catholic canon, the Orthodox, the Protestant, the Jewish, or a critical canon (seeking to use only what has been judged "primary") or a formally theological (on the basis of each one's "gospel within the gospel"). The canon is *chosen.*

"The Christian message," as one doctrine among others, cannot be a solid basis for judging the authenticity (or the continuity) of doctrines, until a further factor is added. That further factor is always the theologian's own insight and judgment as to what the Christian message really is.

No amount of thumping the Bible or bowing to tradition will change this fact. The existing text of the Scripture, far from being "the original Christian message," is only so many marks on paper until a human subject reads it and interprets it in the light of the subject's own self. Neither does tradition preserve "the original Christian message," except insofar as the tradition is actively remembered, studied, appealed to as a norm by selves who have committed themselves freely to that specific tradition (even though they always know the tradition in only a fragmentary and imperfect way).

Scripture and tradition are norms only to the selves who have freely chosen to make them their norms. That free choice cannot be explained on the basis of Scripture and tradition.

Therefore one cannot avoid relativism by appealing to the secure foundation of "the Christian message." In practice that phrase always ends up either standing generally for "everything good"; or else meaning specifically "those parts of the Bible and of early Christian monuments and history which happen, under a particular interpretation, to appeal to the person who is talking."

This is inevitable. It is nothing to be ashamed of. But it must be recognized, and that is what the subject-conscious, self-aware new paradigm of theology is all about.

VI. A SUBJECT-CENTERED ACCOUNT OF THE CONTINUITY OF THEOLOGY

What then is the foundation? And what continuity is possible in theology? I cannot give the entire exposition of that in so short a space as this; but in brief (as Lonergan explains at length) the foundation is the theologian's own *self.* There can be no other.

It is the questioning mind and the never-satisfied intellectual appetite, directing themselves to the infinite horizon of human existing. The foundation is in the steady aspiration to understand—that is, to apply to unending problems of the infinite horizon the only faculties we have for advancing insight and knowledge.

The role of the *past* is not to provide objective norms outside the theologian and the community to whom the theologian speaks. The past fulfills its role when it has formed the theologian and the community to be what they are. The past, as remembered, evokes responses and questions which thrust toward the infinite horizon of human living. The theologian tries honestly to assimilate the past by all available human means, and then reflect on the responses and answer the questions which arise.

The theologian takes the concrete symbols of an individual religion and makes them concepts and categories of a science by treating them not as denotative, but as indicative. They do not define something known, measurable and achieved, but point to what is *to be* achieved. The theologian uses them to express what is to be known when we shall know perfectly.

The symbols, thus, as theological categories, become heuristic, open to many successive explicit and improved, better-formulated contents as one cultural stage succeeds another (just as "fire" remained the name for that which was to be explained in the days of the four elements, in the age of caloric and phlogiston, and of rapid oxidation). One term can suffice, for it is a heuristic term, standing for "whatever is the true explanation of the phenomenon from which we begin." (But the term itself is of secondary importance; of primary importance is the question. So there have been in recent years those Christian theologians who have asked us to give up for a time talking about "God.")

"God" is, in theology, the ultimate explanation of the phenomena from which all our knowing and questioning begin. The term, "God," can be filled in various ways in different succeeding theologies, for "God" has, in theology, the unity of the question.

Theologians in a pre-self-conscious theology could speak as if they were able to appeal to God, God's mind, God's will, as their norm, criterion or measure. But a norm, criterion or measure must be something at our disposal. If it is itself not definable, it cannot be used to define anything else. "God" is always that which we seek; which will fill the hunger and longing our minds and hearts cannot help but feel. A subject-aware theology knows its unity comes from God not as from a norm but as from an aspiration.

"The Christian message" functions in theology in exactly the same way. It is the concrete symbol standing for the call to self-transcendence, to growth toward God.

The continuity of a subject-centered theology, therefore, comes from the inquiring human mind of anyone willing to devote himself or herself to the consistent effort to do theology. For theology is a process, and each practitioner not only may but must enter the process from wherever he or she happens to be. That means "Christian theology" starts from any background that calls itself "Christian" and that sees its own work in terms of loyalty to what it considers "the Christian message." But such theology always takes place in a community of others who are striving to do the same thing, and many of those others start from other places than oneself. And others use other categories, translating other symbols.

Every Christian theologian supposes that, when the content of the Christian symbols has been completely and satisfactorily filled in, that content will also prove to be the explanation of everything from the Christian past which is still remembered and cherished as valuable. And no theologian should be surprised if the full and final content turns out to explain other remembered pasts as well.

NOTES

1 Thomas S. Kuhn, *The Structure of Scientific Revolutions* (International Encyclopedia of Unified Science, Vol. 2, Number 2) Second edition, enlarged. (Chicago: University of Chicago Press, 1962; 1970) p. 175.

2 Ibid., p. 187.

3 Ibid., p. 175.

4 The keynote paper for the East-West conference on "Paradigm Shifts in Buddhism and Christianity: Cultural Systems and the Self" held at the University of Hawaii, January 3–11, 1984, and to be published in the proceedings of that conference.

5 Bernard Lonergan, *Method in Theology*, Ch. V, p. 135.

6 Küng, p. 17.

7 Ibid., p. 18.

8 Ibid., p. 19.

9 Ibid.

10 Ibid., p. 20.

11 Ibid., p. 21.

12 Ibid., p. 26.

X

Theology and the
Secularizing of Truth

MICHAEL O'CALLAGHAN

In his presidential address to the 1983 annual meeting of the American Academy of Religion, Wilfred Cantwell Smith noted his profound agreement with Robert Bellah's analysis of the major attitudes to other cultures that the Modern West has developed.[1] In its initial stage, the Modern West understood itself as quite superior to other cultures, as the paradigm of rationality and of progress to which other cultures aspired with greater or lesser success. A second stage, in part a reaction to the first and in part a result of more recent study, promoted cultural relativism: the Modern West has its own system of values, and other cultures have their own differing systems, and there is no higher viewpoint for evaluating one as better than another. The third stage is advocated by a contemporary minority: disillusioned by the decline of the Modern West, the minority idealizes one of the other cultures as better—so much so, that we should adopt that culture as our very own.[2]

None of these three basic attitudes is adequate, though none is completely ridiculous. A fourth position is both requisite and possible; its scope was sketched by Bellah, and Dr. Smith's paper would both aid in the filling-in of that sketch and direct our vision beyond the fourth stage to a fifth. The fourth stage would have us profit from our deepening cultural sensitivity so as to illuminate better what we in the West have been doing and what has been done to us: knowledge of the rest of the world contributes possibly to critical self-awareness. Dr. Smith's fifth perspective would subsume and transcend all the previous four.[3] This fifth stage, according to Dr. Smith, occurs when a culture moves beyond the attitude, "We can learn from you about ourselves," and begins to realize that "Both you and I, while different,

135

are nonetheless parts of a unified, transcendent whole." It is a movement from saying, "We have something to learn from them, thereby improving ourselves," to a stage when we say, "We are all in this together," where "we" means "we human beings" in all our great diversity, yet as well in our communal humanity.[4]

While fourth-stage thinking seems to be a definite advance over the previous three, it fails to address the crucial question about the authenticity of the Modern West's basic horizon. The basic validity of that horizon is presupposed, so that now this, now that component of another culture is assimilated within the Modern West's basic standpoint. That standpoint, notes Dr. Smith, is profoundly secular: it fails to discern the reality of a transcendent dimension in the universe; its cult of atomistic individuality is blind to communal transcendence in society; and its absence of social sensitivity leads, in turn, to the disparaging of human culture and human history.[5]

But if fourth-stage thinking assumes the validity of the Modern West's secularist horizon, fifth-stage thinking would radically challenge that assumption and horizon. In particular, Dr. Smith would challenge the Modern West's secularizing of truth: its assumption that truth (including the truth of human nature) is fundamentally secular and that religion, accordingly, is something that humans have tacked on to themselves here and there in various forms and for various purposes.[6] Truth, for the Modern West, no longer is higher than us, a heuristic notion to which it is humanizing to aspire; rather, truth is something less than us, a mass-produced conceptualism packaged for a relativist society.[7]

Dr. Smith's reflections on the Modern West, and in particular on the West's secularizing of truth, would seem to have special importance for theology today. "A theology," notes Bernard Lonergan, "mediates between a cultural matrix and the significance and role of a religion in that matrix."[8] But such mediation may be differently conceived. It can be the sort of mediation that promotes cultural superiority or cultural relativism or cultural adulation. Again, theology may be part of a culture that is open to learning from other cultures, but not open to be challenged in its basic horizon by this encounter. Finally, the mediation performed by theology can at once cast suspicion on any cultural horizon assuming its authenticity, and simultaneously strive to recover and promote the truth that human existence is in fact rooted in Transcendence.

The focus of the present paper, accordingly, has to do with the conditions of the possibility for the effective emergence of fifth-stage theological mediation. One's notion of mediation will shape one's notion of theology, and so we shall begin by sketching the sorts of mediation found when we contrast classicist and methodical theologies. Methodical mediation dominates contemporary theologizing, and so is deeply sensitive to cultural diversity: we note this in a second section outlining the methodical mediation effected by concern with the methods of historical-critical scholarship, of dialectic, and of praxis. A final section applauds the validity of such methodical mediation, but then raises the hermeneutical issue of the truth of methodical mediation: a theology rooted in method can avoid secularizing mediation only to the extent it rests on a prior commitment to the reality of Transcedence affirmed by an explicit philosophy of religion. To anticipate, methodical theology as hermeneutic meets very well the needs of fourth-stage mediation; but only attention to Transcendence as hermeneutical will move theology away from secularizing assumptions towards a foundation in metaxical truth.

I. From Logical to Methodical Mediation

Medieval theology was a theoretical enterprise, and its theory was controlled by logic; accordingly, its foundation was a set of logically first propositions from which further propositions could be deduced.[9] Modern theology is becoming a deliberately methodical enterprise, but it is not clear just how this enterprise is to be controlled or where its foundation lies.

Inspired by the coherence and breadth of the Aristotelian corpus, medieval theologians conceived of theology as a science that deduces conclusions from the articles of faith. Revealed truths are the first principles, and their truth, evidence, and necessity are immediately given. In a first moment, the *ordo inventionis*, the theologian moved from revelation to conclusions that have not been revealed; in a second moment, the *ordo disciplinae*, the theologian moved from the conclusions of the *ordo inventionis* to a systematic presentation of the truths that have been revealed.[10] Such, at least, was the mediation effected by Aquinas, for whom logic was a tool, not merely for deducing non-revealed truths from revealed premises, but also for attaining some partial and imperfect understanding of the mysteries of faith that are the revealed truths.

It remains that logic can be used for demonstration alone, and not as well for deepening understanding. Indeed, one school of medieval theologians sought to give logical demonstrations of all revealed truths; from conclusions that had not been revealed, one could move to revealed truths themselves.[11] Nor were these sacralist and fideist tendencies the only possibility; for as long as certitude was the name of the logical game, there was never any lack of medieval thinkers who were happy to draw attention to the limitations of logic and who concluded that no revealed truths could be understood because no revealed truths could be rationally demonstrated.[12]

Scholasticism deteriorated into skepticism, inviting the extremist reaction of reformers who urged either a logical fideism or a return to a commonsensical mediation of Christian faith.[13] But these internal squabbles pale in significance when compared to the revolution occurring within the cultural matrix. Natural science was proclaiming its autonomy from philosophical metaphysics; and philosophy itself declared its independence from both theology and metaphysics.[14] These changes, along with the rise of historical-critical scholarship, ushered in a profoundly new cultural context, signaling a transition from logic to method.

Methodical mediation begins, not with logical propositions, but with concrete realities: sensitively, intellectually, rationally, morally conscious subjects.[15] The mediatory process includes both logical and non-logical operations by these conscious subjects, for logical operations consolidate past achievement, while non-logical operations keep all achievement open to further advance.[16] So it is, that modern science and modern scholarship are ongoing, developing processes; so it is, that modern philosophy, at least since Hegel, has struggled to identify the conditions of the possibility of responsible control of these processes. And so it is, that contemporary theology, though in fact methodical, does not yet know itself as methodical and in consequence is a house divided within itself concerning which of the methods currently operative are to guide the entire theological enterprise.

Before presenting this debate, however, it would be well to underline the significance of a shift from logic to method. In the first place, attention to method places as much emphasis on the authentic or unauthentic subjectivity of theologians as logic placed on the truth or falsity of objective theological propositions. Secondly, a focus on method, while not in the least ignoring logical mediation, nonetheless highlights the non-logical operations that keep theology adding discovery to discovery. Finally, it is method and not logic that allows theology to deal fairly and squarely with human historicity and with the significance and role of Christian commitment in that historicity.

II. FROM METHOD TO METHODS IN THEOLOGY

Theology is becoming more explicitly methodical, but it is not yet clear just how this methodical process is to be controlled. In part, the ambiguity is due to the absence of an adequate philosophy of religion, and to this topic we shall return in our next section. In part, the ambiguity is due to the presence within theology of several quite distinct methods, and a word must now be said about the mediation effected by each.

There are three main methodical contenders to the throne of logic. Theology can come to take a stand on the methods of critical-historical scholarship, on the methods of dialectical evaluation, or on the methods of praxis. The methods of critical-historical scholarship reconstruct for us the commonsense constructions of another place and time. The methods of dialectical evaluation bring into sharp focus, and reduce to their radical origins, the conflicts revealed by such critical-historical reconstruction. The methods of praxis make the reflective and practical judgments of value that promote authenticity in one's cultural and social contexts.[17]

The present question is not whether these three contenders are integral to theological mediation in its new context, for of course they are. Rather, our question has to do with whether or not any one of the three, or even all three taken together, can provide the foundational control of the entire theological enterprise as it shifts from logic to method.

To focus this question it seems important to discuss the function of truth in methodical mediation. Which of the three contenders, if any, are successful in mediating to us religious truth? Our answer, to anticipate, will be to the effect that, although all methods can mediate religious truth, the determination of whether in fact they do so involves a non-methodical (and, it should be noted, a non-logical) hermeneutical commitment. In a word, method (and methods) in theology is (and are) a necessary but not yet sufficient condition for the truth of theological mediation between religion and the significance and role of a religion within a cultural matrix. Method is a necessary condition, for, without method, the theology would be mired in notions of cultural superiority, cultural relativism, or cultural adulation; it is theology's shift to method that has allowed it the historical understanding it needs to break from notions of superiority, the dialectical evaluation it needs to break from notions of relativism, and the attention to praxis it needs to realize that a cultural house can put itself in order, and need not emulate some alien utopian culture. It is method that has allowed theology to become at home in a variety of cultural contexts, and it is method that allows theologians of one context to learn from those in another.

We may ask, accordingly, about the role of each of the three main methods in mediating religious Transcendence. Critical-historical methods, first of all, move us towards objective knowledge of the past religious heritage.[18] They would mediate to us the various constructions of the human spirit in different places and past times, as a distinct community came to interpret itself and its world in reference to Christ Jesus, and as it passed from one generation to the next. Such critical-historical scholarship, however, reconstructs different interpretations and different histories within the Christian heritage. To the extent those differences are not merely genetic or complementary but dialectical, to that extent is the question of historical truth left unresolved. On the basis of critical-historical methods alone, it is by no means clear which interpretation and which history is the authentic carrier or mediator of religious Transcendence in history.[19]

Similarly, dialectical methods take us beyond the fact of conflicting historic and conflicting interpretations to the reasons for the conflict.[20] Such methods are explicitly evaluative, and are concerned with the dialectically opposed horizons that come to light with the application of critical-historical methods. Still, an evaluative dialectic is no guarantee of uniform results; it may indeed mediate to us an encounter with objective values embraced by people in the past religious tradition, just as it may distinguish authentic from unauthentic horizons within that tradition. But what is the criterion for that distinction? On what foundation does the dialectician pronounce one past horizon to be authentic, and another unauthentic?

At some point, then, there is needed an explicit account of the grounding of dialectical method, if dialecticians are not simply to assert their own values as the true ones. This danger of theological subjectivism or dogmatism has led some theologians to ask if perhaps the methods of praxis might provide theology with the foundational control needed in mediating religious Transcendence in history. Here, the emphasis shifts from reflecting on the ambiguity of the given religious historical world to the theoretical and practical judgments of value needed to make history as opposed to just knowing history.[21]

Such methods of praxis include thematizing the horizon of transformative truth, judging the doctrinal truths of the tradition, reconciling those truths with one another and with the current academic context, and communicating effectively the meaning and value of those truths to all levels of society and culture.[22] The first of those four steps is the one that concerns us here: on what foundations are praxis-oriented theologians to thematize the horizon of transformative truth?

Clearly, part of the foundation is the evaluative reconstruction revealed by dialectic. Such is the objective situation of authenticity and unauthenticity that is found in the cumulative religious tradition. Still, a problem remains for, as Habermas has made clear, a purely hermeneutical/dialectical approach all too often can erroneously judge a tradition authentic when in fact it is not, and erroneously judge a tradition unauthentic when in fact it is.[23] What, then, is it that leads us from an evaluative dialectic that reconstructs the past to an evaluation of that evaluative dialectic that grounds authentic and true praxis? As Lonergan points out, the need is for the religious, moral, and intellectual conversion of the theologian as human subject, and it is the thematization by converted theologians of their converted subjectivity that constitutes the foundational step in the four-fold process of theology as mediating Transcendence in history.[24]

Granted that foundational reality is indeed this three-fold conversion of a theologian's human reality,[25] and granted that the objectification or thematization of conversion in the functional specialty, foundations, grounds theological praxis, the nagging question remains: what makes foundational thematization true? One could answer that the presence of conversion is a necessary condition for the truth of foundational thematization, and this would be correct: methodically speaking, the converted self cannot be conceptualized until the grounding performance of conversion occurs.[26] But this appropriation by the theologian of his or her converted self, an appropriation central to foundational theology, presupposes the constitution of the converted self through language in history: hermeneutically speaking, the grounding performance of conversion is itself mediated by the language of the community in history.[27]

Just what it means to say that conversion is mediated by the language of a community in history is the task, not of theology – even in its foundational reflection – but of a philosophy of religion grounded in a fundamental, religious, and hermeneutic ontology.[28] Such a philosophy would explore the necessary, though not sufficient conditions for the possibility of religious conversion expressed in a mythic-symbolic language that is the norm of a particular religious tradition; it cannot, of course, determine the sufficient conditions for religious conversion, for this is hidden in the mystery of divinely transcendent freedom. Accordingly, a philosophy of religion can mediate theology by mediating religious experience, religious meaning, and religious language, while the limits of such mediation can be expressed in terms of the hermeneutic circle constituting the horizon and interpretation of the self.[29]

The shift from logical mediation to methodical mediation implies, therefore, the intermediate step of hermeneutical mediation. Indeed, it might even be said that methodical theology is mediated by hermeneutical philosophy, as well as by critical-historical and dialectical methods. Without the clarifications made available by hermeneutical philosophy, praxis-oriented theologians all too easily can become the religious advocates of an unauthentic cultural matrix, whose unauthentic language is borrowed to thematize a perhaps authentic conversion. Such was the problem identified by Dr. Smith in his account of fourth-stage horizons, and such was the reason he advocated a fifth stage critique of cultural matrices.

III. Towards a Universal Theology

As long as foundational theologians remain uncritical of their linguistic cultural matrix, they run the risk of thematizing conversion in unauthentic categories. If attention to method, and not just to logic, encourages theologians to make conversion a topic of cultural conversation, then perhaps attention to hermeneutics, and in particular to language as symbolic, will lead to a conversion of conversational language.[30]

A foundational hermeneutics of Transcendence is needed if theology is to move from fourth-to fifth-level mediation, to recall once again the comments of Wilfred Cantwell Smith.[31] Specifically, a foundational hermeneutics of Transcendence could lead to the restoration of religious meaning in the secularized world described by Dr. Smith. Just how this might be accomplished is sketched by Dr. Emil Piscitelli, who suggests the following order for foundational inquiry:

1. Is the religious interpretation of human experience meaningful, coherent and true?

2. Is the theistic interpretation of religious, human experience meaningful, coherent, and true?

3. Is the Christian interpretation of theistic, religious, human experience meaningful, coherent, and probable?

The first question asks about the "religious" interpretation of human experience and calls for a fundamental religious ontology. The second question asks about the "theistic" interpretation of religious, human experience and calls for a philosophy of religion including an argument for the existence of God based on a fundamental, religious ontology. The third question asks about the "Christian" interpretation of theistic, religious experience and represents a movement within the foundational horizon (hermeneutic circle) from a philosophy of religion to a foundational theology. Notice that all the questions are radically hermeneutic in the sense that they are oriented to the interpretation of the self in language. All three questions begin from self-transcendence to speak about Transcendence.[32]

A foundational hermeneutic would be underpinned, of course, by critical-historical scholarship and by dialectical evaluation. Its contribution to theology would lie in preparing the way for the thematization of conversion by theologians in the functional specialty, foundations; as such, a foundational hermeneutic would be praxis-oriented, and while this opens up a number of possibilities, one of the chief fruits of hermeneutical inquiry is its potential for moving theology towards the sort of universalist praxis urged by Dr. Smith for fifth-stage religious mediation.

An important step in this move towards universalist praxis would be to indicate how human historicity, human being-in-the-world, is in fact a historicity-in-Transcendence, and not merely a fundamentally secular historicity to which Transcendence may or may not be added, depending on one's success as a secular being. To indicate historicity-in-Transcendence, however, is really to indicate how religious language, and ultimately the word of God embodied in language, is constitutive of religious meaning and of the human horizon as religious; it is to indicate the radical openness of human language to the revelation of the Divine Word and to the historic address and call of the Transcendent Other.[33]

Within the secularist horizon of the Modern West human historicity is a matter of what humanity can make of itself or do with its world; what is needed is a foundational hermeneutic and a praxis-oriented theology that sets forth what Transcendent reality will make of humanity and its world.[34] We must respond to Nietzsche's alternative of total linguistic meaninglessness by setting-forth a way of talking about historicity-in-Transcendence that is both post-logical and post-metaphysical, yet deeply methodical and profoundly religious. It is precisely here that Christian theologians concerned with praxis can and must overcome a foundational pluralism rooted in their use of secularist language, and move towards a foundational unity of human historicity-in-Transcendence made possible by a twofold concern: first, by parabolically employing language, to reveal the poverty of secularist aspirations; and, secondly, by rhetorically employing language to ground the transformation religiously of the human economic, cultural, social, and familial communities.[35]

This twofold concern seems implicit in the current interest in the role of narrative or story in theology. Not without reason did the original disciples of Jesus find that only a "gospel," a narrative of human historicity-in-Transcendence, could do justice to the claims of Jesus in history.[36] Not without reason did Jesus proclaim the rootedness of historicity-in-Transcendence by means of parable and rhetoric: the parable that demolished any effort to reduce human historicity to human secularity,[37] and the rhetoric that told of the rootedness of human historicity in the Transcendent beyond. [38]

For foundational theology to speak both parabolically and rhetorically within a secularist cultural matrix demands attention to the foundational manner in which a cultural matrix interprets itself to itself, and this means attention to the economic matrix of cultural self-interpretation. The modern West is secular, not only in its cultural aspirations, but more deeply in its economic behavior that would ground and justify those secularist cultural aspirations. The narrative of historicity-in-Transcendence, then, will become a praxis-oriented narrative to the degree it is successful in mediating Transcendence within a secularist-oriented economic matrix. Indeed, one might almost say that theology today mediates between a religion and the significance and role of religion in an economic matrix, at least in theology's foundational function.[39]

The economic is the sphere of personal values, and to reverse secularist economics is to promote an economics as if people mattered.[40] But the ultimate reason why people matter is because of their exigence for Transcendence and so to appeal for a foundational religious hermeneutic as part of the necessary but not yet sufficient grounding of a praxis-oriented theology seems eminently reasonable. The suggestion that such a foundational religious hermeneutic and foundational theology become parabolic and rhetorical with respect to secularist economics is only to suggest that foundational praxis concern itself with foundational problems.

Just what all this means in praxis has yet to be articulated in foundational categories, whether religious or theological. But the need, at least, is clear and the challenge is set forth by Lonergan:

From economic theorists we have to demand, along with as many other types of analysis as they please, a new and specific type that reveals how moral precepts have both a basis in economic process and so an effective application to it. From moral theorists we have to to demand, along with their other various forms of wisdom and prudence, specifically economic precepts that arise out of economic process itself and promote its proper functioning.[41]

If the actual task of working out an economic historicity-in-Transcendence has only recently begun, at least the aim of such work has frequently received the attention of the scholarly community[42]. Dr. Smith speaks of a fifth-stage cultural attitude rooted in cultural ecumenism; he has promised an elaboration of this theme in a forthcoming book,[43] but likely his thought will be similar in vision to that of another scholar of religion, Dr. Raimundo Panikkar. Both Smith and Panikkar have been cited by Lonergan since the publication of *Method in Theology*, and their importance seems to lie precisely in their attention to categories of universal religious Transcendence.

In a paper entitled "The Myth of Pluralism: The Tower of Babel—A Meditation on Non-Violence,"[44] Dr. Panikkar recalled the myth of the Tower of Babel in Genesis, chapter 11. It is a myth, notes Panikkar, that reflects countless historical aspirations of Secular Humanity, from ancient Babylon to the Technocrats of modernity. Common to all was the utopian dream of one single secular city, one single secular civilization, one single secular God; the dream has persisted through some sixty centuries of human memory, as humans sought in different ways to build their unitarian tower. Panikkar's question is the question of this present paper on theology and the secularizing of truth; is there no way for us to awaken to the futility of the secularist dream? Is there no way to build, instead, roads of communication that, in time, could lead to communion between and among the different tribes, the different life-styles, the different philosophies, the different religions that inhabit the earth? Must we build an economic and linguistic empire, in order to overcome the present biases and prejudices of the human race?

Panikkar's answer begins with identifying the problem as one of praxis and only secondarily one of theory; any solution, accordingly, is a matter of exercising human responsibility and promoting planetary human coexistence: a praxis, hopefully, that will lead to—and be enhanced by—attention to theory. But Panikkar's praxis would be within a profoundly hermeneutical horizon, for otherwise praxis easily degenerates into secularist superiority, secularist relativism, secularist adultation, or secularist modification.[45]

The problem with a praxis-oriented culture, notes Panikkar, is that it throws us into the arms of one another, so that we no longer can live in geographical boxes, just as we no longer can be segregated into economic capsules, cultural areas, or racial ghettos. Isolation is no longer possible, yet unity is not convincing: the parties have become so dialectically opposed that their unification would demand the destruction of one of the parties—an obviously unacceptable option to the party whose destruction is demanded. The dilemma leads some to embrace a nihilistic despairing of humanity's future, while others turn to common sense and the violence of short-term solutions to produce global harmony by force.

nihilistic withdrawal and commonsense violence, Panikkar reminds us, are simply admissions that we humans no longer know what we have to say or do.[46]

Not without reason has humanity of late come to renewed interest in reflection on itself in the overall context of world civilizations. Such reflection can have three forms: with the Modern West one asks, "What is Man?," and makes Man an object of methodically based interdisciplinary research; with the Modern East one asks, "Who am I?," and strives to reconstruct the human image from this supracosmic intuition. Panikkar himself urges a third question, "Who are you?"; it is a radically different question, for it not only cannot be answered without talking to you, but also requires you as a fellow questioner.

Only by asking "Who are you?" will it gradually dawn on each of us that neither your humanity nor my humanity nor Humanity itself is the whole of Reality: for besides Humanity there is the Cosmic and the Transcendent, and each of us can define ourself only in relation to the whole of this Reality. Panikkar, then, would transform an increasingly intolerable dialectical conflict among the peoples of the world into a dialogical tension among these peoples. By recognizing the human other as a "you" and not an "it" in conversation, we may together reach a mutual recognition of a center which transcends the understanding of it by any individual or any group. Theologically that recognition is the gift of faith, a faith that when acknowledged and embraced will promote our common search for genuinely human values.

One of the main contributions in Panikkar's sketch of a hermeneutically grounded ecumenic and economic praxis concerns the attitude towards evil. He recalls the startling parabolic and rhetoric admonition of Jesus, "Do not resist evil!", "Do not set yourself against the man who wrongs you!"[47]

Jesus warns us that to declare war on evil leads us to become immersed in it and dependent on it, no longer free to live on our own terms. What we must do is realize that the way to struggle with the force of evil is not by dialectically opposing to evil what we believe to be non-evil, but by transforming, converting, convincing, evolving, contesting—and all this mainly from within, as leaven, witness, martyr.[48] The goal is not defeat of the adversary, but a mutual conversion to transcendent value, a mutual withdrawal from our communal unauthenticity.[49]

Panikkar concludes by re-telling the Myth of Babel; in part it reads:

> Come, let us go down there, the Lord said, and confuse their meanings so that when
> they say 'democracy' some may mean people's dictatorship, some licentious individualism,
> some a bowing to the majority, and others the manipulating of public opinion; when
> they say 'justice' some may mean maintenance of the status quo at any cost, some state
> ownership, some upheaval, some violence, and some non-violence; when they say 'love'
> some may mean rape, other flirtation, and still others conquest, pleasure, and even pain,
> self-abnegation, or self-gratification. Apparently they have not yet realized that language is
> the concrete personal symbol and that a *lingua universalis* would not be language.[50]

IV. CONCLUSION

We have been asking about the conditions of the possibility for the effective emergence of fifth-stage theological mediation. The preliminary condition, already met in most of contemporary theology, was the shift from logical to methodical mediation. The second condition is the clarification of the structure of methodical mediation, and in distinguishing a threefold structure built around critical-historical, dialectical, and praxis methods, we acknowledged the achievement of Lonergan and of those inspired by his focus on method in theology. The third condition would complement attention to method with a reflection on method from within the context of a foundational hermeneutics of Transcendence; in some such manner might be illuminated the dialectical process whereby a theologian comes to articulate and thematize religious, moral, and intellectual conversion in categories drawn from the ecumenic and economic human community.

In some such fashion, theology as praxis will come to rest on a solid foundation. It will resist the temptation to sacralize truth, because it will be keenly aware of its own limited understanding and its inevitable complicity in unauthenticity. It will resist the temptation to secularize truth, because it will have roots in Transcendent Mystery. Finally, it will be a theology that is deeply Trinitarian and Incarnational, revealing to a troubled world the Transcendent Symbol in whom the world shares.

NOTES

1 Wilfred Cantwell Smith, "The Modern West in the History of Religion," in *Journal of the American Academy of Religion* 52 (1984), pp. 3–18.

2 Ibid., pp. 3–4.

3 Ibid., p. 5.

4 Ibid.

5 Ibid., pp. 14–17.

6 Ibid., p. 8.

7 Ibid., pp. 17–18. See also Smith's *Towards A World Theology*, Philadelphia: Westminster, 1981; and "The World Church and the World History of Religion," in *CTSA Proceedings* 39 (1984), pp. 52–68.

8 Bernard Lonergan, *Method in Theology*, London: Darton, Longman & Todd, 1972, p. xi.

9 See Bernard Lonergan, "Aquinas Today: Tradition and Innovation," in *The Journal of Religion* 55 (1975), pp. 169–172 (re-printed in *A Third Collection: Papers by Bernard J.F. Lonergan, S.J.*, edited by Frederick E. Crowe, S.J. [New York: Paulist Press, 1985], pp. 35–54); and *Idem.*, "The Mediation of Christ in Prayer" (edited by Mark D. Morelli), in *Method: Journal of Lonergan Studies* 2 (1984), pp. 1–6.

10 See Bernard Lonergan, "Theology and Understanding," in *Collection, Papers by Bernard Lonergan S.J.*, edited by F.E. Crowe, Montreal: Palm, 1967, pp. 127ff.

11 See Etienne Gilson, *Reason and Revelation in the Middle Ages*, New York: Charles Scribner's Sons, 1938, pp. 3–33, esp. 25–27.

12 Ibid., pp. 37–66. For the meaning of "sacralism" and "secularism," see my *Unity in Theology*, Washington: University Press of America, 1980, pp. 53–64.

13   See Bernard Lonergan, *Verbum: Word and Idea in Aquinas*, Notre Dame: University of Notre Dame Press, 1967 (edited by David B. Burrell), p. 211; also Lonergan, *Method, p.* 280, and *Insight: A Study of Human Understanding*, London: Longmans, 1957, pp. 403–404.

14   See Michael C. O'Callaghan, *Unity in Theology*, pp. 65–207, for a full account of this emergence of autonomous specializations; more briefly: Lonergan, "Aquinas Today...," pp. 165–180.

15   See Bernard Lonergan, "Aquinas Today...," p. 174.

16   Ibid., p. 172.

17   See O'Callaghan, *op. cit.*, pp. 307–327.

18   Under the general heading of critical-historical scholarship are included the methods of research, interpretation, and history – the first three functional specialties in Lonergan's theological methodology. In what follows, I employ the example of their operations in Christian theology.

19   See Lonergan, *Method*, pp. 167–173 and 232–233.

20   Ibid., pp. 245–247.

21   See Bernard Lonergan, "The Ongoing Genesis of Methods," in *Studies in Religion/Sciences Religieuses* 6 (1976–1977), p. 352. (Re-printed in *A Third Collection*, pp. 146–165.)

22   See O'Callaghan, *op. cit.*, pp. 385–440.

23   See the remarks of David Tracy, "Theologies of Praxis," in Matthew Lamb (ed.), *Creativity and Method*, Milwaukee: The Marquette University Press, 1981, pp. 42–43.

24   See Lonergan, *Method*, pp. 267–271.

25   Ibid., p. 270.

26   See Emil J. Piscitelli, *Language and Method in the Philosophy of Religion: A Critical Study of the Development of the Philosophy of Bernard Lonergan*, unpublished dissertation, Ann Arbor: University Microfilms International, 1977, p. 624; my debt to Dr. Piscitelli's work will be apparent in the remainder of this paper.

27   Ibid., p. 629.

28   Ibid., pp. 638ff.

29   Ibid., pp. 638–639.

30   See Lonergan, "Aquinas Today...," pp. 170–175.

31   See my remarks in "Rahner and Lonergan on Foundational Theology." in Lamb, *op. cit.*, pp. 123–140. Method, of course, is implicit in Rahner's work, just as hermeneutics is implicit in Lonergan's methodology. Indeed, Frederick Lawrence argues convincingly that Lonergan's method *is* profoundly hermeneutical (see his "Method and Theology as Hermeneutical", in Lamb, *op. cit.*, pp. 79–104). I cannot but agree that, just as metaphysical theory was the hermeneutic principle operative in classical theology, so cognitional theory, precisely as articulated by Lonergan in his invitation to self-appropriate one's own interiority, should be the hermeneutic principle in a methodically understood theology. Lawrence identifies two key dimensions to Lonergan's method as hermeneutic: the cognitional and the existential. Clearly, these are integral to the methodic exigence, and Lawrence is right in his critique of both Kantian neglect of objectivity and of the systematic misinterpretation of subjectivity. Method, as understood by Lonergan, is clearly hermeneutical. In addition to the methodical exigence, however, there is the transcendent exigence that also should function as hermeneutical principle. Granted, transcendence as hermeneutics is indeed implied by Lonergan in the fourth chapter of his *Method in Theology;* my sole aim in this paper is to ask for an explicit account of transcendence as hermeneutical, an account that would complement the methodical concern for cognitional and existential concepts of authenticity demanded by Lawrence with the transcendental symbols of authenticity demanded by Lonergan but not worked out by Lonergan in a philosophy of religion that would say what is meant by the self-appropriation of oneself

as religiously-committed subject. Method as hermeneutic is a prerequisite of fourth-stage theology; transcendence as hermeneutic seems a prerequisite of fifth-stage theology.

32   Piscitelli, *op. cit.,* pp. 814–816.

33   Ibid., pp. 849–850.

34   Ibid., pp . 977–978; within, of course, the dialectical community revealed in the work of critical-historical scholarship and of evaluative dialectic.

35   "Rhetoric" in this context is a transformation of the Greek notion; it would come close to Gadamer's analysis of classical rhetoric, but would integrate Habermas' insistence that a contemporary rhetoric be methodically grounded and hermeneutically expanded to correlate language, work, and power.

36   See Gerhard Lohfink, "Erzahlung als Theologie. Zur sprachlichen Grundstruktur der Evanglien", in *Stimmen der Zeit* 192 (1974), pp. 521–532. John Shea's *Stories of God,* Chicago: The Thomas More Press, 1978, correctly locates narrative as foundational in theology, rather than as simply a tool for effective communication.

37   See Dominic Crossan, *In Parables,* New York: Harper & Row, 1973, esp. pp. 4–36.

38   See all four volumes so far published in Eric Voegelin's *Order and History,* published by the Louisiana State University Press.

39   Lonergan has given considerable attention to economics, but his work remains in manuscript form; for some general comments on that economic work, see Michael Gibbons, "Insight and Emergence," in Lamb, *op. cit.,* pp. 529–541.

40   See E.F. Schumacher, *Small is Beautiful: Economics as if People Mattered,* New York: Harper & Row, 1975.

41   Bernard Lonergan, "Healing and Creating in History," in R.E. O'Connor (ed.), *Bernard Lonergan: 3 Lectures,* Montreal: Thomas More Institute for Adult Education, 1975, pp. 65–66. (Reprinted in *A Third Collection,* pp. 100–109.) Among the economic theorists attending to moral precepts, Jane Jacobs is especially important at the present time.

42   The importance of economic categories is underlined by Matthew Lamb, *Solidarity with Victims,* New York: Crossroad, 1982, pp. 132–133 (plus references there given). On the universal aspect of hermeneutics, see Hans-Georg Gadamer, *Truth and Method,* New York: Seabury, 1975, pp. 431–447.

43   See Smith, *op cit.,* pp. 11–12.

44   Raimundo Panikkar, "The Myth of Pluralism: The Tower of Babel – A Meditation on Non-Violence," in *Cross Currents* 39 (1979), pp. 197–230.

45   Ibid., p. 201. "Praxis," for Panikkar, seems to mean simply unreflective human behaving – what in fact people do; Lonergan's meaning of praxis is methodical, designating a reflection on human behaving that is grounded in one's own cognitional, existential, and Transcendental subjectivity.

46   Ibid., p. 212.

47   Ibid., p. 221.

48   Ibid., p. 222.

49   Ibid., p. 223.

50   Ibid., p. 229.

XI

On Reading The Way to Nicea

CHARLES C. HEFLING, JR.

"AND what is worst of all is to advocate Christianity, not because it is true, but because it might be beneficial."[1] So said T. S. Eliot, and it is a hard saying. Nowadays, advocating Christianity because it is true is fairly asking for trouble, not least from other advocates. The usual strategy of apologetics at present is some sort of appeal to the affective and imaginative dimensions of religious living; to symbols, narrative symbols especially, as uniquely privileged bearers of religious meaning and value; in short, to practical rather than theoretical reasoning. Such an appeal need not entail outright rejection of truth in the sense of cognitive meaning propositionally expressed. The current emphasis on myth and parable can be regarded as a healthy antidote to arid and sometimes arrogant positivism, in which case all that needs to be cleared up is what the more modest, less autocratic role of propositional assertions ought to be within the whole of the theological enterprise.

More often than not, however, those who would stress what Lonergan calls the constitutive and effective meanings of the Christian word take as their text *the letter killeth,* insisting that humanity's relation to transcendence cannot be pinned down with flat yes-or-no statements, that between "objective" or "scientific" truth and the truth of authentic faith a great gulf is fixed, and so on. Hence the familiar dichotomies of biblical *versus* dogmatic theology, charisma *versus* creed, dynamic meaning *versus* static formula, lived faith *versus* abstract assent—the litany goes on. And it is not only the watchdogs of old-fashioned orthodoxy who are in trouble, if these dichotomies are irresolvable. So is Lonergan.

True, it is possible to read *Method in Theology* (apart from the section on the permanence of dogmas, which can be written off as a polite nod to ecclesiastical authority) in a modernist sense. More accurately, "modernist" being an elastic term, it is possible to read *Method* as one more example of the religious-experience-plus-symbolic-expression view of theology.[2] What is not possible to read in the same way is the only extended piece of theology (as distinct from methodology) that Lonergan published in English—*The Way to Nicea.*

This slim book, translated from a Latin treatise that he finished at Rome in 1964, is not Lonergan at his best. Nor, for reasons I will go into below, is it the book he would have written at Toronto or Boston in the 1970s. "Jejune" and "violent" are the words he later used himself to describe how its procedure might appear "to an outsider."[3] All that notwithstanding, *The Way to Nicea* leaves little room for doubt as to whether, in his view, the Christian word is "just the objectification of the gift of God's love (as the modernist might claim)."[4] It is not. The outer word of religious expression does symbolize the content of religious experience, but that is not all it does, and it is not what Lonergan concentrates on. *The Way to Nicea's* emphatic, almost exclusive theme is "the word *as true.*" Nor is there any ambiguity about what is being meant by truth: "if one rejects propositional truth in favour of some other kind of truth, one is not attending to the word of God as true."[5] Thus, perhaps, it is no surprise that *The Way to Nicea* has come in for quite a lot of adverse criticism.

Lonergan's main argument is to the effect that at Nicea the Christian community turned a corner in the still unfinished process of understanding the gospel by which that community was and is constituted. Some of his critics, however, deny that there was any corner to be turned; the rest, although they agree that there was, contend that turning it was a mistake, a defection rather than a development, and among the variations on this latter theme (usually if perhaps unfairly attributed to Harnack) is the longest and most intemperate discussion of *The Way to Nicea* in print.

As portrayed by Joseph S. O'Leary, Lonergan's analysis of the ante-Nicene movement is the epitome of dogmatism in all the most negative senses the word can bear. Behind its emphasis on "the word *as true*" O'Leary detects sins of both omission and commission: on the one hand, "systematic ignorance" and "insidious provinciality" where post-Englightenment philosophy is concerned; on the other, an "unhappy intellectualist itch" that prompts Lonergan "to seek a kind of meaning in revelation which it was never intended to convey,"[6] typical of the "desire to control truth, to tie down the Spirit in propositions, to subject a 'hearing of the Word' to a technological mastery of its meanings," which O'Leary finds in all of Lonergan's work.[7] It may be that such a mathematization of data is possible, even legitimate, in the natural sciences; in theology, however, "it is not so clear that there are scientific patterns of intelligibility to be abstracted from the rich and myth-laden language of the kerygma. Understanding is rather a matter of coping with this richness as one copes with the rich meaning of a work of art."[8] In other words—words that have come to be an incantation—Lonergan has succumbed to forgetfulness of being.

Much of this is rhetoric, of course, and not very profound rhetoric at that; the voice is O'Leary's voice, but the hands are the hands of Heidegger and Nietzsche. Nevertheless, his rather dogmatic attack on dogmatism is significant here for two interrelated reasons. In the first place, O'Leary does manage to indicate, if not exactly clarify, the real issue. The gist of his objections is that Lonergan has chosen the wrong hermeneutical tools. Religion is one thing, the world that natural science investigates (manipulates, O'Leary would say) is something else, and never the twain shall meet. Hence Lonergan's mistake lies in taking "a certain kind of existence . . . as paradigmatic for being in general," namely, the kind that is "affirmed in the rational judgment that such and such a state of affairs is a fact."[9]

Just so. To quote *The Way to Nicea,* "sooner or later one is forced to ask, What is truth? and, What is the relationship between truth and reality?"[10] On the answers to those two questions depends the meaning of every other term, and Lonergan's own answers underpin everything he says about the ante-Nicene movement. Had he responded to the quite different answers on which O'Leary bases his suspicion of "geometrical" dogmas as vehicles of "ineffable" truth, Lonergan himself would no doubt have pointed out the same inconsistency he found in another author's attitude towards judgments propositionally expressed: "So eager has he been to impugn what he considered the Thomist theory of knowledge that he overlooked the fact that he needed a correspondence view of truth to mean what he said."[11]

But, in the second place, even if it should turn out that O'Leary's epistemological position is somewhat less than coherent, it does not follow that he is merely attacking a straw doll. Parts of *The Way to Nicea* do seem to have something of a dogmatic flavor, using the word dyslogistically. Whereas in other works Lonergan's precept for reversing counterpositions is "be attentive, intelligent, reasonable, and responsible," his precept in *The Way to Nicea* is "pay attention to the word as true"—almost as though assent to the cognitive meaning of the Christian message is, in itself, the resolution of basic issues in cognitional theory and epistemology. About this precept I shall have more to say presently, but it is worth noting here that Lonergan delivers it explicitly only in the first section, "Dogmatic Development," which provides O'Leary with four of the five long quotations he dissects and which other critics too, almost without exception, have singled out for scrutiny. Oddly, and a little ironically, the nine sections that follow have been pretty much ignored.

The irony is twofold: section one has not always been there, whereas the rest of what is now *The Way to Nicea* remained virtually unchanged when Lonergan revised it for the version published in 1964 and eventually translated.[12] Evidently he had not changed his mind as to which were the important stages on the way to Nicea. Nor did he. The movement from Tertullian's naive realism to Origen's idealism to the Nicene *homoousios* and Athanasius's rule for interpreting it shows up in several later essays, down to 1976,[13] and there is reason to think that it was partly to substantiate these brief summaries that Lonergan finally agreed to let the first part of *De Deo Trino* be published in translation. In any event there is not much question but that the last nine sections of *The Way to Nicea* are the important thing.

Yet it is also clear that they could not and cannot stand on their own. As Lonergan notes, there is no use trying to understand the ante-Nicene movement (or any other) without some preliminary notion of what to look for; the interpreter needs a heuristic structure—general, anticipatory categories, which serve as the upper blade of a metaphorical scissors, as well as a lower blade consisting of possibly relevant documents. Inasmuch as Lonergan's positions on knowing, reality, and objectivity are, as I have suggested, the most basic components of the upper blade he uses in analyzing the early development of Trinitarian theology, the best and perhaps the only really adequate introduction to *The Way to Nicea* would have been *Insight* itself; it still is, for reasons I will go into later. But for the practical purposes of writing a textbook he had to be content with citing the relevant pages in *Insight* and asking his readers to accept, by way of an orientation to his approach, what the new first section says about "dogmatic development, viewed in its totality." It is unlikely that Lonergan thought of this section as anything but a compromise. Still, there it is, a scandal to his critics and a stumbling block to some of his followers. Compromise or not, section one does set out an interpretive framework for everything that follows; and this framework, in which "the word *as true*" figures so prominently, can be something of a puzzle even for those who know and admire Lonergan's other writings. No one who is at all familiar with *Method,* in particular, is likely to read *The Way to Nicea* without raising in one way or another the question I am concerned with here: how do these two books fit together?

DIALECTIC AND FOUNDATIONS IN *THE WAY TO NICEA*

We have Lonergan's own answer to this question. One of the permanently valid chunks in his Latin writings, he said in a published interview, is the part of *De Deo Trino* which makes use of "this type of interpretation that is concerned with things the thinkers themselves didn't think about."[14] And a brief foreword, written in 1976 for the translation of this part as *The Way to Nicea,* locates his analysis squarely within *Method in Theology's* fourth functional specialty: "we do not propose to add to erudition by research, or to clarify interpretation by study, or to enrich history with fresh information . . . Our purpose is to move on . . . to a *dialectic* that, like an x-ray, sets certain key issues in high relief to concentrate on their oppositions and their interplay."[15]

Both of these statements tally with Lonergan's view that a text is to be understood within an ongoing context which includes what came afterwards as well as what went before.[16] It remains that his "breakthrough" to the full complement of eight specialties occurred only after the final edition of *De Deo Trino* was in print, so that there is a sense in which his retrospective assessment of *The Way to Nicea* as an example of Dialectic is itself an example of Dialectic. It portrays "something better than was the reality" by getting hold of what the thinker, in this case Lonergan himself, was not thinking about, namely, functional specialization as he would later thematize it in *Method.* This is not to say that the assessment is wrong; my suggestion is rather that Dialectic is not the only thing going on in *The Way to Nicea* as it stands.

To put this another way, Lonergan does not always draw *Method's* clear distinction between *indirect* discourse, proper to all four specialties in the first or "mediating" phase of theology, and the *direct* discourse proper to the four further specialties of the second, "mediated" phase. This is particularly evident in section one, where his discussion of what is basically a dialectical method seems to spill over into Foundations and even Doctrines, making it difficult to decide which of two things he means by "pay attention to the word *as true.*" It might mean that the reader is to entertain the possibility that the ante-Nicene authors *were* concerned—indirect discourse—with the cognitive meaning of the gospel. Or it might instead mean that he or she is to concentrate on the fact that the Christian message *does* convey—direct discourse—a meaning that is (among other things) cognitive.

Actually, it means both. The truth of the word of God is not only something affirmed implicitly and unphilosophically in Scripture and the writings of the early fathers; it is also something that has to be affirmed, explicitly, by those who would understand the way to Nicea correctly today. This may or may not qualify as "dogmatism"; it does however echo the frequently quoted passage from a much earlier essay in which Lonergan states in no uncertain terms that "the development of understanding in Christian doctrine regards, not sensible presentations which intellect has to raise to the order of truths, but a divine revelation which already is in the order of truth."[17] But this passage, in turn, affords a useful key to the "prior phase" of Lonergan's work only if the question at issue is stated accurately. It is not a matter of whether belief in a divine revelation ought to be ruled out in advance on the ground that historical investigation can and should be kept free of presuppositions. That is just the Principle of the Empty Head. The only question is whether the non-empty heads of scholarly investigators must profess such a belief in advance on the ground that otherwise their investigations will be irrelevant to theology. What, in other words, is the nature of theological understanding in so far as it is exercised on historical materials of the kind Lonergan is concerned with in *The Way to Nicea*? Is it, in the first instance, a matter of grasping the intelligibility of empirical evidence, which may *also* convey the true word of God, or the intelligibility of a word that has already been acknowledged, for whatever reasons, as a divine revelation?

At issue, then, is what Lonergan once called "the whole problem in modern theology, Protestant and Catholic," namely, the introduction of historical scholarship.[18] What I want to suggest is that the whole problem in modern theology is also the whole problem in *The Way to Nicea*. If Lonergan's argument here occasionally sounds dogmatic, it is not because he accepts the truth of the Christian word. So he does, but that in itself does not explain much. Rather, it is because in 1964 he had not yet fully resolved the methodological question of where judgments of truth stand in relation to historical scholarship: does the doctrinal belief that there has been a divine revelation, a disclosure of meaning that is cognitively true, precede or follow investigation into what the early Christian community was doing as it hammered out its doctrines?

THE PEDAGOGICAL BACKGROUND OF *THE WAY TO NICEA*

Among the things that make this a complicated question is the fact that all of Lonergan's Latin theology was written for an audience rather different from the intended readership of *Insight*. Looking back on his tour of duty as a professor of dogmatic theology,

Lonergan could comment on the impossible conditions under which he had to teach and on the invalidity of having to write a book like *De Deo Trino* at all, its permanently valid chunks notwithstanding.[19] Given the curricular setup that was then in place, there was nothing to do but introduce as much as he could. Ordinarily, however, he was introducing it to second-year seminarians who came to his classes after a year's study of fundamental theology, and there is every reason to suppose that what they had been taught was "foundations in the simple manner."[20]

It would be strange if this situation had left no traces in Lonergan's Latin textbooks. In fact it has, although the most obvious ones do not appear in *The Way to Nicea.* There is, for example, a passage in the first version of *De Deo Trino* where to all appearances Lonergan deduces the fact of dogmatic development from certain "fundamental" doctrines. In order for the truth of the word of God to be apprehended, he writes, reason must be illuminated by faith; but it belongs to reason, so illuminated, to grasp

> that what the word of God implicitly contains can be judged by no wisdom other than God's own; that this divine judgment is known to us in no other way than through the teaching authority of the church; that the church's teaching authority is not exercised except within history and under historical conditions, and that this history, inasmuch as it is both doctrinal and sacred history, is not subject to perpetual doubts. . .[21]

Three doctrines are fairly explicit here—revelation, ecclesial *magisterium,* and special providence—and another, inspiration of Scripture, is presumably involved by implication. As it happens, the same four "fundamental" doctrines turn up on the first page of *The Way to Nicea,* in a footnote that has become mildly notorious. It can be (and has been) construed as proving that Lonergan's analysis of the ante-Nicene movement, far from being an exercise in critical or even dialectical history, is just window-dressing, since the conclusions about doctrinal development that he purports to draw from a scholarly interpretation of the patristic documents are already implied in the "fundamental" doctrines with which, according to this note, he presumes his readers are familiar. In short, he has molded historical evidence to fit a party line.

Possibly. But this is making much of a footnote, and given the consistent stand his earlier essays take on the bankruptcy of abstract deductivism as a theological method, a different construction is, I think, more plausible: even in the part of *De Deo Trino* which he allowed to be translated Lonergan was writing *for* but to nothing like the same extent *from* a horizon in which the traditional foundations of theology stand unshaken. As for "fundamental" doctrines, his students were, in all probability, familiar with them. What this implies, if anything, about the proper way to understand the ante-Nicene movement is a different question, but it is worth pointing out that even if foundations in the simple manner can be used to establish what Newman called an antecedent probability that Christian doctrine has developed, they cannot specify *how* any development that has in fact occurred did occur—which is what Lonergan sets out to do for Nicea's *homoousios.* Knowing what to look for is a far cry from finding anything; there is still plenty of work for historical scholarship.

My point at present is that anyone who reads *The Way to Nicea* will do well to keep in mind this sentence from *Insight:* "the great difficulties of interpretation arise when the new wine of literary, scientific, and philosophic leaders cannot but be poured into the old bottles of established modes of expression."[22] The same goes for new theological wine. But while John Carmody is no doubt right when he says that Lonergan's Latin theology shows "how Rome wanted its seminarians to think,"[23] it also shows how Lonergan was teaching his students to think, as well as how he was thinking himself. Since that is the important thing here, I want to return to the question of development in Lonergan's own position on theological method, and specifically to the way in which, prior to 1965, he went about solving "the whole problem in modern theology."

HISTORICAL THEOLOGY AND THE "WAY OF DISCOVERY"

Descartes's recommendation about taking up questions one at a time is one that Lonergan endorsed by example as well as by precept. His three most important books, as Frederick Crowe has pointed out, move stepwise through the levels of intentionality: *Verbum* concentrates on understanding, *Insight* adds factual judgment, and *Method* goes on to evaluation and decision.[24] Chronologically speaking, *The Way to Nicea* falls just halfway between *Insight* and *Method,* and I submit that it similarly occupies an intermediate position in the development of Lonergan's thinking on theological method. On the one hand, it points ahead to functional specialization, specifically to Dialectic, as his foreword of 1976 suggests. On the other, the methodological sections of *De Deo Trino* itself set out a somewhat different methodological framework, and this immediate context points back to the epilogue of *Insight* and to articles Lonergan published at about the same time. One of these, "Theology and Understanding," is a convenient starting point for tracing the movement of Lonergan's thought during the years of his professorship in Rome.

The title of this long review announces its theme: not demonstration, not conceptualistic deduction, but *understanding* and nothing else is the proper end of systematic or (as Lonergan refers to it here) speculative theology. Syllogism has its role—not the merely factual type of syllogism, which does not promote insight, but the "explanatory" type, which does. Such a syllogism can advance one's understanding in either of two directions, according as its middle term answers the question "Why is it so?" by giving cognitional reasons or ontological reasons. The example Lonergan uses turns up again and again, down to his 1976 essay on Christology: "the phases of the moon are the cause of our knowing that the moon is a sphere, but the sphericity of the moon is the cause of its phases being what they are."[25] The phases are *causae cognoscendi;* as sensible presentations they come first in the order of knowing and take priority *quoad nos.* The sphericity is the *causa essendi,* first in the order of being and prior *quoad se.* Start with the phases, ask what explains them, and you arrive at the "why," the *causa essendi,* by way of a movement of understanding called the *ordo inventionis* or "way of discovery." Inversely, there is a "way of teaching" or *ordo disciplinae,* which starts from what is prior *quoad se* and moves to an explanation of the sensible phenomena.

Although the terminology here may be antique, what it refers to is not. Lonergan observes that the two routes which understanding can take are to be found in modern as well as in Aristotelian science, and that they also have a place in theology. In particular, speculative theology is analogous to the "way of teaching"; it follows the "synthetic or constructive procedure in which human intelligence forms and develops concepts," thereby generating some partial understanding of revealed truth.[26] What speculative theology does not generate is any new ground or motive for affirming this truth. Certitude, the assent of faith, is presumed. As for settling what truths there are to be affirmed, that falls to the "way of discovery," which in this regard takes priority over the "way of teaching."

To these two complementary "ways" correspond the two volumes of *De Deo Trino,* which at one stage in fact bore the subtitles *Pars analytica* and *Pars synthetica* respectively. In the second, longer, and untranslated part of the first volume (finally subtitled *Pars dogmatica*), Lonergan pursues the analytical "way of discovery" in a sequence of five theses, the first of which is this:

> God the Father neither made his own and only Son out of already existing stuff, nor created him out of nothing; rather, the Son is eternally begotten, of the Father's substance and consubstantial with him.[27]

Forty pages of argument follow. After defining his terms Lonergan lists and discusses briefly the authors who oppose the thesis, and then presents a lengthy case built on Scripture and a lengthier one drawing on the patristic literature.

The biblical argument is the important one here. It is no mere catalogue of proof-texts. The point, as always, is to *understand;* in this case, to discern an intrinsic unity in the assertions Scripture makes in many and various ways. This search for insight concludes with a syllogism:

> The Son is consubstantial with the Father, if the same things are said *secundum substantiam* about the Son as are said about the Father. But they are. Therefore he is.[28]

What this explanatory syllogism illustrates is "that the articles of faith"—here, scriptural statements about the Father and about the Son—"are the theologian's *causae cognoscendi,* that they provide the *priora quoad nos,* and that they are first in the *ordo inventionis.* "[29] More significant, in the present context, is the fact that Lonergan is arguing for a thesis that reiterates the principal assertions in the creed of the council of Nicea, by using an explanatory syllogism that reiterates Athanasius's interpretation of the Nicene *homoousios* as shorthand for a second-order proposition—a proposition, that is, which says something about certain propositions contained in Scripture.

What makes this significant is that Lonergan had already shown, in the preceding part of *De Deo Trino,* that the rule of Athanasius and the conciliar decree it explains were the culmination of the way to Nicea. In other words, the *Pars dogmatica* of *De Deo Trino* arrives at one doctrine by two routes. Part one presents the Son's consubstantiality with the Father as the result of a historical process; part two recapitulates that process in Lonergan's own argument for the first thesis. This raises an interesting question: why does *De Deo Trino* go over the same ground twice? True, in the patristic section of his argument for the thesis quoted above, Lonergan does refer back to what is now *The Way to Nicea*. But did he need to? Or is it instead that the thesis is unnecessary, Athanasius and the council of Nicea having already said everything that Lonergan wants to say about the Son's relation to the Father?

Eventually, by endorsing *The Way to Nicea* rather than the dogmatic theses, Lonergan was to take the direction suggested by this second question. There are rather clear indications, however, that in 1964 he was not ready to turn historical scholarship loose on Christian texts, unsupervised by dogmatic theology. The successive revisions he made in both volumes of *De Deo Trino* show, on the contrary, that his aim was to include the study of history *within* dogmatics or, better, to unite the historical and dogmatic "ways of discovery" in one methodical process. Although at first he was inclined to propose a third "way," a *via historica*,[30] he abandoned this scheme soon afterwards in favor of one that has the "way of discovery" (or "way of analysis," as he now preferred to call it) operating in two modes, one historical, the other conceptual. How then are they related?

To this methodological question, Lonergan's most definitive "prior phase" answer appears at the beginning of the second volume, *Pars systematica*, of *De Deo Trino*, which also provides the proximate context of the first volume and thus of *The Way to Nicea*. Not far in the background, however, is the epilogue of *Insight*, which sketches the theological method that Lonergan was still refining up to the breakthrough of 1965.

THEOLOGICAL HISTORY IN *INSIGHT* AND *DE DEO TRINO*

If the whole problem in modern theology is the introduction of historical scholarship, the whole problem in modern historical scholarship, as Lonergan saw it in the early 1960s, is the introduction of a method that is both stable in itself and capable of bringing under control the "flood tide of scholarly diligence." Not until the historical disciplines become methodical, and in that sense scientific, can they be integrated with theology, for "it is primarily through the illumination of method by faith that theology has to exercise her queenly rule."[31]

To that end, Lonergan distinguishes and relates several types of historical movements, three of which are pertinent here. First of all, the shift from commonsense description to explanatory theory has to be distinguished from what he calls a "cross-cultural" movement, in which Christian truths are only transposed from one commonsense context to another—from the cultural matrix of first-century Palestine, say, to that of fourth-century Africa or Asia Minor.[32] Moreover—and this, it will turn out, is the important thing—in theology the shift from what is evident *quoad nos* to things as they are *quoad se* can itself occur in two ways. What Lonergan calls a "theological movement" accomplishes the transition from common sense to theory, but another, "dogmatic movement" takes place when the result of such a transition is pronounced correct by the proper authority.

How *The Way to Nicea* applies these general distinctions to the early history of Trinitarian doctrine needs no elaboration. The writings of Judeo-Christianity do not make even a "cross-cultural" movement, remaining as they do within the commonsense context of scriptural imagery. But from Tertullian to Origen to Arius to Athanasius the movement was, in Lonergan's specialized sense, "theological," while the council of Nicea itself added the "dogmatic" movement when it endorsed the *homoousios*. What may not be so obvious is that these three movements go back to *Insight*. Although the heuristic scheme that Lonergan proposes in *De Deo Trino* uses different terms, Latin ones at that, it matches *Insight's* outline of theological interpretation rather closely. I have put them side by side in the two middle columns of the following table.[33] The fourth column explains their similarity; in both cases Lonergan's analysis of cognitional structure is the foundation.

The Place of Historical Scholarship
in a Methodical Theology:
Insight and *De Deo Trino*

	The Epilogue of *Insight*		*De Deo Trino, Pars systematica*
	NON-THEOLOGICAL	THEOLOGICAL	
LEVEL OF PRESENTATIONS	(1) initial statements addressed to particular audiences	(1) an initial divine revelation	revelation, given to one particular culture
LEVEL OF (COMMONSENSE) UNDERSTANDING	(2) their successive recasting for sequences of other particular audiences	(2) the work of teachers and preachers communicating and applying the initial message to a succession of different audiences	the 'cross-cultural' movement from one *prius quoad nos* to another *prius quoad nos*
LEVEL OF (EXPLANATORY) UNDERSTANDING	(3) the ascent to a universal viewpoint to express the initial statements in a form accessible to any sufficiently cultured audience	(3) the work of the . . . theologian seeking a universal formulation of the truths of faith {through the *philosophia perennis*}	the properly 'theological' movement from *priora quoad nos* to *priora quoad se*
LEVEL OF JUDGMENT	(4) the explanatory unification from the universal viewpoint of the initial statements and all their subsequent re-expressions	{dogmatic decisions and (possibly) the technical theses of the dogmatic theologian as true interpretations} (4) the work of the historical theologian revealing the doctrinal identity in the verbal and conceptual differences of (1), (2), and (3) {from the theologically transformed universal viewpoint}	the 'dogmatic' movement that ratifies or posits as true the results of a shift to *priora quoad se*

What I am suggesting is that in *De Deo Trino* what Lonergan calls the *via historica* is the first cousin, if not the twin, of specifically theological hermeneutics as *Insight* outlines it. How then does theological hermeneutics compare with methodical interpretation elsewhere? As the first two columns of my table indicate, Lonergan observes that they are structurally analogous or "isomorphic." But only isomorphic. There is a difference, which shows up most clearly at the bottom of these two columns, and which needs some explaining.

Interpreters, both theological and non-theological, can be sure that they have not overlooked any possibly relevant interpretation of the data they seek to understand, if and only if they work from a "universal viewpoint" that anticipates in a general way the genetic and dialectical relations that *can* hold between different sequences and levels of expressions of meaning. But while a non-theological interpreter will thus be enabled to understand even the broad lines of "every possible philosophy and metaphysics,"[34] the universal viewpoint must be "theologically transformed" before it can be used to anticipate the meaning of expressions referring to transcendent realities. Thus, in addition to the heuristic tools provided in the first eighteen chapters of *Insight*, theological interpreters will employ the transcendent knowledge, general and special, treated in chapters 19 and 20. They will have affirmed, that is, the existence of a God whose attributes imply that his way of dealing with evil has certain characteristics. Four of these characteristics reappear in the epilogue as part of the framework Lonergan offers for a specifically theological hermeneutics. One is that the divine solution will have a cognitive aspect and will thus involve human intelligence and reasonableness as well as affectivity. Another is that men and women will collaborate in the solution as well as accept it as true. The third is that their collaboration will include "conceiving and expressing the solution in terms of the universal viewpoint," as well as "recasting the expression of the solution into the equivalent expressions of different places, times, classes, and cultures." And, fourth, the solution will have an institutional aspect, an organization capable of making the judgments necessary to prevent the collaboration from straying.

Otherwise stated, God's solution to the problem of evil can be expected to embody not only a "word *as true*" but also the "cross-cultural," "theological," and "dogmatic" movements. So, if acceptance of that solution is one of the prerequisites of properly theological hermeneutics, it would seem that theological historians must accept not only "an initial divine revelation" but also its subsequent developments, including dogmatic definitions.

This begins to explain why, at the level of judgment, the three columns of my table do not line up exactly. The basic question is about criteria: what prompts a *yes* in deciding whether an interpretation of the Christian word is true? On the side of non-theological interpretation things are fairly clear: as with any judgment of fact, the criterion of truth in non-theological interpretation is the "virtually unconditioned" reached when all the relevant questions have been raised and answered. But, as the relevant questions pertain to a process, so does the judgment: what a true interpretation explains correctly is "what was going forward."[35] Moving across to my second column, what Lonergan says about the work of the historical theologian is similar; here too the goal is an explanatory unification of successive expressions. But similarity is not sameness, and the next few lines of *Insight* add a double qualification which makes it clear that where theology is concerned true interpretations are not simply a matter of correct historical explanation. First, non-theological interpreters do not and evidently cannot grasp the unity of meaning expressed in Christian texts, at least not in an explanatory way. They can only "recapture the mentality for which the books of the Old and New Testament were written," and presumably the same goes for other documents. By contrast, secondly, the theological interpreter has a "firmer and broader base" to work from, namely the theologically transformed universal viewpoint.

Having stated these qualifications, and without pausing for a full stop, Lonergan draws this remarkable conclusion: "and so it is that in a pre-eminent and unique manner the dogmatic decision is, and the technical thesis of the dogmatic theologian can be, the true interpretation of Scriptural texts, patristic teaching, and traditional utterances."[36] Are dogmas grist to the historical theologian's mill, or foundations on which the mill itself is built? It is not, I think, too much to say that in *Insight* Lonergan wants to have it both ways. That is why the second column of my table has two items corresponding to the level of judgment, one of them similar to correct historical explanation in the first column, the other similar to the "dogmatic movement" in the third. The two will converge, as presumably they are meant to do, only if the horizon within which historical theologians can arrive at correct explanatory insights already includes the dogmatic decisions of the past—which is almost as much as to say that historians, if they are authentically Christian theologians too, have answers to their questions given to them in advance. For the method they use, however closely it may resemble procedures followed by other historians, is a method illuminated by faith; and in *Insight* that means it is illuminated by an intelligent and reasonable decision to accept as true the results of the very collaboration which, as historical theologians, they are going to investigate.

It will not do to make the epilogue of *Insight* carry more weight than it can bear; Lonergan himself cautions that the parallel set out in my first two columns is not to be pushed in any *a priori* manner. Yet here if anywhere is the root of the "dogmatism," such as it is, in *The Way to Nicea:* historical theologians are a breed apart, distinguished from the rest of the herd by a viewpoint that has been transformed by accepting, among other things, "the word *as true.*" It would be a caricature to conclude that in *Insight* the theological transformation of the universal viewpoint amounts to an endorsement of "foundations in the simple manner." Nevertheless, Lonergan's proof of God's existence in chapter 19 and the next chapter's heuristic anticipation of God's redemptive work do lay the groundwork for a view of theological method which can to some extent be squared with older, classical views. Not that there is anything wrong with the proof as it stands. The anomaly of chapter 19 is that it stands *where* it stands, namely, at the point of transition from a generalized empirical method to a theological method which makes no appeal to religious experience and which operates from the first, not on empirical data, but on truths acknowledged as such.

THE *WAY TO NICEA* IN LIGHT OF *METHOD IN THEOLOGY*

With the advent of functional specialization, all of this changes. Conversion, not proof, provides the specifically theological component in the method of *Method;* arguments like the one in chapter 19 of *Insight* find a new home in the functional specialty Systematics; much of chapter 20 becomes the content of faith, now understood as knowledge born of religious love, so that "be in love" rather than "pay attention to the word as true" is the specifically theological precept; and, most importantly, the two kinds of factual judgment that Lonergan was still endeavoring to combine in *De Deo Trino* are allowed to separate and assigned to different points in the dynamic sequence of methodical operations. What might be called the dogmatic judgment belongs to the direct discourse of Doctrines ; the judgment as to whether reconstructions of "what was going forward" are correct belongs to the indirect discourse of the functional specialty History.

Thus, while historical theologians must certainly know *about* a doctrine in order to study its development, there is no need to sort out in advance who is and who is not a *bona fide* historical theologian. "The historian does history on historical principles"—not religious, still less dogmatic ones.[37] Whether a given historian is or is not an authentic human being or an authentic Christian remains a valid question. Methodologically speaking, however, it comes up only *after* the historian in question has done his or her work, precisely as a historian—not, as both *The Way to Nicea* and the epilogue of *Insight* suggest, before.

As for a universal viewpoint, that is the "high and distant goal" of the *next* functional specialty, Dialectic; as for theologically transforming this comprehensive viewpoint (as Lonergan sometimes refers to it in *Method*), none of the functional specialties does that, because the transformation is not a theological procedure at all. It is a religious event, which takes place, so to say, *between* Dialectic and Foundations, between indirect and direct discourse. Which means it takes place after *The Way to Nicea*, considered precisely as dialectical history. What you make of Lonergan's analysis still depends on the authenticity of your intellectual, moral, and religious horizon; but in *Method* authenticity is primarily a gift, a decision made possible by grace, rather than an intellectual achievement. From that foundation, so different from "foundations in the simple manner," you may go on to judge, not only that what led up to the council of Nicea was the kind of shift Lonergan maintains it was; not only that certain Christian writers, some hundreds of years ago, based what they said about Christ on a message they held to be true as well as salvific; but also that their contribution to the ongoing process which is the Christian church remains valid, that the questions they raised and answered are still meaningful, that the stand they took in answering these questions—the truth of the gospel that had transformed their lives—was the right stand to take. More briefly, you may make the way to Nicea, as mediated by *The Way to Nicea*, part of a heuristic structure for mediating what it means, today, to profess that Jesus Christ is the Son of God.[38] Perhaps you will not ask, as the bishops at Nicea did, whether Christ is a creature; but Lonergan points out that there is an equivalent question: "whether God revealed his love for us by having a man die the death of scourging and crucifixion."[39] So stated, this is by no means an academic quibble. It gets at the very heart of Christian spirituality. For if there is anything specific about the religious experience of Christians, it is that the love of God meets them not only immediately, in the heart-flooding love Lonergan so often refers to, but also mediately, in the human world of words and rites and institutions.

That being so, the question I began with has to be dealt with: does this "outer word" simply disclose and symbolize a generic human relationship to the divine? Or does it also change those who hear it, committing them to a way of life which, on the face of it, promises little in the way of pleasure or profit in any generally accepted sense? The Christian story, after all, is not a success story. If it does effect as well as express a transcendent love—if it is really God who, through this story and all its mediations, draws human hearts into conversation—then "love" means something strange, something which does not fit easily into any of the moral and intellectual horizons modernity offers, and which, to that extent, is difficult to understand. Lonergan's way of understanding it appears in the final thesis of *De Verbo Incarnato* (surely another permanently valid chunk of his Latin theology); but what he there names the "just and mysterious Law of the Cross" makes no sense at all if the man whose cross overcomes the human problem of evil was just a man, much less if the story Christians tell about him is just a story.[40]

The same point can be made the other way round. If, for whatever reason—Lessing's ditch, the reputed demise of metaphysics, religious pluralism—cognitive meaning is excluded from the Christian word at the outset, the result will inevitably be a toning-down of its moral and religious meaning. There is not much of a "disturbing memory" in the tale of an itinerant rabbi executed for blasphemy. In the long run, as the more radical followers of Bultmann saw, there will be no reason to keep the Christian message at all. Demythologization, in Bultmann's sense, invites dekerygmatization,[41] and as Lonergan suggests, there is no reason to think that "a rejection of the message is not also a rejection of the mission."[42] Hence that pungent remark of Eliot's with which I began.

Lonergan's later writings tend to moderate some of *The Way to Nicea*'s claims about the significance of that achievement; in *Method* the early Greek councils are said to display only a slight tincture of theoretically differentiated consciousness, and since there are other differentiations the "discovery of mind" does not account for every development that has occurred in Christian doctrine.[43] It does still explain the *homoousios*, though, as well as the Chalcedonian usage of "person" and "nature," for the context in which these doctrines were framed is the merely logical context of propositional operations. "What is said of the Father is said of the Son too, except for the name *Father*"—that is simply not Greek ontology. But if it is all that *homoousios* meant, then surely Lonergan is correct when he says that this supposedly abstruse doctrine "leaves the believer free to conceive the Father"—and consequently the Son as well—"in scriptural, patristic, medieval, or modern terms; and of course contemporary consciousness, which is historically minded, will be at home in all four."[44] *How* the doctrine can be true is a further question, a question calling for understanding rather than for judgment, which scholasticism answered in the theoretical context of a metaphysics and which Lonergan has answered in the methodical context of an intentionality analysis. But the doctrine itself is accessible to anyone with the normal twelve-year-old's ability to operate on propositions.[45]

This presupposes, of course, that there are propositions to be operated on—that the Christian message does say something *about* something—which amounts to "admitting the possibility and acknowledging the fact that God could and did enter into the division of labor by which men come to know, [and] that his contribution was one that could not be replaced by human effort."[46] The possibility can be ruled out on the ground that the division of labor by which men and women come to know has, in modern times, emptied the world of mystery and freedom, leaving a void that all the technology of enlightened instrumental reason has failed to fill. And, if that were the whole story, human knowing would indeed be the sort of process that nobody would expect to find God contributing to—least of all, contributing himself. But it is not the whole story. If Lonergan is right, it is a cover story, and what it covers up is a history in which position and counterposition, intellectual genuineness and inauthenticity, have long been so intertwined as to make untangling them a massive labor. Simply to cut the knot, by abandoning cognitive meaning to the "real" sciences and setting up shop elsewhere, is to accept on trust a myth that both obscures and at the same time reinforces a principal source of modernity's *malaise:* the hopeless vision of a universe mindlessly grinding along in obedience to iron laws that can be manipulated but never escaped.

How anything like the Incarnation could occur in such a universe, or anything like the Law of the Cross apply to it, is admittedly inconceivable. But if the universe that actually exists is quite different, if it points beyond itself, not despite but because of the fact that its existence is scientifically intelligible, then the possibility of a divine revelation could at least be acknowledged, and from one point of view Lonergan's whole strategy in *Insight* is to allow, if not compel, such an acknowledgment by assembling a view of the universe as intelligible *and* mysterious. His later acknowledgment of the fact that religious conversion normally precedes intellectual conversion does not imply that theology can make do with specifically religious language alone. On the contrary, it is worth emphasizing that virtually all of *Insight*, with the notable exception of chapter 19, is incorporated in *Method's* functional specialty Foundations.[47] Thus if the next functional specialty, Doctrines, affirms as a fact that God has entered the world mediated by meaning, the affirmation will occur in a horizon of intellectual as well as religious authenticity; a horizon, that is, which acknowledges successive higher viewpoints, the complementarity of statistical and classical laws, emergent probability, cycles of progress and decline, and all the rest; in short, a horizon where the whole creation waits with eager longing for the manifestation of the children of God. If the redeemable universe is the intelligible universe as intelligible, and if it is not only redeemable but also redeemed, how could its redemption be either less or otherwise true than its intelligibility?

NOTES

1   T. S. Eliot, *The Idea of a Christian Society* (1940), reprinted in his *Christianity and Culture* (New York: Harcourt Brace Jovanovich, 1968), p. 46.

2   See especially George A. Lindbeck, *The Nature of Doctrine* (Philadelphia: The Westminster Press, 1984), about which I have made some comments in "Turning Liberalism Inside-Out," *Method: Journal of Lonergan Studies* 3, no. 2 (October, 1985), pp. 51–69.

3   Bernard Lonergan, "Foreword," *The Way to Nicea: The Dialectical Development of Trinitarian Theology* (Philadelphia: The Westminster Press, 1976), p. viii. This foreword was written in 1976; the body of the book is a translation by Conn O'Donovan of part one (the *praemittenda* or preliminaries) of *De Deo Trino: Pars dogmatica,* 2nd rev. ed. (Rome: Gregorian University Press, 1964), pp. 17–112.

4   Bernard Lonergan, "Religious Commitment," *The Pilgrim People: A Vision with Hope,* edited by Joseph Papin (Villanova, PA: The Villanova University Press, 1970), p. 68. Much of this essay reappears in *Method's* chapter on "Religion" with only minor changes, one of which is the omission of the parenthesis from the passage I have quoted. See *Method in Theology* (New York: Herder and Herder, 1972), p. 119.

5   *The Way to Nicea,* p. 8.

6   Joseph Stephen O'Leary, "The Hermeneutics of Dogmatism," *Irish Theological Quarterly* 47 (1980), pp. 114; 118, n. 9; 108.

7   Ibid., p. 111.

8   Ibid., p. 103.

9   Ibid., p. 117, n. 7.

10 *The Way to Nicea,* p. 12.

11 "The Dehellenization of Dogma," *A Second Collection,* edited by William F.J. Ryan, S.J. and Bernard J. Tyrrell, S.J. (Philadelphia: The Westminster Press, 1974), p. 15. The author under review is Leslie Dewart.

12 The rather complicated evolution of Lonergan's *De Deo Trino* is outlined in Conn O'Donovan's "Translator's Introduction," *The Way to Nicea,* pp. ix–xvii. For more detailed discussion, see Charles C. Hefling, Jr., "Lonergan on Development: *The Way to Nicea* in Light of His More Recent Methodology" (diss., Boston College-Andover Newton Theological School; Ann Arbor, MI: University Microfilms, no. 8225103).

13 "The Dehellenization of Dogma" (1967), *A Second Collection,* pp. 11–32; "An Interview with Fr. Bernard Lonergan, S.J." (1971), *A Second Collection,* pp. 209–223 (see p. 212); "The Origins of Christian Realism" (1972), *A Second Collection,* pp. 239–261; "Christology Today: Methodological Reflections" (1976), *A Third Collection: Papers by Bernard Lonergan, S.J.,* edited by F.E. Crowe, S.J. (Paramus, N.J.: Paulist Press, 1985), pp. 74–99; see also *Method,* pp. 277, 307, 313.

14 "An Interview with Fr. Bernard Lonergan, S.J." (1971), *A Second Collection,* p. 212; compare *The Way to Nicea,* p. 15.

15 *The Way to Nicea,* p. viii; emphasis added.

16 See *Method,* pp. 312–314.

17 "The Assumption and Theology" (1948), *Collection,* p. 76.

18 "To What Am I Responding in My World?", *The Question as Commitment: A Symposium,* edited by Elaine Cahn and Cathleen Going (Montreal: The Thomas More Institute, 1979), p. 103.

19 See "An Interview with Fr. Bernard Lonergan, S.J.," *A Second Collection,* pp. 211–213; *Philosophy of God, and Theology,* p. 15.

20 See *Method,* p. 270.

21 *De Deo Trino: Pars analytica* (1961), p. 9.

22 *Insight,* p. 572.

23 John Carmody, "The Biblical Foundation and Conclusion of Lonergan's *De Verbo Incarnato,*" *Andover Newton Quarterly* 14 (1974), p. 125.

24 Frederick E. Crowe, *The Lonergan Enterprise* (Cambridge, MA: Cowley Publications, 1980), p. 52.

25 "Theology and Understanding" (1954), *Collection,* p. 127; compare "Christology Today," *A Third Collection,* pp. 79–80.

26 Ibid., p. 130.

27 *De Deo Trino: Pars dogmatica* (1964), p. 114.

28 Ibid., p. 126.

29 "Theology and Understanding," *Collection,* p. 128.

30   Three distinct "ways" appear in the first edition of *Divinarium Personarum conceptio analogica* (1957); see p. 21. See also O'Donovan, "Translator's Introduction," *The Way to Nicea*, pp. xvi–xvii; Crowe, *Lonergan Enterprise*, pp. 19–20.

31   "Theology and Understanding," *Collection*, p. 140.

32   For the sake of what I hope is clarity, I am paraphrasing here. Lonergan actually speaks of a movement from the *prius scripturisticum* to the *prius patristicum*, the *prius* in each case being *quoad nos*. "Commonsense context" seems the closest English substitute. Moreover, here and in the table below I have used "cross-cultural movement" for Lonergan's *motus transculturalis*. "Transcultural," though more literal, would also be misleading, since in *Method* Lonergan uses the word "transcultural" in a rather different way.

33   The third column draws on *De Deo Trino: Pars systematica*, pp. 45–46. The first two columns reproduce Lonergan's enumerations in the epilogue of *Insight*, pp. 739 and 740, with two exceptions. (1) I have amplified the second column, theological hermeneutics, by drawing on the rest of p. 740; these additions, which are not *verbatim*, appear in braces {thus}. (2) In the third item of the second column, Lonergan actually writes "the work of the speculative theologian." But the movement here is *towards* universal expressions, whereas "speculative" theology as Lonergan speaks of it in "Theology and Understanding" (see above) and in the Latin treatises *begins* from these expressions and seeks an understanding of them. For this and other reasons, I am convinced that on p. 740 Lonergan is using "speculative" broadly, in contrast to "practical." There are no other references to speculative *theology* in *Insight*, but see, for this usage, pp. 230, 598, 600, and 697.

34   *Insight*, p. 594; compare pp. xxviii and 748.

35   This, I think, is also the reason why in *Method* Lonergan puts the functional specialty History at the level of factual judgment, whereas Interpretation, which more or less corresponds to the older "positive" theology, is at the level of understanding.

36   *Insight*, p. 740.

37   *Method*, p. 137.

38   I have elaborated this point, as well as some others the present essay has made, in "Redemption and Intellectual Conversion: Notes on Lonergan's 'Christology Today,'" *Lonergan Workshop 5*, edited by Fred Lawrence (Chico, CA: Scholars Press, 1985), pp. 219–261.

39   "Theology and Praxis," *A Third Collection*, p. 198.

40   Relevant here is *Insight's* twenty-seventh clue for identifying the divine solution to the problem of evil. Mystery, in the exact sense that Lonergan defines, is a permanent human need, but if human collaboration is to be intelligent and reasonable, then "the mystery that is the solution . . . must be not fiction but fact, not a story but history" (p. 724).

41   See Schubert M. Ogden's discussion in *Christ Without Myth* (New York: Harper and Brothers, 1961); for Lonergan's quite different use of "demythologization," see *Doctrinal Pluralism* (Milwaukee, WI: Marquette University Press, 1971), pp. 66–71.

42   "The Dehellenization of Dogma," *A Second Collection*, p. 19.

43   *Method*, pp. 278, 307, 319; compare *The Way to Nicea*, pp. 136–137.

44   "The Dehellenization of Dogma," *A Second Collection*, p. 23.

45   Ibid., pp. 23–24.

46   "Belief: Today's Issue," *A Second Collection*, p. 97.

47   See *Method*, pp. 285–288. The two other segments of *Insight* that Lonergan deliberately omits here are chapter 18, "The Possibility of Ethics," which like chapter 19 was added in order to "round off" *Insight* before Lonergan took up his professorial duties in Rome, and the section on belief in chapter 20 (see *Method*, p. 288, n. 15). These are superceded, respectively, by *Method's* chapters on "The Human Good" and "Religion."

XII

Irenaeus' Soteriology:
Transposing the Question

WILLIAM P. LOEWE

I. TRANSPOSING THE QUESTION

THE eminent patrologist Johannes Quasten identified Irenaeus of Lyons as "the founder of Christian theology" because Irenaeus "unmasked Gnosticism as pseudo-Christian" and because, in performing this service, he emerged as "the first author to express in dogmatic terms the whole of Christian doctrine."[1] Although a generation has passed since Quasten proffered this judgement, its basic correctness still stands. One may still agree, three decades later, that Irenaeus' importance rests on the comprehensiveness of his response to the Gnostic threat.

Yet the intervening years have also seen developments that enhance our understanding of the precise character of Irenaeus' response, so that a new articulation of his significance, in terms somewhat different than those employed by Quasten, may be in order. Walter Ong, for example, has been exploring the correlations among communications media, psychological structures, and cultural stages.[2] In the course of his work Ong has stressed the distinction between an oral-narrative mode of thought and the subsequent philosophic, analytic mode that becomes possible once written texts assume a dominant cultural position, while Pheme Perkins has followed up to locate the Gnostics, and, by implication, Irenaeus as well, in the former.[3] Her suggestion sheds no little light on the frustration Irenaeus' allegedly rambling style and inconsistent thinking have occasioned among at least some of his systematically-minded commentators.[4]

The years since Quasten wrote have also of course witnessed a revolution both in Roman Catholic theology generally and particularly with regard to the theological appreciation of the symbolic character of religious discourse and of the mythic amplification of such discourse. Against the background of developments such as these I would propose, as a first presupposition of this paper, that Irenaeus' significance lies first of all in the fact that he responded to the challenge of Gnosticism by forging diverse elements of the Christian tradition into a myth comprehensive enough to match the Gnostic version.[5] What was at stake between Gnosticism and Christianity was, in an oral-narrative culture, the true story about God and humanity. By constructing the Christian story around the notions of divine dispensation, recapitulation, and the Pauline Christ-Adam typology, Irenaeus elaborated a myth which expressed simultaneously the Christian faith and his own creative originality. In a word, Irenaeus met the Gnostic myth with a Christian countermyth, a narrative expression of the role of Jesus in the story of God and God's redemptive dealings with humanity.

This manner of appreciating Irenaeus' significance opens in turn onto new possibilities for the development of Christian soteriology, for it allows one to pose the soteriological question on a new level. On the one hand, if Christian faith prompts one to recognize in Irenaeus' myth the true story of God and humanity, one can go on to ask how Jesus, as a character within the story, effected the salvation of the human race. This is to pose the soteriological question in its classical form. At this level there is little agreement on Irenaeus' soteriology among modern scholars, so that Jean-Pierre Jossua, for example, can state that despite numerous studies on the topic, no final word is in sight.[6]

Much of the difficulty stems, I suspect, from the narrative mode that dominates Irenaeus' thought and from the aesthetic logic by which he can move from image to image in developing a line of argument. Still, a case might nonetheless be mounted that Irenaeus offers partial confirmation of G. Greshake's hypothesis that the key to the unity of Greek patristic soteriology, despite the notorious diversity of that body of literature, lies in the Hellenistic notion of *paideia*.[7] The warrants for such a claim would be two-fold. On the one hand, Irenaeus constructs the full sweep of salvation history as a pedagogical process. On the other, when he arrives at the work of Christ proper, he first transposes to a noetic plane the martial imagery of the *Christus Victor* theme associated with the passion and then integrates the passion itself into a johannine perspective wherein the "lifting up" of the Son of God completes the revelatory mission of the Son begun at the incarnation. By these two moves Irenaeus integrates passion and incarnation within a single noetic soteriology wholly continuous with his pedagogical construction of salvation history. That noetic soteriology forms at least one coherent pattern within his thought on Christ's saving work, though it is still by no means the whole story.[8]

Whatever the merits of the argument just sketched, once the classical form of the soteriological question is recognized as a question about Jesus as a figure within a myth, a new form of the question becomes possible. Rather than inquiring into the soteriology within the story, one may seek to determine what we may call the soteriology beyond the story. This line of inquiry has been framed in various ways of late. David Tracy has commended a hermeneutic that points us to the world or mode of being "in front of" a text.[9] John Shea has elaborated an "intentional" as opposed to an "interventionist" style of interpreting religious texts.[10] Matthew Lamb calls for a "reflectively dialectical orthopraxis."[11]

Irenaeus may indeed express, as Quasten had it, "the whole of Christian doctrine," but he hardly does so "in dogmatic terms"; his mode of expression is first of all symbolic and narrative, that is, mythic. This does not mean, however, that Quasten was necessarily off the mark. Bernard Lonergan would have us recognize in doctrine the expression of the meanings and values that inform Christian praxis, meanings and values the validity of which is patent to faith when faith is conceived as the eyes of love, as the cognitive dimension of the gift of religious conversion.[12]

Lonergan's insight suggests that we may pose the soteriological question as follows. What values are mediated by acceptance of Irenaeus' myth as the true story of God and humanity? What commitments shape the world in which his story invites us to dwell? That is, how does acceptance in faith render Irenaeus' story of salvation a saving story? It is this transposed form of the soteriological question that the present essay seeks to address.

II. IRENAEUS' HERMENEUTICAL FOUNDATIONS

If, as we have suggested, Irenaeus' significance derives first of all from the imaginative power which enabled him to draw his diverse scriptural and traditional sources into a single, comprehensive myth, we may begin by seeking to determine the base or hermeneutical stance that generated the horizon within which he operated. Contemporary hermeneutical theory rightly cautions against any psychologizing attempt to reconstruct an author's interiority. It does, however, allow one to seek in a work clues to the posture implied by the text on the part of its author.

One point of entry to Irenaeus' stance can be won from the single concern that animates the response he directs to both Gnostics and Marcionites. The former reduced the creator God of the Old Testament to an inferior, ignorant, and deluded Demiurge, while at Marcion's hands he became a principle of law and vengeful wrath who stood in opposition to the loving God revealed by Jesus. On each front Irenaeus encountered the same challenge, to secure the identity of God, the Father of Jesus Christ, with God of the Old Testament.

To meet this end Irenaeus marshalls a thoroughly christological reading of the Old Testament. Arguing that the same Word who became incarnate in Christ was present as the Father's instrument at creation and throughout the history of Israel, he assembles a panoply of events and citations which, he would have it, foreshadow and predict in detail various aspects of the future career of the Word incarnate. So ample does Irenaeus find this Old Testament witness to Christ that he can assert that to those steeped in it, like the God-fearer Cornelius whose household Peter baptized (III, 12/7) or the Ethiopean eunuch whom Philip converted (IV,23/2), only one thing was lacking which they did not already possess, knowledge of the incarnate Word himself.

Yet Irenaeus is not naive about his argument from prophecy. Its witness may be abundant, but it is also, he recognizes, of itself quite ambiguous. Each of the patriarchs and prophets may have been granted a vision of some aspect or other of the dispensation of Christ's coming in the flesh (IV,33/10), but the convergence of those fragments upon the historical figure of Christ only becomes clear with hindsight, after the event. Generalizing, Irenaeus can liken the presence of Christ in the Old Testament to a treasure hidden in a field (IV,20/1). Only a Christian reading can locate the treasure and, he adds, it is specifically the cross of Christ which brings the treasure to light.

But how are these assertions to be understood? How, specifically, is the cross related to a Christian, and indeed to Irenaeus' own, understanding of scripture? At this point in our inquiry the soteriological pattern to which we referred earlier assumes relevance. From time to time in his work Irenaeus adopts a johannine perspective on the cross as the "lifting up" of the Son of God. Only the Son knows the things of the Father, and he became incarnate in order to share that knowledge with human beings (V,1/1). On the cross the revelatory function which defines his mission reaches climactic fulfillment. Lifted on high, the Son now draws all human beings to himself. In that action the sovereignty which, as Word, he has always exercised invisibly in the cosmological sphere becomes effective in history as well. Constituted head of the Church, the Son rules by pouring forth the Spirit (III,16/6).

The Spirit in turn enables those men and women who receive him to recognize Jesus as God's Word and Son and moves them to follow Jesus as the revealer of the Father. The revelatory knowledge thus imparted is first of all transformative and practical. Becoming a follower of the Word entails a great change in one's manner of life (III,5/2). One comes to imitate the deeds of Jesus and to perform what he enjoined (V,1/1); through this praxis of discipleship one acquires the knowledge of the Father and of the divine dispensation, of what the Father intended in creating, which it was the Son's mission to communicate.

Irenaeus explicates the transformative character of Christian praxis through a rich cluster of images. By this praxis one is drawn into communion with the Son, and, under the action of the Spirit, is reestablished in the Son's image and likeness. Thus conformed to the eternal Word, men and women receive adoptive sonship. Through the pledge of the Spirit (V,8/1) they are brought to maturity, readied for the future gifts of immortality and incorruptibility, for the fullness of life in possession of the Spirit which is the Father's final will for them.[13]

Irenaeus looks back on the cross as the source of the transforming empowerment experienced in the praxis of discipleship. The cross completes the revelatory career of the Word incarnate and marks his establishment in sovereignty as head of the church and source of the Spirit. It is in this manner that the cross also supplies Irenaeus with the key to his Christian reading of the scriptures. From within the Christian community, illumined by the Spirit of the Father's love, it becomes clear that God's Word has been active since creation, preparing humanity for his coming in the flesh. The Lord's "lifting up" brings to light the unity of the two Testaments as the story of the single divine dispensation, unfolding in good order, by which God has been guiding humanity to its goal. Thus it is the light proceeding from the cross and received in the praxis of discipleship which illumines Irenaeus' imagination as he weaves his various sources into the narrative of the single dispensation of the one God.

Irenaeus' text points to the praxis of Christian discipleship as the foundational hermeneutical base from which he operates. If this is correct, we may proceed to inquire into how Irenaeus' text thematizes the commitments which govern that praxis and which shape as well the world in which his story invites its reader to dwell. What values does Irenaeus' work seek to mediate?

As we approach this question we may anticipate that the results of our inquiry may be unstartlingly familiar. We have already noted J. Quasten's discovery in Irenaeus of a comprehensive statement of Christian doctrine, and we have noted as well how B. Lonergan alerts us to the character of doctrines as the expression, in one or another of the stages of meaning that Lonergan distinguishes, of the judgments of fact and value which inform a way of living. Hence we may anticipate from Irenaeus an expression of the values central to Christian praxis then and now, while the manner of their expression will bear the joint determination of the stage of meaning dominant in Irenaeus' day and the particular concerns which exercised him.

III. VALUE AND THE EYES OF LOVE

"Gloria hominis Deus" (III,20/2). At the outset of his work Irenaeus voices his primary complaint against the Gnostics, that "they also overthrow the faith of many, by drawing them away, under a pretense of (superior) knowledge, from Him who founded and adorned the universe. . ." (I,Pref.,1).[14] Like the serpent in the garden, Irenaeus' adversaries ". . . lead away captive from the truth those who do not retain a stedfast (sic) faith in one God, the Father Almighty, and in one Lord Jesus Christ, the Son of God" (I,3/6). Against them he urges his reader to retain. ". . . unchangeable in his heart the rule of truth which he received at baptism" (I,9/4), according to which rule ". . . there is one God Almighty, who made all things by His Word, and fashioned and formed, out of that which had no existence, all things which exist" (I,22/1).

If the Gnostics ". . . disregard the order and the connection of the Scriptures, and so far as in them lies, dismember and destroy the truth . . ." (I,8/1), the Marcionites likewise ". . . destroy multitudes, wickedly disseminating their own doctrines by the use of a good name (i.e., Christ Jesus), and through means of its beauty and sweetness, extending to their hearers the bitter and malignant poison of the serpent, the great author of apostasy" (I,27/4). In the face of the dual challenge posed by both Gnostics and Marcionites, Irenaeus finds that "it is proper, then, that I should begin with the first and most important head, that is, God the Creator . . ."(II,1/1).

The controversy over the identity of God is for Irenaeus no merely cognitive affair, no abstrusely speculative issue. By nature, he asserts, we belong to God (V,1/1). Obedience to God renders our living authentically human (IV,39/1), and we experience the fullness of authentic human living when we love God with our whole hearts (II,26/1). "It is not possible to live apart from life, and the means of life is found in fellowship with God . . " (IV,20/5). Because "the glory of man is God" (III,20/2), what is at stake in Irenaeus' debate with his opponents is the wholly practical issue of success or failure in human existence. The transcendent God, creator of the universe and of humanity, is the primary and central value in the world of Irenaeus' narrative.

His opponents impose a dual task. With the Gnostics, Irenaeus must affirm the utter transcendence of God, and yet he must also exhibit God, in contrast to their remote, indifferent ultimate principle, as source of a creation over which he has unfailing care. With Marcion Irenaeus must give full weight to the extravagant love and mercy of God, and yet he must also show that for God to be God, he must also be just, a God who respects his creatures sufficiently to hold them accountable for their free decisions. Let us note briefly how Irenaeus carries out this programme.

Behind the Gnostic refusal to identify the true God with the creator of the universe Irenaeus detects a positive motive: ". . . they deny that He Himself made the world, to guard against attributing want of power to Him . . ." (II,13/3). How do the Gnostics come to err? Ironically, Irenaeus charges them with failing to pay due honor to what ostensibly they most cherish, the divine transcendence. This failure, in turn, stems in part from an inability to recognize the limits of the imagination. The Gnostics refuse to attribute creation to God because they ". . . liken Him to needy human beings, and to those who cannot immediately, and without assistance form anything, but require many intermediaries to produce what they intend" (II,2/4). But in his transcendence God remains, even as creator, beyond the grasp of the human imagination: "But He Himself in Himself, after a fashion which we can neither describe nor conceive, predestinating all things, formed them as He pleased . . ." (Ibid). Far from compromising the divine transcendence, the act of creating serves to demonstrate it: "While men, indeed, cannot make anything out of nothing, but only out of matter already existing, yet God is in this point preeminently superior to men, that He Himself called into existence the substance of His creation, when previously it has no existence" (II,10/4).

Contrary to what the Gnostics imagine, creating out of nothing betokens no dependence of God on intermediary agents. Nor does it imply any dependence of God on what he has created. "For God needs none of these things" (I,22/1) runs as a constant refrain throughout Irenaeus' work, whether it be a matter of the whole of creation (loc. cit.), Abraham's friendship (IV,13/4), Israel's love (IV,16/4), or the offering of sacrifice (IV,18/4). Irenaeus dwells on this theme at some length in Book IV,14/1:

> In the beginning, therefore, did God form Adam, not as if He stood in need of
> man, but that He might have (some one) upon whom to confer His benefits. For not
> alone antecedently to Adam, but also before all creation, the Word glorified His Father,
> remaining in Him; and was Himself glorified by the Father, as He did Himself declare:
> "Father, glorify Thou Me with the glory which I had with Thee before the world
> was." Nor did He stand in need of our service when He ordered us to follow Him, but
> He thus bestowed salvation upon ourselves. For to follow the Saviour is to be a partaker
> of salvation, and to follow light is to receive light. But those who are in light do not
> themselves illumine the light, but are illumined and revealed by it: they do certainly
> contribute nothing to it, but, receiving the benefit, they are illumined by the light. Thus
> also, service (rendered) to God does indeed profit God nothing, nor has God need of
> human obedience; but He grants to those who follow and serve Him life and
> incorruption and eternal glory, bestowing benefit upon those who serve (Him), because
> they do serve Him, and upon his followers; but does not receive any benefit from them:
> for He is rich, perfect, and in need of nothing.

Creation in no way compromises the divine transcendence. The unimaginable act of creating from nothing implies no dependence on intermediary instruments. Creatures exist to receive God's benefits, while the Triune God remains *"nullius indigens, sibi sufficiens"* (III,8/3). Creation witnesses, not to the creator's poverty, but to an unfathomable mystery of superabundant generosity. But if God remains thus transcendent, what sort of knowledge of him is possible to his creatures?

Irenaeus affirms that the knowledge of God as creator is a universal possibility. God is thus known to the angels, on account of his providence (II,6/1). The ancients possessed a tradition originating with Adam, of which the prophets reminded Israel, while the heathen learn of God from creation itself, and the church from the tradition of the apostles (II,9/2). Irenaeus regards this revelation of God's existence through creation, to both angels and human beings (II,30/9), as the work of God's Word (IV,6/6). As such, however, it forms but a preliminary stage in the unfolding of the single divine dispensation to be effected through the Word.

Through creation God "has come within reach of human knowledge" as creator, wise, powerful, and good (III,24/2), but only with the coming of the Word in the flesh is God manifest as Son and Father (IV,6/3). As creator God bestowed a "faculty of increase" on human beings (II,28/1), and that faculty reaches its term when "the Lord renders his disciples perfect by their seeking after and finding the Father" (II,18/3). God created human beings for "the greater glory of promotion," and that end comes into reach with the coming of "the Word of God who dwelt in man, and became the son of Man, that He might accustom man to receive God, and God to dwell in man, according to the good pleasure of the Father" (II,20/2).

For Irenaeus knowledge of God is imparted in stages through the revelatory activity of the Word, beginning with creation and culminating in the exaltation of the Son on the cross. In none of this, however, is the divine transcendence compromised. Though the angels know God as creator and ruler, he remains "invisible to them on account of his superiority" (II,6/1). Human knowledge never grasps the "greatness or essence" of God (III,24/2), but what the Word does communicate, in an orderly fashion and at the proper time, is the love of the ever-transcendent mystery.

> And for this reason did the Word become the dispenser of the paternal grace for the benefit of men, for whom He made such great dispensations, revealing God indeed to men, but presenting man to God, and preserving at the same time the invisibility of the Father, lest man should at any time become a despiser of God, and that he might always possess something towards which he might advance . . . (IV,20/7).

"Gloria Dei vivens homo" (IV,20/7). Thus far Irenaeus' narrative of a single divine dispensation—beginning with creation, advancing through patriarchs and prophets, and culminating with Christ's exaltation on the cross—has yielded a central value. Irenaeus' world is grounded in the reality of a God who remains ever-transcendent and yet is known in love through the praxis of Christian discipleship as the "father of all who follow the Word of God" (IV,25/1). Within Irenaeus' narrative, however, besides communicating knowl-

edge of God as Father, the revelatory mission of the incarnate Word has a second focus as well:

> For in times long past, it was *said* that man was created after the image of God, but it was not (actually) *shown;* for the Word was as yet invisible, after whose image man was created. Wherefore did he also easily lose the similitude (V,16/2).

Christ's coming reveals, not only God, but also the full dignity of the human person.

Once again Irenaeus' adversaries serve to bring various dimensions of this value into focus. Let us begin with human bodiliness. Irenaeus' summary of the Gnostic tale of the fall of Sophia affords a glimpse of the existential and psychological origins of the dualism which Gnostics erected between matter and spirit. Concluding his version of the tale Irenaeus notes, ". . . and hence they declare that material substance had its beginning from ignorance and grief, and fear and bewilderment" (I,2/3). His remark lends weight to Hans Jonas' classic interpretation of Gnosticism as a response to an experience of alienation,[15] and it sheds further light on the Gnostic refusal to identify the true God with the creator of the world. Overwhelmed by the pathos of material existence, the Gnostics thought to shield God from responsibility for such misery.

This glimpse of the Gnostic experience is, however, strictly accidental. Irenaeus' work offers no hint that its author shares the pathos from which the Gnostics speak. On the contrary, he delights in extolling the wisdom and diligence of God manifest in material creation. Since God created, the result ". . . must be worthy of the Father" (II,2/3). Therefore Irenaeus affirms the value of precisely those aspects which most distressed the Gnostics. God created the world ". . . according to the conception of his mind, such as it now is, compound, mutable, and transient" (Ibid.). To those who fail to perceive the harmonious order which manifests God's wisdom, Irenaeus recommends an aesthetic analogy. Created things, ". . . when viewed individually, are mutually opposite and inharmonious, just as the sound of the lyre, which consists of many and opposite notes, gives rise to one unbroken melody . . ." (II,25/2).

This theologically grounded vision of the goodness of material creation comes to bear when Irenaeus affirms the integrity of the human person:

> For that flesh which has been moulded is not a perfect man in itself, but the body of a man and a part of a man. Neither is the soul itself, considered apart from itself, the man; but it is the soul of a man, and a part of a man. Neither is the spirit a man, for it is called the spirit and not, a man; but the commingling and union of all these constitutes the perfect man (V,6/1).

Bodiliness is integral to being human, and it is good. Not only is the flesh God's handiwork (IV,Pref./4), the product of divine skill (II, 33/5), but precisely in their bodiliness men and women exhibit the image of God, that is, for Irenaeus, the image of the Word in his incarnate state. Hence, he argues further, the fullness of redemption will embrace the entire person, including the dimension of corporeality; why else would the Word have become incarnate (V,14/2) and why else would he nourish us with his flesh and blood in the Eucharist (IV,18/2-3)?

From Irenaeus we receive perhaps the last unambiguous witness to the goodness of human corporeality before the wave of Platonic revival decisively engaged Christian thought on a new path.[14] In like manner he affirms as well the positive character of human temporality. God ". . . made the things of time for man, so that, coming to maturity in them, he might produce the fruit of immortality . . ." (IV,5/1). Temporality follows from the status of human beings as creatures:

> And in this respect God differs from man, that God indeed makes, but man is made; and truly, He who makes is always the same; but that which is made must receive both beginning, and middle, and addition, and increase . . . man receives increase and advancement towards God. For as God is always the same, so also man, when found in God, shall always go on towards God (IV,11/2; see also IV,38/3).

In creating human beings God ". . . bestowed the faculty of increase on His own creation" (II,28/1). In God's wisdom time provides the medium for the human race to reach maturity according to the dispensation which God has willed for it.

Contrary to the Gnostics Irenaeus refuses to regard either human bodiliness or temporality as defects. Both derive from the wisdom of the creator, and hence they are good. Because "God is superior to nature" (II,29/2), and because ". . . life does not arise from us, not from our own nature, but it is bestowed according to the grace of God" (II,34/3), even human bodiliness is destined to share in final salvation. The path to salvation lies, not along some escape route from the realm of time, but precisely through human temporality, according to the well-ordered divine dispensation. Even in the state of immortality God will remain transcendent, so that even then human advance towards God will be an unending process.

On the basis of their dualism of matter and spirit the Gnostics distinguished three classes of human being. Spiritual persons were destined by nature to escape this world and find bliss in the realm of the divine, while material persons could entertain no hope for salvation. Between these lay the animal class, whose destiny depended on their works (I,6/1-4). Irenaeus counters with the tripartite anthropology we have already cited: spirit, matter, and soul designate, not three classes of human beings, but the components of the perfect individual.

Even though he prizes human bodiliness as bearing the image of God, Irenaeus envisages human corporeality as subordinate within the person to a more crucial dimension, the soul. Indeed, in an occasional passage he seems to identify the powers of the soul, rationality and free will, with the likeness of God of Genesis 1.26 (IV,4/3). This is not, however, his usual line of thought.[17] By nature the human being is composed of body and soul, but when to these Irenaeus adds his third element, spirit, he renders his conception of the human dynamic and historical. God is superior to nature, including human nature, and that superiority comes into play when the divine dispensation orders human beings to a final destiny in which, promoted beyond the limits their nature would impose, they become like

God, immortal and incorruptible. The achievement of that likeness is, for Irenaeus, the special task of the Holy Spirit, and hence he posits, as his third element in the complete or perfect human being, the gift of spirit.

From the perspective of this theologically transformed anthropology the issue raised by both Gnostics and Marcionites comes into clear focus. The former claim for themselves the natural salvation of an elite, while the latter implicitly deny human responsibility by denying to the God of Jesus a judicial function. On both fronts Irenaeus is challenged to defend his understanding of a divine dispensation which has placed the choice of eternal life, the completion of authentically human living animated by the love of God, in the hands of human freedom.

Irenaeus' perspective leaves no neutral ground upon which human freedom may stand. To be merely human, to be body and soul but without the spirit, is to be less than human (V,6/1). This is no remote, speculative possibility. Irenaeus may, in his account of the fall, shift the onus of responsibility onto Satan, excusing Adam for his youthful guilelessness (III,23/5–7), but this in no way mitigates his portrayal of the effects of the fall. In Adam the likeness of God was lost (III,18/1), the human race fell under the power of sin, and salvation became impossible (III,18/2). God permitted the race ". . . to be swallowed up by the great whale, who was the author of transgression . . ." (III,20/1).

In the concrete order human freedom has become impotent. The minds of human beings have been seduced and their hearts darkened, so that they have forgotten the God in whom their fulfillment lies (V,24/3). To the extent that this situation obtains, history has become a reign of sin.

Yet history offers another possibility as well. God remains God, faithful to his creation, not coercing it but ever offering it his counsel (V, 1/1). To counter the cumulative weight of perverted human praxis, God has provided the discipline of the Mosaic law and raised up the voice of prophetic denunciation. And in Christ God has introduced into history a human freedom set free, an actualization of freedom in unreserved love of the Father powerful enough in the Spirit to recall the minds and hearts of the race to its destiny. Irenaeus finds in the incarnate Word God's most eloquent witness to the dignity of human freedom, insofar as Christ's human freedom becomes the means for reversing the effects of Adam's disobedience (III,18/7) and subjecting Satan to humankind (III,23/7).

The narrative matrix of Irenaeus' thought imposes a logic of linear temporality according to which the possibilities of human freedom move from the fall through the Mosaic law to Christ. His work nonetheless offers abundant indications that each stage of the narrative perdures as a continuing possibility in the present. Christ may have conquered Satan, but Irenaeus conceives his adversaries as actualizing again the role of the serpent in the garden (I,3/6; 27/4). In Christ God may have brought the human race to maturity, but that maturity exists as a gift which can always be refused. Flesh and blood cannot possess the kingdom of God without the Spirit of God (V,9/3), but in response to the offer of the Spirit's illumination, "each person (has) a choice of his own, and a free understanding" (V, 27/1).

In his response to Marcion Irenaeus argues that the exercise of judicial power is required precisely by God's goodness (III,23/2–3), but at the same time he thoroughly demythologizes the notion of divine punishment, heightening again the decisive role he attributes to human freedom. If some are excluded from bliss at the final judgment, God "... shall righteously shut out into the darkness which they have chosen for themselves, those who do not believe, and who do consequently avoid His light" (III,6/1). The same dynamic operated in the history of Israel, for "when they turned themselves to make a calf, and had gone back in their minds to Egypt, desiring to be slaves rather than freemen, they were placed for the future in a state of servitude suited to their wish" (IV,15/1). The Marcionites allege that the God of the Old Testament perversely hardened Pharaoh's heart, but, explains Irenaeus, God acted "just as the sun . . . (acts with regard) to those who, by reason of any weakness of their eyes, cannot behold his light" (IV,29/1). He applies the same analogy once more to the damned (IV,39/4) and to Satan (V,26/2). In each case, "God, however, does not punish them immediately of Himself, but their punishment falls upon them because they are destitute of all that is good" (V,27/2).

Bodiliness and temporality provide the arena for the self-disposition of human freedom. As God's creature the human being owes God obedience, but this demand is not, for Irenaeus, an extrinsic imposition. Obedience to God coincides with fidelity to the demands of one's nature, the precepts of which are "implanted in mankind" (IV,15/1). The violation of these precepts renders one, not autonomous, but a slave. Because human beings have in fact chosen servitude, God revealed the Decalogue to remind them of the path along which their true humanity lay, while the prophets proclaimed the requirements of justice among human beings as the key to obeying the will of god (IV,17/1–4).

None of this did Christ abrogate (IV,13/1); what he did reveal was the secret of the divine dispensation whereby the praxis of love of God in deeds of justice among human beings is the seed, pledge, and foretaste of a communion with God which will have no end. The fulfillment of our humanity lies beyond being merely human in the transformation of human beings into the likeness of God.

IV. FURTHER QUESTIONS

At this point of our inquiry we have uncovered a central core of values which generate the world of Irenaeus' narrative. That world is founded on the reality of God as the ever-transcendent mystery who is known in love through the praxis of Christian discipleship as Father by those who, through the impulse of the Spirit, are being conformed to His Word and Son. The reality of God in turn grounds the value of human beings called, in their bodiliness, temporality, and freedom, to the works of justice through which the Spirit of God's love transforms them into the likeness of God. Hence, because his work brings to expression the dialogue of divine love and human freedom which constitute history as a story of sin and redemption, we can agree with Quasten's judgment that Irenaeus expresses "the whole of Christian doctrine."

Irenaeus expresses this central core of values explicitly and quite self-consciously, in response to their contestation by his adversaries. Beyond these consciously known values, however, Matthew Lamb would direct our inquiry to others, operative in Irenaeus' work even if not explicitly thematized. Taking his cue from Lonergan's penetration to the dialectic of intellectual values leading to the Council of Nicea, Lamb suggests an inquiry aimed at "articulating the dialectic of values and disvalues unknown but consciously operative in scriptural and doctrinal orthodoxies."[18] Such a project would complement the theological-anthropological method employed in the present essay with social-critical analysis of the clash between Irenaeus and his adversaries.[19] Among the relevant data would be Irenaeus' allusions to the transformative effect of the Gospel among the barbarian tribes, underscoring peace as a value intrinsic to Christian praxis (e.g., IV,39/4), and his incidental comments on the Roman empire.

Second, both theological-anthropological and social-critical approaches to Irenaeus' work demand, as one moment in their performance, the exercise of an hermeneutic of suspicion. We have argued that Irenaeus' foundations lie in the praxis of Christian disciple-ship, but Bernard Lonergan warns us that religious conversion is always both precarious and dialectical,[20] while David Tracy would have us advert to the inadequacy and even ambiguity of any religious classic.[21] Hence we may anticipate from Irenaeus' work the mediation not only of value but of disvalue as well.

Thus, for example, because he is immersed in an oral-narrative stage of culture, Irenaeus lacks critical purchase on the logic of temporal advance which structures his story, and this lack wins him a place in the trajectory of Christian anti-Semitism. He assumes that Judaism is superseded and obsolete (IV,4/1), repeats the New Testament caricatures of the Pharisees (IV,2/6), and unhesitatingly attributes to the Jews as a group the slaying of their Lord (III,2/6). For Irenaeus the Jews are a people whose "hands are full of blood" (IV,18/4).

Similarly, one notices a casual remark on the Gnostic tale of Sophia. "Her passion, as they declare, gave origin to a female offspring, weak, inferior, unformed, and ineffective" (II,20/3). Does this betray a partiarchal, even misogynist, bias in Irenaeus? The question is worthy of further investigation.

We may conclude with one final indication of the sort of further work which seems in order. In a recent interpretation of the Nag Hammadi literature, Elaine Pagels has drawn attention to the socialpolitical import of the points contested between Gnostics and Christian orthodoxy.[22] She shows, for example, how belief in one God served to legitimize the authority of the monarchic bishop, while insistence on the bodily character of the resur-rection of Christ found a correlate in an apostolic succession of ecclesial officers. Pagels recognizes, though with less than whole-hearted enthusiasm, the sociological and historical efficacy of such ecclesial developments, but something more than pragmatism is called for; the criteria for evaluating the institutional commitments operative in Irenaeus' work require further elaboration and debate. In this manner Pagels' findings can be seen to constitute a first step toward the dialectic of social-critical interpretations suggested by M. Lamb.

NOTES

1 J. Quasten, *Patrology*, Vol. 1 (Utrecht: Spectrum, 1950), p. 294.

2 See W. Ong, *Orality and Literacy: The Technologizing of the Word*, (New York: Methuen, 1982).

3 P. Perkins, *The Gnostic Dialogue: The Early Church and the Crisis of Gnosticism,* (New York: Paulist, 1980), p. 9.

4 See, for example, J. Hochban, "St. Irenaeus and the Atonement," *Theological Studies* 7 (1946), pp. 525-557.

5 For a development of this argument, see W. Loewe, "Myth and Counter-Myth: Irenaeus' Story of Salvation," in J. Kopas, ed., *Interpreting Tradition: The Art of Theological Interpretation* (Chico, CA: Scholars Press, 1984), pp. 39-54.

6 See J. P. Jossua, *Le Salut: incarnation ou mystère pascale,* (Paris: Cerf, 1969), pp. 45-46.

7 G. Greshake, "Der Wandel der Erlösungsvorstellungen in der Theologiegeschichte," in L. Scheffczyk, ed., *Erlösung und Emanzipation. Quaestiones Disputatae 61* (Freiburg: Herder, 1978), pp. 71-82.

8 The textual evidence for this hypothesis may be found in W. Loewe, "*Christus Victor* Revisited: Irenaeus' Soteriology," *Anglican Theological Review* XLVII/1 (1985), pp. 1-15.

9 D. Tracy, *Blessed Rage for Order* (New York: Seabury, 1975), pp. 72-79, 120-145, 204-236.

10 J. Shea, *Stories of God,* (Chicago: Thomas More, 1978) pp. 88-116.

11 M. Lamb, *Solidarity With Victims* (New York: Crossroad, 1982), pp. 134-142.

12 B. Lonergan, *Method in Theology* (New York: Herder and Herder, 1972), pp. 115-120, 295-335.

13 Because of the correlation in Irenaeus' work between ontological and religious-existential categories, it is wrong to interpret him as representative of a "physical" theory of redemption.

14 All citations will be taken from the English translation of the *Adversus Haereses* in Volume 1 of A. Roberts and J. Donaldson, eds., *The Ante-Nicene Fathers* (Grand Rapids: Eerdmanns, 1979). Now that *Sources Chrétiennes* has completed the critical text, a new English version of the work is to be expected.

15 H. Jonas, *The Gnostic Religion* (Boston: Beacon, 1963).

16 Thus, in a passage like Book III,22/2, Irenaeus can insist on precisely those features of Christ's human experience portrayed in the Gospels—hunger, sorrow, weariness, etc.—which proved an embarrassment to the Alexandrians and indeed to the subsequent tradition up to the retrieval of the humanity of Jesus represented by exegetical work like R. Brown's *Jesus, God and Man* (New York: Macmillan, 1967).

17 On Irenaeus' understanding of "the likeness of God," see A. Orbe, *Antropologia de San Ireneo* (Madrid: Biblioteca de autores cristianos, 1969), pp. 118-148.

18 Lamb, *op. cit.,* p. 140.

19 On the Gnostics, this shift may be exemplified by comparing the classic work of H. Jonas with Kurt Rudolph's more recent *Gnosis: The Nature and History of Gnosticism* (ET San Francisco: Harper and Row, 1983).

20 Lonergan, *op. cit.,* pp. 110 ff.

21 D. Tracy, *The Analogical Imagination* (New York: Crossroad, 1981), pp. 167-192.

22 E. Pagels, *The Gnostic Gospels* (New York: Random House, 1979).

XIII

Typologies and the Cross-Cultural Analysis of Mysticism: A Critique

JAMES PRICE

SINCE the appearance of Rudolph Otto's *Mysticism East and West* more than fifty years ago, the use of typologies has dominated the cross-cultural analysis of mysticism.[1] When employed by sensitive interpreters such as Otto and (more recently) Ninian Smart,[2] the approach is very useful for organizing a vast body of complex data and for bringing a spirit of openness and tolerance to interreligious dialogue. This said, it is nevertheless my conviction that the typological approach is fundamentally inadequate to the cross-cultural analysis of mysticism. It is therefore also inadequate as a basis for interreligious dialogue.

In this essay I will contend that the typological approach is inadequate for the simple reason that it is insufficiently precise and that it leads to mistaken conclusions. The inadequacy is inherent in the typological approach itself and is not ascribable to the relative skills of a particular analyst. I will also contend that Bernard Lonergan's methodological turn to the horizon of interiority, while preserving the advantages of a typological approach, provides a more adequate basis for the cross-cultural analysis of mysticism and hence for interreligious dialogue.[3]

I. THE TYPOLOGICAL APPROACH TO MYSTICISM

Max Weber initiated the typological approach to the study of culture, but credit must go to Rudolf Otto for its decisive entry into the analysis of mysticism.[4] On the one hand,

Otto distinguished two basic types of religious experience, the numinous and the mystical.[5] On the other, he distinguished two basic types of mysticism, the introspection of soul mysticism and the unifying vision of God-mysticism.[6] These typological distinctions, despite changes in terminology introduced by subsequent analysts, remain basic to the field to this day.[7]

Like all heuristic structures, a typology provides categories of analysis which facilitate the organization and interpretation of a relevant body of data. To borrow Lonergan's image, it functions like the upper blade of a scissors closing along the lower blade of the data.[8] My intention is to assess the adequacy of this upper blade, but to do so it is necessary to sketch its principal analytical components.

Beginning with Otto, two basic analytical categories are discernible in all the typologies of mysticism. The first is a distinction between inner and outer. This is the basis, for instance, of Otto's distinction between the mystical and the numinous. The numinous is an experience of the holy; an encounter with a being wholly other than oneself and unlike anything else. It has the outer, thunderous quality reported in the experiences of the prophets. In contrast, mystical experience is an inner attainment exemplified by certain transcendent states of consciousness.

Employing the same distinction between inner and outer, Otto also distinguished two basic types of mystical experience. Mysticism as introspection (exemplified by Sankara) is characterized as a "withdrawal from all outward things, [a] retreat into the ground of one's own soul."[9] In contrast, mysticism as unifying vision (exemplified by Eckhart) "knows nothing of inwardness."[10] In this vision, the multiplicity of the world is transcended in an intuition of the fundamental unity, not simply of the world, but of the transcendent One itself.[11]

The second analytical category concerns the nature of the mystical data itself. This involves two related assumptions, both often more implicit than explicit. The first is the assumption that the relevant mystical data is to be understood in some fashion as the object or content of consciousness. That is to say, the typological approach assumes that mystical data consists of accounts which report "experiences of . . ." [something]. This is the case even when it is noted, as it regularly is, that mystical awareness transcends discursive consciousness. The contention is that the content or object of mystical consciousness is grasped not through reason or discursive analysis, but through "intuition."[10]

The second and related assumption is that the doctrinal and metaphysical language used by the mystics provides the basic terms for understanding and analyzing the content of mystical experience. Given that mystical experience is "experience of," a question arises concerning the relation of the doctrinal and metaphysical language used by the mystics to the object of their experience. In answer, two basic positions have emerged.

The first position, variously referred to as the primordial tradition or the perennial philosophy, argues that the common elements of doctrinal and metaphysical language (such as claims for the experience of unity or oneness) point to a "common core" of mystical experience which is culturally invariant. Doctrinal and metaphysical differences are regarded as unimportant, ascribable to the unavoidable influences of differing cultures upon mystics faced with the task of describing and interpreting their mystical experiences. The point, then, is that certain elements of doctrinal language provide the basic terms for understanding and analyzing the content of mystical experience.

A second position has recently emerged to challenge the first, in particular its assumption that doctrines function simply as *post-facto* interpretations of prior, unmediated mystical experiences. For the second position, there are no unmediated mystical experiences. Rather, the doctrinal and metaphysical language of a particular tradition is operative in various ways prior to a mystic's experience and functions to mediate and shape the experience itself. For this position, then, doctrinal and metaphysical differences are of major importance. They are the basis for denying a "common core" to mystical experience, and for asserting instead a plurality of experiences. Thus, for the second position as for the first, doctrinal and metaphysical language is taken as basic for an understanding of the content of mystical experience.

The point I wish to emphasize in this regard is that despite fundamental differences between the two positions—in analytical claims as well as in epistemological assumptions—both positions assume that the doctrinal and metaphysical language used by the mystics provides the basic terms for understanding and analyzing the content of mystical experience. The analytical significance of this assumption will become clear in the subsequent presentation of Lonergan's position. First, however, it is important to assess the adequacy of the upper blade I have just described.

II. The Typological Model: An Illustration and Assessment

If the typological approach to the cross-cultural analysis of mysticism is to be assessed with any specificity, it seems to me necessary to allow its upper blade to slice along the lower blade of mystical data. Following, therefore, are two brief accounts of mystical experience. The first is an example from the Hindu tradition, *The Spiritual Teachings of Ramana Maharshi,* and the second an example from the Christian tradition, *The Cloud of Unknowing.* A full analysis of these texts is not appropriate here, but they will provide a focus for questions and a means for comparing the typological approach with Lonergan's turn to interiority.

(1)

Who am I? The gross body . . . I am not; the five senses . . . I am not; . . . even the mind which thinks, I am not . . . That Awareness which alone remains—that I [the Self] am.

What exists in truth is the Self alone. The world, the individual soul, and God are appearances in it, like silver in mother-of-pearl; these three appear at the same time, and disappear at the same time.

The Self is that where there is absolutely no "I" thought. That is called "Silence." The Self itself is the world; the Self itself is "I"; the Self itself is God; all is Siva, the Self."[13]

(2)

Take care in this exercise and do not labour with your senses or with your imagination in any way at all. For I tell you truly, this exercise cannot be achieved by their labour; so leave them and do not work with them.

You must destroy all knowing and feeling of every kind of creature, but most especially of
yourself. For on the knowledge and experience of yourself depends the knowledge and
experience of all other creatures.
But whenever you are aware that your mind is occupied with no created thing, whether
material or spiritual, . . . then you are above yourself and under your God.
You are above yourself because you are striving by grace to reach a point to which you
cannot come by nature; that is to say, to be made one with God in spirit and in love and
in oneness of wills. You are beneath your God; for though it can be said that during this
time God and yourself are not two but one in spirit . . . nevertheless you are still beneath
him. For he is God by nature.[14]

The simple juxtaposition of these texts in itself suggests a number of comparisons and
contrasts. Given the data, however, the question at hand is: What will the typological upper
blade tell us?

First, by employing the basic distinction between inner and outer, both of these
passages would be identified by all typologists as mystical rather than numinous. Otto, for
instance, would then go on to point out that the data illustrates the two basic types of
mystical experience. The account provided by the *Spiritual Teachings* is an example of soul-
mysticism. It describes an experience of mystical consciousness in which the Self (atman),
detached from the material and intellectual objects of discursive knowing, recognizes itself
alone as truly existing, as therefore God (Siva) and the source of the names of God. The
account provided by the *Cloud of Unknowing* is an example of God-mysticism. It describes an
experience of mystical consciousness in which the mind, also detached from the patterns of
discursive knowing, recognizes itself as united to God, by nature a higher reality.[15]

Second, in the analysis just sketched, it should be noted both that the data is framed as
an "experience of" (Self or God, respectively) and that doctrinal language (Self/Siva/God)
provides the basic terminology for indicating the content of the experiences. As indicated
earlier, there are basically two positions regarding the comparative status of this "content."
Stace, for example, would contend that both accounts illustrate the "common core" of all
mystical experience, a unitary consciousness devoid of empirical and conceptual content. For
Stace, the differences in the interpretive use of doctrinal language (the Self is God; the mind is
united to God) would be regarded as inconsequential.[16] In opposition to Stace, Robert
Gimello, an articulate proponent of the second position, would suggest that while there is
undoubtedly some common factor in the two accounts, the doctrinal differences would
mediate different mystical experiences: an experience of "the Self as all" as distinct from an
experience of "the mind united to God."[17]

Having employed the typological upper blade to organize and interpret the mystical
data, I put my question again, What does this tell us? The typologies provide a rough
categorization of the data along doctrinal lines, but do they offer any basis for critical
comparative analysis? The typological approach involves a careful noting and describing of
similarities and differences in the various types of mystical experience, but does it explain and
relate these similarities and differences? The answer to these questions, it seems, is a clear
"no." The typological approach describes much but explains very little. For this reason I
regard it as inadequate for the cross-cultural analysis of mysticism. Otto, Stace, and Gimello

are all sensitive analysts of religious texts; the problem is the inadequacy of the upper blade itself. It is my contention that a more adequate heuristic structure is provided by Bernard Lonergan, who shifts the basic terms of analysis from doctrines to interiority and thereby from a descriptive to a critical, explanatory framework.

III. INTERIORITY AND THE ANALYSIS OF MYSTICISM

All of Lonergan's work in critical analysis both enjoins and presupposes entry into what he refers to as the horizon of interiority. Thus, an exploration of the usefulness of his thought for the cross-cultural analysis of mysticism must begin with a consideration of that horizon. Lonergan puts it simply. To enter the horizon of interiority is to undertake "the appropriation of one's own conscious and intentional operations."[18] It is to attend to oneself as a conscious subject and to seek to understand and know the data of one's consciousness. To put it less technically, Lonergan's reflections begin from the simple fact that we are conscious beings, that we have minds, and that we use them. "Interiority" is the term he employs to refer to this fact of consciousness and to the patterns in which consciousness operates when we use our minds. Thus, the focus that emerges within the horizon of interiority is not the *object* or *content* of consciousness, but the *operations* of consciousness. Or to put it another way, within interiority, the primary *object* of consciousness is the *operation* of consciousness.[19] Note that this emphasis is different from the typological approach, in which the focus is the content of consciousness. This shift, I will argue, is what makes possible a critically grounded, cross-cultural analysis of mysticism.

To more clearly locate Lonergan's shift, it is important to understand the two ways the issue of religion arises within the horizon of interiority. The first is general. It entails an awareness of limits, and it raises the question of the ground of human consciousness. For once the horizon of interiority has been entered and it is affirmed that as conscious subjects we are spontaneously driven by wonder to seek what is true, motivated by concern to affirm what is worthwhile, and opened by awe to appreciate what is beautiful, a limit question inevitably emerges: Why is this so? How can this be? Lonergan refers to this as the question of God.[20] It is not an answer. It is a question which points toward an unknown horizon, one more encompassing than interiority itself, a "horizon of transcendence" in which human consciousness is grounded.[21]

Once the question of God has emerged within interiority and the possibility of a horizon of transcendence glimpsed, the issue of religion arises in a second, more specific way. The horizon of transcendence becomes the specific focus of attention and a new set of questions emerges: What is the ground of consciousness? How is it experienced? How is it related to human consciousness? In what sense can it be known? How can it be most adequately expressed? Note that this set of questions (albeit articulated in terms of interiority) addresses the major issues raised by the mystics of the various traditions.

It is also important to notice that the set of religious questions articulated above arises spontaneously, systematically and critically within the horizon of interiority. The questions

(What is the ground of consciousness? How is it experienced?) are precise and intelligible. For even if it is not clear what the answers to these questions might be, it is nevertheless clear how such answers could in principle be obtained. One would attend to the relevant data, to the data of consciousness in relation to its transcendent ground. It is this procedure, in fact, which would "critically ground" any forthcoming answers. In the same way, previously formulated answers could also be critically assessed and either corroborated or corrected. In sum, any answer to any question arising explicitly from interiority can in principle be correlated precisely and critically with the relevant data of consciousness. In Lonergan's words: "Critically grounding knowledge isn't finding the ground for knowledge. It's already there. Being critical means eliminating the ordinary nonsense, the systematically misleading images and so on; the mythical account."[22]

Both to clarify this notion more fully, as well as to offer a preliminary comparison of Lonergan's turn to interiority with the typological approach, it seems to me helpful to contrast the set of religious questions that arises within interiority with a formulation of the same based on doctrinal terms. This requires a reformulation of the questions by transposing the basic terms from interiority to doctrines. For example, the question, "What is the ground of consciousness?" is transposed from interiority to (Christian) doctrine as "What is God?" Transposition of the other questions follows a similar pattern. "How is the ground of consciousness experienced?"becomes, "How is God experienced?" "How is the ground of consciousness related to human consciousness?" becomes, "What is the relationship between God and human beings?" "In what sense can the ground of consciousness be known?" becomes, "In what sense can God be known?"

The point of this exercise in transposition is to make it clear that the difference between the two sets of questions lies not in the knowledge they seek, but in the basic terms and relations in which they are formulated. In the set from interiority, the basic term is "consciousness." In the set from doctrines, the basic term is "God." Inconsequential as this difference may seem it nonetheless has significant theoretical ramifications.

First, the difference in basic terms and relations leads to parallel differences in derived terms and relations. This is not difficult to grasp. In the set from interiority, for instance, where "consciousness" is a basic term, "God" is a derived term. What "God" means is specified by the basic terms "consciousness" and "ground of consciousness," which, in turn, are specified by the relevant data of consciousness. In the set from doctrines, however, where "God" is a basic term, the term "mystical consciousness," for example, is a derived term. What "mystical consciousness" means is specified by the meaning of the basic term "God," and this in connection with other basic doctrinal terms such as "grace" and "creation." The two sets of questions, in other words, are inversely related. When the terms and relations of interiority are taken as basic, doctrines are regarded as derived. When the terms and relations of doctrines are taken as basic, interiority is regarded as derived. Again, the difference in these two sets of questions is not in the issues they address or the knowledge they seek; the difference is in the basic terms and relations in which they are formulated.

A second, broader theoretical ramification emerges in comparing the way the two sets of questions function in a cross-cultural context. It is in this regard that the chief difference between Lonergan's approach and the typological approach becomes evident and the significance of the critical grounding which attends the turn to the interiority becomes apparent. For when the basic term is "consciousness," then any human being from any culture and with any religious conviction can in principle attend to his or her own interiority and identify what is meant by the term "consciousness."[23] It is true that there may be terminological confusions and inaccuracies, but these can be clarified and corrected by an appeal to the data of consciousness itself.[24] The same is true when dealing with a relation such as that of consciousness to its transcendent ground. There may indeed be rival claims for accuracy in expressing that relation. But again, the relative adequacy of each of these expressions can be assessed by appealing to the relevant data of consciousness. In this way critical control is both gained and maintained over one's terms and relations.

In the same way, critical control can be extended to derived terms and relations on the level of doctrines and metaphysics. As Lonergan expressed it, "for every term and relation there will exist a corresponding element in intentional consciousness. Accordingly, empty or misleading terms and relations can be eliminated, while valid ones can be elucidated by the conscious intentions from which they are derived. . . ."[25]

When basic terms are drawn from doctrines, the situation is quite different. What is meant by the term "God" is not identifiable in the same way that the term "consciousness" is identifiable. There is no appeal to interiority. This means that even if what is meant by the term "God" is understood (as for instance, it is possible for a Hindu committed to Siva to understand the Christian doctrine of God) there is no common, critical basis either for explaining real differences and dissolving apparent ones, or for assessing the relative adequacy of a particular doctrine. As the analysis of the typological approach makes clear, differences and similarities in doctrine can be carefully described and a spirit of mutual respect can be brought to such comparisons. Basically, however, one is left with two options: either the positions are fundamentally the same or they are fundamentally different. Neither conclusion is explanatory; neither conclusion provides a basis for genuine dialogue.

IV. THE INTERIORITY-BASED APPROACH: AN ILLUSTRATION AND ASSESSMENT

It remains, then, to assess the relative adequacy of the upper blade provided by Lonergan's turn to interiority. As before, I will give it some specificity by employing it to organize and interpret the lower blade of the mystical data provided by the *Spiritual Teachings* and the *Cloud of Unknowing*. A full comparison with the typological approach, however, will not be possible. Lonergan himself never undertook the cross-cultural study of mysticism, and as a result, the particular terms and relations of this upper blade have yet to be specified. It will be possible, however, to indicate the basic methodological approach that Lonergan's upper blade suggests.

The first interpretive task suggested by Lonergan's upper blade would be to clarify the basic terms and relations of interiority evident in each account. In fact, both the *Spiritual Teachings* and the *Cloud* not only permit but enjoin this critical correlation, for both specify their respective accounts of mystical consciousness in terms of interiority.[26] The passages quoted earlier reveal that in neither case are the senses in operation, nor is there any imagining, thinking or feeling. According to the *Spiritual Teachings*, "there is absolutely no 'I' thought" and "Awareness alone remains." According to the *Cloud*, all "knowing and feeling . . . of yourself [is destroyed]" and you become "aware that your mind is occupied with no created thing." A question then arises: Are these experiences the same or different? Both are identified as states which emerge when discursive thought has ceased. The analyst's task would be to determine precisely the relationship between "Awareness," a basic term in the *Spiritual Teachings*, and "the mind occupied with no created thing," a basic term in the *Cloud.*

The point here is not to make this determination—which would require an analysis of the texts quite beyond the scope of this essay—but to indicate that Lonergan's upper blade specifies the procedures for how to find the answers. An analyst would seek to critically ground and correlate both terms in light of the relevant operations of consciousness presented in the texts. The goal would be to develop a critical grammar of the mystical interiority for the two texts and to use this as a basis for comparing them. Thus, one clear advantage of Lonergan's approach over the typological approach is apparent: its ability to explain and specify differences in basic terms and relations in light of their common basis in interiority.

This advantage carries over to the second task of the analyst, the clarification and comparison of the doctrinal language of the texts, that is to say, their derived terms and relations. As previously noted, there are differences on the level of doctrines. For the *Spiritual Teachings*, the claim is that the Self is All. For the *Cloud*, the claim is that the mind is one in spirit with God. In contrast to the typological approach (which would distinguish the two in terms of the inner and outer foci of the doctrinal claims), the approach from interiority would critically correlate the derived doctrinal terminology with the basic terms and relations of interiority. Thus, the analyst would note that in the *Spiritual Teachings* the doctrinal term "Self" is correlative with the emergence of non-sensory, non-discursive Awareness. The analyst would also note that the *Cloud's* doctrinal term "oneness with God" also correlates with an experience in which there is no sense experience, no thought, and no sense of "I." A series of questions then arises: Given discernible similarities in interiority, why are the correlative doctrinal claims different? Are the doctrinal claims based on differences in interiority that would be revealed through further analysis, or are they different accounts of the same experience? If the former, What are the differences? If the latter, Is either account in some way more relatively adequate? Again, the point here is not to answer these questions but to illustrate the way in which Lonergan's upper blade both sets up the questions and directs the inquiry.

In this way Lonergan's turn to interiority proves to be a more adequate heuristic approach to the cross-cultural analysis of mysticism than the one provided by the use of typologies. Like the typological approach, the approach from interiority calls for the even handed, careful reading of texts. It advances beyond typology, however, in that it provides a basis for explaining the real differences in mystical claims and for dissolving the apparent ones. It does so because it takes its basic terms from interiority rather than from doctrines. The result is that in organizing and interpreting the data, the analyst is able to move beyond the distinction between inner and outer to the discernment of a critical grammar of mystical interiority. This, in its turn, can provide a basis for genuine cross-cultural dialogue among the religious traditions of the world.

NOTES

1   Rudolph Otto, *Mysticism East and West* (New York: Macmillan, 1932).

2   Ninian Smart, *Reasons and Faiths* (London: Routledge & Kegan Paul, 1958).

3   Although this essay will focus on the typological approach as it applies to the analysis of mysticism, the critique presented here applies to the typological approach in general.

4   Typologies, of course, were employed prior to Otto, as in W.R. Inge's *Christian Mysticism* (1899), but it is Otto whose influence is dominant.

5   Otto, *The Idea of the Holy,* trans. by John W. Harvey (Oxford: Oxford University Press, 1958).

6   Otto, *Mysticism East and West,* pp. 38–53.

7   Thus, where Otto distinguishes unifying vision and introspection, R. C. Zaehner distinguishes theistic and monistic mysticism in his *Mysticism Sacred and Profane* (Oxford: Clarenden Press, 1957) and W. T. Stace distinguishes extrovertive and introvertive mysticism in his *Mysticism and Philosophy* (New York: Lippincott, 1960).

8   B. Lonergan, S.J., *Method in Theology* (New York: Herder and Herder, 1972), p. 293.

9   Otto, *Mysticism East and West,* p. 40.

10   *Ibid.,* p. 42.

11   Otto delineates three stages in this intuition: (1) a synthesis of multiplicity, (2) a recognition of the unity as One, and (3) a final recognition of the transcendence of the One. (*Ibid.,* pp. 43–53).

12   In the case of Otto, see *Mysticism East and West,* pp. 32–35; 40–42. Compare Stace, *Mysticism and Philosophy,* pp. 85–88, and Steven T. Katz, "Language, Epistemology and Mysticism," in *Mysticism and Philosophical Analysis,* edited by Steven T. Katz, (New York: Oxford University Press, 1978), pp. 25–27.

13   Ramana Maharshi, *The Spiritual Teachings of Ramana Maharshi* (Boulder: Shambala Publications, 1972), pp. 3–4, 10.

14   *The Cloud of Unknowing,* edited with an introduction by James Walsh, preface by Simon Tugwell, (Ramsey, NJ: Paulist Press, 1981), chapter IV, p. 127; XLIII, p. 202; LXVII, p. 249.

15   See Otto, *Mysticism East and West,* pp. 77–85.

16   See Stace, *Mysticism and Philosophy,* pp. 85–111, esp. 100–104.

17   See Robert Gimello, "Mysticism and Meditation," in *Mysticism and Philosophical Analysis,* pp. 175–7.

18   B. Lonergan, S.J., *Philosophy of God and Theology* (Philadelphia: Westminster Press, 1973), p. 49.

19   In Lonergan's terms, to be at home in the horizon of interiority is to have undergone an intellectual conversion and to be operating in terms of method. (*Method in Theology,* p. 238; 261–62)

20   *Ibid.,* pp. 101–103.

21   *Ibid.,* pp. 256–266.

22   B. Lonergan, S.J., *A Second Collection: Papers by Bernard Lonergan, S.J.,* Edited by W. Ryan and B. Tyrrell (Philadelphia: Westminster Press, 1974), p. 229.

23   B. Lonergan, S.J., "Prolegomena to the Study of the Emerging Religious Consciousness of Our

Time," *Studies in Religion/Sciences Religieuses,* vol. 9, n. 3 (1980), p. 15 (reprinted in *A Third Collection: Papers by Bernard J.F. Lonergan, S.J.,* edited by Frederick E. Crowe, S.J. [New York: Paulist Press, 1985], pp. 55–71.)

24   It is not possible, within the scope of this essay, to address the objections that might be raised here from the perspective of analytic philosophy. The main lines of this critique with regard to mysticism can be found in the volume of essays edited by Steven T. Katz (see n. 12 above). The main lines of a reply compatible with the perspective of this essay have been sketched by John F. Haught in *Religion and Self-Acceptance* (Lanham: University Press of America, 1980). See also my reply to Katz in "The Objectivity of Mystical Truth Claims," *The Thomist* 49 (1985), pp. 81–98.

25   B. Lonergan, S.J., *Method in Theology,* p. 343.

26   This is the case not simply for the passages I have cited, but for the texts as a whole. See Maharshi Ramana, *Spiritual Teachings,* pp. 3–44, and *The Cloud of Unknowing.* chaps. 62–68.

XIV

Religious Rhetoric and the Language of Theological Foundations

STEPHEN HAPPEL

"The eloquent divine, then, when he is urging a pactical truth, must not only teach so as to give instruction, and please so as to keep up the attention, but he must also sway the mind so as to subdue the will."

—Augustine, *De Doctrina Christiana,* IV,13.

IN struggling with the prose of Bernard Lonergan, it is important to locate the enterprise he calls foundations in *Method in Theology.*[1] How has the language of theology changed because of the way in which he envisions it? Can we clarify the human grammar he seeks to include within theology? I believe that in the entire text, but especially in the chapters on dialectic and foundations, Lonergan has provided a seminal rhetoric of religious authenticity, where rhetoric means an analysis of the persuasive linguistic arguments toward truthful values. The rhetoric for which he claims currency, however, should not be viewed as ornament or bought as a communicative device for already pre-established doctrines. Rather through his understanding of the conflicts which led to conversion and their expressions in symbol and image, he has generated a syntax and vocabulary for transforming individual and social praxis. In essence, by revitalizing theology as "generalized empirical method," Lonergan has rethought rhetoric as a contemporary public language which integrates both head and heart, truth about reality and the affective desire for that reality.

It was significant that in the portion of the International Symposium on Religion and Culture which studied shifting theological foundations, each position in its own way was concerned with the transformative dimension of religious experience. What kind of language does this entail? Clearly not an observer-free, uninvolved language as in certain formulations of the scientific ideal. Rather the language sought reshapes human beings; it engages their commitment or self-involvement. It clarifies their minds while cleansing their hearts. This language is not only soteriological in the stories it tells, but also healing in the way it operates. The grammar of religious rhetoric includes therapeutic mechanisms which are purifying as well as comforting. The "healing" character of religious stories "breaks the bonds of psychological and social determinisms with the conviction of faith and the power of hope."[2]

It seems legitimate to describe Lonergan's renewed foundations for theology as a rhetoric. This does not deny the status of Lonergan's work in its theoretic or metaphysical claims, but it does argue that the way in which he has performed the theological endeavor places abstract, metaphysical understanding in a derived location in theology. Method, as it is conceived, is founded upon a reflected interiority interacting with religious common sense. But it is the religious life-world as precariously emerging into authenticity, a social praxis which corrects the past cycles of decline and anticipates a realizable utopian future. Method becomes contemporary culture transformed by the Christian religion.

In the interpretation of Lonergan that follows, I will point out the (I) nature of post-classicist rhetoric through the use of I.A. Richards, Paul Ricoeur and Chaim Perelman. Then (II) interpreting dialectic and foundations as functional specialties, I can show their highly rhetorical goals and devices. Thirdly, (III) I will reiterate some remarks concerning the role of linguistic expression for this rhetorical process that occur for Lonergan in image, symbol and Christian sacrament. In this way, it becomes possible to note how Lonergan's understanding (IV) provides a new mode for the interaction of religion and culture.

I. Some Problems in Post-Classicist Rhetoric

Paul Ricoeur offers a neat summary of the role of image in what I call classicist rhetoric.[3] Neglecting important nuances within Aristotelian and Platonic theory, classicist rhetoric assumes that there are proper and improper meanings which belong naturally to words. Dictionary definitions provide proper meaning. Metaphors are improper attributions; and underneath these oblique images, there remain non-figurative meanings. Some semantic void propels speakers or writers into substituting an alien term for what they cannot express properly. This means that the old, borrowed word has deviated from its ordinary, proper usage. The substitution of the loaned word for the absent expression is primarily a matter of personal preference, based upon some underlying reasonable resemblance observed by the speaker. The figurative use of words does not provide any new information; it clothes the nudity of thought.[4]

So when Walt Whitman addresses Abraham Lincoln: "O powerful western fallen star!/ O shades of night—O moody tearful night!/ O great star disappear'd—O the black murk that hides the star.'' (''When Lilacs last in the Dooryard bloom'd''), he could have substituted some proper literal resemblance for the trope. Through emotional bias, he thinks of Lincoln as a slain leader of some magnitude. The underlying resemblance between this and a star's fading brightness creates the metaphor. What is a proper essence of an evening star is improperly attributed to a person. What we know already about Lincoln is decoratively confirmed.

Classicist rhetoric embellished doctrines already held by the speaker.[5] For example, Cicero saw the rhetorician not as someone engaged in the establishment of truth, but as one ''who will say whatever falls to him for presentation, with wise forecast of the whole, order, style, memory, and a certain dignity of delivery.''[6] Public speech struggled to establish an order for the audience's agreement with a pre-determined subject matter. The task required much effort; because Cicero himself was highly skeptical about the possibility of attaining truth philosophically, he demanded of the rhetorician a wide-ranging knowledge of the arguments, examples, and styles which could persuade and please.[7]

Born in the marketplace of political disagreement, rhetoric grew into a body of tropological eloquence whose skeletal structure was constituted by either the audience's preferences or the speaker's force. True ''rhetoric died when the penchant for classifying figures of speech completely supplanted the philosophical sensibility''[8] that had been its internal truth-claim.[9] The nature of persuasive speech became a matter of flattery, seduction or threat—all forms of violence, however subtle.

Classicist rhetoric was, in many senses, the child of late classical skepticism and post-Enlightenment science. The empirical sciences required consistent, repeatable, physical evidence for validation of its premises. Their object was control of nature and prediction of regular consequences. It was important, therefore, to excise as much as was possible, the role of the observer from such a discipline. The status of truth was dependent upon separating the ''objective'' from the ''subjective'' elements. The world of the human sciences, the worlds framed by what Kant called the psychological, cosmological and theological ideas, could no more be proven than disproven through such methods of verification. They were relegated to the realm of the ''subjective,'' and left primarily to the emotional field of interior life.

Religion, ethics, and the history of peoples were not known through philosophy, nor through science, but through rhetoric, where rhetoric meant a language which persuaded us to what we could not know for sure through the empirical methods. Rhetoric did not so much tell us the truth as negotiate for us a highly subjective world with a readily inflatable, verbal, emotional currency. By this accounting, rhetoric became a parlor-room trick to materialize the ghosts lost by other analytic disciplines. Philosophy and theology were not statements about reality, but partial arguments for what was absent in human experience. Eloquence was a fantasy to tease the mind and heart beyond themselves, a seduction without the performance which might make submission pleasurable. Finally, rhetoric degenerated into a collection of tropes which speakers could manipulate to convince audiences.

Therefore as the criterion for truth changed with the Enlightenment from philosophical doctrine to empirical observation, rhetoric regressed so much that it became a substitute language for what could not be more objectively determined. To say something "rhetorically" was to speak in an inflated fashion, without proper, empirical warrants. The human sciences were "reduced" to rhetorical, i.e. partially meretricious explanations. Ciceronean and Humean skepticism about what could certainly be known combined with emotional subjectivity to give rhetoric a tool-like role in language.

Aristotelian rhetoric, on the contrary, was tied to the logic of the probable,[10] the historical and contingent. It sought to convince, first speakers in their discovery, then the audience through their development that particular actions or probable notions should be undertaken. Where philosophy dealt with the necessary, rhetoric articulated the order of the ongoing process of history, though it was not to be seen as a branch of politics.[11]

Poetic metaphor or narrative within rhetoric could assist the speaker and the audience in finding a way of presenting the probable for mimetic catharsis. The metaphors of poetry did not prove or persuade; they made present the possible, thereby providing both forceful argument and a realized experience of the anticipated result in language.[12] Through judicious selection of data,[13] the speaker defined the relevant community of discourse or the audience. Such techniques of "presence," according to Perelman, act directly on our sensibility[14] and are central to an effective rhetoric. Since in the fields of our perception, we do not always attend to some data, various aspects of the speaker's language call our attention to a constantly renewed sense of an object's reality. Syntactic and semantic methods, such as emphasis, repetition, accumulation and accent "set things out in such a way that the matter seems to unfold, and the thing to happen under our eyes."[15] Pragmatic entailments (such as inclusive personal pronouns "we") make the audience a participant in the subject matter.

The use of image in language, therefore, does not simply exemplify the old meaning, but awakens new reality in our experience. Metaphor is the resolution of some clash of literal coherence for the sake of announcing a semantic impertinence.[16] Where classicist rhetoric saw ambiguity as a problem to be overcome, a new rhetoric would see it as indispensable for crucial human utterances.[17]

Whitman's use of the fading western star for Lincoln's absence connotes far more than the literal death of the president. The iconic memories evoke a range of experience which includes both Christ, the morning star rising in our hearts and Lucifer the fallen light-bearer. The sorrow over Lincoln's assassination combines with the twilight of nature to settle the soul and teach it a song of resigned peace. The entry to the poem's experience demands a willingness to undergo the ambiguity of death's absence in order to be released from the anxiety of night's appearance. When such metaphor is used in public speaking, the rhetoric expects a similar response—but as part of a constant reintegration into the ordinary world. The goal of rhetoric is not reverie but action.

Contemporary rhetoric, therefore, views "neutral" scientific speech as a late, if important, human development. Rather than seeing ordinary language as a swamp to be traversed by means of technical expertise of science, we are required to recognize language as essentially metaphorical.[18] Metaphor is not so much a deviation from normally clear speech, as the "omnipresent principle of language's free action."[19]

Language itself as we use it is a speech in which we dwell to persuade ourselves and to argue with others.[20] Assuming images and ideas, we form our identities in the world. We use a tensive speech[21] which awakens in us what could not be articulated otherwise.[22]

A new rhetoric provides both the practice of, and a reflection upon, our experience of ordinary language. It focuses the intersubjective character of speech, describes the logic of that interactive encounter, and articulates the goals and values embodied in the metaphoric and conceptual processes which characterize its operation. Since reflective language is a control of meaning, it also is involved in understanding the relationships between speech and power. A new rhetoric will redescribe the interaction of speaker and audience as mutual, rather than as the conviction of the masses by a single orator. It will note the transformative character of language for the establishment of the grounds, values, and bases of community. Rather than focusing simply upon eloquent tropes of style, it will recognize the intrinsic relationship between truth-claims and metaphors, between the authenticity of the speaker and the values preached. It will offer a critique of the biases of speaker and audience so that a transforming social praxis might be appropriated.

II. DIALECTIC AND FOUNDATIONS: A NEW RHETORIC

Dialectic, as a specialty within theology, attempts a general apologetic;[23] it proceeds toward a comprehensive viewpoint, not in the sense of an idealist cognition recovering itself, but in the sense of a heuristic notion, ever intending further insights, judgments and values. It deals with the conflicts which emerge from earlier phases of the theological endeavor—including the conflicting interpretations of history. But most importantly, it recognizes that some differences of interpretation occur because of fundamental differences in human horizon. Dialectical differences of human interest are not all reconciliable by complementarity. They sometimes conflict in the way the intelligible and the unintelligible do; they contradict each other in action as good and evil do; they can accept or reject divine disclosure in human affairs.[24] This specialty objectifies the subjective conditions through which truth, goodness and beauty appear.[25]

The comprehensive viewpoint toward which dialectic tends does not end in an idea, but in a person. Its goal is encounter. "It is meeting persons, appreciating the values they represent, criticizing their defects, and allowing one's living to be challenged at its very roots by their words and by their deeds."[26] As an evaluative hermeneutics, it focuses upon the choices necessary in oneself and within community to enact the values which appear at stake when human traditions are examined.

In this sense, four general realms mark the differences in horizon which separate one person from another and distinguish one level of personal development from another. They are the intellectual, the moral, the affective and the religious dimensions of life.[27] In each, Lonergan sees the statistical necessity for a sharp about-face from our habitual mode of behavior. Appropriation of one's intellect requires a shift from the belief that knowing is like looking, that objectivity is a matter of seeing what is "out there," to a constant attention to the multiple operations of human knowing and their varied criteria for truth and objectivity. To "acquire mastery in one's own house . . . is to be had only when one knows precisely what one is doing when one is knowing."[28] Moral self-appropriation demands a change from satisfaction of self-interest to dedication to the good of others. Affective appropriation moves from an ignorant unconscious functioning of our internal symbols to the conscious understanding of their operation in our psyches. Religious conversion faces the reality of the transcendent calling us to holiness and responds to that Voice by "falling in love" unrestrictedly with the One who speaks. On the analogy of religious change, Lonergan entitles each radical shift a conversion.

For students of Lonergan, this is repetition; but what is important here is that dialectics, through its analysis, supports and enables these goals to occur. By appealing to the structures of human authenticity, its language furthers appropriation of the intellectual, moral and religious self.[29] In pointing out the ultimate differences, offering examples of value to others, occasioning reflection and self-scrutiny, dialectic provides a way of clarifying both self and other.

In this sense, the techniques of this evaluative hermeneutics sound remarkably like the categories of a new rhetoric: assembly of relevant data, including the interests, desires and biases of both speaker and audience; comparison of viewpoints; reduction to types; classification of material and selection for the sake of argument. The constant withdrawal from inauthenticity at which the method aims provides a rather idealized version of past history as a cumulative weight toward intended values and a somewhat utopian though attainable future as an invitation for further achievement.[30] The first, largely historical, phase of theological method, therefore, funnels the relevant data, interpretations and patterns of conflict so that normative positions may be taken for the sake of future constructive endeavors. By including not only intellectual, moral and affective data, but also religious interests, Lonergan indicates that this rhetoric will invite us into the highest realms of self-transcendence, the turning to God.

Dialectic and foundations permit a clarification of both oneself and one's community. The personal identity of the theologian and the intersubjectivity of communities are moved toward authentic self-transcendence. It seems that Lonergan is "setting up an artistic, a rhetorical, an argumentative development of language" before he establishes "a metaphysical account of mind," as he says of the Greeks.[31] Just as the linguistic context for the scientific analysis of cognition is an articulated rhetoric which operates as the structure of the life-world or common sense, so in the study of religion, a religious rhetoric which studies movements toward transcendence must precede scientific understanding. Authentic rhetoric is not a study of ornamental communicative devices. Rather it contains an analysis of the images, gestures and partial logics through which truth is attained in our common religious world.

When Lonergan maintains that "genuine objectivity is the fruit of authentic subjectivity,"[32] he goes on to say that ascertaining the real requires the converting affect, intellect, decision and religious sense. Lonergan develops an ontological rhetoric which, through its differentiation of interiority and its proper appropriation transforms common sense and theory. Common sense and theory grounded in an ontological interiority become the dominant entry into a disclosure of differentiated transcendence itself. Intersubjective interiority in our religious common sense has become the primary metaphor for the presence of God.

Dialectic and foundations permit us to understand why this is so. They are a self-implying rhetoric; no interpretation of religion or of any cultural artifact allows initial neutrality. Dialectic and foundations are an audience-implying discourse; they reflect the interaction of subjects in community as well as intend God's presence. The first language of rhetorical expression, as we shall see, is image, symbol and story. Only later do conceptual clarification and analytic judgment emerge.

The specialties, dialectic and foundations, name a dual movement—what the classical tradition would have understood by a transformed metaphysics of interiority as well as a rhetorical maieutic which can assist in the achievement of the developmental task. The therapeutic, indeed ultimately soteriological, character of dialectic recognizes that the language of religion (certainly that of Christianity) is both enlightening (telling the truth about the self, world and God) and healing (reversing communal and interior patterns of decline into sin).

Foundations is the thematization of the process of development or decline. This specialty provides a language for truths known, the decisions taken and the values chosen. First will appear the incarnate articulation of the religious and human reality that a religious person is.[33] When this consciousness is differentiated, it will exist in interlocking vocabularies and grammars which describe the multiple facets of individual and communal experience. General categories which focus experiences, conceptualizations, judgments and decisions common among theology and other disciplines will be examined. General categories will offer clarity about what counts in one's wider world; special categories will speak of the specific religious tradition from which one comes and in which one studies and will issue in explicit commitment to that tradition.[34] Foundations makes clear the claims, as well as the truth of the claims, of those conversions which occur as the basis for authentic dialectics.

But the first language of theological foundations is prayer, the symbolic utterance of an address toward the ultimate Other. What follows this, for the theologian, are the general and specific categories which will explicate this experience of adoration.

III. The Sacraments as Symbols in Religious Rhetoric

I will not repeat clarifications concerning image, symbol and sacrament in Lonergan which I have made in other contexts;[35] but it is important to summarize my discussion to locate its role within interpretation of Lonergan's use of language.

Images are a name we give to an intentional operation within the perceptual flow. There is (1) image as image, "sensible content as operative on the sensitive level"; (2) image as symbol which corresponds to activities or elements on the intellectual level, a heuristic factor in discerning the unknown; and (3) image as sign or signal, in which intelligence abstracts the import of an image.[36] Images are necessary in human knowing and cannot ultimately be transcended. Images do not disappear from consciousness in the human quest for understanding—they remain present, but as "held" in differing ways.

Though Lonergan often stresses the way in which signals are the material for the higher viewpoints achieved in knowledge,[37] he also speaks of the ways in which images anticipate mystery.[38] In this sense, there are no neutral images. They either promote self-appropriation or they discourage it. Mystery is image on the way to self-integration; myth is the use of images in a non-heuristic fashion, as an end product of human knowledge.[39] Myth is image become motionless idol.

When Lonergan describes the way in which images function as symbols in consciousness, he stresses their polysemy, their ability to carry all levels of understanding, and the fact that they do not operate under the law of contradiction.[40] When we link our feelings, our actions and our thinking to their originating and expressive images, we enable symbolic self-appropriation to take place.[41]

The artist intensifies these dramatic patterns of our experience. The factors by which an artist produces a representation—psychic distance from the field of feelings, embodiment in a commanding form, and idealizing the original experiential pattern—invite the new viewer or listener to participate in the aesthetic symbol.

These symbols function not only within the psyche of individuals, but also in the communal framework of societies. The basic problem, Lonergan says, is "to discover the dynamic images that both correspond to intellectual contents, orientations and determinations yet also possess in the sensitive field the power to issue forth not only in words but also in deeds."[42] In our society, symbols either promote the cycles of decline or assist in the transformation of the universe. These symbolic images will be related to art and literature, theatre and broadcasting, journalism and history, academy and university, and a breadth of public opinion.[43]

The symbols of individual and social conversion are the language which thematizes the process of dialectics in its foundational phase. From the intersubjective prethematic "we" which founds community through the articulated love which focuses friendship, family and social bonds, to the triune love of a communal God flowing through the hearts of believers, there appear the images of converting love. "Being in love is properly itself, not in the isolated individual, but only in a plurality of persons that disclose their love to one another."[44]

In the earliest phases of his work, Lonergan was aware of the role of symbol as an expression of affective religious life. In an unpublished tract of 1943–44, Lonergan discussed the interaction among Christ's originating sacrificial experience, the ritual action of the community, and the extra-sacramental experience of the Christian church through the language of symbol.[45] Indeed, his definition of symbol is determined by its theological usage. Like Rahner's formulation of symbol,[46] Lonergan's application sees symbol as the objective disclosure through which a being expresses or reproduces itself in a lower order of reality. The symbolic disclosure is appropriate if there is a proportionate relationship which can be described: but it does not necessarily seem that the resemblance is determined antecedently. Proportionate symbols have a natural and spontaneous affinity for their spiritual meaning. So Lonergan sees ways in which the Last Supper is the proper symbol of Christ's sacrificial offering of himself.

The links between individuals and their symbolic self-expression are not extrinsic. There is an internal "conjunction" between the image used and the meaning intended. The ways in which symbolic images function in this context and later in Lonergan's thought[47] are not dissimilar. There is a recognition of the ambiguous shape of images, their need to be inserted into the ongoing process of human signification. In fact, it is precisely the religious, indeed divine meaning intended which places symbolic images into the transforming process of events.[48]

Sacrament becomes the essential example of religious image. Because Christian conversion is fundamentally intersubjective, image-laden, embodied discourse, it requires the thematization of ritual, worship and prayer as its proper expression. Such social symbols become the common intending by the community of the one Other who transforms all our images. Christians learn that they do not achieve this presence to God by themselves alone. Address to and through Christ, who took upon himself our subjectivity, is the proper symbol of our communal mediation of identity as believers.[49]

All Christian prayer involves this mediation through the subject-to-subject encounter with Christ. Sacrament, moreover, is the paradigmatic instance of this prayer; the normative experience of ecclesial life is the sacramental expression of faith. This is not simply a virtual world, a possible world projected before the participants by which they are judged but in which they do not participate. Rather Christian sacraments achieve incrementally that which they signify. Like any effective language of words and gestures, they engage the participants in cathartic confrontation and healing.[50] In another context, I have called this ritual process emancipatory praxis, rememorative creativity, and prescriptive achievement.[51] The sacraments are not simply an imagistic moralism, making the participants feel guilty. If this were so, if sacraments could only inform us about what they could not even partially deliver, they would indeed be propaganda, emotional and cognitive imperialism of the worst order. "The willingness to undergo the ritual praxis is the offering of oneself to transformation by an other (the community and God)."[52]

Adoring silence, the enjoyment of union with another, may be the primary expression of Christian conversion—the simple turning to the other in love, without demand, without recrimination, without need of approval or blame to "justify" one's voiced admiration; yet the embodied thanksgiving forms the one who engages in it. The words heard are recognized through the ecclesial tradition as the voice of God in Christ. The gestures enacted are known as the healing and forgiving hand of Jesus. The interactive public language of the community informs our private conversations. It articulates the religious rhetoric of love. It sets things to unfold before our eyes and ears so that we cannot mistake ourselves or the One who is speaking.

IV. RHETORIC, RELIGION AND CULTURE

By situating Bernard Lonergan's analysis of dialectic and foundations in the context of contemporary rhetorical theory, I have not denied the philosophically analytic character of his work. What I have argued, however, is that this sometimes seemingly intellectualist analysis has a major role to play in the interpretation of our common culture. Rhetoric is the analysis of the language of the marketplace. It attempts to understand the structures which persuade, dissuade, invite and betray our social praxis.

Every discourse which does not claim an impersonal validity belongs to rhetoric. As soon as a communication tries to influence one or more persons, to orient their thinking, to excite or calm their emotions, to guide their actions, it belongs to the realm of rhetoric. Dialectic, the technique of controversy, is included as one part of this larger realm.[53] Some ancient rhetorics seemed to be based upon social flattery or cultural fascism. Contemporary rhetoric, following certain aspects of Aristotle, aims much higher. It hopes to provide a grammar for authentic value, the communication of truth, and the pleasing achievement of both truth and goodness.

Lonergan's generalized empirical method integrates this contemporary reading of language into theology and offers an ontological grounding for regularly subjectivist interpretations of value, interiority and the truth claims of discourse. When Perelman describes the new rhetoric as "non-demonstrative discourse," aimed at persuasion and conviction, whatever the audience addressed and whatever the subject matter,[54] he wants to leave aside all philosophical investigations which pretend scientific demonstration. He argues that it is the divine hypothesis of an all knowing absolute God which justifies this false understanding of observerless science. Generalized empirical method does not permit us to see knowing as not self-implying; yet at the same time, it also does not collapse knowing our world into a subjectivist principle. Though no mathematical rationalism,[55] Lonergan's method argues for the achievement of an authentic knowledge of what is really true, good and the beautiful—all in the face of divine Transcendence.

Lonergan's understanding of the ontological role of image in perception, art, the recovery of psyche and the conversion to God allows a correction of Ricoeur's emphasis upon the "possible" world manifest in metaphoric disclosure. By grounding the image in cognition, the ongoing pursuit of value, by recognizing that there are no neutral images, that each is either on its way to mystification or to mystery, Lonergan confronts certain problems with Ricoeur's notion of the "work of resemblance" and "split reference" as the proclamation of freedom in a virtual world.[56]

On the other hand, expansion of Lonergan's notions of symbol and art as metaphoric disclosure through use of Langer, Ricoeur and others, and extension of his notion of the intersubjective expressions of conversion permit location of the enterprise within an ongoing process of the transformation of our common social, linguistic praxis.

Lonergan portrays the structures of a new religious rhetoric in dialectic and foundations which thematize the work of image and symbol, concept, judgment, and decision within our ordinary Christian discourse. Rhetoric includes an analysis of religious intersubjectivity, its expressions (conversion, prayer and sacrament); a description of the world disclosed by these thematizations; the changes which occur in both subjects and their world by participation in these languages; the conditions under which religious truth-claims can emerge in analytic language and some clarity about what counts as religious evidence. Lonergan's interpretation requires revision of the praxis of sacrament, ecclesial polity, and the function of Christianity within secular, post-Christian and non-Christian cultures. Bad rhetoric perverts culture, leading it toward further decline; good rhetoric transforms and enables culture to participate in Mystery.

Religion often plays the role in our world of nostalgic keeper of antiquities or of scolding nurse to the moral values of the future. If Christianity is to take more than an alienated back seat in the driving of contemporary life, then it must speak a convincing rhetoric. Such a language will thematize human interaction with attention to both speaker and audience, where each is informed by the data of history, where vital, social and personal values are expressed, and where differentiations include address by the One who loves all without prejudice to friend or enemy. Where classicist rhetoric thought of itself as perpetuating a normative culture available to the orator, but not to the populace, Lonergan's analysis of rhetoric envisions a collaborative endeavor among speakers of a common language of values, such that their participation in God transforms both individuals and world.

NOTES

1 What Father Frederick Crowe has argued in *The Lonergan Enterprise* (Cambridge, Mass.: Cowley, 1980) pp. 1–41, is pertinent to my remarks here. Where Father Crowe attempts to locate Lonergan in terms of Aristotle's *Organon* and Bacon's *Novum Organum*, I am concerned to understand the kinds of language Lonergan uses in his reformulation of theology.

2 Bernard Lonergan, *Three Lectures* (Montreal: Thomas More Institute, 1975), p. 63; hereafter Lonergan *Lectures.*

3 The distinction between classicist and historical consciousness applies to linguistic usage (See Stephen Happel, "Classicist Culture and the Nature of Worship," *Heythrop Journal* 21 (1980), 293–296 where it is applied to worship and the relevant sources for this distinction are cited). Classicist language presumes uniform meanings and decries variety; historically conscious language revels in linguistic change and the charms of neologisms.

4 Paul Ricoeur, *The Rule of Metaphor: Multidisciplinary Studies of the Creation of Meaning in Language,* trans. Robert Czerny with Kathleen McLaughlin and John Costello. (Toronto: University of Toronto Press, 1977), pp. 45–46, hereafter RM.

5 Ibid., p. 9.

6 Daniel Fogarty, *Roots for a New Rhetoric.* (New York: Russell, 1968), p. 16; but see James J. Murphy, *Rhetoric in the Middle Ages: A History of Rhetorical Theory from Saint Augustine to the Renaissance.* (Berkeley, CA.: University of California Press, 1974), pp. 9–21; hereafter Murphy, *Rhetoric.*

7 Marcia Colish, *The Mirror of Language: A Study in the Medieval Theory of Knowledge.* (Lincoln, Neb.: University of Nebraska Press, 1983).

8 Ricoeur, RM, p. 10.

9 Harry Caplan, *Of Eloquence: Studies in Ancient and Medieval Rhetoric* (Ithaca, N.Y.: Cornell University Press, 1970), pp. 160–195.

10 Ricoeur, RM, p. 12.

11 Murphy, *Rhetoric* p. 7.

12 Ricoeur, RM, p. 13; see also *idem, Time and Narrative,* trans. Kathleen McLaughlin and David Pellauer. (Chicago: University of Chicago Press, 1984) pp. 31–87 and *idem, Temps et Recit* Tome II. (Paris: Seuil, 1985), esp. 92–149, 233–234.

13 Chaim Perelman and L. Olbrechts-Tyteca, *The New Rhetoric: A Treatise on Argument.* (London: University of Notre Dame Press, 1971), p. 116; hereafter Perelman, NR.

14 Ibid.

15 Chaim Perelman, *The Realm of Rhetoric,* trans. William Kluback. (London: University of Notre Dame Press, 1982), p. 38; hereafter Perelman, RR; see also Ricoeur, RM, pp. 187–215.

16 Ricoeur, RM. 190.

17 I.A. Richards, *Philosophy of Rhetoric.* (New York: Oxford University Press, 1936), p. 40; hereafter Richards, PR.

18 Ibid., p. 89.

19 Ibid., p. 90.

20 Kenneth Burke, *A Rhetoric of Motives.* (Berkeley, Ca.: University of California Press, 1969), esp. pp. 37–39; see also Richards' remarks concerning psychoanalytic transference as metaphors, PR, p. 135.

21 Richards, PR, p. 125.

22 Ibid., p. 100.

23 Bernard Lonergan, *Method in Theology* (London: Darton, Longman, and Todd, 1972), p. 130; hereafter Lonergan, MT.

24 Ibid., p. 236.

25 Ibid., p. 235.

26 Ibid., p. 247.

27 Ibid., pp. 237–242.

28 Ibid., pp. 239–240.

29 Ibid., p. 254.

30 Ibid., p. 251.

31 Ibid., p. 261.

32 Ibid., p. 292.

33 Ibid., p. 270.

34 Ibid., p. 292.

35 See Stephen Happel, "Sacrament: Symbol of Conversion," *Creativity and Method: Essays in Honor of Bernard Lonergan,* ed. Matthew L. Lamb. (Milwaukee, Wis.: Marquette University Press, 1981), pp. 275–290 and *idem,* "Whether Sacraments Liberate Communities: Some Reflections upon Images as an Agent in Achieving Freedom," *Lonergan Workshop V,* ed. Frederick Lawrence (Chico, CA: Scholars Press, 1985), pp. 197–217.

36 Bernard Lonergan, *Understanding and Being: An Introduction and Companion to Insight,* ed. Elizabeth A. Morrelli and Mark D. Morelli. (New York: Edwin Mellen Press, 1980), pp. 178–182; hereafter Lonergan, UB; Lonergan, MT, pp. 76–81; and Bernard Lonergan, *Collection: Papers by Bernard Lonergan, S.J.,* ed. Frederick Crowe, S.J. (New York: Herder, 1967), p. 243; hereafter Lonergan, C I.

37 Lonergan, UB, p. 99; C I, p. 4–5, MT, p. 187.

38 Lonergan, UB, p. 268; Bernard Lonergan, *Insight: A Study of Human Understanding.* (New York: Longmans, 1957), p. 547; hereafter Lonergan, I.

39 Lonergan, I, p. 538.

40 Lonergan, UB, p. 268.

41 Ibid., p. 270.

42 Lonergan, I, p. 561.

43 Ibid., p. 236–41.

44 Lonergan, MT, p. 283.

45 Lonergan, *Lectures,* p. 14; *De Notione Sacrificii,* ed. Frederick E. Crowe, Conn O'Donovan and Giovanni Sala (1943–44) (Toronto: Regis College, 1973).

46 Karl Rahner, "The Theology of the Symbol," *Theological Investigations,* trans. Kevin Smyth. (Baltimore: Helicon Press, 1966), IV, pp. 221–252.

47 Bernard Lonergan, *De Verbo Incarnato* (Rome: Gregorian University Press, 1964), Part V, pp. 534–5; MT, p. 66.

48 Bernard Lonergan, "The Mediation of Christ in Prayer," Lonergan Center Archives (TC 373), Regis College, Toronto. (Reprinted in *Method: Journal of Lonergan Studies,* vol. 2, n. 1 [March 1984], pp. 1–20).

49 Ibid.

50 T.J. Scheff, *Catharsis in Healing Ritual and Drama* (Berkeley, CA.: University of California Press, 1979), pp. 111–179.

51 Stephen Happel, "The 'Bent World': Sacrament as Orthopraxis," *CTSA Proceedings,* 35 (June, 1980), p. 96.

52 Ibid., p. 98.

53 Perelman, RR, p. 162.

54 Ibid., p. 5.

55 Ibid., p. 157.

56 Ricoeur, RM, 216–256.

XV

The Spiritual Authority of the Bible

SEAN MCEVENUE

THE Bible is undoubtedly a collection of literary texts, and as a book it is certainly a classic. Rather it is *the* classic. However, in the Church, and within Theology, there has been an added character to the Bible, namely its authority. Whatever one's precise doctrine about "revelation," "inspiration," or "word of God," Jewish and Christian readers of the Bible recognize in it a normativity of a kind which they do not recognize in any other book. In so far as currently popular ideas about "reading the Bible as literature" might imply abandoning this recognition, then such reading will neither be religious nor theological.

I believe it is worth the trouble to be specific about one key difference in the approach. A literary reading of Milton, or a production of a Shakesperian play, aims at stimulating the listener. It is an artistic act, expressive of meaning in some full sense. The text is one element in that meaning, and it is chosen because of its powers. It may not matter whether the resulting meaning for the listener is related to what Milton or Shakespeare historically intended. What does matter is the degree of stimulation afforded the listener. If a given reader or actor can read the text in a number of ways, and evoke a variety of meanings from it, exciting a variety of responses from the listeners, this will be virtuosity. Any suggestion that one meaning is correct, and another somehow incorrect, will be universally scoffed at.[1] The text may even be changed for aesthetic reasons. The original meaning of the text, and the original author of the text are deemed irretrievable on the one hand, and irrelevant on the other.[2] The text may have power, but not authority over either reader or listener. We do not submit to limits of meaning in literature, nor are we measured by it. We may learn from it, enjoy it, respect it. We are

205

not ruled by it. This distinction was recognized long ago, when for example Ezechiel is listened to as a troubador rather than as a prophet (Ez 33:31-32).

Such an approach to the Bible will not be acceptable to the theologian or to the religious reader. One goes to the Bible in order to learn something true. One is prepared for a conversion, for a demand to change one's life, for a radical challenge. One recognizes the authority of a past moment, in which somehow history, and a human author, and a divine intervention combined to change reality and meaning in a normative manner. One desires, not merely to enjoy this text, but rather to relive, or to participate in, the new reality to which it testifies.

A comparison with legal texts may be helpful here. Biblical texts in a context of ecclesiastical theology are like constitutions or pacts or contracts in a courtroom context, in that they possess an historical authority. These texts are normative and constitutive of a social reality which results from them. Their original meaning was freighted with the authority of the writer, whether the writer was understood to be God, or Moses, or a king or prophet, or a government, or a conqueror. Therefore the author's intention, however uncertain the exact identity of the actual writer, is the normative meaning. Any subsequent misreading of such texts, no matter how creative or useful, are subject to refutation by appeal to the literal sense of the original. Judges and lawyers know as much about historical-critical method as do exegetes.

I. THE PROBLEM

It must be admitted, however, that over the past thirty years biblical scholarship has spent much of its time in exile from the context of ecclesiastical theology. Rather it has been in servitude to comparative philology, or to archeology, or to ancient near-eastern history.[3] At present it risks a new slavery in departments of literary studies.[4] And even within the context of theology the sovereign role of scripture has been undermined by the inconsistent and even abusive methodologies of theologians.[5] Sometimes its authority has been simply denied.[6] Something is wrong with biblical exegesis! Clearly it needs to rediscover itself. Otherwise the Bible itself may be reduced to the level of popular culture, while theology spins off into space without historical root.

Limitations of "Original Meaning"

The triumph of modern biblical scholarship has been to recover the original contexts and meanings of biblical texts. It comes then as an unwelcome shock to note that throughout the history of Judaism and Christianity the original contexts and meanings of the Bible have *not* been normative! The original *texts* have been revered, but the original *meanings* have been overlooked.

The very idea of distinguishing between an original meaning and a convenient contemporary reinterpretation seems to have had no weight at all before the 19th century.

Within the Old Testament context, or the Biblical context, or the Patristic context, or Medieveal Exegesis, or the Renaissance reform scholars, or in other words within the historical period in which the body of Jewish and Christian belief was explicitly formed on the basis of biblical faith, critical historical awareness was almost entirely absent.[7] And most recently both the great biblical scholar Brevard Childs and the great literary scholar Northrop Frye have proposed a form of return to the innocence of old which followed Augustine in finding the New Testament foreshadowed in the Old, and the Old Testament revealed in the New.[8]

It may be helpful to recall one concrete example. Psalm 8:4–6 is cited as an authority in Heb 2:6–9. Psalm 8 had recalled Gen 1 in order to reflect on the wonder of mankind which was created in the image and likeness of God, an idea which the psalm expresses by saying that man is made "little less than God." The epistle to the Hebrews cites an inadequate Greek translation of Ps 8, misunderstands the words "son of man" to mean an individual, disregards the clear intention of the Psalmist to discuss mankind in general, and applies the text to Jesus who, as the text runs, "for a little while" was made less than angels in order to be exalted afterwards. The inspired author of the epistle to the Hebrews explicitly cites a familiar text *verbatim* in a sense which it originally could not have had, in order to make a point about Jesus.[9]

What matters here is not to note something about the superiority of modern exegesis; rather, quite the contrary, it is to point out that the original meaning was not normative in this case. And this case exemplifies the rule rather than the exception. For us, for contemporary scholars, for sophisticated theology, the original meaning has become important, and even intellectually preemptive. But we must recognize that, where the Bible has been normative, the original text was normative, while the original meaning was not. We must recall just how normative that original text has been. Certainly the Jewish communities preserved their books with incredible fidelity: from editors of Old Testament books who juxtaposed contradictory sources without harmonizing them, through the masoretes who counted words to make sure none was omitted, and right up to the modern Israelis who amid the turmoil of war in 1948 send an expedition to Aleppo to seize a codex preserved in a monastery there. This tradition finds dramatic expression in Jesus's insistence that not a jot or tittle of the sacred text might be taken away (Mt 5:18; Lk 16:16–17), and in the citation of Dt 4:2 in Rev 22:18–19. As for the Christian communities, despite Paul's warning that "the letter killeth while the Spirit giveth life," our scholarly editions of the Vulgate, the Septuagint, the Samaritan pentateuch, the Hebrew Bible, and the New Testament, carry no monastic traditions of dedicated copyists, and continue the earlier work of establishing and fixing the Christian canon. The material text surely is normative.

Still the material text was preserved precisely because of its meaning. It must follow that some meaning of the original text has been authoritative. If not the articulated content, then what content? And we must not take refuge in the shapelessness of the sea of tradition, or in the illusion of a total truth in the canon as a whole.[10] For, if the articulated content of the original biblical text has not been normative, then subsequent misinterpretations or misunderstandings of that text, which are found in later biblical authors or editors, have not been any more normative.

The Authority of Scripture in General

What then is the authority of Scripture? The question sounds simple, demanding a straight answer. But the word "authority" here covers an uncharted area of culture. The Bible is written largely in the form of stories, poems, laws, and exhortations. Biblical scholarship has come a long way towards a definition of the literary forms found in the Bible, but critical theory has only recently addressed the question of the relation between art and culture, literature and civilization. And this precisely is the larger question within which the authority of Scripture must be examined, both historically as to what it has been, and theoretically as to what it should be.

It may be useful to see this question in the words of a prominent contemporary literary critic, namely Jonathan Culler:

> There are many tasks that confront criticism, many things we need to advance our understanding of literature, but one thing we do not need is more interpretations of literary works . . . . We have no convincing account of the role or function of literature in society or social consciousness. We have only fragmentary or anecdotal histories of literature as an institution: we need a fuller exploration of its historical relation to the other forms of discourse through which the world is organized and human activities are given meaning. We need a more sophisticated and apposite account of the role of literature in the psychological economies of both writers and readers; in particular we ought to understand much more than we do about the effect of *fictional* discourses . . .
> What is the status and what is the role of fictions, or, to pose the same kind of problem in another way, what are the relations (the historical, the psychic, the social relationships) between the real and the fictive? What are the ways of moving between life and art? What operations or figures articulate this movement? Have we in fact progressed beyond Freud's simple distinction between the figures of condensation and displacement? Finally, or perhaps in sum, we need a typology of discourse and a theory of the relations (both mimetic and nonmimetic) between literature and the other modes of discourse which make up the text of intersubjective experience.[11]

Of course the Bible cannot be described as fiction. And, as literature, it is unique. Still, in asking about its authority we must recognize this larger cultural context.

Now the Bible's authority is not that of the letter of the law. Nor is the Bible a collection of dogmas, or even doctrines. We must ask then what precise aspect of biblical meaning exercises authority? We have ruled out original articulated meaning, and later expressed in intrabiblical interpretations, because these never have been normative. Must we then turn to unarticulated, implicit, or subliminal messages in Scripture, and to effects of which the reader is unaware? Has the authority of Scripture been applied, not to what Scripture said, but rather to what the texts do to the reader without our adverting to its influence? Should we look to affects rather than ideas? to conversion rather than truths?

The answer must be "yes," in some degree, no matter how painful such an admission may be to scholars trained for exact definitions, and for objective data.[12]

In sketching this answer we shall proceed in two steps. First, we shall attempt to show that what the text does to us is determined by an unnamed, unarticulated, and very elusive *"speaker"* who addresses us from the text, and controls our response, and in effect exercises subliminal authority. Second, we shall point to one kind of unarticulated message of that speaker, which will be present in each text, and which will be both normative and important theologically. This kind of message we shall call *"spirituality."*

II. EXEGETICAL ANSWER: THE SPEAKER

The Subliminal Effects of the Speaker in Literature

In speaking of meaning it is helpful to distinguish two poles: meaning as it occurs in the text, which is derived from the author and what lies behind him, and meaning as it occurs in the reader. The title of this section begins with the reader, speaking of the effects of literature.

It must be further noted that the word "subliminal" in this discussion does not mean unconscious. Rather it intends to designate a range of awareness stretching from merely potential awareness on the one hand, all the way to full but implicit awareness on the other. Awareness may be considered implicit when verbal articulation is lacking. Take for example a simple sentence such as "Victory at last." The reader is conscious of an articulated meaning, and could easily define each of its terms. However, if the sentence "Victory at last" is understood to be spoken by a belligerent clown like Jackie Gleason or Popeye, then there result further nuances of meaning which are harder to define: an expectancy of reversal in Popeye's good fortune, for example, and a feeling of humourous bombast. The reader is aware of these "effects" of the sentence, but no words name them and the reader will not advert to them explicitly unless asked about them. They remain implicit or subliminal. Now if the sentence "Victory at last" is placed in the mouth of Hitler, the reader will experience immediate anger, or rage, or perhaps terror, or else a bitter awareness of irony. These effects will be harder to define, and will easily remain subliminal. And if it is to be General MacArthur who says "Victory at last" as he alights in Tokyo, the effects in a post-Vietnam reader will be a still more elusive combination of triumph and irony, a combination which may defy articulation.[13] Or, finally, if in a novel a father or mother figure is made to say "Victory at last," some readers might even require the aid of psycho-analysis to articulate the literary effects they experience. An analogous range of subliminal awareness would exist in the author who chooses words and places them in contexts.

Traditional exegesis has always accepted some responsibility for the nuances, or colourings, or levels of meaning provided by the text, and experienced as subliminal effects of this kind. Form criticism, in more recent times, has added further dimensions by drawing attention to the literary forms, and to their appropriate contexts or *"Sitz-im-*

Leben.'' The speaker of a text is not a personnage named in a text, but rather it is the voice of the text itself; a voice which addresses the reader and elicits a particular response; a voice which, however elusive, must remain identical with itself and coherent if the text is to retain its unity. The speaker's tone of voice is shaped by the literary forms given it, and by the social context in which it is understood to be speaking.

The *"speaker"* of a text must be understood to have several phases. The first phase, or most immediate to the reader, will be the *literary form* of the text in question. The form will be considered a phase of the speaker because if, for example, the form is a limerick or a joke, then the speaker assumes a certain tone of voice, a certain *persona* or stance. This is never thematized in the text, and yet picking up this tone, or "getting the joke," is essential to understanding the text. The second phase of the speaker may be a *personage* like Popeye, who is represented as speaking certain sentences. A third phase of the speaker will be the *unnamed narrator*, a most elusive figure who assures the unity of an action, who knows the times and places of a narrative and who distributes to its various personages the information each will have. The unnamed narrator must remain utterly coherent if the story is to be unified and imaginatively credible. The unnamed narrator may be identical with the speaker if the text is only a story. Otherwise the speaker will contain the unnamed narrator, while establishing a separate identity by adding a framework of some kind, or a comment, or even just a title. Finally, the fourth phase of the speaker will be the *historical author* whose historical reality may or may not be very evident and very important.

Let us see the four phases in a single example, namely the sentence "Let there be light" in Gen 1:3. Phase one of the speaker is the peculiar tone of a literary form consisting of seven patterned days of creation. Phase two of the speaker is the personage, God. Phase three is the unnamed narrator who is neither man nor God, but who is reassuringly present at the moment of creation and throughout the Priestly narrative. Phase four appears to be a 6th century exiled Jew, experiencing chaos and despair, and still finding reasons to hope in the future of Israel. All of these phases merge in the one voice of the text which addresses us, and which produces literary effects. These effects usually remain subliminal.

If a Jew, or Christian reads this text as authoritative, he or she will be subliminally moved by the voice of the speaker in ways which one would not easily define. Now it is quite possible that an obtuse reader would not experience much of the subliminal effects, or that a perverse reader would experience totally inappropriate subliminal effects. However distortion in the reader does not affect the subliminal meaning in the text itself. The subliminal meaning of "Let there be light" is not a doctrine of creation, much less an explanation of the origin of light; rather it is a personal sharing of the Priestly Writer's faith in God's limitless power to illuminate the dark.

Before the age of printing, the unnamed narrator was the dominant phase of the speaker, because texts were not known as texts but rather they were heard as read in public. The voice of the reader (or singer or chanter) would be heard as that of the unnamed narrator. What limitless authority might be felt in that situation!

In view of the traditional concern among biblical scholars after Gutenberg accurately to situate the historical author on the one hand, and in view of current trends, following Gadamer and Derrida, towards giving to the text a life independent of historical authors on the other, a special word about the historical author may be necessary.

It is the historical author who unites all the phases of the "speaker" into one voice. Clearly the author creates and maintains the unnamed narrator (phase three) as a unifying control over the text. If, for example, a current movie presents a war in the present tense, and yet casts it in the 16th century, then the viewer will participate with the unnamed narrator as though its perils were real and the issue uncertain, all the while keeping an aesthetic distance with the current author who lives long after the danger is past. In this way, the voice of the unnamed narrator is retained, and yet radically modified by the voice of the historical author. Similarly the author modifies the voice of any personage (phase two) in the text. If, for example, an iconoclast like Bunuel has God say "Let there be light" in one of his films, God's voice will be radically different from the voice in Gen. 1:3. And, finally, in using literary forms (phase one), an historical author will inevitably modify them, at least subtly, either by emphasizing some aspect of the form over the other, or by placing the form in a larger context, or by applying the form to some content for which it has not hitherto seemed appropriate. [14] Such subtle changes constitute the originality of the author, require his/her brilliance, and above all lead the reader to perceive the author's perspective and focus. When the reader experiences this fourth phase of the speaker, and hears the text in this voice, only then does he fully experience the subliminal effects of the text.

At stake here is not merely aesthetic completeness, but also theological truth. For even if the fourth phase of the speaker remains subliminal, still current philosophy and theology have created a space for subliminal meaning in the realm of truth. I refer here to Bernard Lonergan, and to Joseph Blenkinsopp.

Bernard Lonergan's publication in 1972 of the book *Method in Theology* marked the end of a pseudo-objective, or empiricist, approach to Theology. [15] He says little specifically about the Bible, but a great deal about reading texts. According to Lonergan, the theologian must read the tradition on any given question, i.e., the authors who have treated it, including the Biblical authors, the Fathers, and so forth. In this research, the theologian must not only understand these authors, but also take a stand by agreeing or disagreeing with them. Lonergan treats this process in a chapter which is not entitled "Controversy" as one might expect, but rather "Dialectic." According to Lonergan, one's decision to agree or disagree will not be based only on the validity or invalidity of the arguments, but rather on the validity or invalidity of the authors. The focus is not on the logic of a position, or on the data or scholarship adduced for it, but rather on what Lonergan calls the "conversion" of the author, a conversion in three parts: "intellectual conversion," "moral conversion," and "religious conversion." Of course logic and data will also be scrutinized in themselves and for clues as to "conversion." The approach is distinctly *ad hominem*. These conversions will never be thematized in the author's texts, but will remain implicit. To use our word, they will be subliminal. And yet upon them will depend a theologian's conclusion about the truth of doctrines. [16]

The Bible is a special case, in that it teaches little doctrine, and is concerned rather with stories, or poetry, or exhortation. Joseph Blenkinsopp uses the word "prophecy" to designate what is common to all biblical writers.[17] He points out the contradictions in the articulated meanings of the Old Testament. For example he writes: "What these writings attest to is rather a plurality of "religions" or religious viewpoints, generally quite diverse and sometimes mutually exclusive."[18] But he finds all the texts in the canon share a single authority which he describes as follows:

> The conclusion to which these considerations lead is that the canon is prophetic insofar as the claim to authority which underlies it in one way or another is the claim to a hearing actually staked by the prophets. This claim arises out of personal experience, often of an extraordinary nature, but always within the context of a community sharing a memory and therefore mediating a common tradition. It also tends toward the formation of a new community which embodies the prophetic claim. To speak of the Bible as 'the word of God' is to affirm or imply its authoritative and prophetic character. It is this which made it possible for the author of the Epistle to the Hebrews, for example, to refer to all previous revelations as God speaking to the fathers through the prophets (Heb 1:1), and we have seen that the rabbis were in essential agreement.[19]

What precisely does Blenkinsopp understand this authority to be, an authority found in historical writers, law collectors, wisdom writers and prophets alike? This is his answer: "Unlike the priests and scribes, the prophets were not provided with their audience by virtue of a legitimate and acknowledged office. They had to establish their own credentials and stake their own claims by virtue of whatever *self-authenticating* character their words possessed."[20]

In these reflections, Blenkinsopp is dealing with community, and with canon. Still his position is worth noting for its implications regarding subliminal meaning. For Blenkinsopp the truth, or revelation, of Scripture does not lie in its articulated religious teachings, which may be contradictory at times, but rather in the authenticity of its authors, an authenticity which the community is able to recognize. For Blenkinsopp, the historical author for the Bible as a whole is a collective prophet, or in our terminology a divine "speaker" personally experienced in equal fashion by a series of historical authors, and authentically expressed in their texts.

It is clear that both the author and the reader create and hear the text within a community and in complex relationships with the community. This dimension of the human person, and of meaning, must remain constantly in view in reflections such as these, even though it cannot be articulated at every point of the discussion. Social dimensions complete, but do not alter, the psychological dimension which is the focus of the present analysis.

Concern for the "historical author" is like respect for philosophy. Some may claim the historical author is irrelevant to the meaning of a text, just as others repudiate the very possibility of philosophical doctrines. But this is to choose to be blind. We all have a philosophical doctrine which controls our thinking, whether we advert to it or not.

Similarly, in reading a text, we all project into it an historical author who controls our reading. Fundamentalists project a 19th century historian. Christian Marxists tend to project a 20th century reformer. Exegetes look very sensitively for traces of the real historical author, in order to break out of contemporary idolatries and to recover the meaning of the text.[21]

III. THEOLOGICAL ANSWER: SPIRITUAL TEACHING

The Teachings of the Biblical Texts

So much for the elusive and subliminal. Is it possible to arrive at articulated theology? Is it possible to suggest a methodologically precise exegetical approach, which will discern and name those subliminal meanings of Scripture which have been normative in Judaism and Christianity, or which should be normative? The rest of this paper will attempt to define one approach of this kind.

There will be three major steps in this approach. First, one must begin with existing historical critical methodology. There can be no short cut in this regard. One must begin exegetically by discerning the articulated meanings, defining them accurately in their historical contexts. This is the only known method for reading out of oneself and into the text, an asceticism all the more necessary as one is reading for spiritual meanings, where our interior inauthenticities drive us unawares to misunderstand and misinterpret.

A second step will consist of naming the speaker in all its four phases, and of articulating as clearly as possible the subliminal meaning of the text. Traditional exegesis has done some of this work, but it may be helpful to distinguish now the first step from the second, at least in order to assure that due place is given to the second.

A third step will consist, not of understanding the speaker further, but rather of asking a theological question of the speaker. Note, that we ask the speaker, not the text, since we have seen that the text's articulated content has never been normative. Note, second, that not all questions will be fruitful, as the speaker may not have addressed some of them at all. However, one can indicate at least one theological question which will always be fruitful: *in what realm of experience does God reveal himself?* or in other words, *in what realm of activity is God salvific?*

The answers to these questions are implicit in all biblical texts, and have been subliminally read by Jews and Christians through the centuries. These answers most certainly have been normative in the evolution of Western society. There are two questions, but they are in continuity with each other because revelation and salvation relate to each other as knowledge of God and the data for that knowledge.

The various answers given to these questions by the different biblical speakers constitute various biblical spiritualities. A final section of this analysis will define terms, and apply our method to a specific text, namely Ex 15.

The Spiritual Teaching of A specific Text

Before beginning, two terms need to be defined: the notion of "realm" and the notion of "spirituality."

By *realm* is meant a group of activities, symbols, and meanings which is coherent within itself, complete, and distinct from other similar groups. For example music is a distinct realm of human activity and experience. Science is another. Sports is another. Each has its own objectives, its own jargon and conventions of expression, and its own material support system.

The notion of *spirituality* is that which is found in phrases such as "Jesuit spirituality" or "Carmelite spirituality" or "Hasidic spirituality," and it involves a specific approach to prayer along with a specific style of life, or an asceticism.

It will be helpful to distinguish between the spirituality in itself, and the asceticism which depends on it. We may define spirituality as *a foundational stance of expectancy regarding divine revelation or divine intervention.* Asceticism then will be understood to mean the self-discipline, or a set of practices, which are adopted because of one's spirituality. (For example, if one's spirituality leads one to expect revelation or salvation only at the moment of death, then one's asceticism might exclude involvement in family or in politics.)

Spirituality will be *foundational* in that it relates to ultimate value and proceeds from the deepest foundation of one's potentially conscious self. Being foundational it will govern all dependent operations.[22] It will be a *stance* rather than a doctrine or truth, in that it may or may not become the object of explicit intellectual appropriation, even though it will always command intellectual activities. It is a stance of *expectancy* in that its object is finally transcendent, never definitively possessed, and always in this life to be readdressed in ongoing experience.

Spiritualities will be differentiated then by the "realms" in which God is expected to reveal himself or to intervene. These realms may be diverse, even widely diverse. For example war is one realm in which God might intervene or appear. If one has a foundational stance of expectancy that God will intervene in war, then a military asceticism will be reasonable. Mental prayer, or mystic union, is a quite different realm, defining a spirituality which might lead to the asceticism of monastic life. Israel's holy war spirituality, as we shall see in Ex 15, expects God to intervene before the battle by melting the heart of the enemy. In Islam on the other hand, if there is a holy war or *jihad,* then the decisive intervention of Allah will be at the moment of death when the faithful soldier is carried off to his reward. An entirely different asceticism is demanded in each case: in Israel one must practice passivity during the battle, and religious ritual after it; in Islam, one must exercise suicidal courage, throwing oneself heroically into danger.

We shall attempt to apply this approach, or method, to a relatively short text, by way of example. For the first step, i.e., historical-critical information about the meaning of the text, we will simply rely on existing scholarship. In this case, Ex 15:1-21, we shall rely on a recent study of this text by Frank Cross, Jr.[23]

We may begin then with the first phase of the speaker, the literary form. The text presents a narrative of the celebrations of a victory song in honour of a god of war. The song of the prophetess Deborah in Judges 5 is perhaps the closest parallel. First the text of the song itself is heard being sung in a cultic setting, where Moses and the people recall the annihilation of Pharaoh's army at the Reed Sea, and then the gathering of Yahweh's people on the mountain of God.[24] There then follows in prose a sort of corrective commentary (vv 19-21), in which is recalled first the tradition that the miracle at the Reed Sea consisted not only of the annihilation of the Egyptians, but also of the wondrous saving of Israel; and second the original setting of this celebration, i.e., a special cultic act involving only women. This allows for the repetition of the first couplet of the song, forming an inclusion.

The song is carried by three images of archetypal power. The first half of the song (vv 1-12) presents Yahweh as a god of war, an Ares or a Wotan, giving him a shrill war cry, *ga oh ga ah* (v 1), and praising him as a "man of war" (v 3). Also in the first part of the song God's radical power is imaged as power over primal water. Water is normally an image of rebirth, or of a chaos which God turns to order, an element in which a man or woman floats softly to the surface and to the light. Here, because of Yahweh's right hand, the Egyptians sink like stone in the water (v 5, and again in v 8), the water turns into a ravenous underworld (v 12), and Yahweh mobilizes the water to fight actively against the Egyptians (v B). In the second half of the song (vv 13-18) a third archetypal image carries the meaning: while other peoples watch in amazement, Yahweh brings his own people over the Jordan (v 16), and establishes them on his holy mountain (vv 17-18).[25]

The second phase of the speaker, the personages, softens these effects. Moses and the people first, and then Miriam with her drum and her women recall the past in song. We are not directly present to the events themselves, but only to their celebration. Moses and the people are figures who are assimilated to roles in the Jerusalem temple liturgy, roles played possibly by the king and a group of singers. Miriam as the "prophetess" and her companions sing the opening verse, whose meaning is here interpreted by the whole song which we have just read. They do not gloat over the victory as does Deborah in Judges 5, but rather they ask for Yahweh's continued protection of Israel as in the days of the Reed Sea. This role is akin to the intercessory prophetic role characteristic of the Ephraimite tradition.[26]

In the third phase of the speaker, the unnamed narrator, we are given even more distance from the violence of the song itself. The narrator has just terminated his account of the events at the Reed Sea. He now proceeds to a creative reflection about them, using a familiar song, and linking together the crossing of the Sea with hitherto separate traditions, i.e., the entry into the promised land and the gathering of God's people on a holy mountain. With this consideration the narrator concludes the Exodus story, and gives it a very distinctive composite meaning. (In the ensuing chapters, the narrator turns to other themes and traditions, i.e. the desert stories and the Sinai pericope). By choosing to recall two very different cultic settings for the song, the narrator achieves a substantial aesthetic distance.

Finally we must consider the fourth phase of the speaker, the historical author. If we take this to be the Pentateuchal editor-author, and place him or her with Israel in exile, apparently removed from God's holy mountain forever, then the text moves up into a very ethereal realm indeed. It becomes a remote memory, an eschatological hope, with mythical meaning and archetypal power. If we take the historical author to be the architects of the Christian Bible, then even greater distance is achieved.

What *spirituality* is carried by the text? In what realm is God expected to appear? Certainly the realm will be situated where there is a final conflict between God and God's enemies, and where at the same time God is drawing his people to himself in a sacral sphere. Obviously the Last Judgment is a realm which realizes this scenario perfectly. There are other possibilities as well. If one focuses on the Pentateuchal editor-author, then one might think of a concrete Zionist hope: God will intervene when the Jews are restored to Jerusalem. However, the distancing of the text from historical reality could justify less sharply defined expectancies: God will be expected to intervene to save any Jewish community facing persecution, or to save his Church at odds with any secular power, and so on.

The Christian community developed a lot of war imagery around Christ and his enemy Satan. A classical text for this is, for example, Ignatius Loyola's meditation on "The Two Standards," in the "second week" of his *Spiritual Exercises*. This text portrays the "chief of all enemies" in the Babylonian plain, seated on a fiery throne, surrounded with smoke, horrible and terrifying to behold, summoning his followers to war under his banner. And on the other side it presents "Christ, our Lord" in a delightful field near Jerusalem, humble, most attractive in appearance, friendly, and sending his own on an opposed mission under his banner. In meditating on these images, one making the *Exercises* is invited to apply them to any concrete circumstances of his or her own life and times.

What *asceticism* will be demanded by this spirituality? The Christian image of the meek and lowly Christ in these contexts teaches that warring under his banner involves the way of the cross, and demands humility, poverty and self-denial. At first glance this seems at odds with the god of war depicted in Ex 15: as though Ex 15 asked the reader to be warlike as our heavenly protector is warlike! The fact is, however, that Ex 15 asks no such thing. Rather it portrays God's people as passive in the war, as exulting in God's power without having or needing any of their own. What is demanded of the reader is trust in God's power, a practice of cultic celebration, fidelity to the community which God has formed on his mountain. This is the asceticism of the lamb, or the trusting and pious faithful. And it is interesting to see how the later Christian tradition, while rearranging the original images, retains the normative subliminal meaning, i.e. the original spirituality and asceticism.

This spirituality, like other biblical spiritualities, may be invoked with powerful effect by any spiritual or political leader whose people read the Bible. Recently Ronald Reagan, President of the United States, invoked the spirituality of Ex 15 when he depicted the Soviet Union as "the dark empire." One is easily led to think of the cosmic power of an atomic war, of the enemies of God being destroyed, and of America as God's holy mountain with God's chosen people gathered there. We are drawn to wave the flag, trust the government, leave the power to God alone. The Bible contains alternative, and opposed, spiritualities which may equally be invoked by someone else. It is a task for biblical scholars to describe the various spiritual teachings of the Bible, in order to make them all available, and in this way to restore biblical truth.

NOTES

1   For a useful survey of current critical theory, cf. Frank Lentricchia, *After the New Criticism,* (Chicago: University of Chicago Press, 1980); and Elmer Borklund, *Contemporary Literary Critics,* (London: St. James Press, and New York: St. Martin's Press, 1977). An exception to this attitude is E.D. Hirsch, *Validity in Interpretation,* (Yale University Press, 1960). Lentricchia characterizes Hirsch's view as "the hermeneutic of innocence"!

2   The idea that poets do not understand their own meaning goes back at least to Plato's *Republic,* bk X. Over the past 50 years, because of the towering influence of F.R. Leavis, and the so-called "New Criticism," it has become less and less fashionable to be concerned about the historical context and the historical author. Only the "Geneva School" of "critics of consciousness," led by George Poulet, resisted this tide. H.G. Gadamer's influential work, *Warheit und Methode,* (Tubingen: Mohr-Siebeck, 1960), with its insistence on the independent life of the text itself after the moment of its publication, gave sharper focus to these perspectives.

3   Cf. Brevard Childs, *Biblical Theology in Crisis,* (Philadelphia: Westminster Press, 1979), pp. 97-98.

4   The growth of the idea of treating the Bible as literature has perhaps reached a climax in the publication of Northrop Frye's *The Great Code, The Bible and Literature* (Toronto: Academic Press, 1982). Frye creates a new discipline, dealing with imagery without historical ("centrifugal" is his term) context or reference.

5   Cf. David Kelsey, *The Uses of Scripture in Recent Theology* (Philadelphia: Fortress Press, 1975).

6   Cf. Bernard Lonergan, *Method in Theology* (London: Dartman, Longman and Todd, 1972), p. 276. Lonergan presents a challenge which, if not met, will entail a rejection of the authority of Scripture. This study is an attempt to meet that challenge. His challenge is close to that of Brevard Childs, in that he points out the chasm between historical-critical exegesis and theology.

7   For an excellent demonstration of this fact, cf. Brevard Childs, *The Book of Exodus, A Critical Theological Commentary* (Philadelphia: Westminster Press, 1974). In treating each pericope, Childs provides a series of what he calls "contexts" or later interpretations, which diverge astoundingly from each other and from the original meaning. For another striking demonstration, cf. Gerald T. Sheppard, *Wisdom as a Hermeneutical Construct, A Study in the Sapientializing of the Old Testament* (BZAW 151) (Berlin and New York: Walter de Gruyer, 1980). An excellent study of this fact is to be found in Hans Frei, *The Eclipse of Biblical Narrative* (Yale University Press, 1974).

8   Cf. Brevard Childs *Theology in Crisis,* especially pp. 107-122, where Childs retains an acute sense of historical context, and proposes mutual illumination of the Old by the New, of the New by the Old, through a dialectic process. Cf. also N. Frye, *The Great Code, passim,* especially p. 78.

9   This striking example is worked out in detail in Brevard Childs, *Theology in Crisis,* pp. 151-163. Such use of Scripture by later biblical authors, which is not interpretation but rather re-interpretation, was the rule and not the exception. The range is limitless: for example editorial gloss effecting a change in meaning, as in Gen 22 where the Elohist's searing tale about trusting God radically is shifted to trust in the merits of Abraham, by the editorial addition of vv 15-18; didactic comment in

the light of synthesizing categories such as "faith" in Heb 11, or "wisdom" in Sir 44–50; daring *non-sequitur* as in Dt 4:10–24; the rewriting of an old story to carry a new *tendenz* as in Dt 1:19–46 (which rewrites Num 13–14 to emphasize the guilt of the people); the editorial formation of a new synthesis out of older, sometimes unrelated materials, as in the Pentateuch, the Deuteronomistic History, the book of Jeremiah, etc.; a radical re-editing of an earlier complex to create a different message, as in Chronicles; and finally a kaleidoscope of interpretative modes evidenced in Qumran and the New Testament. For the New Testament, Childs presents a representative bibliography in *Biblical Theology in Crisis*, footnote 16, p. 241. For Qumran and the "intertestamental" period, cf. for example Maurya P. Horgan, *Pesharim: Qumran Interpretation of Biblical Books*. (CBQ Monograph Series 8) (Washington, 1979), especially Part II, pp. 229–259, with its useful bibliography.

10   For a fuller refutation of the possibility of using the canon as a whole for context, cf. S. McEvenue, "The Old Testament, Scripture or Theology," *Interpretation*, 1981, especially pp. 236–239.

11   Jonathan Culler, *The Pursuit of Signs: Semiotics, Literature, Deconstruction* (Cornell University Press, 1981), p. 6.

12   The position which I shall propose is far from isolated, though it must be carefully distinguished from others which share a single trait. For example the deconstructionist Geoffrey Hartman, in the Preface of a collection of essays entitled *Deconstruction and Criticism* (New York: Continuum Publishing Co., 1979), p. vii heads in the same direction but with very different intent. Northrop Frye develops a literary understanding of Scripture based on archetypal images which at times may not be at all evident to the reader. This position was brilliantly presented in *Anatomy of Criticism, Four Essays*, (Princeton University Press, 1957) and then again in a more doctrinaire fashion in *The Great Code*. Finally "structuralist" reading of Scripture, whether focused on surface or on deep structures, deals with subliminal meaning and effects of the text. Cf. Robert Polzin, *Biblical Structuralism, Method and Subjectivity in the Study of Ancient Texts*, with its useful bibliography. The possibility, method, and limits of a structuralist poetics have been laid out with welcome clarity by Jonathan Culler, *Structuralist Poetics, Structuralism, Linguistics and the Study of Literature* (London: Routledge and Kegan Paul, 1975).

13   It may be precisely the need to give expression to such subtle and complex knowledge which leads some authors to write fiction and poetry, rather than descriptive or scientific prose. Cf. Cleanth Brooks, "The Heresy of Paraphrase," in *The Well Wrought Urn* (New York and London: Harcourt Brace Jovanovitch, 1947, 1975) for a compelling demonstration of the impossibility of saying what a poem means in any other words.

14   The work of Claus Westermann, for example in his commentary on Isaiah 40–66 (Philadelphia: Westminster Press, 1969) has made extensive use of this kind of observation.

15   This work applied to theology ideas most of which he had worked out in his earlier book, *Insight: An Essay in Human Understanding* (New York: Philosophical Library, 1958), written in the same city and published one year before Frye's *Anatomy*.

16   Cf. Bernard Lonergan, *Method in Theology*, pp. 235–266.

17   Cf. Joseph Blenkinsopp, *Prophecy and Canon, A Contribution to the Study of Jewish Origins* (University of Notre Dame Press, 1977).

18   Cf. *Ibid.*, p. 6.

19   Cf. *Ibid.*, p. 147.

20   Cf. *Ibid.*, p. 144

21   It may be helpful finally to adduce evidence that historical authors themselves *intend* the subliminal meaning, rather than the articulated ones, and that the method proposed here is not

drawn only from the ideosyncratic needs of a biblical scholar. Doris Lessing, in a novel first published in 1962 entitled *The Golden Notebook*, puts the following analysis on the lips of a novelist named Anne: "The novel is 'about' a colour problem. I said nothing in it that wasn't true. But the emotion it came out of was something frightening, the unhealthy, feverish illicit excitement of wartime, a lying nostalgia, a longing for license, for freedom, for the jungle, for formlessness. It is so clear to me that I cannot read that novel without feeling ashamed, as if I were in a street naked. Yet no one else seems to see it. Not one of the reviewers saw it . . . . And it would be that emotion which would make those fifty books novels and not reportage." (Bantam paperback edition, p. 63.) What Lessing calls "emotion" is clearly a foundational stance which remained subliminal for the "reviewers," but which for the author was the real meaning. An exegesis which overlooked the *Sitz-im-Leben* of the historical author, i.e., war in Europe, would radically miss the point, reducing the novel to reportage! The 4th phase of the speaker gives the essential clue. If that clue were missing, still a very perceptive reading might correctly identify the stance, and even identify the historical context of the author, i.e., reestablish the clue.

22   The notions of "realm" and of "foundation" are drawn from Bernard Lonergan, *Method in Theology, passim*, but especially pp. 272 and 267–269.

23   F.M. Cross, "The Song of the Sea," in *Canaanite Myth and Hebrew Epic, Essays in the History of the Religion of Israel* (Harvard University Press, 1973), pp. 121–144. This study seems to compel assent. For further discussion and bibliography, cf. Brevard Childs, commentary on Exodus cited in note 7 above, pp. 240–248.

24   For details of the form cf. F. Cross, *op. cit.*

25   For an elaboration of this image, and a study of its origins, cf. Richard J. Clifford, *The Cosmic Mountain in Canaan and the Old Testament* (Harvard University Press, 1972).

26   Cf. the discussion of the "Ephraimite Tradition" in Robert R. Wilson, *Prophecy and Society in Ancient Israel*, (Philadelphia: Fortress Press, 1980), pp. indicated in the index under the entry "Intercession."

XVI

What Makes a Story Interesting?

Tad Dunne, S.J.

WHEN we think of interesting stories, we might think of characters and plots, comedies and tragedies, suspense and surprise. These form some of the structural elements of stories. But structures do not make a story interesting. The characters, the plot, the style are all shaped by some subtle sequence of events that the author wants to portray. And these events are not merely the interactions between people. In the best stories external behaviors point to more recondite events in the hearts of people as they struggle with their own selves. These inner events appeal to similar inner events in the people who hear the story, making them listen very attentively. So I would like to begin my reflections by defining the sort of events that make a story interesting. Then I will discuss the different ways in which fiction, myth, and historiography are interesting. That discussion will lead to the theological question whether all of history should be conceived as a story.

I. Mystery and Mysteries

For methodological purposes, Lonergan refers to God as "transcendent mystery."[1] But because concrete events can do more than anything else to stir the transcendent movements in our souls that orient us towards God, we can also call the more crucial events "mysteries."[2] I am not thinking here of detective mysteries; these are puzzles that

221

admit clear answers. I am thinking rather of the impenetrable events portrayed in the "mysteries" of the rosary, or the "mystery" plays of medieval times.

So a mystery would be an event in which a human is touched by the divine, regardless of whether or not its story talks about "God." The stories that speak of mysteries in this sense symbolize for us, in palpable, concrete terms, our touch with the singular Mystery we are made to love. We find examples of this everywhere in our tradition. Israel praises God by telling stories of what God has done. Each Evangelist has his own narrative about the mysteries of the life of Christ. The Church tells of the lives of the saints. Each one of us tells of a personal call to holiness, of when and where it happened. Even within a more secular narrative, we are touched by the story of an anti-nuclear demonstrator speaking so gently to belligerent police officers you would think they were family. Or we find some poignant piece of fiction, and we read the story to a friend in the hospital, knowing very well that it says something absolutely true about real life in a way that factual reporting never could. Like the one Mystery, each of our mysteries holds ever more meaning and can be told and retold without exhausting it. Mysteries, in this sense, are always about what Scripture calls salvation or redemption because they save us from meaninglessness and redeem us from despair.

The know-it-alls among us are impatient with good stories because they prefer certitudes to mysteries. They hope to slice some moral from the heart of a story or enshrine some pithy line on a poster. But such categorial reductions of good stories can never exhaust their meaning. Flannery O'Connor has made this point well: "When you can state the theme of a story, when you can separate it from the story itself, then you can be sure the story is not a very good one."[3] And yet on the other hand, no single event or set of events, nor any of their stories can ever exhaust the total potentiality of complete intelligibility, existence or goodness. So "events" that we find important enough to tell a story about stand halfway between what Scholastics call the categorials and the transcendentals. In other words, good stories are more than we can handle, and yet fail to slake our thirst for Mystery. Good stories, like good liturgies, span the chasm between divine Mystery and human reckoning.

Not all human events are expressed in stories. This does not necessarily mean that only certain events are mysteries and the rest of life just ordinary or obvious. But we often act as though this were the case. We think of certain "religious" events as so extraordinary that we expect the normal laws of physics and history to have been abrogated for a brief, astonishing moment. We then tend to call certain events "divine interventions," as though we had been, up to that point, surrounded by the obvious and not really living in a universal darkness packed with divinity but masked by ambiguous color, sound, movement, and smell.

So we must seriously consider the possibility that all events are mysteries. They bring reality upon the mind, but the reality passes on, leaving the mind with more questions than answers. For the religious lover, all events are words of a lover. They do not possess intelligibility except what comes from a loving intelligence. They are not real except what depends completely on an existence that cannot have been called into existence. They do not possess any worth except what is positively intended and appreciated, desired and welcomed by a lover who cannot will anything but the good. And these events, these "words of a lover," are salvific words because they reveal life as a tightrope and yet beckon us to walk forward anyway.

It is no easy matter to sense the mysterious in every ordinary event. Among Christians it has been customary to refer to doctrines and miracles as "mysteries." For example, the divinity of Christ is a mystery; the raising of Lazarus is a mystery. But we should be careful not to associate mystery with mere perplexity in our minds. In their origins, mysteries are historical events that waken our wonder. And the historical event itself is a saving encounter with the one transcendent Mystery in a specific time and place. When it comes to teaching doctrines about God and establishing certain doctrines as authoritative, we always come back to the stories of the events. Likewise, miracles and visions, impressive though they be, are neither the exclusive nor the normal way in which we encounter divine Mystery. They may seem "mysterious," but they are not necessarily "mysteries" in our sense because they often lack the transcendent punch of even an ordinary "I'm sorry; will you forgive me?"

Also, I do not think it is helpful to speak of the Church as a mystery, or of a person as a "something" which is among the mysteries. Not that they are not involved in mystery; quite the opposite. But in order to understand the Church and a person as related to divine Mystery, we really do not get very far by subsuming their reality under a metaphysical concept of mystery.

By attending to events first, we may be able to give an account of storytelling that is consonant with Lonergan's world-view. From the explanatory viewpoint which he has worked out in *Insight*, one understands "things" by understanding the recurring events that condition their existence.[4] In a similar fashion, might we say that we reach the divine Mystery in ordinary "things" by seeing the unique *historical* events that condition their existence. This would explain why we are more effectively knocked over by a story than by a formal analysis. It is the narrated event that brings the mystery of God home. In other words, the "mystery" of the Church or of any human person has to be understood within the framework of something historical—that is, "storied." It is difficult to believe that Christianity could survive in a culture that emphasized its doctrines and codes of behavior but never told any stories. Indeed, maybe that is why Christianity is not surviving in some cultures.

If by "mysteries" we mean practically any events in which humans encounter the divine, then we can expect to find faith, charity, and hope at their core. These, after all, are exactly the movements of the soul which respond to divine Mystery and which we cannot rationally produce or explain. It is because of the faith, charity, and hope in us that the story of the event amazes us. For example, a story of someone seeing value where another misses it (faith), of commitment and fidelity beyond what can reasonably be expected (charity), or of long-suffering without a great deal of assurance that everything will turn out for the best (hope). Not that all amazing stories have to be success stories. The story of Judas can shake us just as thoroughly as the story of Peter. Both are about salvation. But just as long as we can sense that these movements of the soul are at stake in a story, we are on tiptoe to see its outcome.

Part of the universal power of mysteries lies in the fact that hearing the story of the event can become another mystery. That is, the event of *hearing* about an encounter with God can itself become an encounter with God. For example, as Israel recited past deeds of the Lord or as Paul preached the past events of Christ's Paschal mystery, hearers encountered the living God in their present and were converted. Or to take a more extended example, many early Christians, having heard the Good News, became chaste. Augustine, having heard the Good News and of their chastity, became chaste. Millions of Christians since then, having heard the Good News and of early Christian chastity, and of Augustine's chastity, became chaste. It is in this fashion that mysteries reproduce themselves, as the ''event'' of the original encounter expands into an ever-broadening and all-encompassing story of God encountering souls in flesh and blood. The mysteries of our faith, then, are not finished events. They are open events. The self-sacrifice of Jesus truly lives, not merely as a model for us to imitate—it is that—but as a growing organism continuing to live in history, making not many mysteries but ultimately one mystery.

Now besides looking at the future of mysteries as they are retold, we should also look at how they began. I have been speaking as though the original historical event—the ''mystery''—occurred before any story of the event emerged. But let us look more closely at the beginnings of the story. Is there really any event we can properly call historical in which the people involved did not already have some understanding, in dramatic terms, of what was going on? Perhaps Moses on Sinai or Jesus in the desert encountered God before they told anyone else the story. But unless they themselves understood the ''event'' as a story, their experience would have remained just experience. The story, then, is already present in any historical event. An event literally would not mean anything to the people involved if this were not the case. This story-making activity is present in all significant historical events, not merely religious ones. But what this says about religious mysteries in particular is this: In claiming that God has encountered us in this time and place, we must recognize that the original story-making activity is intrinsic to the encounter. God cannot begin to mean anything to us except as protagonist or antagonist in a story. Any properly human effect God can impress on flesh depends very strictly on storytelling.

Right from the beginning, then, religious experience is always a matter of insight into the meaning of the experience. That insight, in turn, is made possible only by faith, the ''eyes of the heart.'' And that faith is made possible by the love we bear for transcendent Mystery. So the stories in our religious tradition are made possible by both an outer occurrence and an inner love. Indeed, it is inner love that wants to bring the mystery of a historical occurrence to the open expression of story. And as one generation succeeds another, the storytelling itself becomes the outer historical occurrence of kerygma addressing the inner love and faith of a historically continuous community.

II. FICTION, EMBLEM, HISTORY

Now there are many kinds of stories, ranging from sheer fiction on one end of the scale to critical historiography on the other. And yet, despite the surface differences between fiction and fact, we usually find in both the spinners of yarns and in the scholarly historians a common spirit, a common goal. Not that they make up stories, certainly, but they touch that part of human life that is mysteriously unrepeatable.

For historians, the unrepeatable is what defines their field of investigation, distinguishing them from the sociologists, the anthropologists, or the psychologists: these specialize in finding patterns or laws at work over a number of different events. Historians do offer some explanations of a general nature, and the best historians will put their finger on developments unnoticed by all the participants in some sequence of events. But even these developments possess a unique character, so that both the quirkiness of an individual's behavior and the strange turnings of a community's development just stare us in the face, repudiating anyone who might say "I told you so."

We humans are, all of us, idiosyncratic. We are odd, even to ourselves. No one of us understands much of what he or she has done, still less what he or she will do come life's next surprise. Besides, when our private purposes get thrown together with the purposes of others, the outcomes seem to go beyond the purposes of any one of us. Hegel marveled how this conglomeration of human intentions produces results that nobody intended. But he flinched in the face of this mystery; he felt that we should imagine a "Cunning of Reason" working some transtemporal process of historical advance.

A more realistic approach to history ought instead to end up amazed, dumbfounded, revolted, or awe-struck over what goes on in the human soul. The more realistic the historian, the more respect will be paid to the uncategorizable, the grotesque, the queer, the fascinating. We readers of history should be profoundly moved at the potentialities that lie within the reach of our own kind, and I am thinking not just of the horrors of genocide but also of the wonderful oddity of those people who never seem to fit. Individuals are far more diverse in their values than advertising corporations and statistic-gathering companies would have us believe. These are the people that actually live the lives of a culture, making a culture a profound yet always elusive object of inquiry.

In the manuals that explain how historians do their work, we usually find a distinction between the written "history" that appears in book form and the actual "history" that the book is about. Historians investigate actual history and produce written "histories." Now there is more to this distinction than meets the eye. Most world leaders, and other people for whom self-importance is very important, can be found everywhere in written histories. After all, they aspire to go down in history, meaning in the books and in the memories of ordinary men and women. But the actual history that goes on under the eye of the historian moves much more along the lines of those people whose self-image is *not* important. The "Will of the People" is surely a larger factor in the unfolding of a culture's history than are the individuals intent on following or shaping that will. It requires a conversion of sorts to see this and to accept it, particularly if one is enamored of one's own self-image. True, people for whom self-image is important are usually influential. They do make an impact. They do make history. But historians need to be ready to see the difference between progress and decline. They need to see that progress results not from narcissists but from authentic persons and that decline results from unauthenticity, whether in the famous egoists or in the secret ones. This is what actual history is all about. It is a drama where four billion people play a part and everyone is trying to write the script as the scenes unfold.

Writers of fiction also concentrate on the unrepeatable, but they do so in a way that complements the work of historians. The fidelity of historians to making sense of evidence sets a limit to how far they can probe the inner intentions, fears, and hopes of individuals. The evidence of human interiority, after all, is notoriously ambiguous. Often enough we feel constrained to render our innards ambiguous on purpose. The fiction writer sails right over that limit and freely contructs inner worlds that give some sense to outer behavior. The story ought to be plausible, and so the writer's own inner experience is the major resource for making that sense. But it need not be predictable. On the contrary, the best writers know very well how surprising the human spirit can be, whether with malice or with grace.

So it can be said that there is truth in fiction. But by "truth," we do not mean an accurate reporting of evidence, nor even a plausible explanation of the events that really happened in a specific time and place. Truth in fiction is about the *possibilities* of the human soul. Truth in profound fiction is particularly about the soul's *mysterious* possibilities, which is the same as saying that fiction rings "true" when it deals with the soul's stretching towards self-transcendence and with how people negotiate their faith, charity, and hope. Fiction seldom talks in these terms. Even our own definitions of these terms have to be drawn partly from fictional accounts of how we experience these movements of the soul that surprise us. But is it not the case that fiction fundamentally makes palpable the human struggle to discern value amid chaos (faith), to honor the mysterious in another person (charity), and to endure life's troubles (hope)? Whether or not the characters in the story succeed does not matter. The good story is concerned with seeing, not with teaching lessons. So the truth of fiction can be tragic as well as comic, ironic as well as romantic.

Lying halfway between historical accounts and fictional accounts, there is yet a third major kind of story that bears elements of both fact and fiction. I am thinking of what cultural anthropologists call the "myth." But since this term often connotes sheer fiction, perhaps it would be better to speak in terms of "emblem" and give it a definition of our own.

An emblem is an event understood as an instance of an archetypical event. For example: Russia "Declares War." His parents were "Lost at Sea." She was "Born Again." This is the "Paschal Mystery." Couple finds "Buried Treasure." Lincoln "Freed the Slaves." He was "Possessed by the Devil." Like fiction and history, emblems too can touch mystery. To understand this it will by helpful to compare emblems with histories.

A history is an event understood as something new. It does not admit to headlines and capital letters. It is full of context, names and places, the flow of time, interruptions, dead-ends, and ambiguity. In contrast, an emblem is a portrayal of an event as though its archetype occurred before. It will contain familiar patterns and clear lessons.

Here are some common examples. A Christmas dinner, as it is actually being eaten, is a history. But it quickly passes into an emblem, joining all the Christmas dinners gone before and yet to come. The day Mother and Dad met was likewise briefly a history but soon an emblem. Liturgy is meant to be an emblem. It should take history and lift it up to purified form, inserting the everyday into the eternal. Newspaper headlines are usually emblems, and in the for-profit-only newpapers, the stories beneath them are too. Headlines in the more serious papers are less often emblematic, and their stories try to fill in all the relevant context.

Emblems leave us in quite a different frame of mind than histories. Emblems tend to eliminate questions about what the people involved thought about the matter as it was unfolding. Histories rather tend to lay out data that may or may not prove relevant. Emblems reinforce old lessons. Histories do not so much teach a lesson as temper enthusiasm, qualify judgments, delay reactions, wait upon wisdom to respect the impenetrable. Still, the study of history always runs the danger of slipping into emblems. We often read such headlines as "El Salvador is Becoming Another Viet Nam" or "The P.L.O. Want Another Holocaust." Their tragic nature urges survivors to learn a lesson for the future, lest "it happen again."

Both emblems and histories honor the mysterious, though in different ways. Emblems are not fussy about details. Any clue that even suggests an emblem is enough impetus to canonize the story in archetypical form and leave behind any evidence that fails to fit. So emblems honor the mysterious by oversimplifying, which carries with it the hope that beneath life's complexities reality actually *is* simple. History, in contrast, tries to respect all the data, without any rigid canon of selection. So there is a surfeit of palpable detail; the air is redolent with a smell we cannot name; we are left wondering about what everything means. Histories are pieces of eternity with strange-shaped edges. So histories honor the mysterious by pointing to a thousand unexplainable pieces, while emblems carry all eternity in themselves. History, in that sense, is an ongoing inquiry, while emblems are finished answers. Histories are conjectures. Emblems are successfully told stories, final and certain.

Still, neither emblem nor history can exhaust the meaning of an event. They each halt before the mysterious in human affairs in their own way. The emblem oversimplifies the story. It places the story in a myth of eternal recurrence, but the myth does not explain anything; it serves as a mere heuristic for the realities that lie hidden beneath what appears on the surface. History does attempt to explain things, but it unabashedly leaves all sorts of loose ends, regarding all of history as a single whole, though what those connections may be is anybody's guess.

Among the Gospels, Mark's leans towards the historical while John's is more emblematic. In Mark, we find details that are never followed up: Jesus' mother and relatives try to reach him; Jesus commands a cured blind man not to enter his village; a young man is stripped of his linen cloth and runs naked out of the story. All of this heightens the effect Mark wants to impress on us: "Who is this, that the wind and sea obey him?" In John, on the other hand, the man born blind reappears, as do Mary, Lazarus, and Mary Magdalene. Each of the five miracles in John comes to a nice finish. We are not left wondering "What happened *after* that?" But the miracle-stories are signs of something mysterious *above* that, something that recurs in the lives of all who seek God. And yet, in spite of these differences, each kind of story packs its own brand of dynamite. The historical accounts of salvation leave us with an overwhelming sense that something profound really happened, and that our normal expectations can be blown apart at any minute. Emblematic accounts give us an assurance that what happened is of enduring significance, that the ordinary contains the extraordinary. In most Christian stories, histories make us feel less secure while emblems make us feel more secure.

All three forms of stories—fiction, emblem, history—usually talk about misfortune and sin. And insofar as they do, they also raise hopes for redemption from these evils. The better historians, the ones who avoid projecting emblematic myths onto concrete events, very gingerly suggest why things happened and hardly ever predict what will happen. They are more interested in human character or the lack of it, in the intricacies of a particular sequence of events. Still, they cannot delve very deeply into the mysteries of human persons without running the danger of speculative psychologizing. So they tend to treat both evil and redemption as emerging from an inner depth of specific people which is left as inaccessible.

As we saw above, these inner depths are the province of fiction. Fiction writers do not speculate on what people silently think and feel; they just tell us. They easily portray some people as mean or malicious and others as weak and afraid—a distinction beyond easy reach of the historian.

Emblems too can be very bold. They can represent outer calamity (Napoleon's Walerloo) or inner struggle (Benedict Arnold, Traitor). In any case, they offer simple pictures of both sin and grace. Let us examine how well or poorly our emblems for them represent what is really going on.

III. Emblems of Evil and Redemption

From Old Testament times up to our recent past, spiritual writers relied heavily on emblematic stories for talking about evil. The source of evil was a powerful and cunning person called the Devil, who assails all people, from Judas to Jesus, with temptations. The final end of evil was considered to be an Apocalypse. For some that meant an actual day of the week in which the world as we know it would collapse and some completely new evil-free existence would begin. Today, we have some reflective distance on such emblems. Both believers and non-believers recognize that the stories belong to myth, not history, though believers also recognize the value of such myth for talking about the mysterious character of redemption within history.

But emblems of the Devil and Apocalypse have recently given way, again in the minds of both believers and non-believers, to another pair of emblems—Neurosis and Economic Forces. The guilt of the individual over wrongdoing has been forgiven by Freud; it is Neurosis that deserves the blame. Likewise the social guilt over social evil has been forgiven by Marx; Economic Forces deserve the blame. The Day of Reckoning for human living has become the Psychological Depression or the Economic Depression. Even though neurosis and the economy surely deserve the best analysis we can bring to bear, they have become overwhelming personal and social emblems that fix our attention on a clearly-defined enemy, a conspiracy, an It that is guilty, not us. We are still trying to say "The Devil made me do it."

Redemption in these latter-day emblems is proclaimed a matter of psychoanalysis or sociological research, in which the root of evil presumably will be uncovered, followed by an intelligent therapy or social reform. But both this analysis and this redemption, like some extreme forms of belief in Satan and the Apocalypse, give evil a reality it would not otherwise possess.

Lonergan has pointed out that basic human evil is the disobedience to the transcendental precepts, Be attentive, Be intelligent, Be reasonable, Be responsible, Be in love. Fundamentally, therefore, evil is not the positive existence of some power or force, even though when we are in the dramatic pattern of experience it may feel like it. Basic evil is the absence of events in consciousness which ought to be occurring. So any emblems of evil that suggest a concrete existing origin—whether as the person of the Devil or as a psychological or social mechanism—always run the Manichaean danger of dividing the universe into the two equally real and opposing forces of good and of evil.

Having reified evil, these emblems then suggest that evil must be understandable (on the correct inference that if something exists, there are reasons or causes for it). So psychologists and economists analyze. They expect that all problems have explanations and that once they hit upon a correct explanation, the solution to a problem will be obvious. But in reality, human evil has no explanation. If that were not so, there would be no sin. Certainly there exist problems that do admit explanations, but any such explanations must end where the irrational disobedience of the transcendental precepts begins.

Finally, a reified and an understandable evil has to look, feel and smell like something. What by judgment we affirm is real, and by insight we understand, must have some locatable data for us to experience. So the emblems of evil easily take over our imaginations. People imagine that they can "see" the Devil, "smell" malice, "feel" the forces of evil in particular situations.

Then, in the name of goodness, the lofty-minded deem certain individuals, certain nations, certain economic institutions as evil, plain and simple. From there, sabotage, torture, murder or genocide become virtue for those brave souls carrying out this mad apostolate.

If evil is ontologically a vacuum but psychologically a massive force, what emblem could possibly suffice? Should there not be a symbolic representation of the ontological "missing factor" in evil? I suggest that we return to the notion of the Devil—but with a careful proviso. Among the more astute insights of Christian wisdom there is the principle that the Devil is a Teller of Lies. This suggests two things.

First, in any temptation, we suffer some illusion or other. That is, our perception of other people, of ourselves, or of the comforts of life is off the mark. We must humbly admit that this Liar has already told false stories that we have taken as true. That is, we are already biased in the ways we view the world and appreciate what we think are its values. We cannot rely on reason alone to reveal what is truly worthwhile; we must also rely on the value judgments that flow from transcendent love—in other words, on faith. We should turn to the fictions, the emblems, and the histories that reveal divine Mystery. We can turn to them with some good measure of confidence because we do have the gift of faith—the heart's eye that sees from a higher viewpoint than that Liar's false stories. So our faith is not exactly opposed to a "Devil" but rather opposed to the lies about reality that plague us. Besides that, as long as we suffer a contracted perception of reality as we wait for faith to do its work, we also rely on the gift of hope to give us the affective anchor that keeps us from jumping to rash conclusions about the truth.

Second, considered as a Teller of Lies, the Devil can do nothing but work with the truth. The Devil can neither force any external act nor prevent any interior act of attention, intelligence, reason, responsibility, or love. It is very important to keep this in mind, because this Liar's first story usually runs, "I have more power than you do." Once we believe that some evil power can force us to disobey our own love of truth and goodness, we are sunk. So when we are assailed by temptation, besides relying on the power of faith to supplant that Liar's false stories with true ones, we should follow the ancient practical advice, "Don't listen, because in what you hear there will be a lie."

If we take seriously the notion of the Teller of Lies as the antagonist in emblems of evil, then we will see that the Devil is a storyteller too. Within the dramatic pattern of experience, therefore, the human struggle for authenticity will mean choosing between several possible stories. Every single significant event in our lives is capable of being told in at least two different stories—as a story of Chaos or of Cosmos, of Despair or Hope, of Sin or Grace—and which story we choose depends on how accustomed we are to recognizing the movements of faith, charity, and hope within ourselves. This takes time to learn, both in each person's life and in the lifetime of a culture as it enlarges its deposit of wisdom. And unfortunately it is usually by our mistakes that we learn to discern the spirits. Ignatius of Loyola has said that we can tell the Devils by their trails.[5] That is, we learn to discriminate true stories from false ones only after we have already believed the false ones for a time.

What possible emblem of true stories do we have to test the false ones against? Above all, we Christians have the Paschal Mystery, that is, the story of the man to whom we owe absolute faith, charity, and hope being abducted, tortured, impaled with spikes, and left to die without the comfort of friends. But this man who himself had absolute faith in God, absolute charity towards even his enemies, and absolute hope that sin's bondage would be broken within history, was raised up by God and given the name to which every knee shall bend. The story of his life is history—the kind of history that leaves the sincere hearer shaking in wonderment over the limitless authority and the equally limitless kindness of this man. The story of his Resurrection and Ascension is an emblem, but the kind that holds out for our imaginations a vivid picture of the secure power of faith, charity, and hope over the darkness of evil and of the actual freedom Jesus now enjoys as Lord of Heaven and Earth.

Some readers may be uneasy with the suggestion that we regard the stories of Jesus' resurrection appearances as emblems and not as history. We do not mean to imply that nothing happened to Jesus in history after his death. Something surely happened to his body; all early accounts mention an empty tomb. Yet the Resurrection which the first Christians proclaimed was regarded as the Father's work, not the work of Jesus. As the Father's work, it must escape all human attempts to put it into ready-made categories. As a real event that saves humanity, it can be known *as salvific* only through faith, charity, and hope, not through the categories generated from normal attention, intelligence, reason, and responsibility. That is why the accounts of the resurrection appearances differ so widely from one another.

Furthermore, to regard the stories as emblems in no way diminishes their truth value. We in the West think of ourselves as so enlightened by the Enlightenment that we keep ourselves at arm's length from emblems, myths, and symbols. For example, once we recognized that the Genesis story of creation is a "myth," or that the Devil is a "symbol," we have tended to look elsewhere for explanations of creation and sin. But the distinction between history and emblem is not founded on the difference between truth and falsehood. Rather it is founded on the distinction between understanding a situation as unique and understanding it as universal. The Fall of Adam and Eve and the seductions of the Tempter are stories written to illumine our present universal condition of being free in principle but slaves in fact. Likewise, no one expects to repeat the unique life of Jesus in its detail, and yet we do hope to repeat the universal pattern of his Paschal Mystery. To really live that out, we need to return to the myths, emblems, and symbols, not with the undifferentiated approach of a child, but with the profounder approach of an adult who knows how necessary emblems are for keeping contact with Mystery.

Now evil and redemption can appear not only in histories and in stories that are emblems but also in those myths that are fictional in content but emblematic in purpose: the plays of Shakespeare, the *Divine Comedy* of Dante, the Greek plays, Eliot's *The Waste Land*, operas, and so on. They too deal with the recurring patterns of how people confront evil. One of the masters of literary criticism, Northrop Frye, classifies such fictions into four basic plots.[6] And his classification is ingenious inasmuch as it looks at what pressures the stories lay on the desires and the dreads within the reader's soul—which, of course, is right up our alley. If we examine these four kinds of plots, we can discern four distinct ways in which hearing a story can be a 'mystery' for the hearer, that is, can be an event that raises the issue of malice and liberation.

First, in the comic, (lyric) plot, human desire feels itself overcoming the forces of human dread. Its happy characters are blessed with luck and with the delightful surprises of springtime, where the dread of winter is melting away. Second, in the romantic plot, desire has mastered dread, and it does so not by luck but by the courage and strength of the story's characters. Romantic stories are summertime stories. Third, in the tragic plot, dread begins to mount over the forces of desire as otherwise strong characters are trammeled by their own situations and by the growing forces of determinism. It is autumn, or more significantly, Fall. And fourth, in the ironic, or satiric plot, dread reigns supreme over desire as all hope seems lost. Winter has set in and characters can only wait for something like spring's comic surprises.

While these plots are most clearly found in fiction, they are also found in emblems and even in histories. To take a few examples from Scripture, the story of Philip visiting the eunuch in the carriage is comic; it begins with a lucky meeting and ends on an upbeat, full of hope in future developments. The Book of Revelation is romantic; it portrays all human desires as fulfilled and all dread as banished. The story of the Rich Young Man is tragic; he comes on the scene with strength, but his own history proves to be his weakness. We do not know his future, but it does not look very promising for him. Ecclesiastes ("Vanity of vanities; all is vanity!") is irony; dread reigns over desire; nothing can be counted on as absolute.

Any plot can tell a mystery. In different ways, they each can serve to jar the reader into awareness of the insecurity of life and the inner tug towards transcendent love. The comic or lyric plot is founded on luck, a sudden appearance of salvation not out of human strength but from the mysterious blessings of nature—surely a reminder that we cannot redeem ourselves by dint of effort. Even the more happy romantic plots render the reader happy only during the storytelling. He or she must return to the business of living, knowing very well that the story is not one's own. In tragedies, the reader recognizes the all-too-familiar experience of being caught up and crunched by one's past. And ironies seem to play our tired, endless song exactly as we feel it.

Still, even though the major plots can attune us to the mysteries of everyday life, it is important to see that most stories do not directly help us discern how to act. The dialectic of desire and dread that underlies all plots is not a dialectic between good and evil. Desire and dread are morally neutral. We can desire evil as well as good; we can dread holiness as well as malice. So meaningful stories do not necessarily give moral clarity. Often they merely recall the pulls and counterpulls of the soul and leave us wondering which is which.

It is only when a culture perceives moral clarity in stories that it canonizes those stories. It says, "These stories can be counted on to represent a view of how desire and dread ought to work in human souls." And thus it produces its Bible and its list of canonized saints. All cultures canonize some of their literature, art, and biographies with a view to passing some moral judgment on their worth. Outside of these canonical stories, however, the spiritually integrated man or woman must listen to all stories—fiction, emblem, or history—with a critical ear. The people who tell the stories, after all, may or may not be converted. That is, they may fail in intellectual conversion and think of the real as little more than the palpable. Or they may fail in moral conversion and confuse the truly good with the merely satisfying. Or they may fail in religious conversion and hate the soul's transcendent ascent towards divine Mystery.

On the other hand, in practically all cases of really profound stories told by truly wise men or women, their contemporaries were so immersed in their traditional values that they failed to see new greatness among them. In other words, while a culture regularly criticizes its own literature, great literature has the power to criticize its own culture. Thus we should maintain a dialectical attitude not only towards the inner stories that make up our personal temptations. We should listen to all fiction, emblems, and histories with an ear that discerns the threefold conversion.

IV. Is History a Story?

Up to this point, our reflections on stories in terms of desire and dread have been about stories within history. The question naturally arises whether all of history itself is a story with a plot. One does not have to read Northrop Frye to wonder what a large-scale depiction of the human struggle between desire and dread should look like. Why do all nations that rise also fall? Is all history just irony? Or can we really look forward to a time within history when every tear will be wiped away? Will the story of history, in other words, prove to be romantic? Between these extremes we find some philosophers proclaiming that what is going on in the global community is a progressive integration, while others think it is a slow disintegration. That is, some think history itself is comic and others think it is tragic. Surely there are stories of redemption within history, but will all of history coalesce into one romantic epic of redemption?

We Christians tend to regard history as a comic plot for the time being—the good we desire is winning over the evil we dread—and eventually as a romantic plot where the desired good triumphs once and for all. This is a dangerous view. It shares with all gnosticisms an overemphasis on a pre-ordained plot and a forgetfulness of the dialectic of desire and dread writhing in every person. The untamed inner tension between the mundane and the transcendent becomes tranquilized by some explanation that points outward: ''We are restless because . . . ''—as if our restlessness originated at some point in past history and just carries on like a vestigial organ in the body that might just as well be cut out. Such explanations of our disquiet usually name some element of humanity as The Enemy and preach a redemption through rejecting that element and embracing some redeeming secret.[7]

So, for example, many of us have been taught to treat sexual desire as a permanent threat to the romantic plot of God's plan. Similarly, the medieval world thought of monarchy as the only redemption of anarchy[8] and took the Ptolemaic hierarchies in the sky as its cosmological emblem of order. Only recently have Christians begun to regard their sexual experiences and their social pluralisms not as emblems of evil in themselves but merely as the stages whereupon a more fundamental struggle for order takes place. But even these recent developments have not clearly enough acknowledged the often painful transcendental precepts as the hearty core of all that is sound and worthy.

A Christian theology of history cannot be a story, not even a simple collection of stories. It will contain stories, but the form of the whole is larger than story. We do not know what that form is, of course, and that is the most obvious feature of human existence in history—having to live in an order larger than any we know. We are in the middle of the ''history'' and its outcome is not yet determined.

On this issue, we humans are divided, because the tension of having to live within an order whose ultimate shape escapes us brings every adult to the brink of decision wherein he or she must decide whether to act as though there really is such an overarching order to human history. Some will choose to obey merely the order at hand, spending their lives in reaction to the known demands that surround them, and suppressing their wonder about larger issues. Others will choose to believe in an ultimate order, in a real and concrete integration of all history in which the merely happenstance and the unfortunate blind alleys will reveal their hidden meanings. But to choose this path is to live in hope. It is *hope* that enables them to live in history without reducing history to a mirror of one of its stories.

If a theology of history must look beyond story-plots for its order, it should equally look beyond geometric images. Even the famous linear or progressive view of history, which Judeo-Christianity regards as a liberation from the Hellenistic cyclic view, is a naive and dangerous alliance between living history and dead geometry. In the linear view, the key events in history are laid along a time line. Civilizations rise and fall, but progress-minded historians record the events for no other reason than that the great achievements may not be lost and that old errors may not be repeated. Prosperity and great cultural foundations are the simple consequences of hard work and human commitment—and the only consequences worth thinking about. (Even most pessimists today adhere to the linear view in the sense that they measure events sheerly in terms of their outcomes.)

But what happened to those who paid the costs? In most actual cases, our great cultural foundations also depended on slavery, mass robbery, institutionalized lying, and rivers of blood. I think of the underpaid Romanians who made the shirts I wear, the Native Americans from whom was stolen the land I stand on, the American soldiers in Viet Nam who died to keep alive the myth of American moral superiority. The linear view has no answer to the questions these people pose. The significance of their lives lies blasted on charred and bloody soil—soil which the progressivist regards as just so much fertilizer.

An equally dangerous alternative to the linear view of history for Christians is what we might call the transcendent view. In this view, all human events are regarded as linked straight up to divinity. Men and women are portrayed as searching for meaning, as being drawn towards an interior conversion that liberates their minds and hearts from illusion and compulsion. The question here is not "What have we produced?" but "Are we obedient within?" This view is able to provide a partial answer to those men and women who paid the costs for the comfort of others, but such an answer is barely accessible to historians. Indeed, the answer to the question, "Are we obedient within?" can be reached only by those who pose it for themselves.

But even this more spiritual view of history is far too bound to its geometric image of the vertical line, in spite of the fact that St. John the Evangelist and St. Augustine can be counted among its proponents. It ignores the reality of social and cultural progress within history. It inhibits the further question, "What difference will it make to your loved ones if you are obedient within?" We can just imagine how delighted the Children of Darkness must be to hear that the Children of Light can so easily be ripped off because they profess no interest in the future.

We are forced to the conclusion that history itself, considered as a single story, should not be thought of as ultimately comic or romantic, let alone tragic or ironic. Nor should we imagine history sheerly in geometric terms as either a recurring circle of rise and fall, or as a horizontal line of progress or as a vertical line of transcendence. Whatever we think about history's ultimate shape, we should be aware that most of our understanding is analogical. That is, we think of historical process in the commonsense terms of myths, narratives, gods above and humans below, or else in the even more simplistic terms borrowed from geometry.

The question whether history itself must be a single story or must be some kind of line needs to be transposed from the realm of common sense to the realm of theory. And once we do that, we leave the dramatic pattern of experience and enter the intellectual pattern. The question then becomes not "What *must* history be?" but rather "What in fact is the nature of historical process?" It is a question for understanding, not imagination—a question about the intelligibility immanent to all historical process, not about certitude, predictions, dramatizations, or geometric projections.

Once we ask about intrinsic intelligibility, we can easily clarify the character of all views by appealing to Lonergan's four methods of pursuing questions.[9] The intelligibility immanent to historical process is not the classical intelligibility of cyclic theories of time. Nor is it the statistical intelligibility of the transcendent views, which regard only particular instances and not the human order as a whole. Nor is it the genetic intelligibility of the progressivist views, which disregard bias and sin. Rather it is the dialectical intelligibility of an ongoing struggle between authenticity and unauthenticity.[10]

Still, we need a commonsense metaphor to represent this dialectical theology of history. Perhaps the best metaphor, replacing cycles, horizontal lines, and vertical lines, is the metaphor of a dialog between God and us. In that dialog, however, we should be careful not to model it strictly on human conversation. In dialogs between humans, each hears the other's words through one's own spirit. But in the divine-human dialog, we hear the Word of God through the Spirit of God.[11] It is that unfinished story which makes all the stories in our history so interesting.

NOTES

1 *Method in Theology* (New York: Herder and Herder, 1972), p. 341.

2 This definition of "mysteries" has been provoked by, but is not identical to, Quentin Quesnell's definition in his "Beliefs and Authenticity," in Matthew L. Lamb, ed., *Creativity and Method: Essays in Honor of Bernard Lonergan* (Milwaukee: Marquette University Press, 1981), pp. 173-183.

3 *Mystery and Manners,* eds. Sally and Robert Fitzgerald (New York: Farrar, Strauss & Geroux, 1957), p. 96.

4 See Joseph Flanagan, "Body to Thing" in *Creativity and Method,* pp. 495-507.

5 "When the enemy of our human nature has been detected and recognized by the trail of evil marking his course and by the wicked end to which he leads us, it will be profitable for one who has been tempted to review immediately the whole course of the temptation." *Spiritual Exercises of St. Ignatius,* trans. Louis J. Puhl (Westminster, Maryland: The Newman Press, 1959), para. 334, p. 148.

6 Northrop Frye, *Anatomy of Criticism* (Princeton: Princeton University Press, 1957), pp. 158-239.

7   These reflections on gnosticism and the more authentic alternative of living in the tension between the mundane and the transcendent have been inspired by the works of Eric Voegelin. In particular, see *Order and History IV: The Ecumenic Age* (Baton Rouge, LA: Louisiana State University Press, 1974), p. 9.

8   For an analysis of the danger of regarding monarchy as the only alternative to anarchy, see Matthew L. Lamb, "Christianity Within the Political Dialectics of Community and Empire," *Method: Journal of Lonergan Studies* 1/1 (Spring 1983) 1–30, esp. p. 11.

9   For a summary view of these four kinds of anticipated intelligibility, see Lonergan's *Insight* (New York: Philosophical Library, 1957), pp. 485, 607.

10   See Lonergan's "Healing and Creating in History," in F.E. Crowe, ed., *A Third Collection: Papers by Bernard J.F. Lonergan, S.J.* (New York: Paulist, 1985), pp. 100–103.

11   For more on the trinitarian structures of history, see my article, "Trinity and History," *Theological Studies* 45/1 (March 1984), pp. 139–152.

XVII

The Communication of A Dangerous Memory

Sebastian Moore

I suspect that not nearly enough thought has been given to the idea that Jesus had a consciousness greatly beyond the normal. I recall that J.G. Bennet discerned six levels of consciousness and placed Jesus, alone, at a seventh. But his approach is unusual—at least in theology departments! I think of Jesus as a quantum leap in human intensity, syphoned off into dogma. I am excited that Rosemary Haughton takes a very similar way in "The Passionate God."

The reason for our reluctance to go this route is probably the fear that it will lead to saying that Jesus is only more developed than others, not the unique person he is in Christian belief. But it is a curious way of thinking of Jesus' preeminence that dictates indifference to the factual impact of that preeminence on the ordinary run of humans—like asserting the presence of an earthquake not on the Richter scale. Christian belief depends entirely on what Johann-Baptist Metz calls a dangerous memory. Its massive formulas embody centuries of reflection on that memory, that original impact of one life on a few other lives, that has quite changed the world.

It has been believed of Jesus since the beginning that he was without sin. The late Bishop Robinson, a scripture scholar, used to remark on the fact that there is no record of this belief ever having been contested. We are more vulnerable morally than in any other way, so that anyone's goodness can be to some extent impugned. Yet no one, it seems, was able to do this in the case of Jesus. Iris Murdoch says that Socrates is the only other historical figure famous mainly for goodness. Indeed his virtue was never impugned either. But then the claim to sinlessness was never made for him, a claim that *asks* for rebuttal, for someone to say "Don't give me that! What about . . .?" In the case of Jesus, we have the extremely provoking claim, and silence on the part of the critics.

Now since sin was the early, pre-psychological name for the negative, anti-life, anti-growth tendency in us, and since our many schools of psychology have recognized in this tendency a matter of crucial importance, one who believes today that Jesus was sinless is making an enormous *psychological* assertion. He or she is describing a human psyche unimpeded by that huge inertial force that operates below the level where we distinguish between sins and mistakes, that deep reluctance to understand, to change, and to grow, that instigation of the flight from understanding. We shall have to exercise our creative imagination to fill out the description of such a psyche.

For about ten years now, I have been basing my Christology on the sinlessness of Jesus. But it is only recently that I have been able, with the aid of this concept, to elucidate the central mystery of Christianity, the saving death itself. This has become possible because I have at last reached the beginning of an adequate concept of original or generic sin, of the root of that human tragedy that is enacted everywhere before our eyes, on our television screens, and in the silence of our hearts.

Sin is a deep-seated refusal to grow. This refusal arises out of that lack of full love of ourselves and of our lives which begins with a less-than-complete negotiation of the separation crisis and of the subsequent Oedipal crisis. Because we do not completely negotiate these socio-dramatic crises, we remain to some extent fixated on the social scene in which they are set, forever trying to finish the job with mother, with father, with family, with society, with culture. That is our original or generic sin: a state of arrested development.

Sin, being evil, never fully reveals itself, its manner of working. We think we have caught it when we call it self-centeredness. What we miss, by this description, is that self-centeredness is essentially dependent on others for its satisfaction. One thinks of Osmund in Henry James' "Portrait of a Lady," whose pride and disdain depend on the society he despises. Sin is the implicit measure of the self by others, on which all the pretensions of the self are built. Sin is not a disregard for others: it is a misregard for others. It is a centering on myself *on the beam* of others. And the beam is not noticed—the failure to notice it being sin in action. Thus the socio-centrism, the anthropocentrism, of sin is never observed—until finally its effects reveal themselves in genocide in its many forms. What of course refuses, in its own interest, to reveal itself to us, is the self-contradiction.

Now this state of arrested development, initiated in a partially flunked growth crisis, means that instead of our basic sense of the goodness and greatness of our life directing us to look beyond the human to the all-embracing mystery, our reduced sense of our goodness continues forever to wrestle with the socio-dramatic context never transcended. In this way we create our own limit for desire, the human world with its endless history of injustice and revenge. Far beyond this limit, stands our real limit, death.

It is this gap between our self-created limit and the death that truly limits us that accounts for the impossibly ambivalent attitude we have to death. Who can make sense of the way we view death, of what death looks like to us? Who can find any coherence in this mixture of remoteness and unavoidableness?

Now a person without sin, a person free of our inbuilt self-contradiction will not have this ambivalent attitude to death. This person's desire is powered by an unimpeded sense of his goodness and so does not meander into the endless and immemorial human labyrinth. It reaches out to infinity, and acknowledges death as its only limit.

And how does this limit appear to our sinless one? Certainly not as the threat that death is to us who have defined ourselves short of it. It will not seem "tragic." It will not suggest the "pompe funèbre." On the contrary, it will signal the person's participation in a universe of death and birth. On the other hand, it certainly will not make the person's unlimited desire seem to no purpose. *That* message, of the ultimate hopelessness of it all, is the message of death to the sinful consciousness, a point that Shakespeare makes clear—though not to all—by having Macbeth, the man given over to evil, speak the famous nihilistic lines "Tomorrow and tomorrow and tomorrow." Nihilism is the projection of the failure of our self-made, anthropocentric project *onto* death, charging the cosmos itself with our own failure. So great was the military self-esteem of the French that they would say, after every defeat, "Nous sommes trahis!" On the contrary, the sinless person for whom life is limitless desire will see death as the gateway to new life *for desire,* as death is the gateway to new life at every level of being. Death will be the process that desire, to be all of itself, wants to surrender to. Desire, appropriated, finally intends a cosmic existence, to which death is the opening—but real death, not that weird spectral figure projected out of our sociocentrism, not the "rire éternelle" that Valery saw in the sunlight on his "Cimetière Marin." For the sinless person, death will be consummation.

But will this be a solitary consummation, something for himself alone? At the level of consciousness we are trying to envision, the concept is quite incoherent. The question "What will become *of me* ?", asked in respect of death, comes from within the citadel of sociocentric consciousness, so it is asked not of death but of the blurred death that we thence envision. For it is the conspiratorially willed remoteness of death that itself makes us strangers to each other and thus invites us to ask a solitary's question of death. The person for whom death, genuinely, feels to be consummation exists in a quite other relationship to all other persons. In this person the feeling whose damming up separates us from one another and from our death runs free. *The same feeling* that senses death as consummation runs out to others whom fear witholds from this consummation and each other. For the sinless one, death is the consummation of his passion for humanity.

The earliest Christian hymn, quoted by Paul in Philippians 2, 6ff, the earliest liturgical evidence of the dangerous memory, sees Jesus not merely as *accepting* death on a cross but as *choosing* it, the point being that, being sinless ("in the form of God") he didn't have to die but chose to out of love. I have argued that we can, and must, reject the anthropology implied here, a naive conjecture on the prelapsarian condition, while maintaining, and entering more deeply into, the basic insight, the dangerous memory, of the man who died atrociously out of love for us, the person whose embrace of death as consummation and whose embrace of us alienated humans was one embrace. I would say that "the loving choice of death by the immortal one" is an incorrect conceptualization of the basic insight into "the loving death of the sinless one" or better "the death of the sinless one as an act of love not of necessity."

But the worst has yet to be considered. The worst is that it is as alienated from death, as enclosed in our self-made human enclave, that we see disaster as simply incompatible with a loving creator. One thing our terrible century is forcing upon theologians is unanimity concerning theodicy—that there isn't an adequate one. As Vernon Gregson puts it: "Ricoeur daringly but I believe truthfully suggests that only when we ourselves have achieved the capacity for offered suffering will the world not be too wicked for God to be good, and even then there will remain the little children . . . ." Thus the love of God cannot show itself in this world unless our fundamental numbness is thawed out. The thawing-out is effected by the resurrection encounters, the experienced divine endorsement of the compassionate death. The compassionate death is the human dimension of a mystery whose God-dimension is a self-identifying of God with the suffering of his creatures. The divine compassion shows itself in the raising from the grave of the one whom love for humankind drove to a horrendous death. It shows itself in this way as far more "pathetic" than any speculation can conceive.

The urgency for "recovering" the *consciousness* of Jesus is coming from the realization that only out of a new consciousness can a world on the brink of disaster be saved. I mean, that the search for the consciousness of Jesus is perforce a search within our consciousness. In its pursuit we are perforce hinting at a potential in our own consciousness. We are seeking within ourselves for that spark of reawakened compassion that blazed up in Jesus. In abandoning the Christological chimera that I have compared with an earthquake not on the Richter scale, we are engaged in spiritual self-searching. And now that the church, in its most visible form, is engaging in the quest for peace and justice, it is becoming clear that the basis for this labour, if it is not to be a mere dogmatic formula, must be an existentially embraced style of consciousness and cognate action, a burning human center such as Gandhi could have recognized.

The center is essential. We do not know how we are to save the world, but we do know that this is impossible save from this center whence sin is swallowed up in life. Even non-violence is not enough, albeit it is far beyond where most of us have yet reached. (How far we have to go is indicated by the fact that the recent national convention of the National Catholic Education Association did not devote one hour to it.) But even non-violence leaves death unappropriated and evil thus still loose. For the non-violent person places the onus of his or her death on the inflictor, unless he or she can take the further step, the Jesus step, of appropriating his death in love for the inflictor and for all people.

These reflections have some application to the menace of nuclear annihilation. Robert J. Lifton, who has gone further than anyone in the psychological analysis of this menace, speaks of it as producing a psychic numbing. I would account for this numbing in the following way. Our style of consciousness makes death remote, and our whole bias is to keep it that way. Thus when new and strange historical circumstances bring death right up close, the only way to "keep it that way" is to become, ourselves, numb in regard to it. This numbness is an accentuation of the lack of deepest feeling which is our "fallen" condition. In its thrall, we are furthest from the redemptive, self-sacrificing stance. But this means, conversely, that the self-sacrificing stance is the only exorcism of the nuclear menace. The spectre and the sacrifice are mutually exclusive possessors of the human soul.

At this end-time, in this twilight of "scores of centuries", the crucified Logos and the deafening denial of all meaning confront one another in the fearful soul. There is but one way to throw off the demon of a new pervasive nihilism. It is "to let that mind be in you which also was in Christ Jesus." In that shared mind alone is eternal life—that eternal life whose natural symbol in the continuity of generations is swallowed by the image of mass-annihilation and planetary winter.

What we are about, in these reflections, is the recovery of a *subject* for the saving death, a consciousness in which death consummates a person for humankind. This consciousness is beyond our rational comprehension, because it is within us almost too deep for our recovery—almost, but not quite, and the "not quite" is precisely that margin of us where we awaken to the dangerous memory. I have tried to express this in a poem, which I cite at the end. This consciousness, this subject of the new death in love, was at pains to impress itself onto that memory: for not only did he *undergo* that death: he *enacted* it, breaking the bread and saying "My body given!", and deepening the drama with the cup of wine as the spilled blood.

Unfortunately, just when we need its healing symbolic communication, the Eucharist is in poor shape—the worse for wear after twenty years of insensitive and uneducated experiment. We should be very open to the Spirit to show us how to find again, in the breaking of bread, that mind and that memory.

Finally, let me try to state the version of Lonergan's "Law of the Cross" that is implicit in these reflections: Sin subjects us to death by making of it the triumphant alien, the final unmeaning, agent of an ambiguous God. Sin is taken away, therefore, by the embrace of death in love for us its helpless subjects, whose hearts can thus open to the unambiguously compassionate one.

I find it necessary to break down Lonergan's opening statement: Sin leads to death. In the logic of Lonergan's whole life work, I have to see the drama of sin and death at the level of existential meaning rather than at the level of an ontology for which death came only with sin: the ontology of Paul and of that early hymn: an ontology whose abandonment does not make void, but invites us to deepen, the crucial insight to which it gave inadequate expression.

I have a deeper soul
that, to my surprise,
is not surprised at injury or wrong:
it prizes only life,
to it, right is dead.
Strive to live where life is:
leave chosen anxieties.

There is such room at this unvisited depth
that none would leave it for the world of right:
strange castle, where the cells are liberty,
the furnished rooms our prison.

Orientations in
the Human Sciences

XVIII

Explanation in the Social Sciences

W. Mathews, S. J.

Introduction

THE confusion surrounding the problem of the structure of explanation in the social sciences is well known.[1] The present paper will outline a specific proposal concerning the nature of such explanation. It does so in the conviction that there is such an explanatory structure, and that a clarification of its nature is one of the really great intellectual challenges of the end of the present century. In whatever area of experience we are involved, without understanding we are blocked, we cannot go on, nor project our way forward. The world economy illustrates this fact with depressing clarity at the present moment. The recession is a blockade in social processes caused largely, but not totally, by an inadequate understanding of finance. It is not simply that current financial procedures are on occasions being mismanaged. The fact is that what is understood by finance is, in many instances, hindering rather than helping economic processes. A creative effort is needed to expand the concept in order to bring about wider patterns of economic growth. Part of the problem of arriving at a better understanding of finance is that of understanding what constitutes an explanation in the social sciences. Until that wider problem has been resolved many areas of social life, economic growth being one of them, are blocked. The central importance of the problem should then be obvious.

A comparative study of the tacit explanatory structure of two of Lonergan's major works, *Method in Theology* and *An Essay in Circulation Analysis,* suggests a clue.[2] Both those

245

works acknowledge the enormous socio-historical complexity of the economic and theological communities. Both effectively ask, "Is there a framework for collaborative creativity to be discovered in those communities?"[3] An answer to that question would constitute a type of explanation. Although the actual answers offered in each instance differ totally in content, their structure is similar. The one presents a possible explanation of the economic community, the other of the theological community. The analysis will open up the parallels.

I. Explanatory Structures in Method
and Circulation Analysis

At the heart of *Method in Theology* is what might be termed an explanation of the theological community, in one of its aspects, in terms of functional specialties, a system of distinct but functionally related methods of inquiry. Research is one particular method of inquiry, interpretation another, history yet another. The theological community is constituted, not by a single method of inquiry, but rather by an interrelated set of special methods. The particular methods can be termed the variables of the community. They can take as many substitutions as there are particular problems appropriate to the method. But the variables are not isolated. Answers to the questions of research generate questions for interpretation. The questions of interpretation are a function of the findings of research. As wonder is the backbone of every cognitive method of inquiry, the social variables are intrinsically human, constituted by meaning, and unrestrictedly dynamic.[4]

The theological is a particular community of inquirers. The community of scientists, historians, and persons of common sense would constitute other such communities. By extension there arises a possibility of a comparable definition of such communities, again in terms of a functionally interrelated set of methods of inquiry. The scientific community is slowly being recognized as constituted, not by a single but rather by a plurality of types of questioning. Statistical modes of inquiry and explanation, which deal with chance and randomness, have separated themselves off from the earlier classical notions of science and demanded their own autonomy.[5] The study of development and of evolution have revealed that there is involved in them problems not reducible to classical or statistical questioning and modes of analysis.[6] So there arises the possibility that the scientific community could likewise be explained in terms of a distinct though related set of cognitive methods, classical, statistical, genetic, dialectical, and evolutionary. Those methods can be considered as the variables of the community. The number of substitutions that can be made in classical or statistical methods of inquiry is openended. Answers to classical types of questions in turn give rise to functionally interrelated statistical types of questions.[7] So there emerges the suggestion that the scientific community could be explained in terms of a functionally related set of methods or types of questioning. Again, as wonder is the backbone of every cognitive method, such variables will be intrinsically human, constituted by meaning, and unrestrictedly dynamic.

At the heart of *An Essay in Circulation Analysis* is an explanation of the economic community, in one of its aspects, in terms of a system of functional relations between the dynamic and meaningful human activities, producing producer and consumer goods, exchanging money for goods and services, and financing economic expansion, the basic activities of an economy.[8] Production is one activity of the members of the economic community. Within the productive activity both producer and consumer goods are produced. The production of specific producer and consumer goods would constitute particular substitutions in the economic variables, consumer and producer production. The possible standard of living stands in a functional relation with the available producer goods in operation. Their emergence in the economic process results in an amplification or multiplication of the possible consumer goods which can be produced. Equally, the exchange of money for goods is also an economic operation. The total quantity of money in an economy can vary. As such, it is a variable, different total quantities constituting different substitutions. Such money can be exchanged for consumer or producer goods, can be paid in salaries, saved, invested, and so forth. Each of those monetary operations, in aggregate, is functionally related with the production of a standard of living.[9] There are then a finite set of significant monetary operations or variables in an exchange economy. Within those aggregate operations certain patterns of substitution can cause stagnation, others growth, others recessions.[10]

What is distinctive about the given of a human community is that it is constituted by meaningful activities. Both the cognitional activities of the members of the scientific and theological communities, and the production, exchange and financial activities of the members of the economic community, are meaningful.[11] Those meaningful activities are not performed by any single member of those communities. Rather they are a social and historical collaboration. The question arises, "Are those meaningful activities as socially distributed, unrelated atoms of meaning, or are there patterns of relations among them?" It is the present contention that they are related. An understanding of those relations will constitute a possible explanation of those communities. Most generally it could be formulated as:

> One possible type of explanation of a human community is constituted by the determination of the appropriate dynamic system of significant variables, and their correlative functional relations, among meaningful human activities of the members of the community.

Meaningful activities are not unrelated. The understanding of those relations will amount to an objectification of a framework for meaningful collaborative creativity. The specific variables sought and which will go into the explanation will obviously vary, depending on whether it is the economic or the cognitive dimension of the community which one wishes to explain. Yet at the same time, the explanatory structure in terms of a system of verifiable functionally related variables is identical in each case.

In order to appreciate this proposal what is needed is a comprehensive and dynamic image of what it is that is being explained, of diverse economic, scientific, and theological communities, and their developments within history. W. W. Rostow in his *The World Economy*[12] sketches in very broad outline, the stages of economic growth in the economies of twenty countries. He builds up an image of a series of economic communities such as Great Britain, the United States, France, Japan, Mexico, China, Egypt, and so forth. Each of those economic communities has its own particular point of take off, specific geographical, natural and cultural resources, and mode of development. The anticipated explanation we are seeking will grant full autonomy to such diverse communities. Yet it will also hold that the same set of dynamic and meaningful human variables can be operative in their development. There can be discerned in them particular substitutions in the variables, producing consumer and producer goods, quantity of money, finance, etc. That understanding, far from constricting a community, will in fact be profoundly liberating. It will articulate the dynamic and meaningful norms which constitute its life principle.

The suggestion of a clue in Lonergan's works as to the nature of explanation in social theory will no doubt surprise many. After all has not much of the interest in his thought been concerned with his breakthrough in the understanding of our individuality? Self-appropriation is a very personal and private invitation to discover something about oneself.[13] Although it requires a sufficiently cultured consciousness, that is to say developed participation in the social enterprises of science and common sense living, the emphasis seems to be very much on the individual.[14] Conversion is a major theological category. But is not conversion something personal and individual? We don't normally think of it as a social attribute but rather as a personal process, despite the fact that through conversion we enter into a community of like-minded people. Finally, Lonergan's concern with method seems largely a concern to help individuals to be authentic in their search for the truth.

The dichotomy between the personal and the social perspectives is a major problem of all current philosophical investigations, human studies and social sciences. We can no longer rest in the present polarised options which are our inheritance. They must be transcended. In the sense of Progoff, it seems that the categories or variables of the social sciences, if they are to be genuinely human, must be both personal and transpersonal.[15] They must be basic attributes of an individual, and yet at the same time of every individual. If this is possible then the bridge between the personalist and socialist approaches might possibly be crossed. In the movement from *Insight* to *Method in Theology* Lonergan seems to be tacitly bridging the personalist/socialist gap. *Insight* seems an extremely personalist orientated work. The central invitation is to self-appropriation. In that one discovers a basic truth about oneself. But it is also a transpersonal truth, a truth about every other person. When an individual has understood the creative and unchanging norms of his own mind, and the attributes of the world that correspond to them, then he has understood something about the common mental and ontological framework of the whole human community.[16] *Method in Theology* builds on that personal and transpersonal truth. In *Method* the community of theologians is understood in terms of cognitional structure. To the extent that *Method* can be considered an explanation of the theological community, to that extent it bridges the personalist/socialist divide. In *An Essay in Circulation Analysis* the starting point is the economic community and its production structure. But it is not paralleled in Lonergan's work by an appropriation, on the personal level, of the productive activity.[17] There the link between the personalist and socialist dimensions has not yet been established.

II. The "Why?" Question

An explanation of one kind or another is a response to a question. Philosophers of science, with their concern with verification and falsification, or the social framework of scientific inquiry, have not paid nearly enough attention to the anticipatory structures of scientific questions. Accordingly, the present section will attempt to complement the previous one on the matter of explanation by relating it to the anticipations of a particular type of question, the "why" question. In this way a further perspective on the problem of explanation in the social sciences will be opened up.

There are many particular forms of the "why" question,[18] one of which will be our focal interest. There are then such forms as:

Why did P do A?
   tackle that project or question etc.
Why did P do A rather than B?
   tackle that project or question rather than . .
Why did a community do C
   produce D rather than E?
   tackle such and such a question rather than another?
Why is there F rather than G?
Why is there anything rather than nothing?

Several of these questions, with their concern with both individual and social motives, are of central importance in social studies. The present study, while totally acknowledging their centrality, will be concerned with a distinct though related form of the why question which can be expressed as:

Why is this an X rather than a Y?

Some substitutions in the question, initially from the non-human and non-social realm, will clarify its meaning:

Why is this a circle rather than an ellipse?
Why is this an ellipse rather than a hyperbola?
Why is this a geometry?

In the particular form of the "why" question we are considering, the anticipated answer is: Because of such and such a set of relations rather than any other. So a circle is a circle rather than anything else because it is constituted by a unique set of relations between a centre, radii and a plane curve, which constitute it as such rather than as anything else. The same holds true for the ellipse, hyperbola, and the infinity of the polyhedra. Depending on the field of one's interests, each can make his or her own substitutions in the question: a Xerox machine, car, computer, chemical element, biological species, etc. This particular form of the why question and its anticipations is to be differentiated from a related form which would anticipate an answer in terms of purpose or use. The set of relations that constitute a Xerox machine or a computer are one thing, the use or purpose of the machine or computer, though related, is another.

In the above list of questions the shift from the second to the third is of great importance. The first two are concerned with the relations constitutive of particular geometrical objects. But the third is concerned with the system of relations constitutive of a geometry. That system of relations will distinguish it from chemistry or biology, for instance. The same shift can occur in questions that emerge in the social sciences. Some of them will be concerned with the relations constitutive of particular economic activities, others will be concerned with the network of relations constitutive of an economy. The search for a system of relations rather than for particular relations will emerge as a central problem in the social sciences. When the system has been established the science is established. The system determines the context in which particular individual problems within the individual sciences are approached.

Consider next further substitutions which are related to the activities of members of the theological or scholarly communities:

Why is this an instance of research questioning rather than of interpretative or historical questioning?

Why is this an instance of foundational questioning rather than of systematic questioning, etc?

Why is this a theological community?

Why is this a theological rather than a non-theological community?

The suggestion is that the answer, in every instance, will be in terms of one particular type or set of relations rather than another. Thus the questioning of research is characterized by a particular type of given and a particular type of expectation. The same holds true for the questioning of interpretation, history, foundations, and systematics. Again, the first two substitutions can be answered through the determination of particular relations. The third substitution will be answered through the determination of a system of relations, in this instance a system of types of questioning. That system, when articulated, will establish the context within which particular questions are resolved. A theological community can then be understood in terms of a system of types of questioning, questioning itself being considered as a basic human rather than a non-human activity.

Further substitutions in the why question can be considered which are related to the cognitive activities of the scientific community:

Why is this an instance of statistical questioning rather than any other type?

Why is this an instance of classical questioning rather than any other type?

Why is this an instance of development questioning rather than any other type?
Why is this an instance of evolutionary questioning rather than any other type?
Why is this a scientific community?
Why is this a scientific community rather than some other type of community?

The first four types of substitution will be answered in terms of the set of relations appropriate to the specific type of scientific inquiry, the given or object of the questioning and the type of anticipation involved. The fifth question will be answered in terms of the system of sets of relations appropriate to the set of methods of inquiry which constitute the scientific community.

A final set of substitutions can be considered which relate to the activities of the members of the economic community:

Why is this an instance of manufacturing a producer good?
Why is this an instance of manufacturing a consumer good?
Why is this a sale rather than something else?
Why is this an instance of saving?
Why is this an economic community rather than something else?

The first four substitutions are concerned with particular economic activities and objects, and will find their answer in terms of a specific set of appropriate relations. The final question is concerned with the system of relations that constitutes, not a particular economic activitiy, but rather the whole economic process. It anticipates the discovery of a dynamic system of economic relations. When established, such a system will determine the context from which particular economic problems are approached.

An important concern of the substitution has been to establish, within its own domain,[19] the wide ranging generality of the "why" question. It seems that it can be validly asked about all things that differ, "why" is this an X rather than a Y? The contention is that it does not make sense to limit the field of that type of question to, for instance, the objects of the natural sciences. We can just as validly ask, "why is this an economic or scientific or theological community rather than something else?" as we can ask, "why is this a geometry or a chemical element or a biological organism?" For each significantly different object or domain, the particular relations anticipated in the question will differ. But what will not differ is the anticipation of relations or of a system of relations. It can now be suggested that one possible way of interpreting Lonergan's *Method in Theology* and *An Essay in Circulation Analysis* is as answers to the question:

Why is this a theological community rather than anything else?
Why is this an economic community rather than anything else?

His answer in each case would run: because of a specific system of functional relations among the appropriate significant human variables or meaningful activities of those communities.

The resolution of a major foundational question in a science, the why question concerned with the system of relations rather than those of a particular object, is an historical narrative. In economics it is the sort of narrative that Schumpeter was attempting to articulate in his massive *History of Economic Analysis*.[20] In such a history there will be pre-system, periods which end with emergence of a system, periods of normal science, periods of development or revolution, and so forth. But in the unfolding history perhaps it can be suggested that although the meaning of the why question might expand, it is never discarded. It is the trunk on which the science grows.

III. VARIABLES AND SYSTEMS OF VARIABLES

A variable would seem to have at least four basic characteristics. Firstly, it can take an indefinite number of substitutions in the appropriate domain. Secondly, it stands in a functional relation with a set of other variables such that corresponding to particular substitutions in any variable are functionally related substitutions in the other variables. In this sense it is a function of other correlative variables.[21] Thirdly, although a variable varies through substitution, paradoxically the attribute it specifies is an invariant of the process in which the substitutions take place. Thus in a gas, although the pressure, temperature, and volume all vary, what is invariant is that the gas is constituted by its temperature, pressure, and volume. The particular questions which a scientific community raise, or the products which an economic community produce vary. But what does not vary in the community is the activity of questioning or of production. Fourthly, a variable, and the system of relations within which it stands with other variables, must be open to verification in experience. In the natural sciences the data are the data of sense. But in the human sciences it must be expanded to include meaningful activities, the data of conscious and intentional living. So verification procedures will employ what Lonergan has termed a generalized empirical method which operates in relation to the data of consciousness.[22]

The field of substitution in certain variables, x and t and f and a in physics, is a continuum. In chemistry the substitutions which the four quantum numbers, $n, l, m,$ and $s,$ can take, are discrete multiples of a basic unit. The domain of substitution in human variables such as classical or statistical questioning, would be the whole field of classical and statistical problems.

Considering the questioning activity as a basic social variable, some possible substitutions in types of questioning and questions will illustrate the matter. The most general form of the type of questioning involved in classical inquiry could be expressed as:

Why is this an X rather than a Y?

The whole of the previous section of the paper was an exploration of various substitutions in that particular variable. The most general form of the type of questioning involved in statistical inquiry could be expressed as:

What is the probability of Ei of the class E?

This type of questioning is concerned with discovering the probability or ideal frequency of occurrence $p(Ei)$ of the event Ei of the class E of events. It can take as many substitutions as there are statistical problems. Where classical questioning anticipates a system of relations in the given, statistical questioning acknowledges that the given is random, and that it is a mistake to search for a system of relations. Where classical questioning is concerned with the relations constitutive of things, statistical questioning is concerned with understanding the probabilities of occurrence of the same things and relations. In genetics, for instance, it is concerned with discovering the normative frequency of occurrence of biological organisms or their genetic attributes.

In scholarship and theology the most general form of some of the basic methods or types of questioning could be written as:

Who was the author of such and such a text and when?
What did the author mean by the text?
What was going forward in history?

Particular substitutions would be, "who was the author of certain of the so-called Pauline Epistles?", "what did Paul mean by the 'old' and the 'new' man, or Nicea by 'consubstantial'?", "what was going forward in early Christian history?", "what has been going forward in history since the Reformation?", and so forth. There are then as many substitutions in the variables as there are distinct textual, exegetical, and historical questions. In reality a substitution takes place in those social variables when a member or members of the communities of inquirers engage in the proportionate form of questioning, in conjunction with specific problems. This illuminates the distinction between human and non-human variables. Hopefully it supports the suggestion that special methods of inquiry are the variables of the various cognitive communities.

Where cognitive communities are concerned with knowing and knowledge, economic communities are concerned with the production of a standard of living. Possible variables in such communities would be:

producing producer goods (aggregates)
producing consumer goods (aggregates)
purchasing producer goods/consumer goods (aggregates)
wages, prices, saving, investment (aggregates)
interest rates, the quantity of money

As the cognitive variables can take substitutions from the whole field of proportionate problems, so also it would appear that the first two human activities on our list can take on as many substitutions as there are distinct aggregates of producer and consumer goods to be produced in an economy at different times. Consumer goods will be entities such as clothes, houses, household implements, cars, and so forth. Producer goods in the nineteenth century would be entities such as steam engines and textile mills. In the twentieth century they would be entities such as robots and computers. Each can supply their own illustrations. Both consumer and producer goods will vary from region to region and from civilization to civilization. Such variations illustrate what might be meant by substitutions in an economic variable. The quantity of money in an economy can also vary over a domain. Producing producer and consumer goods, and varying the quantity of money, would then seem three possible significant variables of the economic community. Why questions such as, "why is this an economic community, a scientific or theological community, a chemistry, mechanics, etc.?", anticipate their resolution, not in terms of a number of variables, but more precisely, in terms of the discovery of a system of such variables. What is meant by a system of relations is in need of considerable clarification. The variables of a science are not isolated, atomic. Every substitution in a variable stands in a functional relation with a substitution in a correlative variable or set of correlative variables. The set together make up the rule of the entity. The major breakthroughs in science, at every level, are in the discovery or revision, not of single variables, or even of a number of variables and their interrelatedness, but rather of complete systems of interdependent variables. Such discovery is profoundly constitutive of the proportionate science. Historically, Newton and Bohr were key figures in the determination of such systems for the sciences of mechanics and chemistry.[23]

As in the natural sciences, so also in the social, the ultimate movement towards explanation is towards a systematic viewpoint. It is the present suggestion that such a shift in viewpoint is occurring in Lonergan's *An Essay in Circulation Analysis* and *Method in Theology*. The anticipation is of the discovery, not simply of one or two human variables and their interrelatedness, but rather of the system of relations among a set of human variables.

The problem can be illustrated by considering the operation of money in a developed exchange economy. A person with money knows within certain limits what specific entities it relates to. He knows what concrete consumer commodities he or she can buy with it, what investments could be made with it, what salaries could be paid with it, and so forth. In such knowledge and operation, the field of questioning interest is pragmatically limited to what is important for business. The understanding is also of the concrete and particular uses of money in a given situation, rather than of the general relations constitutive of money. There is involved a limited understanding of the relations constitutive of money. On the other hand those limited experiences could lead one to wonder, what are the totality of significant operations which money can perform in an exchange economy? In the early, intermediate, and final versions of the circulation diagram we see Lonergan attempting to classify such a series of operations, the significant aggregate monetary circuits in an economy.[24] Money can be exchanged for consumer or producer goods, for wages for the manufacturing of consumer or producer goods, for savings, investment, and so forth. Each of those different operations in aggregate is a possible significant variable of the exchange economy. The specific aggregate of consumer spending stands in a functional relation with the variables constitutive of the production relation with the variables constitutive of the production process and the other monetary variables. Explaining the economy, understanding the relations between the significant variables, is like moving from a limited understanding of a number of terms and relations in a mathematical series to grasping the principle of the whole series. But here the "terms in the series" will be specific economies, and the systematic principles will relate to them as the dynamic principles. It could be argued that the historical substitutions in the variables, production, exchange, and finance, in the economies of the twenty countries considered by W. W. Rostow, stand in a similar relation to the economic system in Lonergan's *An Essay in Circulation Analysis* as the kinematical equations stand to Newton's dynamic principles.

A similar movement towards a systematic viewpoint can be detected in Lonergan's efforts to understand the theological community. In his early work on the Trinity in Rome, Lonergan recognised that theology was constituted by more than a single method of inquiry.[25] In 1964 he had succeeded in differentiating four methods.[26] In 1965, with his insight into the functional specialties, he arrived at the systematic viewpoint articulated in *Method in Theology*. There the theological community is understood in terms of a dynamically interrelated system of special methods or variables. That viewpoint, far from attempting to enclose theology in a straight jacket, articulates the dynamic norms under which any number of culturally distinct theological communities might develop. But it will not determine the historical details of their development. A similar systematic understanding of the scientific community also becomes possible in terms of the inter-related methods, classical, statistical, developmental, and evolutionary.

The present study has suggested that wonder and production are human variables. Under no circumstances are they to be considered as the only ones. It is up to the social sciences to discover the full range of significant human variables. As those variables are dynamic, the attainment of the systematic viewpoint would objectify the dynamic norms of the community, the principles of community authenticity. Far from chaining up the members, it would objectify a framework for collaborative creativity in which their wonder, productivity, and other comparable activities could prosper.

IV. HUMAN VARIABLES AND RELATIONS

Having articulated a basic heuristic of the social sciences, it will be helpful to list some points about human variables that stand in need of clarification. A first problem area is that of the distinction between human and non-human variables. A physical movement or a chemical element is one thing, the language we use to talk about them is another. That language use as meaningful does not constitute a movement or an element. But it is consti-tutive of the properly human realm, the community of physicists and chemists, for instance.

> Hence there is a radical difference between the data of natural science and the data of human science. The physicist, chemist, biologist verifies his hypotheses in what is given just as it is given. The human scientist can verify only in data that besides being given have a meaning. Physicists, chemists, engineers might enter a court of law, but after making all their measurements and calculations they could not declare that it was a court of law.(27)

There is a related need to classify the whole realm of meaningful activities. Analytical philosophers are strong on the analysis of language, but weak on the analysis of preconceptual operations such as wonder and insight. Lonergan asserts clearly that production is a meaningful activity, a view not shared by all:

> Beyond the world we know about, there is the further world we make. But what we make, we first intend. We imagine, we plan, we investigate possibilities, we weigh pros and cons, we enter into contracts, we have countless orders given and executed. From the beginning to the end of the process, we are engaged in acts of meaning; . . .(28)

The meaningful elements of working need elaboration.

Secondly, there is a need to clarify the distinction between social and functional relations. Briefly stated, social relations are relations between individuals, between an individual and a group, or between groups. The terms or poles that enter into the relations are then individuals or groups. Functional relations are relations between meaningful activities such as questioning, understanding, thinking, speaking, judging, deciding, or between the special methods of inquiry of theology and science, or between producing consumer or producer products. Particular University Faculties are not mentioned in *Method in Theology*. Relations of role or status, etc., between individuals in departments and between the members of departments in Faculties would constitute social relations. Individual persons are the terms or poles that enter into such relations. On the other hand, relations between research, interpretation, history and dialectic, are relations between interrelated meaningful activities.

Similar considerations apply to the economic community. *An Essay in Circulation Analysis* makes no mention of particular banks or firms, of unions or management, or of individuals in the productive process. Relations of role or status, etc., between particular individuals and unions, between unions and management, between individuals or companies and banks, in the production process constitute social relations. Again, the poles or terms of the relations are individuals or groups. Functional relations differ in that the terms or poles in the relations are interrelated meaningful activities such as production, exchange, or finance. In both the theological and economic communities, the significant functional relations among the variables are utterly different from the significant social relations among the individuals and social groups.

Functional relations are intrinsic to such social processes as producing a standard of living, doing science, doing theology. They are the set of internal relations among the meaningful activities which constitute those processes. Lonergan proposes that the theological process is constituted by eight interdependent methods of inquiry, research, interpretation, history, dialectic, foundations, doctrines, systematics, and communications. That set of functional relations, if verified, would constitute the theological process. Similarly, the functional relations among production, exchange, and finance, if verified, would constitute the economic process of producing a standard of living. As functional relations are intrinsic to the process so also they reveal its autonomy. Politicians and religious authorities can obviously establish directions within the economic and theological processes. But those involvements, if they are to be genuine, must not interfere with the internal autonomy of the processes as established in the functional relations. The economic process has its own internal autonomy which must be respected by politicians, management, and unions, be they socialist or capitalist.

Hand in hand with those functional relations, but quite distinct from them are the social relations by means of which the communities relate to the production, scientific, and theological processes. Social relations can vary from place to place, and culture to culture. They will be different at different stages of scientific and industrial progress, a fact brought out by the study of the trade union movement. Reflection on the current employment situation brings out the distinction between those two kinds of relations. With the ever increasing mechanisation of the production process it is now clear that a high standard of living can be produced for all. That production process has an internal structure and autonomy which must be respected. But what is also clear is that one and the same production process can be operated with vastly different social patterns of work. The social distribution of work and employment pertains to social relations. Its structure, unlike that of the production or theological processes, has to be freely chosen and established by the socio-political communities.

To what extent would the determination of the appropriate functional relations for a social realm determine or even guarantee future social progress in that realm? In response a distinction has to be drawn between two forms of the "why" question. An answer to a why question such as "why is this an X rather than a Y?", says nothing at all to questions such as, "why did A do P?", or "what economic products are we going to produce?", or "what research or interpretative questions are we going to tackle?" The determination of the functional relations leaves all such specific matters indeterminate. It is up to the members of the community, freely, to make their options. Determining the really significant questions which the theological community ought to confront in an era, or equivalently, the productive challenges which the global economic community should face up to, is a matter of high morality. However, while the functional specialties might have nothing to say about such projects, they have everything to say about the way in which they are to be achieved. With all the good will in the world an economic community could plan its future projects. Yet without understanding the functional relations between production, exchange, and finance, it is inherently a victim of stagnation, booms and slumps, and worst of all, recessions. For the functional relations specify the processes by means of which the projects are worked out.

An analogy will help. Consider a car. One can pose the question, "why is this a car rather than something else?" The answer will be in terms of a system of relations appropriate to the car. When one understands them one understands the structural relations of the car. However, that knowledge will not enable one to determine where any driver might drive the car. It will enable one to say when it is being wrongly driven. But it leaves utterly indeterminate answers to questions about where the car was and will be driven. On the other hand it does make clear that anytime the car is being driven anywhere, a certain pattern of dynamic relations among the mechanical parts of the car is operative. It gives one mastery over those relations. Having made a decision to drive from A to B, that knowledge will both guide the manner in which it is driven and insure, in the case of mechanical failure, that the car will arrive at its destination.

The kind of explanation sought in the social sciences will then have a crucial role to play in promoting social processes. It will predict in the economic community the circumstances under which progress towards economic goals could stagnate, be caught in a trade cycle, a recession, or ideally, progress through a pure cycle.[29] Similar observations apply to science and theology, interpreted as social processes. If they are both constituted by an interrelated set of methods of inquiry, then to the extent that the social process allows full scope to all the methods and their relations, will science or theology progress through the equivalent of the pure cycle in economics. To the extent that some or many of those methods and the relations between them are ignored, will such social processes stagnate, be caught in booms and slumps, or even recessions. If all the functional specialties are covered in the theological community there will result something akin to a pure cycle of progress. If not, there will be blind spots in the horizon.

The aim of the paper has been to introduce and explore a possible explanatory structure or heuristic for the social sciences. An analysis of similarities in *Method in Theology* and *An Essay in Circulation Analysis* resulted in a proposal. One possible aim in the social sciences is to understand dynamic systems of functional relations among meaningful human activities of the members of the community. Now that the position has been articulated, the further task of relating it to parallel efforts among social scientists remains to be performed. The remainder of the paper linked the suggested type of explanation with a form of the why question. It follows that although the proposal was formulated with respect to the theological and economic communities, its field of relevance is more general. Other types of communities or dimensions of the human community can be approached with the same expectation.

NOTES

1 The literature on the subject is vast. Anthony Giddens in his *Central Problems in Social Theory* (London: The Macmillan Press, 1979), Chapter 7 provides a useful statement about the present state of the discipline.

2 *Method in Theology* (London: Darton, Longman & Todd, 1972); *An Essay in Circulation Analysis* (1944, 1978, 1980, 1982). (At the moment it is not yet published but texts are available at the Lonergan Centres in Toronto, Boston, Santa Clara, Dublin, and elsewhere.)

3 *Method*, p. xi. Lonergan does not state this about *An Essay in Circulation Analysis* but I would like to suggest that it is not a bad standpoint from which to approach it.

4 *Insight: A Study of Human Understanding*, (London: Longman's, Green and Co., 1957), Chapter XII, especially sections 2 and 5.

5 See Walter Heitler, "The Departure from Classical Thought in Modern Physics," in P.A. Schilpp, ed., *Albert Einstein: Philosopher-Scientist*, 3rd ed. (La Salle: Open Court Publ. Co., 1971), pp. 179-198.

6 On the structure of development see Ira Progoff, *The Practice of Process Meditation* (New York: Dialogue House Library, 1981), Chapter 3; on evolutionary questioning see David Hull, *Philosophy of Biological Science* (New Jersey: Prentice Hall, 1974), Chapter 2.

7 *Insight*, Chapter IV argues that classical and statistical modes of questioning and analysis are complementary. Every answer to a classical question generates a statistical one, and vice versa. To

establish that complementarity is really to prove that they are functionally related variables of the scientific community.

8 *An Essay in Circulation Analysis,* 1982 on pps. 10 to 13 introduces the terms: production, exchange, and finance. Sections 4 to 9 of the text deal with production, sections 10 to 12 with exchange, and section 13, with finance. The terms, production, exchange, and finance, are not the names of single variables in economics, but rather of blocks of variables. When interpreting their use in this essay this point must be borne in mind.

9 Ibid., section 10, pp. 40f.

10 Ibid., section 13, especially pp. 55, 60–66.

11 *Method in Theology,* Chapter 3, section 8.

12 W. W. Rostow, *The World Economy* (Austin and London: University of Texas Press, 1978), Part Five.

13 *Insight,* xix. "In the third place, more than all else, the aim of the book is to issue an invitation to a personal, decisive act."

14 Ibid., xxviii. In the build up to the judgement of self-appropriation, Lonergan in Chapters I to V invites us to participate in the activities of the members of the mathematical and scientific communities; in chapters VI and VII, he invites us to reflect on our involvement in our everyday common sense worlds. So although self-appropriation is a personal act, it presupposes involvement in a social context.

15 *At a Journal Workshop* (New York: Dialogue House Library, 1975), Chapters 17 and 18, and *Process Meditation* (New York: Dialogue House Library, 1981), Chapter 9, on the personal and transpersonal.

16 See W. Mathews, "Method and the Social Appropriation of Reality" in *Method and Creativity,* edited by Matthew Lamb (Milwaukee: Marquette University Press, 1981), Section III, especially pp. 432–3 where the point about connecting the personal with the transpersonal is developed. The present essay is a sequel to that earlier one.

17 *Insight* was largely concerned with appropriating the cognitive function of meaning, although pp. 601f is expanding into the field of activity. *Collection* pp. 253f., adds to the world we know, the world we make. *Method in Theology,* pp. 77–8 gives as much emphasis to the efficient as to the cognitive function of meaning. In those later writings Lonergan is asserting that work and economic activity are as meaningful as cognition. To appropriate the efficient function, to answer the question, 'What am I doing when I am working?' would involve, for instance, appropriating the whole bodily dimension of work and productive activity, and would require a study comparable to *Insight.* This has to be undertaken in the context of such studies of work and creativity as Buber's *I and Thou* (Edinburgh: T. & T. Clark, 1966), especially pp. 9–10; Progoff, *At a Journal Workshop,* Chapter 12; and Hannah Arendt, *The Human Condition* (Chicago: University of Chicago Press, 1958).

18 Aristotle, *Physics,* 194b, 15–35, *Metaphysics,* 1041, 10f.

19 There are many other forms of basic questions other than the why form. There is the 'how often?' form which underpins statistics, the developmental and evolutionary forms which underpin development and evolution. No claim is being made that the why question is the only form of basic question. On the other hand, despite the fact that it is one of many, when validly posed it cannot be avoided.

20 Schumpeter, *History of Economic Analysis* (London: George Allen and Unwin, 1961). To this must be added Collingwood's point that a basic "why" question is really a complex of sub-questions and answers (*Autobiography* [Oxford: Oxford University Press, 1970], Chapter V, especially p. 37 f.) The sciences in their history allow the sub-questions to emerge and be resolved. For a study of the

narrative by means of which the science of chemistry became established see Mathews, Price and Ford, *The Nature of Scientific Discovery* (SISCON report, the University of Manchester, 1979), part 2.
21   The term function, poses a number of problems. In the natural sciences we say that a variable y is a function of x, $y = f(x)$. Corresponding to substitutions in one variable are functionally related substitutions in the other. The present usage is closer to that than what is known in sociology as functionalism. See R. K. Merton, *Social Theory and Social Structure* (New York: The Free Press, 1957), pp. 20f, where five senses of the word, function, are outlined. Merton acknowledges that the boundaries between the variable and the sociological senses of function are not clear (p. 21). The matter needs further clarification but the evidence seems to suggest that they are very different. So the present position is not to be equated with functionalism. See also Achinstein, *The Nature of Explanation* (London and New York: Oxford University Press, 1983).
22   *Insight*, 243f.
23   For the story of the quest for and the discovery of the systematic viewpoint in chemistry see Mathews, Price and Ford, op. cit., pp. 131-153. For an appreciation of how the systematic viewpoint, when reached transforms the whole problem-solving framework of the science see G.I. Browne, *A new Guide to Valency Theory* (London: Longmans, 1968), pp. 18f.
24   A first version occurs on p. 41 of the 1944 and p. 42 of the 1977 texts. In the notes for the Spring Course in 1979 there is an intermediate revision. For the final version see p. 54 of the 1982 text.
25   His early reflections on theological method are in Chapter one of *Divinarum Personarum Conceptionem Analogicam* (Rome: Gregorian University Press, 1959), and *De Deo Trino, Pars Prima* (Rome: Gregorian University Press, 1964). There is occurring in those works the process of differentiating doctrines and sytematics from history.
26   In July 13-17, 1964 at an Institute on *Method in Theology* at Georgetown University, Lonergan had differentiated four theological tasks or methods: foundations, positive theology, doctrines and systematics. An advertisement describing the titles of the lectures at this Institute may be consulted in the Lonergan Centres, as well as some notes taken at it. It is obvious that at this stage Lonergan was in search of the complete set of theological methods and their systematic interdependence.
27   *Collection*, p. 244.
28   Ibid., p. 253.
29   On cycles see *An Essay in Circulation Analysis*, 1982, section 8, pp. 35f.

XIX

Affective Conversion: The Transformation of Desire

WALTER E. CONN

WHEN philosophical emphases shift from human nature to human history and from the human soul to the human subject, the meaning of the personal subject's experienced life moves from the wings to center stage.[1] Once this transposition from the abstract and static to the concrete and dynamic occurs, the drama inevitably focuses on the realities of personal development and conversion.[2] And within this new focus on the transformation of personal experience, one of the major challenges of interpretation facing the critic is the radical personal reality Bernard Lonergan has called affective conversion.[3] Here I want to suggest that affective conversion is a transformation of desire: a turning from possessive desire to desire for generosity; a reorientation from the possessiveness rooted in obsessive concern for one's own needs to the self-giving of intimate love and generative care of others.[4]

I. FALLING-IN-LOVE

A person is affectively self-transcendent, Lonergan points out, when the isolation of the individual is broken and he or she spontaneously acts not just for self but for others as well. Further, when a person falls in love, his or her love is embodied not just in this or that act or even in any series of acts, but in a dynamic state of being-in-love. Such being-in-love is the concrete first principle from which a person's affective life flows: "one's desires

261

and fears, one's joys and sorrows, one's discernment of values, one's decisions and deeds."[5] Falling-in-love, in other words, is a more or less radical transformation of a person's life: affective conversion.[6] Such conversion turns one's self, shifts one's orientation, from an absorption in one's own interests to concern for the good of others. If moral conversion is the recognition of the possibility, thus the felt challenge, of becoming a living principle of benevolence and beneficience, affective conversion is the transformation of personal being which actualizes that possibility, which makes effective response to that challenge a reality. Rooted in the peaceful joy and bliss of affective conversion, therefore, is the concrete possibility of overcoming moral impotence, of not only being able to make a decision to commit oneself to a course of action or direction of life judged worthwhile and personally appropriate, but of being able to execute that decision over the long haul against serious obstacles.[7]

The reality of falling-in-love, of course, has as many versions as there are love stories.[8] There is the beaming love of young parents for their newborn child; there is the love of sons and daughters for mothers and fathers which grows through years of responding to the wonders of parental self-transcendence. Such familial self-transcendence grounds the possibility, too, of the intimate love between a woman and a man—from the boundless dreams and reckless self-giving of young lovers to the gentle touch and knowing smiles of a peaceful couple remembering a half-century through which they have grown together in each other's love.

Life, of course, is made of more than love stories. Right alongside are ugly tales of hatred and brutality, misunderstanding and resentment, indifference and bitter disappointment—tales which too often end without a hint of forgiveness, reconciliation, hope. At the end of a century that has witnessed human atrocities of the most staggering proportions, a story that ignores the full potential of the human heart for evil is less credible than a fairy tale.[9] Still, if life is not an innocent story in which prince charmings and fairy godmothers always emerge triumphant, there are indeed instances of self-transcending love. As the lives of individuals as different as Martin Luther King and Mother Teresa of Calcutta remind us, when the mutual love of families and friends is authentic it does not remain absorbed in an *egoisme a deux* or three or more, but reaches out beyond itself to the neighbor, not to "humanity," but to the concrete person in need, whoever or wherever that person is.

Now, as imaginatively suggestive as the phrase "falling-in-love" is, without further precision it is far too ambiguous to provide a critical understanding of affective conversion. "Love" simply means too many very different things to adequately ground so central a human reality as affective conversion. Erich Fromm speaks of five loves (brotherly, motherly, erotic, self-love, and love of God); Paul Tillich lists four (libido, eros, philia, and agape), as does C. S. Lewis (affection, eros distinguished from venus, friendship, and charity); the Scholastics specify three (*concupiscentia, benevolentia,* and *amicitia*); Anders Nygren and Denis de Rougement insist on the dichotomy of two loves, eros and agape, while Martin D'Arcy and Robert Johann, following Augustine and Aquinas, attempt their synthesis; the fundamental unity of love, finally, is maintained by George Tavard.[10]

By "love" Lonergan clearly means the active, other-oriented principle of beneficence and benevolence, but this meaning is confused by his use of the phrase "*falling*-in-love," with all its connotations of passivity and sentimentality. A critical interpretation of affective conversion demands a careful examination of affectivity in general and of love in particular. [11]

II. Cognitive Interpretation of Affectivity

Lonergan's interpretation of affectivity focuses on feelings as sources of value. Distinct from feelings of directly physiological origin, feelings capable of disclosing value are *intentional* responses of the whole person. Such fully personal feelings arise out of cognitive activities like perceiving and imagining, and are thus related not just to causes and ends but to intentional objects as responses. [12]

Although this interpretation of feeling as intentional response is based directly on Dietrich von Hildebrand's (and indirectly Max Scheler's) rather distinctive phenomenological analysis, it relates very positively to the major line of contemporary psychological theories of emotions which stresses their *cognitive* character. [13] Indeed, its roots in the *philosophia perennis* are manifest in the work of Magda Arnold, the principal psychological proponent of the cognitive theory of emotions, who explicitly derives her fundamental approach from Aristotle and Aquinas. [14]

This link to the philosophical tradition can be discerned in Arnold's definition of emotion as "a felt tendency toward anything appraised as good, and away from anything appraised as bad." [15] In this view of emotion, whatever is perceived, remembered, imagined will be appraised; if the object is appraised as desirable or harmful, an action tendency is aroused. Arnold regards the physiological changes that are so impressive in emotion as ancillary to the felt action tendency; both originate from the appraisal. In Arnold's vocabulary, emotions aim at possession or avoidance of objects, while the term "feeling" designates "those affective states where the psychological reference is principally to the subject." [16] Feelings reflect the individual's inner state of functioning.

An essential dimension of this perspective on emotion is what Arnold calls affective memory. Distinct from modality-specific memory such as visual or auditory, affective memory is "the living record of the emotional life history of each person." [17] Unlike modality-specific memory which is usually lost quickly, affective memory is always at our disposal, and in appraisals it relives the original acceptance or rejection (a dog-bite in early childhood, for example) in a new but similar situation. Though appraisals organize emotions, and emotions organize the actions they urge, from the perspective of the person motions can be perceived as interfering and disturbing if they urge in a direction different from that indicated by deliberate judgment. But, as the diabetic who resists the temptation of the delicious but dangerous dessert exemplifies, even the intuitive appraisal leading to strong desire is not necessarily final. Intuitive appraisal produces an action impulse, but in the end it is the motive established by conscious judgment and deliberate decision that determines action. [18] In Arnold's perspective, then, emotions are cognitive in a two-fold sense: they depend on cognitive activities for their objects, and they are fundamentally constituted by intuitive appraisals which are not only cognitive but evaluative.

Richard Lazarus also holds that emotions and cognitions are inseparable. He assumes that emotions arise from how a person construes the outcome of his or her transaction with the environment.[19] In this view, cognitive processes "create the emotional response out of the organism-environment transaction and shape it into anger, fear, grief, etc."[20] Extending Arnold's basic cognitive approach, Lazarus argues that the pattern of arousal observed in emotion derives from impulses to action generated not only by the individual's appraised situation, but also by the evaluated possibilities available for action. An important part of the cognitive dimension of emotions, in other words, are the reappraisals based on feedback processes. Along with direct actions (attack, avoidance), reappraisals constitute the basic coping processes available to the individual. Lazarus also stresses the beliefs, attitudes, etc. of the individual as important conditions of appraisals along with situational factors.

Among psychologists offering a cognitive interpretation of emotions, James Averill is distinctive for his social constructivist view. For him, not only do cognitive structures provide the basis for the appraisals of stimuli, but the functional significance of emotional response is to be found largely within the sociocultural system. With regard to subjective experience within emotion, Averill makes the important claim that a person interprets his or her own experience as emotional much as an actor interprets a role "with feeling,"[21] The passivity commonly associated with emotions, for example, is not intrinsic to the response, according to Averill, but is an interpretation. Here, then, we have a view of emotions as cognitive not just in the sense of being dependent on cognitive activities, or even of incorporating appraisal as a constitutive component, but as essentially an act of creative interpretation of experience.

III. AFFECTIVITY AS CONSTITUTIVE OF IDENTITY

Psychologists are not alone in their emphasis on the cognitive dimension of emotion. Indeed, it is a contemporary philosopher, Robert Solomon, who has been most insistent on this theme over the course of two books and several articles.

The aim of Solomon's major study, *The Passions*, is to return to the passions the central and defining role in our lives. "Our passions constitute our lives," says Solomon, they alone provide our lives with meaning. Emotions, he argues, are "the very core of our existence, the system of meanings and values within which our lives either develop and grow or starve and stagnate." Focusing on the cognitive theme in particular, Solomon stresses that emotions are "our own *judgments*, with which we structure the world to our purposes, . . . and ultimately 'constitute' not only our world but ourselves."[22] As judgments, then, emotions are both evaluative and constitutive. They are the source of most of our values. Our emotions would transform the world. Indeed, emotional expression is an attempt to make the world the way it *ought* to be.[23]

Solomon aims at a marriage of the passions and reason in a new romanticism, in which the passions are illuminated, enlightened by reflection, supported by deliberation.

For unlike other judgments, emotions are unarticulated, unreflective, undeliberated. Because they are already made when we come to reflect on them, emotions can appear to happen to us.[24] But it is Solomon's basic point to insist that we make our emotions—we make ourselves angry, we make ourselves depressed, we make ourselves fall in love—and thus we are responsible for them.

Again, in line with his general analysis of emotion, Solomon wants to insist that love is something we actively *do,* not some passive thing that happens to us. Despite all the sentimental rhetoric to the contrary, we do not *fall* in love, we rather judge, decide, choose to love. Thus, we are responsible for our loving.[25] Solomon's point is that we do not simply come upon and fall captive to, but that we *constitute* the charms and virtues of the person we *choose* to love. Love, like other emotions, is a set of constitutive judgments, in this case "to the effect that we *will* see in this person every possible virtue, ignore or overlook every possible vice, celebrating faults as well as charms in the context of his or her total personality."[26] The virtues and charms lovers "discover," then, are actually created through interpretation. It is the interpretation that is discovered. Even the parameters of one's love are a set of self-legislated ideals and standards. Like the other emotions, love establishes a framework, a set of standards within which we commit ourselves, and "to which the world, other people, and, most importantly, our Selves are expected to comply."[27]

Deciding to love means many things, says Solomon, but most of all it means that "one stops thinking in terms of self-interest as the criterion for making decisions."[28] It means ceasing to think of independence as the ideal of self-identity. Paradoxically, it means dropping the goal of self-esteem, despite love's very strategy of maximizing self-esteem. Ideally, of course, in the shared self of the loveworld, to maximize the self-esteem of one's lover is to maximize one's own self-esteem.

Much of what masquerades as love—dependency, possessiveness, for example—is not love at all. For Solomon, "Love is intimacy and trust; love is mutual respect and admiration; love is the insistence on mutual independence and autonomy, free from possessiveness but charged with desire; love is unqualified acceptance of the other's welfare and happiness as one's own."[29] Love is not possessiveness; love only begins where possessive desire ends. Love is not dependency; love is an emotion of strength. Those who think they need love the most are the least likely to love, because though they may be ready to give themselves, they have so little self to give. And neither, according to Solomon, is love self-love. Self-love is not love at all, but idolatry. In self-love one loves merely the *image* of the self, not the self; the self as object, not as subject.[30]

For Solomon, then, emotions are not only radically cognitive, but through unreflective interpretation, judgment, decision, and choice are also fundamentally constitutive of our human world. Emotions are not essentially at odds with reason; rather, in reflection lies the possibility of emotional transformation. If emotions have in common the power of self-creation, romantic love is singular in that its creation is a radically transforming recreation of a shared self in a shared world with a shared interest.

IV. ROMANTIC LOVE: PASSION AND DECISION

The self-transforming power of romantic love is also central to the theological analysis of Rosemary Haughton's *The Passionate God*. Haughton's thesis is that we can make sense of how God loves by looking at the way people love, particularly the way of love called passionate. By "passionate" Haughton means to evoke something "in motion—strong, wanting, needy, concentrated towards a very deep encounter." For her "passion" also means a certain "helplessness, a suffering and undergoing for the sake of what is desired and, implicitly, the possibility of a tragic outcome."[31]

Romantic love is bodily, sexual (though not necessarily genital) love; it is concentrated on the experience of passion; it is not platonically "spiritual." But as fully human love, it is a radical realization of spirit in the flesh. In this passionate love, Haughton stresses, lovers come to self-awareness in the awareness of the beloved; they are defined in the very exchange of life that is love.

Haughton discerns four key moments in the pattern or sequence of Romantic breakthrough.[32] First there is *remote preparation*, probably a lengthy process of vague restlessness, desire, longing (adolescence, for example) which creates a situation for *immediate preparation*, the weak spot or vulnerable point. Here something happens which "shakes the person loose from normal expectations and settled attitudes"—a book, a vacation, a disaster, an encounter with "the" person. Whatever the occasion, when it occurs there is recognition, and the response to it transforms vague longing into intense passion: "the thrust of the whole personality towards the strange 'home' it perceives." But the recognition is so profound, so complete as to be ineffable, and is thus experienced as a gap, a void. Passion is the thrust which leaps that void, without guarantee or even knowledge; it is a leap of faith. The actual *breakthrough*, then, is this difficult, painful self-giving—across a gap of "un-knowing"—towards an intensely desired wholeness. The final moment identified by Haughton involves follow-through. How will the *language* of an individual's community help that person to interpret the experience of breakthrough? This element of communal language is vital because on the question of interpretation depends the crucial issue of what one will *do* about the breakthrough. The question of action points to what Haughton takes to be the most important element of Romantic doctrine, the element that the French originators of courtly love referred to as *amour voulu*: dedicated service of commitment.

Haughton's view of romantic love as *amour voulu* clearly goes beyond that of Solomon, whose most recent account rejects commitment of any kind as the very opposite of love, not its fulfillment.[33] But just as clearly, her interpretation reflects the essence of Solomon's understanding of love as not only a creative transformation of oneself and one's world but as itself open to transformation through reflection and deliberation.

Indeed, Haughton's analysis of conversion in her *Transformation of Man* characterizes it precisely as a radical breakthrough of *love*. Transformation only occurs within a context of formation, she maintains, within the "personality formed through time-conditioned stages of development." But formation is always a matter of fairness, order, self-interest, whereas transformation is a response to the "demand for the decision to love." Conversion is a giving of love, a giving of self in love, a "personal decision of self-surrender."[34]

In asserting that "transformation occurs in the moment of self-surrender to love," Haughton takes her stand within a virtuous circle.[35] For only the individuated self, distinguished in self-awareness, is capable of self-giving. But real self-knowledge, which weakens the defenses against the outside world, can only be accepted by one who has experienced him or herself *as loved*. So loving requires self-surrender; but self-surrender requires being loved. "Self-awareness as separate is the prerequisite of self-giving love," but the required awareness of self as separate is the genuine self-knowledge of humility; "it is not the withdrawal of pride that defends the beleaguered citadel but the confidence of being valued that makes openness possible without fear."[36]

The transforming decision of love is a "total gift of the whole person," unconditional and unreflective. It is not just a decision to behave differently, but a faithful "commitment to the unknown."[37] "Only the knowledge of *being loved* has the power to set free into faith," says Haughton; alone each of us is helpless. Therefore "Someone already transformed by love is needed, in order to convey an assurance of love sufficiently strong to penetrate the defenses of the flesh in another and let loose the power of the spirit," Haughton explains. "This is the work of the community of love." The point to be stressed here is that the support of love must be simply for the sake of love, with its radical given-ness, at-riskness. Support given out of self-confidence is possessive, it wants to control growth. "Support given for love is willing to see the support no longer needed," it has its source not in oneself but in the power of love shared, which is never possessed by always given.[38]

This, indeed, is the fundamental point of Haughton's *Love*, which seems to distinguish genuine love from its counterfeit. The basic problem in specifying the nature of love, as Haughton sees it, is that if love simply means even the rather advanced notion of a "drive towards, or desire for, a wider, deeper, more important 'beyond' in human life," it can include the demonic devotion of a Hitler as well as the compassionate devotion of a Mother Teresa. Some further, critical specification is needed. In her reading of the mystics especially, Haughton discerns a fundamental criterion: "you can tell genuine love because it opens out and gives itself." In contrast, "You can recognize false 'love' because it encloses itself, and seeks to grow by grabbing and snatching and keeping." The attempt to possess is anti-love, while real love is not only the desire for the "other" or "beyond", but the impulse to give oneself to that "otherness." It may be impossible to draw this line neatly through complex human experience, but distinction does provide a standard for judgment. Love is genuine to the degree that it is open, self-giving, generous; false to the extent that it is closed, possessive, controlling.[39]

Mystical love's attachment to something beyond the human helps Haughton to recognize that *all* genuine love "actually reaches further than the human object." "Love that stops short at its human object," she explains, "is liable to become anti-love, because it depends on the existence of its object as *lovable*, that is, as a sort of object of worship." If necessary, it will *force* the beloved to remain lovable. The possessive mother who wants a dependent child to cherish is only the most obvious example of this "love" syndrome that takes its immediate object as its god and becomes anti-love, often destroying the beloved and warping the lover.[40]

But genuine love refuses to worship a limited good, no matter how lovable. It remains responsive to the demand of the call for "something more," the demand to "leave all things," to "go out," to "give oneself." If love goes beyond its immediate object, it is also experienced as originating beyond one's very self and existing beyond one's control; one experiences oneself as almost literally seized by the power of love's demand. Yet the power of the demand is felt so forcefully not because it comes from the outside as a foreign invader, but precisely because it is the fundamental drive, the activity of the spirit of one's person, arising from the depths of one's very being. The demand of such a drive can be resisted, but only at the cost of destroying something of one's deepest reality—thus the sense of being *seized*. Response to this demand, on the other hand, creates the person, says Haughton, for it means going beyond ourselves to others in responding to situations that call for love, thereby actually becoming the self-transcending persons we are capable of being.[41]

V. PERSONAL TRANSFORMATION: DESIRE, COMMITMENT, SERVICE

Clearly, there are important differences between the reflections on love of Haughton and Solomon. But both make up a source from which we may draw some basic points of interpretation. First, love is passionate; it is not a bloodless act of cerebral will. Second, as emotion, love is not blind, it has a cognitive character. Love is a passionate interpretation, judgment, decision, choice—unreflective and therefore undifferentiated (feeling, knowing, choosing are one). Third, though unreflective, love can be influenced, even transformed by reflection. Fourth, and perhaps most important, love, though a passionate desire, must be distinguished clearly from *possessive* desire. Solomon says love begins where possessive desire ends. Haughton names possessiveness anti-love. Both reflect the fundamental distinction we saw earlier in de Rivera's structural theory of emotion between love (self moving towards other: giving) and desire (self moving other towards self: getting).

I have thoroughly reviewed the interpretations Solomon and Haughton give of love because of the striking possibilities they offer for understanding the dynamics of affective conversion. By paying serious attention to the passionate reality of Romantic love they have managed to transcend the tangles of the usual theological discussions of love which revolve upon the relation between eros and agape. Indeed, they have disclosed at the heart of an authentic human love a single source from which spring the movements of both desire and self-giving. Desire and self-giving are not identical, but neither are they inevitably at odds with each other. Indeed, George Tavard insists that human love is inseparably other-desire and self-gift.[42] Desire can be possessive, but it need not be. Self-giving can be personally destructive, but this is not necessary. Eros, as Paul Tillich has shown so clearly, can be desire for value: the true, the good, the beautiful.[43] And as Haughton points out, self-giving can be the fulfillment of the self-transcending person. In fully human love, the two movements specified by de Rivera as desire and love reinforce each other in the single drive for value that moves a person beyond him or her self. Far from being necessarily at odds, then, genuine desire and authentic self-giving become one in the realization of self-transcendence. As Robert Johann argues, eros can be *desire for generosity.*[44]

Despite the self-transcending possibilities of desire, however, Haughton is acutely aware of how easily desire can distort itself into indulgent possessiveness. Thus while the intense *passion* of desire is necessary for authentic love, it is not sufficient. Truly human love also requires what the courtly poets called *amour voulu:* the deliberate self-giving of the lover in the decision of commitment. By transforming passion into a definitive orientation, such decision constitutes the whole person in terms of a love reaching for ultimate value, and commits her or him to express this being-in-love in action for the good of the beloved.[45]

What light, finally, does this analysis of love contribute towards clarifying the fundamental reality of affective conversion? The major point I want to emphasize is the two-fold character of affective conversion—its dual dimensions. Affective conversion must be understood as a matter of *both passion and commitment.*

Affective conversion belongs to the interior world of feeling—one falls-in-love; but it is not simply a matter of passion. Again, affective conversion requires deliberate decision—one commits oneself to the beloved; but it is no ethereal, disembodied act of will. Because affective conversion is a transformation of the whole person, it involves both intuitive passion and deliberate commitment.

Affective conversion does mean "falling-in-love," with all the specifications of that phrase we have examined in the views of Haughton, Solomon, and the cognitive interpreters of emotion. One *"falls"*-in-love precisely because love is passionate—the unreflective desire to give oneself in which the self is experienced as passive and helpless because the desire is experienced as originating and existing beyond—and therefore outside the control of—the reflectively conscious self. Haughton reminds us that, in the case of love, beyond the reflectively conscious self means not external to the person, but from within the interior depths of the person, the drive of the spirit of one's very being for self-transcendence. Unless one passionately falls-in-love, unless one unreflectively desires to give oneself in a way that involves one's own meaning and value—indeed, one's identity and self-esteem, then one can expect the deliberate, reflective decision to love and will the good of another, though sincere, to be at best a beautifully crafted, highly polished veneer, unlikely over the long term to stand up under the hard knocks and constant pressure of tough, everyday use. Affective conversion is a reorientation of the whole person, but especially of those pre-reflective desires which must support our reflectively conscious decisions, choices, and loving commitments.

If reflective commitment to love be merely surface reality when unsupported by pre-reflective passion, it is also true that feeling needs the guidance and stability of reflective commitment. Passion is neither blind nor weak, but it is often near-sighted and short-lived. We may not be able to *make* ourselves fall-in-love at will, but when it happens that we do desire to give ourselves passionately, reflection and deliberation can, as Solomon argues, both illuminate and strengthen our pre-reflective responses. "Since emotions are aroused by appraisal, and appraisal depends on what is experienced, remembered, imagined," Arnold explains that we can have at least indirect control over our emotions by using our imagination to influence appraisal.[46] Along the same line, Lonergan, while recognizing that feelings are fundamentally spontaneous inasmuch as they do not lie under the command of decision, points out that "once they have arisen, they may be reinforced by advertence and approval, and they may be curtailed by disapproval and distraction. Such reinforcement and curtailment," he suggests, "will not only encourage some feelings and discourage others but will also modify one's spontaneous scale of preferences."[47] Both Donald Gelpi and Paul Philibert have illuminated this crucial area by stressing Carl Rogers' process approach to the appropriation of affectivity.[48] Reflection, as Solomon, further insists, not only considers emotions, but, through criticism and reinforcement, transforms them.

Affective conversion *is* the transformation of our deepest life of feeling. Without the radical reorientation of our passionate desires from obsession with self-needs to concern for the needs of others, there is no affective conversion. But because fundamental conversion is always a fully personal reality, affective conversion is not exclusively a matter of passion, feeling, emotion. The centrifugal reorientation of the passionate desires of our affective life, having been nudged and coaxed, briefed and guided by reflection, finally needs to be thoroughly personalized in the decision of commitment to love. Such commitment is powerful when it crystalizes the other-centered reorientation of feeling. Still, loving commitment is directed toward service; the criterion, then, for passionate commitment to others, for authentic affective conversion, lies in action.

The transformative influence of reflective criticism and deliberate commitment on our feelings notwithstanding, the principal operator of affective conversion remains the symbol. The carriers of meaning in the internal communication between mind and heart and body, symbols are images that evoke feelings and are evoked by them.[49] Thus, if affective development and conversion effect a transvaluation of symbols, it is also the case that they are initiated by the transforming symbols communicated externally through various intersubjective, artistic, religious, and, especially, personally incarnated embodiments. In all these and other forms, imaginative symbols of self-transcendence speak to the internal tensions, incompatibilities, conflicts, struggles, destructions of our psychic life inaccessible to the logical discourse of reflection. Only concrete, undifferentiated symbols speak the natural language of the pre-reflective heart (where feeling, knowing, and choosing are one). Both pre-reflective, undifferentiated symbols and the logical discourse of critical reflection are related to feeling, but whereas reflection is the distant cousin that speaks a foreign language, imaginative symbols are "family," and affective conversion is first of all a family affair. This significance of the symbol has recently been rediscovered in an important way by those ethicists who stress the role of story in the formation of character.[50]

If we add active service to the two dimensions of affective conversion already discussed, we can summarize the essence of affective conversion by saying that it is "signed" in the other-centered transformation of feeling effected by symbols and guided by reflection, "sealed" in the deliberate decision of commitment to love, and "delivered" in the action of loving service.

1 For Lonergan's analysis of the shift from classicist to contemporary culture, see Bernard Lonergan, "The Transition from a Classicist World-View to Historical-Mindedness" and "The Future of Thomism" in his *A Second Collection,* ed. W. F. J. Ryan and B. J. Tyrrell (London: Darton, Longman & Todd, 1974), pp. 1–10 and 43–53. In the latter essay Lonergan specifies the transition in terms of five distinct shifts of emphasis: 1) from logic to method; 2) from an Aristotelian to a modern conception of science; 3) from a metaphysics of the soul to the self-appropriation of the subject; 4) from human nature to human history; and 5) from first principles to transcendental method.

2 For Lonergan's basic statements of intellectual, moral, and religious conversions, see Bernard Lonergan, *Method in Theology* (New York: Herder and Herder, 1972), pp. 238–43. Among the many discussions of Lonergan's general notion of conversion, see Charles E. Curran, "Christian Conversion in the Writings of Bernard Lonergan" in Philip McShane, ed., *Foundations of Theology: Papers from the International Lonergan Congress 1970* (Notre Dame, IN: University of Notre Dame Press, 1972), pp. 41–59; Kevin J. Colleran, "Bernard Lonergan on Conversion," *Dunwoodie Review* 11 (January 1971): 3–23; Donal Dorr, "Conversion" in Patrick Corcoran, ed., *Looking at Lonergan's Method* (Dublin: Talbot, 1975), pp. 175–186; and Michael L. Rende, "The Development and the Unity of Lonergan's Notion of Conversion," *Method* 1/2 (October 1983): 158–73. For a correlation of the basic conversions with the fundamental patterns of personal development delineated by Erik Erikson, Jean Piaget, and Lawrence Kohlberg, see Walter E. Conn, *Conscience: Development and Self-Transcendence* (Birmingham, AL: Religious Education Press, 1981).

3 On affective conversion, see Bernard Lonergan, "Natural Right and Historical Mindedness," *Proceedings of the American Catholic Philosophical Association* 51 (1977): 132–43; and Walter E. Conn, "Bernard Lonergan's Analysis of Conversion," *Angelicum* 53/3 (1976): 362–404, at 389–90.

4 Readers familiar with the work of Erik Erikson will recognize in intimate love and generative care reference to the young adult and adult stages of his psychosocial life cycle, following on the crisis of identity and anticipating that of integrity; see Erik H. Erikson, *Childhood and Society* (2nd ed.; New York: Norton, 1963, 1950), pp. 247–74, and *Insight and Responsibility* (New York: Norton, 1964), pp. 111–34.

5 Lonergan, *Method in Theology,* p. 105.

6 See Lonergan, "Natural Right and Historical Mindedness," pp. 140–41. Lonergan's treatment of affective conversion is clearly the least developed of the conversions; one must rely on his rather brief discussions of falling-in-love, as I do in the present attempt at systematic analysis. While my discussions of the other conversions deliberately introduce innovations into Lonergan's original perspectives, the process here is more clearly one of creative development from a minimal starting point. For a somewhat different version of affective conversion stressing the centrality of decision, see Donald L. Gelpi, *Charism and Sacrament* (New York: Paulist, 1976), p. 17 ("Affective conversion is the decision to assume personal responsibility for my emotional growth and development"), *Experiencing God: A Theology of Human Emergence* (New York: Paulist, 1978), pp. 179–81 (where eight stages of affective conversion are outlined following the seven stages of therapeutic process in Carl R. Rogers, *On Becoming a Person: A Therapist's View of Psychotherapy* (Boston: Houghton Mifflin, 1961), pp. 125–59), and "Conversion: The Challenge of Contemporary Charismatic Piety," *Theological Studies* 43/4 (December 1982): 606–28, esp. 613–16. Another excellent treatment of affective conversion in Christian terms complementary to the present discussion is William Johnston, *The Mirror Mind:*

Spirituality and Transformation (San Francisco: Harper & Row, 1981), esp. ch. 6, "Transformation of Feeling."

Significantly different from affective conversion in the sense developed here, though often confused with it, is psychic conversion: see Robert M. Doran, "Psychic Conversion," *Thomist* 41 (April 1977): 200–36, *Subject and Psyche: Ricoeur, Jung, and the Search for Foundations* (Washington, DC: University Press of America, 1977), and *Psychic Conversion and Theological Foundations: Toward a Reorientation of the Human Sciences*, AAR Studies in Religion 25 (Chico, CA: Scholars Press, 1981), esp. pp. 178–93. In the latter work, Doran explains that this conversion, which releases the capacity for internal symbolic communication (p. 178), has religious, moral, and intellectual conversions as conditions for its possibility (p. 184). To use the terms of the present study, then, it *seems* that psychic conversion would be some form of explicitly critical affective conversion—the extension of cognitive (intellectual) conversion into the domain of preconscious affectivity through the symbolic imagination. Also see Bernard Lonergan, "Reality, Myth, Symbol" in Alan M. Olson, ed., *Myth, Symbol, and Reality* (Notre Dame, IN: University of Notre Dame Press, 1980), pp. 31–37, at 37. Another important treatment of the topic along different lines is Bernard J. Tyrrell's discussion of "psychological conversion" and "conversion from addiction" along with religious and moral conversions in his *Christotheraphy II: The Fasting and Feasting Heart* (New York: Paulist, 1982), pp. 10–23.

In my interpretation, conversion is not identical with self-appropriation. I distinguish conversion as the transformation of one's horizon from the critical appropriation of that transformation: only critical versions of conversion are forms of self-appropriation (thus affective conversion may or may not be a form of self-appropriation, but it seems that psychic conversion is by definition). Further, my interpretation does not focus on only one factor (e.g., deciding) as the defining element in all the conversions. While all the basic dimensions, including decision, are involved in every form of conversion, each conversion is specified by a particular element (e.g., as deciding is primary in moral conversion, so understanding and judging play important roles in affective conversion, but to focus on them as definitive is to miss the transformation of desire that is central to affective conversion).

7 On moral impotence as the existential gap between actual and hypothetical effective freedom in terms of incomplete willingness, see Lonergan, *Insight*, p. 627. From this perspective affective conversion is a transformation of willingness. On willingness and the various attempts to escape the exigence for self-consistency in knowing and deciding (avoidance of self-consciousness, rationalization, and moral renunciation), see *ibid.*, pp. 598–600.

8 See Lonergan, *Method in Theology*, pp. 105, 289.

9 For Lonergan on alienation, basic sin, evil, social surd, breakdown, and decline, see his *Insight: A Study of Human Understanding* (2nd ed.; New York: Philosophical Library, 1958, 1957), pp. 228–32, 666–68, 688–93, and *Method in Theology*, pp. 39–40, 53–55, 117–18, 242–44, 364. For Lonergan's analysis of dramatic, individual, group, and general bias, see *Insight*, pp. 191–206, 218–242. Also see William P. Loewe, "Dialectics of Sin: Lonergan's *Insight* and the Critical Theory of Max Horkheimer," *Anglican Theological Review* 61 (1979): 224–45.

10. See Erich Fromm, *The Art of Loving* (2nd ed.; New York: Bantam Books, 1963, 1956), pp. 38–69; Paul Tillich, *Love, Power, and Justice: Ontological Analyses and Ethical Applications* (New York: Oxford University Press Galaxy, 1960, 1954), pp. 28–33; C. S. Lewis, *The Four Loves* (London: Collins Fontana, 1963 1960); Andrew Nygren, *Agape and Eros*, trans. P. S. Watson (2nd ed.; New York: Harper & Row Torchbooks, 1969 original Swedish 1930, 1936; first English 1932, 1938, 1939; 2nd 1953), pp. 53–55; Denis de Rougemont, *Love in the Western*

World, trans. M. Belgion (2nd ed.; Garden City, NY: Doubleday Anchor, 1957 original French 1939, first English 1940, 2nd 1956), pp. 51–61; M. C. D'Arcy, *The Mind and Heart of Love* (2nd ed.; New York: Meridian, 1956, 1945); Robert O. Johann, *The Meaning of Love: An Essay Towards a Metaphysics of Intersubjectivity* (New York: Paulist, 1966), pp. 74–75; and George Tavard, *A Way of Love* (Maryknoll, NY: Orbis, 1977), p. 66. One of the most valuable integrating theological analyses of love (human loves prepare for agape) is Daniel Day Williams, *The Spirit and the Forms of Love* (New York: Harper & Row, 1968), where love in the Christian tradition is distinguished as Augustinian, Franciscan, and evangelical (pp. 52–89). Of the many excellent studies on Augustine, whose caritas synthesis set the terms of the succeeding discussion, see Oliver O'Donovan, *The Problem of Self-Love in St. Augustine* (New Haven, CT: Yale University Press, 1980), which considers four aspects of love: cosmic, positive, rational, and benevolent, pp. 10–36. For a valuable analysis of love in Aquinas, see Frederick E. Crowe, "Complacency and Concern in the Thought of St. Thomas," *Theological Studies* 20 (March 1959): 1–39; 20 (June 1959): 198–230; 20 (September 1959); 343–95, with a perceptive critique of Nygren at 353–63. For a study informed by the contemporary philosophical perspective, see Gene Outka, *Agape: An Ethical Analysis* (New Haven, CT: Yale University Press, 1972).

11   In addition to the authors cited here and below, see the following for valuable contextual and critical discussions: James Hillman, *Emotion: A Comprehensive Phenomenology of Theories and Their Meanings for Therapy* (Evanston, IL: Northwestern University Press, 1961); Anthony Kenny, *Action, Emotion and Will* (New York: Humanities Press, 1963); J. R. S. Wilson, *Emotion and Object* (Cambridge: Cambridge University Press, 1972); W. W. Fortenbaugh, *Aristotle on Emotion* (London: Duckworth, 1975); William Lyons, *Emotion* (Cambridge: University Press, 1980); and Robert C. Roberts, *Spirituality and Human Emotion* (Grand Rapids, MI: Eerdmans, 1982); also see these helpful collections of essays: Bernard Weiner, ed., *Cognitive Views of Human Motivation* (New York: Academic Press, 1974); D. K. Candland et al., *Emotion* (Monterey, CA: Brooks/Cole, 1977); Ashley Montagu, ed., *The Practice of Love* (Englewood Cliffs, NJ: Prentice-Hall, 1975); and Kenneth S. Pope et al., eds., *On Love and Loving: Psychological Perspective on the Nature and Experience of Romantic Love* (San Francisco: Jossey-Bass, 1980).

12   See Lonergan, *Method in Theology*, p. 30.

13   See ibid., p. 31. Also see Max Scheler, *Formalism in Ethics and a Non-Formal Ethics of Value*, trans. M. Frings and R. Funk (Evanston, IL: Northwestern University Press, 1973, original German 1913, 1916, and "Ordo Amoris" in his *Selected Philosophical Essays*, ed. and trans. D. R. Lachterman (Evanston, IL: Northwestern University Press, 1973), pp. 98–135; Manfred S. Frings, *Max Scheler* (Pittsburgh, PA: Duquesne University Press, 1965), esp. chs. 3, 4, 6; Edward V. Vacek, "Scheler's Phenomenology of Love," *Journal of Religion* 62 (April 1982): 156–77; Dietrich von Hildebrand, *Christian Ethics* (New York: David McKay, 1953), ch. 17, "Value Response," pp. 191–243, esp. 191–97, 214–15; and Dietrich von Hildebrand, "The Role of Affectivity in Morality," *Proceedings of the American Catholic Philosophical Association* 32 (1958): 85–95.

14   Magda B. Arnold, *Emotion and Personality* (2 vols.; New York: Columbia University Press, 1960), 1:93–95.

15   Magda B. Arnold, "Perennial Problems in the Field of Emotion" in Magda B. Arnold, ed., *Feelings and Emotions: The Loyola Symposium* (New York: Academic Press, 1970), pp. 169–85, at 176.

16   M. B. Arnold and J. A. Gasson, "Feelings and Emotion as Dynamic Factors in Personal-

ity Integration" in Magda B. Arnold, ed., *The Nature of Emotion: Selected Readings* (Baltimore: Penguin, 1968), pp. 203–21, at 210.

17 Arnold, "Perennial Problems," p. 177.

18 Ibid., p. 179.

19 Richard S. Lazarus, Allan D. Kanner, and Susan Folkman, "Emotions: A Cognitive-Phenomenological Analysis" in Robert Plutchik and Henry Kellerman, eds., *Emotion: Theory, Research, and Experience, 1: Theories of Emotion* (New York: Academic Press, 1980), pp. 189–217, at 198, 192.

20 Richard S. Lazarus, James R. Averill, and Edward M. Opton, Jr., "Towards a Cognitive Theory of Emotion" in Arnold, ed., *Feelings and Emotions*, pp. 207–32, at 219.

21 James R. Averill, "A Constructivist View of Emotion" in Plutchik and Kellerman, eds., *Emotion*, pp. 305–39, at 305. For interpretations of specific emotions, also see Averill and R. Boothroyd, "On Falling in Love in Conformance with the Romantic Ideal," *Motivation and Emotion* 1 (1977): 235–47; and Averill, "Anger" in Richard A. Dienstbier, ed., *Nebraska Symposium on Motivation 1978* (Lincoln: University of Nebraska Press, 1979), pp. 1–80.

22 Robert C. Solomon, *The Passions: The Myth and Nature of Human Emotion* (Garden City, NY: Doubleday Anchor, 1976), pp. xiv, xvii.

23 Ibid., p. 229.

24 Ibid., pp. 191–92.

25 Robert C. Solomon, *Love: Emotion, Myth and Metaphor* (Garden City, NY: Doubleday Anchor, 1981), pp. 202, 213. Also see Robert C. Solomon, "Emotions and Choice" in Amelie Rorty, ed., *Explaining Emotions* (Berkeley: University of California Press, 1980), pp. 251–81.

26 Ibid., p. 201.

27 Ibid., pp. 202–03.

28 Ibid., p. 223.

29 Solomon, *Passions*, p. 337.

30 Ibid., p. 359. For a different perspective on self-love, see Fromm, *Art of Loving*, pp. 48–53, where self-love is defined in contrast to selfishness, and affirmed.

Solomon's entire discussion of love, of course, focuses on romantic love, a point that needs emphasis when he states, e.g., that love is not dependent, an obvious characteristic of a child's love. For an analysis that explicitly recognizes need love, see Otto Bird, "The Complexity of Love," *Thought* 39 (June 1964): 210–20, which shows three basic forms of love (gift, appreciative, need) blending to give four familiar types (gift and appreciation: friendship; gift and need: affection; appreciative and need: romantic; gift, appreciative, and need: charity); see Lewis, *Four Loves*, pp. 7–14.

31 Rosemary Haughton, *The Passionate God* (New York: Paulist, 1981), p. 6; for critical discussion of this book, see the Review Symposium with essays by Joann Wolski Conn, Lawrence S. Cunningham, Pheme Perkins, and Brian O. McDermott, and Haughton's response in *Horizons* 10/1 (Spring 1983): 124–40; also see Dennis P. McCann, "Rosemary Haughton: The Passionate Theologian," *Anglican Theological Review* 65/2 (April 1983), 206–13.

32 Ibid., pp. 58–61.

33 Solomon, *Love*, pp. 224–27. By denying commitment in love Solomon wants to emphasize that, whatever commitments may be added, in itself love makes no promises, offers no guarantee of future love. Commitment in this sense of promise of future love is different from the commitment of the self in the very decision of love that Solomon recognizes (*Passions,*

pp. 416–17). For a Jungian version of the standard interpretation of romantic love in opposition to the committed love of human relationship, see Robert A. Johnson, *WE: Understanding the Psychology of Romantic Love* (San Francisco: Harper & Row, 1983), pp. 99–104. Johnson sees romantic love as a necessary stage in psychological evolution, but insists that it must be clearly distinguished from committed love so that the latter may flourish and that the true significance of romantic love, its spiritual aspiration for inner wholeness and transcendence, may be followed into the interior world of religious experience (pp. 52–58, 131–32). The opposition of these loves is upheld on different grounds in Francesco Alberoni, *Falling in Love*, trans. L. Venuti (New York: Random House, 1983 original Italian 1981). On this point M. C. Dillon argues that romantic love and enduring love are mutually exclusive and that taken by themselves neither can be fulfilling; he proposes a third, authentic, love—an active, dialogic, responsible, developing love rooted in the self-transcendence of mutual affirmation: see "Romantic Love, Enduring Love, and Authentic Love," *Soundings* 66/2 (Summer 1983): 133–51. For the classic analysis of the medieval origins of romantic love, see C. S. Lewis, *The Allegory of Love: A Study in Medieval Tradition* (Oxford: Oxford University Press, 1936).

34 Rosemary Haughton, *The Transformation of Man: A Study of Conversion and Community* (New York: Paulist, 1967), pp. 32, 34.

35 Ibid., p. 80.

36 Ibid., pp. 38, 110.

37 Ibid., pp. 80, 174.

38 Ibid., pp. 80, 115.

39 Rosemary Haughton, *Love* (Baltimore, MD: Penguin, 1971, 1970), pp. 170, 173, 174, 175.

40 Ibid., p. 176.

41 Ibid., p. 183.

42 Tavard, *Way of Love*, pp. 66, 92.

43 Tillich, *Love, Power, and Justice*, pp. 30–31.

44 Johann, *Meaning of Love*, p. 74.

45 For an approach that sets the question of love in terms of the relationship between heart and will (will alone; heart alone, heart, then will; or will, then heart), and opts for the priority of will (will, then heart), see Andrew Tallon, "Love and the Logic of the Heart," *Listening* 18/1 (Winter 1983) 5–22, at 8–11. Also see M. Scott Peck, *The Road Less Travelled* (New York: Simon & Schuster Touchstone, 1978), who argues that "Genuine love is volitional rather than emotional" (p. 119). For Peck, love is "the will to extend one's self for the purpose of nurturing one's own or another's spiritual growth" (p. 81). In contrast, falling-in-love is not an act of will, for Peck, not an extension but a collapse of ego boundaries (p. 89). In terms of the present interpretation, Peck may be contrasting the passion and commitment seen here as complementary moments in affective conversion. Indeed, collapse of ego boundaries may be a condition for the self-transcendence of affective conversion.

46 Magda B. Arnold, "Human Emotion and Action" in Theodore Mischel, ed., *Human Action: Conceptual and Empirical Issues* (New York: Academic Press, 1969), pp. 167–97, at 188.

47 Lonergan, *Method in Theology*, p. 32. Also see Richard S. Peters, "The Education of the Emotions" in Arnold, ed., *Feelings and Emotions*, pp. 187–203.

48 See Gelpi, *Experiencing God*, pp. 179–81; and Paul Philibert, "Conscience: Developmental Perspective from Rogers and Kohlberg," *Horizons* 6/1 (Spring 1979): 1–25, at 3–10; also see Rogers, *On Becoming a Person*, pp. 125–59.

49 See Lonergan, *Method in Theology*, pp. 64–67, and *Insight*, pp. 533, 547, 561–62, 723.

50   See, e.g., Stanley Hauerwas, "The Self as Story: A Reconsideration of the Relation of Religion and Morality from the Agent's Perspective" in his *Vision and Virtue* (Notre Dame, IN: Fides, 1974), pp. 68–89, "Character, Narrative, and Growth in the Christian Life" in his *A Community of Character* (Notre Dame, IN: University of Notre Dame Press, 1981), pp. 129–52, esp. 143–49, and "Constancy and Forgiveness: The Novel as a School for Virtue," *Notre Dame English Journal* 15/3 (Summer 1983): 23–54.

XX

The Nuclear Issue
and the Human Sciences

GEOFFREY PRICE

AT the end of 1983, a year of widespread concern at the possibility of nuclear conflict, the London *Times Higher Education Supplement* noted with dismay the diminishing ability of the intellectual community to clarify the moral issues that arise from the application of its own theoretical knowledge in the construction of atomic weapons. With the growth of the technocratic ambitions of the university over the last century, its moral ambitions had atrophied.[1] What is the role of the human sciences in face of these challenges? Is the issue adequately conceived as one of the "expansion of the moral imagination" of the intellectual community, as the leader suggests? Or is it one in which the contemporary human sciences themselves sustain in our culture the politics of will and force which so deeply affects the use of science in innovation?

Lonergan makes a contrast between Malinowski's findings on the world-view of the Trobriand islanders, and the tacit outlook of industrialized cultures, which is valuable in this context. The everyday skills of survival in a simple agricultural community in the Pacific are exercised in the context of an assumed structure of myth and magic. The aid of the gods can be sought for impending disasters beyond human control, but their existence does not affect the everyday tasks of making and doing.[2] Industrial cultures can be seen as exhibiting a sophisticated form of the same split mentality. The arts of making and doing have reached extraordinary levels of complexity and extent. But our philosophic representation of the status of scientific knowledge tends to support beliefs which are positivist, pragmatist and antimetaphysical. Instead of myth and magic as the counterpart of the world of everyday

277

living, we have antimyth and antimagic: a blank.[3] The resulting cultural vacuum in the general population is very prone to subversion by irrational mass movements. If we consider the problem of the threat of nuclear weaponry in these terms, we will need to inquire into the tacit beliefs and expectations that flourish behind the "public" positivism of industrial societies.

This paper suggests that the current pattern of nuclear confrontation can be understood as the culmination of a particular complex of ideas in the field of religion and culture, which have consequences in the twentieth-century pattern of instability towards total war. Those ideas will be examined first in the language of religious experience, then in the corresponding patterns of personal relations, and finally in their consequences for conceptions of war and international relations. It seeks to understand how far that complex of ideas has come to pervade the contemporary social sciences within the intellectual community. It then suggests that the true task of the human sciences involves the healing of political and international patterns based on the acting out of mythologies of passion and human perfectibility, and the recovery of intelligent and responsible awareness of the world of concrete human community and relationships. It concurs with MacIntyre that the intellectual situation is now such that we must shoulder again the task which the church undertook at the end of the Roman *imperium*: to construct and preserve communities in which the recognition of persons as neighbors is the ground of commitment to the common good.[4] Thus it argues that Lonergan's heuristic of progress in history as the emergence of such communities of openness is crucial to the reorientation of the human sciences in the present crisis.

I. LIBERATION AND PERSONHOOD IN PATTERNS OF RELIGIOUS EXPERIENCE

As a first step, we may consider the divergence between world-affirmation and world-rejection that underlies differing approaches to religious experience. R. C. Zaehner's classic study of the varieties of mystical experience distinguishes those monistic forms which embody the longing for the primitive innocence of the self as it issues from its creator, and the theistic forms which rest upon the discovery that the human image is only re-made through the death of its own self-centeredness, and the healing of its capacity for loving relationships with God and one's neighbor.

Monistic mysticism takes two principal forms. The first is that which oscillates between the "natural" pole of absorption into world process, bringing an over-riding sense of the unity of all things, and the "closed-in" pole of the isolated self, suffering the loss of that original participation, and experiencing the unreality of existence in moments of extreme isolation and depression. The second form focusses not on absorption in or alienation from the world of the senses, but on the achievement of indifference to and withdrawal from that world. By isolating consciousness from all contact with the natural world and unconscious imagery, it aims at the settling in quietness of its own immortal self.[5]

This "way of renunciation" takes many forms in different religious traditions. The world of the body may be regarded, as in Samkhya Yoga in the Hindu tradition, as a kindly and purposeful agency in which the soul is entangled, but which will cooperate in its eventual release.[6] If the bodily world is regarded with more radical pessimism, then severer forms of asceticism appear, as in the elaborate dualism of Mani.[7] In Mediterranean gnosticism, mankind is divided into categories according to the capacity for embodying the spark of the eternal soul. In its Christianized form, Marcion's gnostic church similarly divided humanity into the elect, the ordinary believer and the infidel. Because the body was the sphere of the retributive creator-God, marriage and generation were to be avoided by those in search of salvation.[8] This theme reappears as Christian heresy in southern Europe in the early medieval period: the Catharites distinguished between the Perfect and the believers, and practised among the former the strictest sexual and dietary asceticism.[9] The fundamental outlook of this "way" is constant: the soul seeks to achieve absolute unity, the negation of the suffering multiplicity of present human existence.[10] It counts the world well lost in search of that goal, and its search is without return.[11] Such a mysticism is ever at odds with the fulfillment and loving reproduction of the body; its keynote is the anguish of confinement in the realm of matter. The ascent to perfection may be through the progressive death of a deliberate ascetic path, or it may in the limit be counted as the longed-for reward of self-destroying passion.[12]

The fundamental contrast between such a representation of existence and the theistic outlook is that for the latter, "there is very little that the soul can itself do, for it is God Himself who works in (it) and makes (it) fit for union."[13] Moreover, our end is not the recovery of the calm of original innocence; that is to confuse union with nature, or the soul's experience of disentanglement from desire, for the discovery of God.[14] Rather, our end is the restoration of relationship with God; of that restoration, the symbol is a death which is the renunciation of the creature's claim to independent existence, and a resurrection which marks the transition from false life to true existence in loving friendship with the Creator.[15] Thus the motif of theistic experience is not flight and liberation, but recreation. What the theist means by "death to self" is the beginning of new life in present existence: not the soul's disembodiment from the world, but its return in force into the midst of the world. Ressurection is *in* the body: those who pass through such a death find that it is the *beginning* of life, brought by the spirit to their true self and to the world.[16] The consequences of these two strands in the sphere of social relations are profound, and to these we must now turn.

II. THE SOCIAL RELATIONS OF PASSION AND OF LOVE

de Rougemont's study *Passion and Society* takes the rise of the Tristan legend as symbolizing the relations between the sexes which were yearned for, however unsuccessfully, in the dominant social caste of twelfth and thirteenth-century European society, the courtly, chivalric society.[17] Although the rule of chivalry is now long past, he argues that its attitudes to love and marriage have continued to work their way through Western societies. The original legend acted to contain and control a passionate form of love which is in sharp contrast to the relation of marriage; it is a love which is not a love of each for the other, as that other really is; each loves the other from the standpoint of self. Such a longing for the experience of passion more than for the object of love, courts suffering. It represents its ultimate willingness to meet death, in the end of Tristan and Iseult for whom reunion is impossible within the constraints of the marriage relations which at the end hold them apart, and whose death symbolizes their only path to ecstasy.[18] Personal relations thus become the field in which the *askesis* typical of unitive mysticism is sought. The path to enlightenment is a path of reunion with the divine; it renounces the bodily world, and it turns from the individuals to be found in the social realm as manifesting the imperfect multiplicity that pervades temporal existence.[19] Accordingly, the lovers in the Tristan romance are compelled to pursue the intensity of passion, not its completion in the establishment of relations between persons.[20]

By contrast, the social relations characteristic of theistic mysticism are a complete inversion of this longing for release from the body. To experience the divine love is to experience the death of the solitary, desirous self, but it also means the birth of our neighbor. The object of the love thus generated, is not the subject in love with its own experience, but the other who is met in the exchange of friendship. In Christian symbolism, the sign of love is no longer the infinite passion of a soul in quest of light, but the marriage of Christ and the Church. As forgiven and reconciled, we are still human; there is no divinization; but we no longer live for ourselves alone. There is no fusion, or ecstatic dissolving of the self in God; the divine love is the beginning of a *new* life, a life created by the act of communion; and for a real communion, there are required two participants, each present to the other. It is thus that in the divine love we each find the other to be our neighbor.[21] Thus, instead of seeing the world as past all possible redemption, theistic mysticism takes the test of the reality of the religious experience to be those acts of neighborly love that follow from it. Thus, as de Rougemont argues, the two forms of mysticism differ most as regards humility. The language of the romance is steeped in the language of knightly pride. At its extreme, the prowess of love appears as the material sign of a process of divinization. When Christianity is transposed into such terms, antipathy towards bodily existence reappears as Docetic Christology. The outcome of orthodox theistic mysticism, by contrast, is life lived in clear-sighted intelligent obedience towards the needs of the world of our neighbor.[22]

III. PASSION AND WARFARE

The chivalrous code of courtly society covered both the arts of love and of war. As Huizinga argued, in each case it served the needs of social order by elevating passion to the level of a rite. For the aristocracy, it provided a culture of their own, in opposition to secular authority, from which to draw their standards of conduct.[23] The effect was apparent in the detailed rules of personal combat, in the fighting of battles and in politics. The ceremonial of the tournament was the physical representation of the style of personal relations symbolized in *Tristan*. There, the outcome of passion in conflict to death was revealed, albeit in veiled form as a sacred ceremony.[24] Warfare was invested with great formality; when the chivalrous code was followed, the essence of tactical practice was to disorganize the enemy's forces and to make prisoners, whose lives were protected. Towns might be besieged many times, but never destroyed; duels between commanders were in honour, and sufficed to bring a campaign to a close.[25] Thus the detailed regulation of war served to check the violent impulses of aristocratic blood, just as the Tristan myth served to control and conceal the world-renouncing aspirations of passionate love.[26] The tournament and the war of knightly honour nevertheless represented a pole of aspiration for passion, and as Huizinga notes, the church's hostility to tournaments revealed an awareness of the threat of heretical myth that it embodied.[27]

With the invention of mechanized forms of warfare, the chivalrous symbolism that restrained the world-renouncing askesis of love and conflict alike, slowly lost its control.[28] The invention of artillery tended to transform soldiers acting with honor into anonymous troops, disciplined and uniform, feeling neither anger nor pity while performing mechanical movements intended to deal death at a distance.[29] For an intermediate period, de Rougemont argues, the main effort was devoted to controlling the mechanical monster in order that as many as possible of the humane features of war might be preserved. The rules of tactics and strategy were multiplied, so as to allow the intellect and "valour" of the commanders to retain a semblance of supremacy.[30] In that way, war recovered the aspect of a game, thereby confining the lawless force within a framework that was all the more vital in face of inhuman weapons of combat. With the advent of revolutionary war in France, however, the violence that had been pinned down by the classical formality of warfare was released, revealing the true aims of passion. As Camus says, there had been regicides before, but 1789 is the start of modern times, because the men of that time wanted to introduce to the historical scene the forces of rebellion and negation that had previously been confined to fantasy, drama and intellectual discussion.[31] The attack of the modern regicides upon the political order implied that peoples create themselves before creating kings. The will of the people, proclaimed sovereign, revealed the aspiration of humanity to achieve existence as a divine entity.[32] The consequence for warfare was that passion was translated to the level of the people as a whole.[33] De Rougemont points out the parallel between such warfare and the passion of the Tristan legend, a passion which is at bottom narcissism, the lover's self-magnification, far more than a relation with the beloved.

> Nationalistic ardour too is a self-elevation, a narcissistic love on the part of the collective self. No doubt its relation with others is seldom averred to be love; nearly always hate is what first appears, and what is proclaimed. But hate of the other is likewise always present in the transports of passionate love.[34]

In its readiness for war at any risk, the nascent nation unconsciously expressed a willingness to court the risk of death, and even to meet death, rather than surrender the passion which is at core the desire for collective divinization. "Thus Nation and War are connected, as Love and Death are connected."[35]

Thus arises the condition which Voegelin describes as the obsession with replacing the world of reality with the transfigured dream-world of gnostic imagination.[36] Its consequence in the nineteenth century was the association between French and German nationalism and the essentially passionate idealism of Fichte and Hegel. In consequence, war took on more and more the character of the conflict of opposing religions. The "enemy" is that group, internal or external, which fails to assent to the ideal world projected as the nation's imagined reality. Thus we have the wars of national independence of the early nineteenth century, themselves succeeded by the prosaic transposition of romantic nationalism onto the calculations of international competition that underlay the later wars of imperial expansion. The making of a still greater conflict in Europe was not long delayed: a conflict which Heine in 1891 predicted would make the French Revolution seem an innocent idyll.

> With the battle of Verdun in 1916, which the Germans called the Battle of War Material, it must seem," wrote de Rougemont, "that the resemblance instituted by chivalry between the *modes* of love and war came to an end.[37]

The attempt to regulate war, first by the chivalrous code, and then by secularized rules, had taken centuries to break down, but only in our time has there been witnessed the assault of total war upon the whole live might of the enemy—the workmen, the factories, the civilian support population, the homes and transport. The use of impersonal mechanical technique in dealing death from afar—at Verdun, the Somme, Passchendaele, . . . Dresden, Hiroshima, Nagasaki . . . has no equivalent in any imaginable code. "Total war eludes both man and instinct; it turns upon passion, its begetter."[38]

We have therefore the paradox that in the pursuit of dreams of perfectibility—the universal reign of Jacobin liberty, national identity or revolutionary fraternity—the death-dealing intention characteristic of self-love is finally exhibited. At the risk of total destruction in the actual world, the protagonists attempt to secure their "doctrine" by universal domination. But this is an endless task: As Camus points out,

> To insure man's control of the world it is necessary to suppress in the world and in man, everything that escapes the empire, everything that does not come under the reign of quantity: and this is an endless undertaking. The empire must embrace time, space and people which comprise the three dimensions of history. It is simultaneously war, obscurantism and tyranny, desperately affirming that one day it will be liberty, fraternity and truth . . . .[39]

Nevertheless, one further development is possible. Since the pursuit of total war abandons every claim of chivalrous warfare to represent, control and channel the fantasies of world-renouncing love, the aspirations of passion have to be channeled through the politics of the collective. The Nation, or the Party, takes on the embodiment of heroic aspiration. The pressures on individuals to adopt those ideals are intensified through the collective self-representations of the mass-media. States which are increasingly totalitarian view each other with rivalry and conflict. The invention of nuclear weapons has already made possible the most appalling total war, and their use has heightened fear which itself becomes part of the cycle of ideological competition. Because overt war is unthinkable, much of the force of international rivalry is transferred to the maintenance of internal myths. The negation of actual war increases the level of psychological compulsion, within and without the nation, to conform to the dream-world of its passionate aspiration. Camus pointed out the significance of propaganda in such a context:

> The empire presupposes a negation and a certainty: the certainty of the infinite malleability of man, and the negation of human nature. Propaganda techniques serve to measure the degree of this malleability, and try to make reflection and conditioned reflex coincide.[40]

IV. THE HUMAN SCIENCES BETWEEN TWO WORLDS

We have thus in the religious sphere, in styles of personal relations, and in the practice of war, two underlying orientations: one towards the imagined divinization of the self or the collective, and one towards the acknowledgement of the dignity of the neighbor, and the values of bodily existence. Can this conclusion be paralleled by MacIntyre's finding that the social and political sciences since the Enlightenment postulate the existence of an "emotivist" self, for whom there are no mutual links of reason and dialogue with the neighbor?

MacIntyre notes that in pre-modern societies individuals inherit a particular space within an interlocking set of social relationships; to move through life is not to occupy that position unchanged, but to develop, so that one's own story and that of the community interlock. In the transition to modernity, the passing of that notion of the person is celebrated not as a loss but as a gain: the freeing of the individual from the constraints of social hierarchies. The specifically modern notion of the self presumes the capacity to judge social situations from a purely universal point of view, detached from all particularity. This disjunction between inner and outer life is mirrored in contemporary social life, where two principal modes of social life seem open to us: the realm of the collective organization, whose sovereignty serves to limit the arbitrary actions of individuals, and the realm of the personal, where choices can be exercised in a limited sphere but the goals of the collective remain untouched.

The irrationality of theories of moral judgement based on the "emotivist" notion of the self was clearly understood by Nietzsche. What, though, is to take their place?

> The rational and rationally-justified autonomous moral subject of the eighteenth century is a fiction; so, Nietzsche resolves, let us make ourselves into autonomous moral subjects by some gigantic and heroic act of the will. . . .[41]

Within the predominantly Weberian terms of the contemporary human sciences, Nietzsche's problems remain unanswered, and his solutions defy reason.

> Consequently it is possible to predict with some confidence that in the apparently quite unlikely context of bureaucratically managed modern societies, there will periodically emerge social movements informed by just that kind of prophetic irrationalism of which Nietzsche's thought is the ancestor.[42]

Nietzsche's stance is passionate in the sense we have described: it presumes that, in defiance of the constraints of mundane existence, the imagined project of the apotheosis of will can be brought to fulfillment. That is the stance we have seen in prophetic nationalism, which, recognizing its implicit defiance of worldly constraints, courts its own death as preferable to the failure to live out its romantic dream. MacIntyre argues that there are two fundamental options within the human sciences: either to follow through the aspirations and the collapse of the different versions of the Enlightenment project, or to hold that that project was not only mistaken, but should never have been undertaken in the first place.[43] The Nietzschean great man is the culmination of emotivism: he cannot enter into relationships mediated by shared standards; he is his only authority, and in his relations with others exercises that authority. Against that stance, MacIntyre argues that the human sciences have to recover the classical discovery that the human good is pursued through the sharing of goods, rather than in the pursuit of individual will. We are never able to avoid living in the concrete circumstances of a community; the pre-modern realization that the individual's search for the good is conducted in a context defined by the traditions and relationships he inherits, is an inescapable starting point for the human sciences.

On that argument, the intellectual community has itself to appreciate that the divergence between the world-denying, passionate philosophies of man, and the notion of incarnate sharing in the common good as the model of political order, affects the human sciences themselves. If that community is to contribute to the healing of the international tensions that tend towards total war, it must be able to point to the sources and intentions of the politics of that passionate national rivalry which is the arena for the conflict of ideologies. Just as in a divided family, opposing members see the moves of others as potential aggression, and react with paranoia, so international relations are beset by selective misinterpretation, grounded both in past memories, and in the fears and hatred that fuel the clash of rival myths. The task of the human sciences is to promote the transition from the passionately-held utopias of collective national aggrandizement, to that acceptance of finitude and mutual dependence which is the foundation of ordered community.

Lonergan's first major contribution to this problem is parallel to the notion of therapeutic intervention in a divided family. He points out that what is needed is a capacity to put up untiring resistance to the rationalizations that each party to a dispute uses to justify their attempt to win power over their enemies. Instead of becoming involved in the short-term practicalities of international policing operations—however necessary they are—such intervention will inquire into the fundamental sources of the conflict. It will seek to break the vicious circle of rationalizations which screen from each warring party the true character of their opponent; it will promote intelligent perceptions of how to resolve the disputes that would otherwise remain suppressed in the interplay of fears and desires. Such a task requires many persons, and to their function Lonergan gives the name "cosmopolis"; but this does not imply an "interventionist" institution that mediates in every type of conflict. Rather, because the dominance exerted by individual or group-egoism invites its own reversal, the function of cosmopolis is not to oppose such movements directly, but to preserve intelligent and reasonable dialogue in the public realm from the imaginary projections of the will to power. "Unless cosmopolis undertakes this essential task, it fails in its mission. One shift of power is followed by another, and if the myths of the first survive, the myths of the second will take their stance on earlier nonsense to bring forth worse nonsense still."[44]

How though can the ultimate requirement of cosmopolis be met—that it be free of the rationalizations and projections that form the multitude of conflicting perspectives around it? Without a critique of history, attempts at the intelligent direction of history are always in danger of reinforcing unsuspected oversights. What can be set against the passionate and self-absorbed nationalism that we have diagnosed as opening the way to the "total-war" mentalities of the twentieth century?

Lonergan goes to the root of this problem by developing a philosophy of social progress whose roots are in the orthodox understanding of love as the mutual recognition of personhood, rather than the ascetical understanding of love as the occasion of the soul's ascent from embodiment.

Marriage is a microcosm of true community: it is the "real apprehension, the intense appetition, the full expression of union with another self."[45] It is "the efficacious sacrament of the realization of another self in Christ";[46] thus it is a hard-won achievement in which one realizes the existence of another, apprehends their personhood, and thereby constitutes a larger unity with them.[47] Thus Lonergan's relational idea of marriage differs profoundly from the unitive; his analysis of the mutual creation of community is an extension of Aristotle's teaching that as we are to ourselves, so we are to our friend. In the sharing of our self-consciousness in mutual activities, arises the exchange of beliefs about the meaning of life which results in the setting of mutual goals.

Here is the foundation on which Lonergan builds his account of progress and decline in history. " . . . Wherever such common conscience and consciousness develop, there is the focal point in human history where the dialectic of decline is offset and the highest ends of man are approached."[48] The field of personal self-transcendence is not the self-realization in which the death-confronting ascetic traditions have sought release from the bonds of the body; rather, it is reached in the field of mutual relations between persons, where love moves from attraction to friendship, charity and thus to the achievement of unity.[49] Whereas the Tristan myth represents the desire to prevent the lower world from encroaching on the realm of the spirit, the friendship of relational love is a willingness to accept the concrete particularity of the other. Thus Lonergan's stance accords with the position that de Rougemont takes in arguing that faithfulness to friendship seeks the good of the beloved: and

. . . when it acts in behalf of that good, it is creating in its own presence the neighbor. It is by this roundabout way through the other that the self rises into being a person—beyond its own happiness. Thus as persons a married couple live as a mutual creation, and to become persons is the double achievement of "active love." [50]

Yet Lonergan goes further, identifying the emergence of such mutuality as the point at which a further level of love can be discerned: the axial meaning of life as the turning of humanity and God to each other in mutual love and reconciliation.

Then their mutual actuation of a common consciousness and conscience will be a rejection of the world's dialectical rationalizations, a focal point in the stream of history for the fostering of growth in the mind and heart of Christ, a pursuit of the highest human and eternal ends. [51]

In Lonergan's subsequent work it becomes clear that such being-in-community is a model not only for the integration of persons in marriage, but also of the integration of a plurality of persons.

Within each individual, vertical finality heads for self-transcendence. In an aggregate of self-transcending individuals there is the significant coincidental manifold in which can emerge a new creation. Possibility yields to fact and fact bears witness to its originality and power in the fidelity that makes families, in the loyalty that makes peoples, in the faith that makes religions. [52]

Thus even in outline, we can discern the orientation in history which Lonergan provides if the human sciences are indeed to exercise a "therapeutic" role in effecting a transition from the death-courting politics of national aggrandizement, to the mutual recognition of humanity that is the starting point of ordered interpersonal and international existence.

On the eve of World War II, de Rougemont considered that the antagonism of Eros and Agape was the antagonism of two religions that were struggling for the upper hand in the West. [53] The situation today is graver still; a further outbreak in the international realm of the rivalries of Eros, would almost certainly extinguish all human life. How can the human sciences begin to foster the transition that is now so urgently needed from the politics of quasi-religious or religious nationalism, to patterns of international dialogue that are rooted in respect for the common humanity of all communities?

THE HEALING OF PASSION

When individuals suppress their own capacity for loving and are estranged from others, they often make the contrary attempt to find satisfaction in controlling those around them. If that strategy fails, they experience others as a threat; feeling diminished, they tend to react by hostility. Comparable patterns occur in the behavior of nations. Camus points out that the failure of the internationalist aspirations of the nineteenth-century socialistic movement, and the intervention of the West against the 1917 Soviet revolution, led the revolutionaries to conclude that war and nationalism were in the same category as the class struggle.[54] In consequence, the logic of accumulation that characterized their liberal capitalist opponents was mirrored in the behavior of the socialist powers, as each fought for survival in the face of hostility. Such a process forces both sides into slavery to the requirements of production. Thus even "peacetime" life is invaded by the passionate will to power, undermining the humanity of each side.[55]

As in an interpersonal quarrel, the gulf widens between intelligent accurate perception of the other and their fear-laden image, so in the international sphere, historical and current constructs of the opponent's intentions are readily distorted. The military historian Michael Howard pointed out in his Bernard Brodie memorial lecture in 1980 that

> . . . One of the oldest "lessons of history" is that the armaments of an adversary always seem brutal and threatening, adjectives that always seem tendentious and absurd when applied to our own.[56]

In the healing of conflict in the interpersonal sphere, the transition from inner fantasy—or fear-oriented behavior to intelligent awareness of and sharing with the other is slow and difficult. The same problem is endemic in the international sphere, and the same need is apparent for a therapeutic intervention which does not solve the parties' problems directly, but which suggests another way of looking at them.[57] Fingarette's account of the role of the therapist in the interpersonal sphere provides a starting point for reflection: he acts as an "enlightened- agonist" who offers love while remaining divided from the clash of motives in the patient. He knows that the subject who acts out in a conflict the range of hopes and fear which form part of their own inner fantasy-world, is unfree. They cannot see what is new and unique in each situation, but only the elements which recall issues which subconsciously they imagine to have a bearing on present circumstances.[58] Passionate love, as explored by de Rougemont, is another outcome of the same "encapsulated" existence: the other is treated, not as capable of being really loved, but an eclipsed, partial form of the true being which fantasy searched for. Thus does such a relationship conceal a hatred and fear of the other—only to be revealed in the transposition of passionate love into war. In the international sphere, the consequence is just such patterns of distorted, fear-filled perception that we have noted.

The task of the therapist is rendered still harder in modern Western societies, which assign reality to the external, "physical" world, and conform to the "anti-myth" of positivism by assigning to the non-logical inner world a secondary status as "psychological" or subjective. Correspondingly, forms of art and therapy which enable the person to go through the suffering involved in recognizing the hidden world and living beyond its enslaving effect, are rare.[59] Nevertheless, the task is to bring the person to a realization of the lives of fantasy to which, below the level of everyday consciousness, their life is oriented; to appreciate their effect in estranging them from present existence; and to move to an integration in which they can distinguish realistically between past, present and future.[60] Moreover, it is emergence from bondage to solipsistic fantasies which in the person's life coincides with a new relationship to real neighbors. In de Rougemont's terms, the individual moves from the relationships of eros to those of agape. As Fingarette puts it,

> Instead of being an "it," serving as the instrument of fantasy gratifications, the other person becomes a potential "Thou." This process is the natural concomitant of release from the various "Me's," the binding ideas of self, and the liberation of the generative "I." The "Thou" and the "I" are integral to each other. The gesture towards the real other can only be taken as there is an "I," a person free to be open to the reality which comes.[61]

Thus the person slowly gives up the use of others as puppets in their inner fantasy lives; they come to respect the reality and autonomy of the other. At the same time they come to see themselves as separate, autonomous and capable of shaping their own existence.

At the present time, urban planners are coming to recognize that a parallel movement—the acceptance of "otherness" as a basis for communication, and with it the possibility of overcoming conflict by a mutual desire to continue in the life of dialogue—is crucial to urbanized societies.[62] We find ourselves painfully trying to rebuild real communities within the larger social bodies. All too often, our capacity for dialogue is stunted; we remain preoccupied; we fly either into the inner fantasy of individualism, or the collective fantasy of the mass. "The community of 'otherness' stands in uncompromising opposition to this tendency," writes Maurice Friedman. "I have freedom, but I am not the whole of reality, and I find my existence in going out to meet what is not myself."[63]

The same problems are apparent at the level of the reduction of international tension. The pressure to live within the collective fantasies of the masses is present in all societies, but it has been intensified in the West by the rise of quasi-religious myths as the guiding force of international conflict, culminating in the twentieth- century experience of total war. Collective existence as lived out within such national myths is symbolized in the everyday world by a plethora of stereotypes in news reportage, elementary history, humour, drama, military tradition, diplomatic convention, and political analysis. The distortion of perception characteristic of ideological conflict is apparent in the tendency to represent competing national religious and political myths as belonging to a wholly unacceptable, sub-human way of life.[64] In the circumstances of impending or actual conflict, the national myth is deliberately controlled and expanded through propaganda.

In such a situation, the social sciences may tacitly concur with the irrational, self-preoccupied character of national myths of enshrining within social theory the "emotivist" image of humanity in which self-affirmation predominates over dialogue and reason. Or they may act by analogy with the therapist, dealing not with the problem as it is perceived by the actors, but by suggesting that the situation is one of systematic oversight and misinterpretation of experience. The magnitude of the historical and theoretical reorientation that this task involves in the social sciences is made clear by MacIntyre's work, whose complementarity to Lonergan's analysis of social progress and decline deserves further study. The task of the social, political and diplomatic historian in disentangling the true sequence of events from their ideological distortion is equally crucial in enabling a sane grasp by a community of its own development in relation to that of its neighbors. We open here upon the task of dramatist, novelist or documentary writer in enabling a nation to look at suppressed elements in past behavior, and to appreciate its involvement in collective myths—ideological, colonial, racist—that unconsciously shape its contemporary existence. Here too lies the task of the politician and diplomat who is free from involvement in the substitute religions of nationalism, and is able to promote the "recognition of otherness" in responsible dialogue between neighboring communities for the maintenance of international order.

Fingarette's image of the "enlightened-agonist" recalls to us the patient search for understanding that grounds Lonergan's achievement of a heuristic of social progress that can undergird this process of "conversion to the other" from the original self-centeredness of narcissistic fantasy that affects individual and communal life alike. Still more, as Lonergan always reminds us, do we realize how deeply we need the saving meeting of God with man lived out in the way of Christ's love for the other. Only by that way can we truly be drawn from our entrapment—as persons, communities and nations—in the world of self-oriented behavior, to the recognition of our true being in God as our lover. Only by that way can there be a healing of the nations.

NOTES

1 "Editorial: The Year of the Bomb," *The Times Higher Education Supplement*, December 24, 1983, p. 24.

2 Bronislaw Malinowski, *Magic Science and Religion* (New York, Doubleday: 1954), pp. 17 ff.

3 Bernard Lonergan, *Understanding and Being: An Introduction and Companion to Insight*, ed. Elizabeth A. Morelli and Mark M. Morelli (Lewiston, New York: Edwin Mellen Press, 1980), p. 122.

4 Alasdair MacIntyre, *After Virtue: A Study in Moral Theory* (London: Duckworth, 1981), p. 245.

5 Robert C. Zachner *Mysticism Sacred and Profane*, London: Oxford University Press, 1957), pp. 38, 44, 149.

6 Ibid., pp. 98–99, 129–146.

7 Steven Runciman, *The Medieval Manichee* (Cambridge: Cambridge University Press, 1983), pp. 5–17.

8 Ibid., p. 9.

9 Ronald L. Knox, *Enthusiasm: A Chapter in the History of Religious* (Oxford: Claredon Press, 1950), pp. 92–98. For further detailed evidence see: M. D. Lambert, *Medieval Heresy: Popular Movements from Bogomil to Hus* (London: Arnold, 1977); R. I. Moore, *The Origins of European Dissent*, (Harmondsworth: Allen Lane, 1977); J. B. Russell, *Dissent and Reform in the Early Middle Ages* (Berkeley: University of California Press, 1965); and W. Wakefield, *Heresy, Crusade and Inquisition in Southern France, 1100–1250* (London: Allen and Unwin, 1974).

10 Eric R. Dodds, *The Greeks and the Irrational* (Berkeley: The University of California Press, 1951), p. 139.

11 Paul Ricoeur, *The Symbolism of Evil*, tr. E. Buchanan (Boston: Beacon Press, 1969), pp. 283–287, 300.

12 Knox, *Enthusiasm*, pp. 96–97.

13 Zaehner, *Mysticism Sacred and Profane*, p. 192.

14 Ibid., pp. 202–204.

15 Ibid., p. 195.

16 Denis de Rougemont, *Passion and Society*, tr. M. Belgion (London: Faber and Faber, 1950), p. 68.

17 The reception of de Rougemont's thesis, and the evidence supporting it, may be assessed in R. Boase, *The Origins and Meaning of Courtly Love: A Critical Study of European Scholarship* (Manchester and Totawa, N. J.: Manchester University Press and Rowman and Littlefield, 1977). The present argument accords generally with the conclusions of the following: E. Gilson, *The Mystical Theology of St. Bernard*, tr. A. C. H. Downes (London: Sheed and Ward, 1940), Appendix IV, "St. Bernard and Courtly Love"; C. Dawson, "The Origins of the Romantic Tradition," in C. Dawson, *Medieval Religion* (London: Sheed and Ward, 1935), pp. 123–154; A. J. Denomy, "An Inquiry into the Origins of Courtly Love," *Medieval Studies* 6 (1944), pp. 175–260; A. J. Denomy, "Fin' Amors: The Pure Love of the Troubadours," *Medieval Studies*, 7 (1945), pp. 139–207; and M. W. Askew, "Courtly Love: Neurosis as Institution," *Psychoanalytic Review*, 52 (1965), pp. 19–29.

18 de Rougemont, *Passion and Society* pp. 50–52

19 Ibid., p. 70.

20 Ibid., pp. 149–150.

21 Ibid., pp. 68, 71.

22 Ibid., p. 150.

23 Johann Huizinga, *The Waning of the Middle Ages*, tr. F. Hopman (New York: Doubleday, 1954), p. 96a.

24 Ibid., p. 67.

25 Jacob Burkhardt, *The Civilization of Italy in the Renaissance*, tr. S. G. C. Middlemore (Oxford: Phaidon Press, 1945), p. 189.

26 Johann Huizinga, *Homo Ludens* (London: Routledge, 1949), p. 116. See, "The Political and Military Significance of Chivalric Ideas in the Middle Ages," in J. Huizinga, *Men and Ideas: History, the Middle Ages and the Renaissance*, tr. J. S. Holmes and H. van der Marle (London: Eyre and Spottiswoode, 1960). Huizinga's treatment is generally borne out by more detailed work; see J. F. Verbruggen, *The Art of Warfare in Western Europe During the Middle Ages* (Amsterdam: North Holland, 1977), Vol. I, Ch. 2, "The Knight;" and R. Barber, *The Knight and Chivalry* (London: Longmans, 1970).

27 *The Waning of the Middle Ages*, p. 71.

28 Raymond L. Kilgour, *The Decline of Chivalry as Shown in the French Literature of the Late Middle Ages* (Cambridge, Mass.: Harvard University Press, 1937), p. 38.

29 The fifteenth-century treatise of Jean de Bueil, *Le Jouvencel*, argues that jousting is a waste of time, and that the knight has to be a professional soldier after all. For detailed discussion, see Barber, *The Knight and Chivalry*, p. 334 and Kilgour, *op. cit.* For a critical assessment of this thesis in the context of Huizinga's work, see M. Vale, *War and Chivalry* (London: Duckworth, 1981), pp. 147–174.

30 de Rougemont, *Passion and Society*, p. 254.

31 Ibid., p. 82.

32 Ibid., pp. 85–87.

33 Ibid., p. 85.

34 Ibid., p. 260.

35 Ibid., p. 261.

36 Eric Voegelin, *The New Science of Politics* (Chicago: The University of Chicago Press, 1952), p. 169.

37 de Rougemont, *Passion and Society,* p. 264; compare H. Heine, *Religion and Philosophy in Germany* (London: English and Foreign Philosophical Library, 1882; reprinted, Boston: Beacon Press, 1959), pp. 158–162.

38 de Rougemont, *Passion and Society,* p. 265.

39 Albert Camus, *The Rebel,* trans. A. Bower (Harmondsworth: Peregrine Books, 1962), p. 201.

40 Ibid., p. 204.

41 MacIntyre, *After Virtue,* p. 107.

42 Ibid., p. 108.

43 Ibid., p. 11.

44 Bernard Lonergan, *Insight: A Study of Human Understanding* (London: Darton, Longman and Todd, 1957), p. 240.

45 Bernard Lonergan, *Collection: Papers by Bernard Lonergan, S. J.* ed. F. E. Crowe, S. J. (Montreal: Palm Publishers, 1967), p. 32.

46 Ibid., p. 33.

47 Thomas Dunne, "Lonergan on Social Progress and Community" (Ph. D. Thesis, University of St. Michael's College, Toronto, 1975), p. 31.

48 Ibid., p. 33.

49 Lonergan, *Collection,* pp. 23, 29–37

50 de Rougemont, *Passion and Society,* p. 310.

51 Lonergan, *Collection,* p. 37.

52 B. Lonergan, "Mission and Spirit," in P. Huizing and W. Bassett, eds., *Experience of the Spirit,* G. Combet and L. Fabre, eds., *Healing and the Spirit,* (*Concilium,* vol. 9/10, n. 10) (New York: The Seabury Press, 1974/6), pp. 69–78.

53 de Rougemont, *Passion and Society,* p. 315.

54 Albert Camus, *The Rebel,* p. 201.

55 Ibid., p. 186.

56 In Robert Scheer, *With Enough Shovels: Reagan, Bush and Nuclear War* (London: Secker and Warburg, 1982), p. 50.

57 Tom Crabtree, "The Nuclear Family," *New Society,* 67, no. 1110 (March 1, 1984), p. 321.

58 Herbert Fingarette, *The Self in Transformation: Psychoanalysis, Philosophy and the Life of the Spirit* (New York: Harper and Row, 1965), p. 211.

59 Ibid., p. 198.

60 Ibid., p. 211.

61 Ibid., p. 244.

62 John Friedmann, *Retracking America: A Theory of Transactive Planning* (New York: Doubleday and Co., 1973), p. 185.

63 Maurice Friedman, *The Hidden Image* (New York: Delta, 1974), p. 366.

64 Erich Neumann, *Depth Psychology and a New Ethic* (London: Hodder and Stoughton, 1967), pp. 52–55.

XXI

Military and Deterrence Strategy
and the "Dialectic of Community"

KENNETH R. MELCHIN

AMONG Catholic theologians in North America the most dramatic entry into the heated debate over the morality of nuclear war fighting and deterrance has been the American Bishops with their 1983 pastoral letter, "The Challenge of Peace."[1] For as well as attracting considerable publicity in their efforts to address the details of a concrete political issue the bishops have crystallized and ratified a trend towards a change in the more traditional Catholic "just war" thinking on the morality of war.[2] The problems in thinking through the morality of nuclear war fighting and deterrence have forced many Christians to adopt a form of pacifism, either as an absolute stance against any resort to violence or as a modified "nuclear pacifism." And in Catholic circles the more traditional just war moral reasoning which had occupied the center stage for such a long time is now being challenged or transformed through the influence of such pacifist thinking and living.

The approach taken by the American bishops is similar to that taken by David Hollenbach in his book *Nuclear Ethics*.[3] It is a form of nuclear pacifism which uses the structure of just war reasoning but which appeals to the magnitude of the destructive capacity of nuclear weapons and the probabilities of uncontrollable escalation to argue against the morality of a range of particular war fighting and deterrence strategies and policies. While the bishops do not adopt the absolute stance of the pacifist's rejection of proportionate reasoning on the use of violent force, nonetheless they do seem to share the pacifist's disenchantment with the efficacy of violence and they encourage the promotion of non-violent means of conflict resolution. The absolute Christian pacifist rejects violence on *a priori*

293

religious grounds whereas the bishops take their stand on the grounds of means-ends proportionate reason and on experience drawn from the lessons of contemporary history.
However, as David Hollenbach argues, even the absolute pacifist makes an implicit or an
explicit "prudential" judgment about the long term negative effects resulting from the
resort to violence as a means of conflict resolution.[5] And this assumption remains an
empirical claim about the "spiral of violence" as a psychological or historical fact about
man and modern warfare regardless of whether or not it is held for religious reasons.

My concern in the analysis which follows is with the theoretical and empirical foundations for this claim about the "spiral of violence" which the threat and the use of
modern weaponry seems to promote, and with the role which this claim plays within the
structure of just war reasoning. One of the criteria which continually confounds just-war
theorists is the proviso "reasonable hope of success." For the ethicist is forced to estimate,
on the basis of precious little evidence, how deterrence measures will or will not contribute to the likelihood of war, whether limited war strategies will escalate to total war, and
how the continuing development of new weapons systems will affect the relative states of
international instability. I would argue that a major flaw in the just-war theories to date is
their inability to handle a dynamic, historical analysis of the course of developments, both
within war or deterrence contexts and over the longer historical term of military and
political relations and non-relations. Just-war analysis is essentially a static analysis which
must draw a line across any historical continuum and assess the relative goals and costs at
that point. In its present form just-war analysis does not lend itself to longer-term visions
of historical vectors or trends. And generally just-war analysts do not engage in attempts
to explain apparent statistical trends in an appeal to the appropriate explanatory conjugates
of systematically operative dynamic cycles. I do not think it is an accident that some just-
war thinkers through history have tended to justify more and more bizarre forms of
human (or inhuman) violence. For the dynamic course of successions of wars tends to
inflate the causes for which war measures can be justified.

Bernard Lonergan has a brief sketch of a structured dynamic cycle, which results from
what he has called the "dialectic of community." The elements of this dialectic are
gleaned from his analysis of the structure of intersubjectively operative practical or
common sense intelligence. I will summarize briefly his analysis and develop it by
introducing some insights from the work of George Herbert Mead as modified by the
American social ethicist, Gibson Winter. Following this search for the relevant explanatory conjugates, I will appeal to some noted historians to show how the history of technological war in the twentieth century bears some evidence of the systematic operation of
the dynamic cycle explained here.

If the general intent of just-war theories can be understood as a search through human
history, the human psyche, and human logic for descriptive and explanatory criteria for a
judgment of value, then this analysis constitutes a contribution to just-war thinking so
conceived. However, my hunch is that the introduction of a dynamic cycle analysis into
just-war theory, could well transform our entire way of thinking about just cause, proportionality and probability of success. And, even if the rule of non-violence does not become
an absolute rule, as the extreme pacifist might wish, I would suggest that the pacifist's

claim to an insight into "the spiral of violence" may well be vindicated. However, a more precise specification of possible and probable conclusions must be left to a later point in this and in further continuing analyses.

I. THE DIALECTIC OF COMMUNITY AND THE PRINCIPLE OF MUTUALITY

The dialectical structure of the intersubjective operation of practical intelligence is sketched in *Insight*[6], chapter seven. But its dynamic operation can be understood better with the introduction of the three-stage structure of sociality developed by Gibson Winter in *Elements for a Social Ethic*.[7]

Practical intelligence proceeds as a probable emergence of subjective and intersubjective unities and schemes. This is to say that responsibly chosen courses of action are neither systematic outcomes of classical laws nor are they the result of purely random or non-systematic convergences of classical laws. Rather the neural manifold of the subject is the locus of a very large aggregate of classes of events recurring with more or less stable f-probabilities each of which is linked with other distinct sets of events, occurring within and outside of the subject's envelope of skin via one or more recurrence schemes. There emerges in this aggregate both spontaneously structured unities linking groups of events in the manifold and temporally ordered sets of such unities which themselves assume the structure of a recurrent scheme or skill. And because the temporally ordered skills and sets of skills can order both sensory-motor events and cognitionally integrative unities, the acquisition of cognitional and responsible skills themselves can operate reflexively to shift the f-probabilities associated with the occurrence and recurrence of classes of cognitional and responsible events.

While such cognitional and responsible skills have the minor effect of bringing onto the scene of world process both the insights and judgments of truth and the practical courses of action which f-probably follow upon insights and judgments of value, they also have the major effect of constituting the subsequent habitual spontaneity of the dramatic subject. And it is the habitual spontaneity which continuously or recurrently orders and censors subsequent neural events, preparing, as it were, the materials for subsequent insights and judgments. While the trend in ethics has been to advert to this minor effect of the exercise of such skills, this study will hope to illustrate why attention to this major effect is now called for within the discipline of ethics.[8] It is the inertial character of past experience, past insights and judgments, past responsible practice which accounts for the dynamic nature of Lonergan's explanation of "dialectic."

For the sake of greater precision, let us say that a dialectic is a concrete unfolding of linked but opposed principles of change. Thus, there will be a dialectic, if
(1) there is an aggregate of events of a determinate character,
(2) the events may be traced to either or both of two principles,
(3) the principles are opposed yet bound together, and
(4) they are modified by the changes that successively result from them.[9]

In the dialectic of the dramatic subject the two principles are identified by Lonergan as "the neural demand functions and the exercise of the constructive or repressive censorship."[10] The dynamic course of this dialectic involves past instances of the operation of the censor constituting inertially the subsequent state of the neural manifold in the face of a new ordering possibility presented by the demand functions of new experiences mediated to the manifold. Inasmuch as the neural manifold does not tolerate any and all integrative possibilities, there will be a dynamic tension in which failures at appropriate integration will drive towards reversal and in which newly acquired experiences, which have been made possible through previous integrative occurrences (either successful or unsuccessful), set up an exigence for new integrative possibilities. Thus the course of the dialectic will be a set of oscillations in a cumulatively developing (or declining) expansion in the integrative complexity of the subject's neural manifold.[11]

While the dialectic of the dramatic subject could explain the course of one person's life, Lonergan introduces the notion of dialectic into his account of the dynamics of social process to explain the relative stability of and the systematic oscillations in f-probabilities of recurrences of classes of events in society and in history. And it is here that his account of "intersubjectivity" and "the dialectic of community" in *Insight* can be complemented and expanded with the introduction of elements from the work of Gibson Winter. In his account of the dialectic of community Lonergan identifies the two principles of the dialectic of community as "human intersubjectivity and practical common sense." And by "human intersubjectivity" Lonergan is referring to the adaptation of sensitive spontaneity to the rhythms and routines of family, tribe, clan, nation and culture.[12] But I would suggest that the shifts in f-probably recurring classes of spontaneous inclination and insight and the emergent schemes of social interrelations which Lonergan names the "good of order" can be explained more fully by identifying a new, distinct "principle" operative in the life of the dramatic subject, a "principle" which accounts for the distinctiveness of the dialectic of community.[13] Quite simple this "principle" is the presence of another human subject as an independent locus of integration within the experiential range of the subject. This integrative "principle" is operative in a fashion which is distinct from (if not unrelated to) the subject's own trial and error exercise and development of skills because of his or her curious capacity for what George Herbert Mead has called "role-taking" or "attitude-taking"[14] and what Albert Bandura has called "learning through modeling."[15] The human bears the remarkable capability of appropriating, at times almost wholesale, an integrative affective, cognitional, practical unity of another person, given the appropriate fulfilling conditions. It is this capacity which plays the key role in Gibson Winter's reconstruction of Mead's structure of human sociality.[16]

While Lonergan turned to Piaget, in *Method*, to illustrate evidence of the subject's trial and error assimilation and adjustment scheme as the dynamic structure in which integrative unities and skills emerge and develop,[17] Winter turned to Mead's gesture-interpretative response scheme as the dynamic structure in which the subject adapts his or her sensitive, meaningful, responsible spontaneity to the routines of the social group.[18] In Mead's original scheme the subject is "socialized" as gestures initiated by him- or herself are interpreted by members of the group and as the subject appropriates the group's interpretation of the meaning of the gesture as the self's own meaning. This appropriation involves a role-taking act in which the subject "sees" him- or herself through the "eyes" of the generalized other.[19] Winter saw this account to place too much emphasis upon the one-way socialization process and he sought a corrective to Mead by introducing a distinct third moment in the scheme (a unification) and by distinguishing a prior underlying relatedness or "We-Relation" which functions as a common experiential ground to which both parties appeal in a dialectical drive to unification.[20] But along with Mead, Winter appreciated the significance of the role-taking or attitude-taking action as essential for explaining the structure of human sociality.

I would suggest that this role-taking capability can be understood within Lonergan's emergent probability structure of the dialectic of the social subject as explaining a shift in the flows of f-probabilities associated with classes of socially recurrent meanings and routines. And I think that Albert Bandura and his associates are correct in seeking to understand social learning theory as complementing the work of Piaget and as correcting some misinterpretations of experimental data.[21] I would suggest that the exemplary behavior of another person functions as the clue does in scientific inquiry to shift the attention of the subject to a specific range of integrative possibilities, and that the subsequent patterning or role-taking does not so much supplant the trial and error discovery process as it does accelerate the probabilities of a narrow range of integrative possibilities. However this acceleration and concentration is sufficiently dramatic in its import upon learning and development as to warrant explaining the role-taking as involving the introduction of a distinct integrating "principle" in the dialectic of community.[22] Along with the experiential exigencies of the subject's neural manifold and the ordering appetite of the subject's intelligent engagement with his or her environment there stands the host of affective, intelligent and practical/responsible integrative routines of a group which are mediated to the subject's neural manifold by other human subjects through the three-fold scheme of gesture, interpretive response, and drive to unification involving successions of reciprocal role-taking events. This distinct "principle" (most fundamentally the fact of another subject as integrating principle) is neither purely sensitive spontaneity nor does it head unequivocally towards the intentional term of practical intelligence's pursuit of objective value. Rather this principle makes of the dialectic of community a double dialectic, based upon three distinct but interrelated principles, headed for two distinct intentional terms or goals which seek to be integrated into the "good of order." The two intentional goals are (1) the responsible object of practical intelligence, i.e. the grasp and actuation of truth and value, and (2) the intersubjective unification of two subjects *as subjects* in authentic mutuality, affirmation and love.[23]

The possibility of a collective unification of subjects in both intentional goals, in which a confirmation in authentic mutuality is at once a collective affirmation of a common set of intelligible meanings and values is, I would suggest, what Eric Voegelin sought to understand with his term "representation" in *The New Science of Politics*. And because a value is a fourth level course of action such a collective affirmation or representation is at once an "articulation" of the society in which the society is organized for collective action as a unified body.[24] But beyond this the unification of subjects in socially ratified practice also creates the conditions of stability of recurring classes of social, economic and political practice. And with the proliferation of such recurrent events it is merely a matter of time before sets of events link together into emergent recurrence schemes which none have devised and which none have understood. At this point it is essential that the twin goals of mutuality and intelligence become the objects of explicit attention in society. For collaborative schemes have become the conditions for the maintenance of daily routines. And the ongoing adaptation of such schemes to the dialectically and developmentally shifting conditions of life requires the wide-scale participation of all involved. What was operative only implicitly in the genesis of societal schemes must become the object of education in more complex societies.

The temporal distribution of the three stages of the intersubjective scheme explains the developmental growth processes wherein the lived example and the pedagogy of a mentor presents a state of virtue and skill towards which a person progressively aspires. And here as often as not it is the drive towards the goal of mutual confirmation which keeps the subject progressing in his or her capacities to grasp and realize value. But as well, this temporal distribution also explains the course of competitive games, personal and social conflicts and wars. And here one of the more dramatic instances of the shift from competitive situations which promote the course of progress to those which impede it can be understood in terms of the presence of a bias or deformation in the drive towards one of the two intentional objects of the double dialectic, the goal of authentic mutuality, the mutual recognition of two subjects as operators, as principles of originating value. Lonergan's notion of the group bias with its corresponding shorter cycle of oscillations between progress and decline can be understood in this case not so much as the intrusion of intersubjective spontaneity into the collective exercise of common sense[25] but rather as a deformation in the object of intersubjective mutuality with its ensuing circumscription and deformation of the horizons and operations of practical intelligence. This analysis would also suggest the possibility of a further classification of types of group bias in terms of the presence or absence of deformations in one or more of the three basic principles.

It is in terms of the double dialectic of community and its ensuing oscillations which arise with the presence of group bias that I will attempt an analysis of the curious history of the two "great" wars of the twentieth century and the novel form of conflict which the presence of nuclear weapons has introduced onto the scene of world process. Lonergan's intent in presenting the shorter cycle in *Insight* was to explain how the oscillations of the shorter cycle contributed to the acceleration of the longer cycle of decline, in which theory progressively adjusts its data base, its aims and its explanatory conjugates to the deteriorating experience of life.[26] My aim here will be limited to the more modest effort of pointing out the relevant historical evidence and suggesting some lines of import for theory.

II. WAR AND DETERRENCE IN THE TWENTIETH CENTURY

While the course of World War I was launched in a flurry of music and flag-waving, Bernard Brodie's account of those first months in 1914 portrays graphically the radical transformation of warfare which was the result of the introduction of the first piece of modern technology, the machine gun.

As it turned out, imprudence against the machine gun was outrageous folly. When the French armies in 1914 went charging off to the east while the Germans wheeled down on their flank and rear, they met a scourge of fire in the opening battles of the frontiers that sent them reeling backward with appalling losses. They were barely able to regroup for the Battle of the Marne, which stopped the German advance. The battles of the Marne and the frontiers cost each side 500,000 casualties, a larger figure than that which represented the whole manpower of the Prussian army in the Austro-Prussian War of 1866.

By late 1914 the armies were already stalemated. The firepower of the machine gun was so devastating that armies could no longer live upon the surface of the battlefield. As General J.F.C. Fuller put it, "there was no choice but to go under the surface; consequently trenches five hundred miles long were dug, and armies went to earth like foxes—each side turned itself into an immense spider and spun hundreds of thousands of miles of steel web around its entrenchments." Soon the trench barrier extended from Switzerland to the North Sea. The fronts became flankless, and penetration became the tactical problem.[27]

It was at this point that the relentless search for a resolution of "the tactical problem" of "penetration" set the dialectic of community into a curious scheme. Since the machine gun could kill footsoldiers but could not at this time take out other machine guns, both sides harnessed the best scientific minds at their disposal to devise an antidote to this immobilizing disease. Artillery turned the battlefields into oceans of mud and advances in artillery and explosive shells accelerated this capacity. But to no avail. For advances on one side were simply met with responses in kind. Poison gases were devised to asphyxiate the soldiers in the trenches. But this only accelerated improvements in gas mask technology, the promotion of reciprocal gas warfare technology, and further stimulated the ingenuity of intelligence agents to penetrate the inner circles of the enemy's strategic planning. The end of the stalemate on land only came about when the exhausted and demoralized German troops met the British Fourth Army led by 450 armoured tanks at Amiens on August 8, 1918, and the German General Erich Ludendorff abandoned hope of victory.[28]

Similar cycles of accelerating technology, generating a prolongation of the stalemate and the multiplication of senseless casualties, characterized the progress of the war at sea and the initiation of a new theater of war, in the air. The submarine terrorized the British fleet and laid waste millions of tons of commercial shipping until mines, escorted convoys, the hydrophone, the depth bomb, the torpedo, and aerial detection and bombing techniques, began to offset advances in submarine technology and to redress the initial imbalances.[29] And in the air the progress of the conflict in Europe saw the virtual birth of modern aircraft technology and the first attempts at what would become the key to the course of the Second War, massive area bombing of civilian populations.[30] If the First War can be said to have been "won" it was so won principally as a result of the Allies' ability to squeeze the Germans into a sustained semi-starvation through the maintenance of their naval blockade.[31] In the long war of attrition the winner was the side which could continue feeding the bodies and the spirits of the citizens who propelled the economic, technological, industrial war machine.

In terms of the schematic structure of the dialectic of community outlined above, the presence of warfare technology in 1914 fulfilled the conditions for the emergence and per-petuation of a systematically recurrent cycle of degenerating intersubjective exchange, progressing and accelerating in the context of a virtual stalemate in the participants' efforts to secure the initially stated objectives of war. Given the fulfilling condition of relatively equal industrial and technological capacities, the first resort to the rule of force ratified an abandonment of the goal of authentic mutuality and mobilized practical intelligence in the service of effecting unification in the subjugation of the opposing party as a principle of articulation.

The key to the perpetuation of the vicious circle of technological warfare is this fact that the two parties have forsaken this goal of mutuality, giving rise to their resolute and single-minded commitment to the rule of force as the only means for securing the goals of policy or for deterring an aggressor committed to such goals.[32] Given the acceleration of hostilities the likelihood of the two parties agreeing upon the cessation of war in the absence of a significant advantage gained becomes progressively lower. For high costs have already been paid and the cessation of conflict in the absence of secured advantage would make these costs purely waste. Given the balance in technological and industrial capacity the possibility of a long-term advantage accruing to one side is improbable. And as the losses or costs mount in the war of technology the initial means-ends calculus which justified going to war gives way to a rationale in which some benefit is sought either to offset accrued losses or at minimum to demobilize an aggressor committed to such a calculus. As losses mount, the magnitude of the end or goal swells to include losses or costs incurred in battle and thus are rationally justified by the just-war theorist the imple-mentation of more and more extraordinary means.[33] In addition the use of force becomes the *only* means for ensuring the very survival of oneself. For the aggressor fights to the death. The goals of policy are consolidated to include the very survival of its author, the state. And so the new ends can progressively justify virtually any means in the calculus of proportionality.[34]

Such is the course of war in a technological era. Two operative characteristics distinguish this cycle of war from wars of previous ages. The first is the order of magnitude of the destructive capacities. The earliest stages of technological wars yield substantial changes in the means-ends proportionalities. As long as the goal of mutuality is abandoned a cycle begins in which progressively more devastating means are justified. Quickly a situation arises in which sufficient devastation warrants the justified payment of extraordinary costs on all sides, regardless of the initial state of values differences. The magnitude of this devastation fulfills the conditions for the emergence of the rigid dynamic cycle. For high costs paid justify progressively more costly means, even for the defendant who seeks only to immobilize an aggressor. The cycle dictates its own rigid set of terms to the just-war theorist. And the key which locks all parties into the brutal scheme is the abandonment of the goal of mutuality, the resolute commitment to the rule of force.

The second characteristic of technological war is the new actors. The combatants now include the scientists competing in destructive hardware and software, the industrial planners who compete in their efforts to manufacture the fruits of the scientists' planning, and the men, women and children who work in the factories. All citizens have become soldiers and thus the defeat of any one side requires either bringing this entire army to its knees or persuading the opponent's populace that its goals are not worth the costs. When the exclusion of mutuality persists the dynamic cycle of technological war only stops when one party is immobilized in its entire capacity to fulfill its next-stage contribution to the ongoing cycle.

Given some sustained economic, technological and industrial capacity on both sides, no significant strategic or technological advancement will succeed in gaining a long-term advantage. For given the maintenance of the fulfilling conditions every innovation will be met with a response. And while individual battles or successions of battles will suggest an advantage to one or another side, such individual instances are non-systematic deviations from an accelerating statistical norm whose dynamic stability is ensured by the generality of the immanent norms of infinitely ingenious, theoretical and practical intelligence operating within the constraints of a deformation in the goal of mutuality. So the course of war, in the long run, will be sustained by the various parties' capacities to maintain their economic, technological and industrial capacities.

In the Second World War Hitler understood the real dangers of the war of attrition. And he sought to avoid this longer degeneration through the implementation of two principles, the ferocious onslaught of the blitzkrieg designed to demoralize the opponents' will, and the maintenance of a state of surprise through the implementation of intelligence cipher technology.[35] On both counts he underestimated the resilience of the opponent's technological capacity and the vengeance which his own methods would elicit.[36] And so the first years of the 1940's initiated another war of attrition in which the cycles of technology took hold and the opponents devastated the world with their ever more ferocious powers. Bernard Brodie's chronicle of the technological cycle elicits in the reader a fascination, a pride, and even an admiration both for the beauty of the new inventions and for the undeniable genius of the technological artists. And this swelling appreciation easily renders one oblivious to the horrors which such creations made possible. From successive advancements in aircraft technology to the development of radar detection technology, antiaircraft artillery, and the electronic proximity fuse; from the developments in submarine technology and naval warfare tactics to the progressive perfection of sonar, depth charges, aircraft detection techniques, and Operations Research or "game theory" submarine hunting techniques; from developments in tanks, gunnery, shells, and land strategy to reciprocal detection and defense equipment and techniques on land, the competitive technological cycle accelerated upwards culminating in the Nazi's development of rocketry and the Allies' victory in the race to the atomic bomb.[37] And while the "stalemate" of the Second War took a substantially different form than the trench warfare of the First, an end to the cycle had to await a virtually total collapse in Germany's and Japan's physical and "morale" capabilities for keeping the economic, industrial, technological military machine in motion. In the view of some commentators the Allies' demands for unconditional surrender from the Germans and similar demands from Japan, coupled with the atomic bombings of Hiroshima and Nagasaki, tended to have the inverse effects of strengthening the two nations' wills to fight to the very death, keeping the spiraling scheme in motion.[38]

The famous British strategist Sir Basil Liddell Hart recognizes some of these elements of the operation of the accelerating dialectic of community in technological war. He notes the degree to which " . . . [f]orce is a vicious circle—or rather, a spiral . . . " and remarks on how the brutality of force or extraordinary demands for surrender only accelerate the opponents' resolve to respond in kind or to continue the fight to the death.[39] His notion of "grand strategy" admits the degree to which nations will mobilize their complete political, social, economic, industrial and military resources to the pursuit of the ends of policy. To call for "grand strategy" is to demand that these resources be coordinated in the context of a systematic program.[40] However, Liddell Hart's analysis tends to downplay the decisive role of the technological dialectic in explaining the course of the two wars.[41] And here I would suggest that his own approach to strategy understates the degree to which the dynamic course of technological wars progressively precludes the probabilities for limiting armed conflict once begun.[42]

What is fascinating about Hitler's mobilization of society, economy and polity in the psychological war of will is that in his recognition of the dead-end war of attrition Hitler's approach through World War II marked the beginning of a shift away from direct battlefield conflict, towards the cold war of "deterrence strategy" which has marked the decades since 1945. Hitler's strategic shift away from exclusive focus upon the battlefield to a systematic concern for terrorizing the opponent's entire population into submission with a minimum use of psychologically calculated force foreshadowed the war of nerves which ensued after 1945.[43] This strategic shift away from exclusive focus upon the battlefield seems only to have transposed the locus of the continuing spiral of technological war. And while the efforts at mutual deterrence through nuclear arms has kept the world from full scale nuclear conflict between the superpowers, the global technological dialectic, begun in 1914, continues through a curious flexibility in shifting alliances. Furthermore Liddell Hart has noted that "to the extent that [the H-bomb] reduces the likelihood of all-out war, it *increases* the possibilities of 'limited' war pursued by indirect and widespread local aggression."[44] The recent history in which the superpowers have progressively subsumed the host of local conflicts in Southeast Asia, in the Middle East, and in Latin America into their ideological conflicts bears witness to a growing trend towards "limited wars" exacerbating the risk of total war.[45] And I would suggest that unless the cycle is understood such events will continue accelerating the dangers in this ongoing dialectic, especially now that all fingers are maintained on a 6–12 minute nuclear hairtrigger in Europe.

The course of the technological dialectic since 1945 is well known to all.[46] From the three 13 kiloton bombs possessed in 1945, the Americans expanded their arsenals to between 100 and 200 bombs in 1949 when the Soviets detonated their first atomic explosive. Only a year separated the Americans' detonation of the first thermonuclear device from the Soviet's first explosion of comparable size. By 1957 the Soviets were in a position to test a new and profoundly more threatening delivery device, the intercontinental ballistic missile. And with the launching of Sputnik I in that same year, their promise of gaining an advantage in communication and detection methods fueled the mobilization of the formidable American space program. By 1963 the Americans had in excess of 4,000 nuclear warheads or bombs, 1,300 strategic bombers and over 475 missile delivery vehicles. Technological advancements on both sides since the early 1960's have included MIRV'ed warheads (multiple, independently targetable re-entry vehicles, groups of which are launched by a single booster rocket and each of which carries a targetable fusion warhead); nuclear submarines which carry dozens of rocket launchers and hundreds of warheads, and which can remain submerged, undetectable for months at a time, traversing the surface of the globe; medium range missiles which can be exchanged between Europe and the Soviet Union within six to twelve minutes; cruise missiles which fly below the altitude of radar detection, at subsonic speeds, flying over hills, and around mountains, guided by sophisticated guidance mechanisms; and huge heavy booster rockets which can deliver ten, twenty and more warheads to anywhere in the world, which can be moved about to avoid detection and verification, and which can land each warhead within hundreds of meters of any chosen target. Coupled with these developments in "hardware" were the "software" developments in deterrence strategy. "Mutually Assured Destruction," "Flexible Response," and "Counterforce Strategy," are some of the code names for progressively more sophisticated, graduated political and war-fighting programs. Sophisticated, satellite-assisted surveillance systems are in operation on both sides, round the clock; hosts of nuclear armed bombers are maintained in the air at all times awaiting the moment when they will fail to receive a command to return to base; and unimaginably huge networks of "intelligence" agents work day and night round the earth to ensure that what each side thinks the other side is thinking, is in fact in line with what is thought.

All of this evidence brings one to a conclusion which stands even more alarming than one might anticipate. For the anticipations since 1918 have been that the endless powers of destruction which have been made possible by the infinite resources of theoretical intelligence—a theoretical intelligence characterized by the systematic neglect of its own subject and by abdication of responsibility for fourth-level intentionality —would make armed conflict obsolete. However as the superpowers continue to make available to selected combatants in manifold minor conflicts throughout the world the best in modern warfare technology, in return for some limited commitment to their respective superpower goals, the indirect war escalates in the technological recurrence scheme which the dialectic of community has become since 1914. To argue that the "nuclear firebreak" will never be crossed by reasonable men is to ignore the surd which is introduced in the traditional means-ends calculus when the goal of authentic mutuality is abandoned and the rigid dialectical scheme is begun.

Since the Second War the then British Prime Minister Chamberlain has been held in contempt for failing naively to recognize Hitler's fanatical rise to power. I would suggest that Chamberlain's responses can be understood more compassionately as the result of the failure of intelligence combined with his own efforts to pursue the principle of mutuality. Some aspects of the folly of the First War were well recognized by 1939 and Chamberlain's efforts were mobilized to avoid resort to the rule of force. Hitler, like a good practitioner of the Eastern martial arts, skillfully used Chamberlain's failures in intelligence against the Allies in the implementation of his own form of strategy. Likewise the Americans in their relations with the Soviets have sought to learn from history by avoiding duplicating

Chamberlain's mistake. But nuclear deterrence strategy rests, if not upon a complete abandonment of the object of mutuality, then upon its deformation. For while war has not been declared formally between the U.S. and the Soviet Union since 1945, the entire course of political relations has been conducted under the threat of war, in the context of a preparation for war, through the cycle of competing efforts to gain the advantage should war break out, and in the midst of the endless series of indirect wars in the southern and eastern hemisphere. Both parties in the conflict have declared their foundational values or interests to be non-negotiable. And far from seeking to explore the relative contributions and deficiencies of the political proposals and concerns of involved parties, international diplomacy between the NATO countries and the Warsaw Pact countries have been conducted, for the most part, under a presumption of mutual hostilities. Deterrence strategy abandons a full commitment to the goal of mutuality in the name of intelligence learning from the mistakes of more recent history.

The time has come to face the problem of the technologically-mediated dialectic of community in all of its hideous proportion. Neither principle of practical intelligence nor mutuality, can be sacrificed without making the situation worse. And when one party (at least) stands committed to a repudiation of the object of authentic intersubjective mutuality then the historical situation becomes radically ambiguous. For an appeal to the role of force must now be understood, not only as a possible solution, but also as the central contributor to the dynamic escalation of the problem.

III. IMPLICATIONS FOR JUST-WAR THEORY

As was noted in the introductory comments above, the implications to be drawn for just-war thinking from this and from related analyses can only be sketched briefly here. But one conclusion looms large. Just-war theory has as its foundation a presumption against the rule of violent force and seeks to set forth criteria for deciding when and how this presumption can be overriden in the pursuit of ends or goals which must be of proportionately great enough value to warrant the costs paid. In other words just-war theory will only ratify the resort to force if the long-term evils ensuing from a decision against such resort can be judged decisively to be greater than the evils wrought by the violence itself. I would submit that the application of this analysis of the dynamic structure of the dialectic of community to the recent history of war and deterrence gives rise to some concrete evidence and a correlative explanatory framework for assessing the degree of evil which will follow systematically upon the resort to the rule of force in a technological age, given the fulfilling conditions. The dynamic cycle of escalation is not an indirect, merely coincidental consequent of the resort to limited war or of the maintenance of current forms of deterrence strategy. Rather an abandonment or a significant deformation in the goal or object of authentic, intersubjective mutuality, as defined here, constitutes the fulfilling condition for linking directly or *systematically* the events in the dialectical scheme. Just-war thinkers can no longer limit the scope of their analyses to theoretically circumscribed hypotheses about possible *in bello* scenarios. Likewise deterrence strategists can no longer exclude from their analyses the longer term cycle of escalating tensions which follow systematically upon the maintenance of deterrence measures which ratify an exclusion or a deformation (or even minimize the relevance) of the principle of mutuality.

I would argue that the long term costs paid both in nuclear war-fighting strategies and in deterrence strategies are much greater than what some just-war theorists have assessed. Whether a careful analysis of the probable outcomes of specific war-fighting and deterrence options would reveal that no such options could be justified, cannot be foreseen at this point.[47] I would argue that such analyses must come to terms with the evidence suggested here. And in the course of such analyses it should become clear to the theorist that the implementation of the rule of force involves the repudiation of the very value which it seeks to defend, i.e. the mutual recognition of all participating subjects' right and responsibility to "free" (liberated) self-articulation in the intersubjective scheme of gesture and response. I would suggest that this recognition should occasion the re-thinking of the foundations of democracy. And perhaps this re-thinking could be conceived as a collaborative effort unifying the participants in the current international disputes.

Concerning the justifiability of war-fighting options, the usual argument of proponents of such options includes an appeal to a so-called "political realism." It is often argued that this is an imperfect world and a "realistic" approach to this world requires admitting that sometimes drastic measures are necessary in the face of enemies who themselves give no consideration to values which we would espouse. The suggestion which follows from the above analysis of the dialectic of community is that the "realist" proposes a measure for stopping or deterring an enemy which is in fact significantly "unrealistic." For this analysis would suggest that the abandonment of the goal of mutuality locks all parties into a scheme in which conditions on all sides degenerate systematically. Clearly more must be said here. But it is the systematic character of the operation of the scheme which must be understood. Correlatively it would appear that the truly "realistic" option open to a participant who would assume responsibility for the long-term good of civilization demands the active pursuit of the well-being of the "opponent" in an intersubjective scheme of political, diplomatic relations which explicitly promote his or her own role in shaping the course of such a scheme. While the "realist" might claim that a "rational self-interest" theory of international relations is at once the best one can expect in an imperfect world and an adequate means for handling international disputes, I would suggest that the results of this analysis challenge this claim to adequacy and force us to re-think what can be expected. For the course of the dialectically operative scheme would seem to be neither "rational" nor in anyone's "self-interest."

Concerning deterrence options, Hollenbach is certainly correct in admitting that such strategies with their weapons systems are currently in place. In addition he is correct in demanding that just-war thinking chart a course towards the reversal of the recent history of degenerating international relations. But his discussion of the nature and structure of deterrence needs to be complemented by an analysis of the precise way in which deterrence efforts to avoid resort to the rule of force set up their own systematically operative scheme;

a scheme which itself contributes to exacerbating the state of international conflicts. Deterrence, with its bilateral (but not mutual) circumscription of the limits within which international relations will be conducted, and with its correlative threats to complete abandonment of the goal of mutuality, tends towards a systematic presumption of worst-case scenarios. This tendency has the effect of taking what just-war theory outlaws except as last resort, and promoting it to a permanent place in the center of all diplomatic activities. This transposition gives rise to the mutual mistrust which dynamizes contemporary east-west diplomatic activity. And the anticipation of worst cases contributes progressively to their own self-fulfillment. Again the central element in the analysis is the deformation in the principle of mutuality which links the events in the degenerating scheme systematically.

One final word must be said concerning the implications for just-war theory. The repudiation of another person as a locus of responsibility or value will result in the contribution to social, historical decline discussed here, i.e. the ensuing dialectical course of conflicts which have been the object of this analysis. But this repudiation also has a less obvious, but perhaps more serious contribution to decline. This second contribution follows from Lonergan's emphasis upon the subjectively self-constituting dimension of social morality. A subject's decision and consequent implementation of a course of action has the effect of constituting the subject as an operator, an agent, an initiator of such an action. And the dynamic tendency of such a constitution, all things being equal, is to set the subject towards the perpetuation of the vector set by the introduction of this new element into his or her range of decision options. The point here is that in addition to the accelerating calculus in which mounting costs paid progressively justify the implementation of more extraordinary means in the dialectical scheme, there is also a process of wide-scale subjective "formation" going on in war and in deterrence. For one's decisions alter one's subsequent spontaneous engagement in the world, they shape the anticipations with which one meets the data of experience and they constitute the range of recurrent, reflex response options within one's "horizons."

Just-war theorists must take account of the systematic effect of this self-constitution in our proportionality calculus in two ways. (1) We must include consideration of the destructive psychic effects on a culture or civilization of waging war and preparing for war, in our means-ends assessments of proportionate goods and evils. (2) We must actively include in our proposals for dealing with past and present war activities, programs for wide-scale "psyche therapy" or salvific reconciliation to render ourselves and other inheritors of the legacy of twentieth century wars capable of meeting the shifting exigencies of the next century. While Robert J. Lifton[48] can be cited as one thinker who is attending to this psychological impact resulting from the sustained threat of nuclear war, I can only suggest his work at this point as a possible fruitful direction for study.

The reader might detect, through the pages of this discussion, the influence of a strong commitment to the relevance of Christian love as a central element in the route towards the reversal of current trends. While the precise nature or form which this love must take is not yet clear I would argue that the evidence and the analysis presented here should argue for its centrality in any theory which would be adequate to the exigencies of the contemporary situation.

Lonergan has argued in his account of the longer cycle of decline that the most dramatic form of decline ensues when theory adjusts itself to the current state of practice.[49] If the state of current world affairs can be explained in terms of corrupted theories claiming their legitimacy in an appeal to the degenerate state of political practice, then I would submit this study as indicating the presence of evidence which would reveal the inadequacy of such theories. For while the evidence of degenerate man is rampant, I would suggest that a full appreciation of the scale and the import of this degeneracy leads to conclusions which are contrary to the anticipations of current theories, and thus to a search for new foundations for reversal. The implicit commitment to the relevance of Christian love, reflected here, is based upon the recognition that this evidence of degenerate practice, while profound in its import, is not the whole evidence on God or on Man.

NOTES

1   National Conference of Catholic Bishops, "The Challenge of Peace," in Philip J. Murnion, ed., *Catholics and Nuclear War,* (New York: Crossroad, 1983) pp. 245–338.

2   For a discussion of the legitimacy of the bishops' response to a concrete political issue see Richard McCormick, "Notes on Moral Theology: 1983," *Theological Studies,* vol. 45 (1984), pp. 124–125. On recent shifts in the approach to war in the Roman Catholic tradition see J. Bryan Hehir, "The Just-War Ethic and Catholic Theology: Dynamics of Change and Continuity," in *War or Peace,* ed. T. Shannon (Maryknoll: Orbis Books, 1980), pp. 19–21. On the contribution of the American Bishops' pastoral to this shift see David Hollenbach, "'The Challenge of Peace' in the Context of Recent Church Teachings,'' in Murnion, ed. *Catholics and Nuclear War,* pp. 3–15. For critical discussion of recent attempts to think through the relationship between the pacifist and just-war approaches in the contemporary nuclear context see K.R. Melchin, "Just-War, Pacifism, and the Ethics of Nuclear Policy," in *Eglise et Theologie,* vol. 17 (Jan., 1986), forthcoming.

3   D. Hollenbach, *Nuclear Ethics* (New York: Paulist Press, 1983).

4   See, for example, "The Challenge of Peace," pars. 111–121, 221–230, 285.

5   Hollenbach, *Nuclear Ethics,* p. 21.

6   B.J.F. Lonergan, S.J., *Insight: A Study of Human Understanding* (New York: Philosophical Library, 1957).

7   Gibson Winter, *Elements for a Social Ethic* (New York: Macmillan, 1968). For a more detailed account of the relevance of emergent probability in understanding Lonergan's account of the structure of practical intelligence, see K. Melchin, *History, Ethics and Emergent Probability,* (Lanham, M.D.: University Press of America, forthcoming, 1986), ch. 5.

8   This is the significance of Lonergan's emphasis upon "conversions" and "originating value" in *Method in Theology* (New York: Herder and Herder, 1972) and *Insight* (ch. 18).

9   *Insight,* p. 217.

10   Ibid.

11   On progress and decline and the foundations of value in Lonergans's work, see Melchin, *History, Ethics and Emergent Probability,* ch. 6.

12   *Insight,* pp. 217, 212–213.

13   The word "principle" is not an entirely adequate term here, but in the absence of an alternative I have chosen to set it in quotation marks. In Lonergan's usage the word "principle" generally designates an integrated set of terms, fixed in their interrelations by an insight or set of linked insights, whose partial terms have an existential or experiential reference. (*Insight*, pp. 304–309) But in his definition of dialectic Lonergan seems to be referring to a special set of principles. "But prior to analysis, to concepts, to judgments, there are the native endowments of intelligence and reasonableness and the inherent structures of cognitional process. These are the real principles on which the rest depend." (p. 308) Clearly the presence of another person as a locus of integration within my own experiential horizon does not constitute a change in or an expansion of the structure of cognition. Rather such a person introduces a systematic shift in the exigences of the neural demand functions. But this shift, I would argue, is sufficiently intelligible and dramatic in its import to call it a "principle" in the more general sense of the term.

14   George Herbert Mead, *On Social Psychology* (Chicago: University of Chicago Press, 1977), pp. 33 ff.

15   Albert Bandura, *Social Learning Theory* (Englewood Cliffs: Prentice-Hall, 1977), pp. 22 ff.

16   There is some evidence that Lonergan appreciated the significance of role-taking in *Method;* see ch. 3 and p. 357.

17   *Method*, pp. 27 ff.

18   Gibson Winter, *Elements for a Social Ethic*, pp. 23 ff., 99 ff.

19   Ibid., pp. 23–29, 99–100.

20   Ibid., pp. 99 ff.

21   Albert Bandura, *Social Learning Theory*, pp. 30–34.

22   For a more detailed discussion here see Melchin, *History, Ethics and Emergent Probability*, chs. 6 and 7.

23   I would say there are two intentional terms or goals because the experiential exigences of the neural demand functions will be present in all activities. Thus the experiential demands, E, will interact dialectically with the "principle" of mutuality, M, and with the integrating and censoring activities of intelligence, I, to yield the two dialectics with their respective terms or goals. The "good of order" demands the integration of all three principles.

24   Eric Voegelin, *The New Science of Politics* (Chicago: University of Chicago Press, 1952), ch. 1.

26   Ibid., ch. 7

27   Bernard and Fawn M. Brodie, *From Crossbow to H-Bomb* (Indiana: Indiana University Press, 1973), p. 190.

28   Ibid., pp. 189–199.

29   Ibid., pp. 180–189.

30   Ibid., pp. 173–180.

31   Basil Liddell Hart, *Strategy*, (New York: Praeger, 1972), pp. 202–203, 214–219.

32   I would suggest that political theories like those of Clausewitz (*On War*, ed. A. Rapoport [Harmondsworth: Penguin Books, 1983]), which allow or promote resort to war as a continuation of policy are dangerously flawed. For they fail to come to terms with the import of the goal of mutuality. Cf. Lonergan, where he has spoken of an acceleration of the "longer cycle of decline" which results when theory adjusts itself to common practice (*Insight*, pp. 225–234).

33   I would suggest that the excessive demands made upon the Germans, following upon World War I, to pay for the horrendous damages wrought throughout the war, were an example of this dynamic "logic" of just-war proportionality. And most commentators are in agreement that the settlements following the first World War contributed significantly to the outbreak of the Second.

34 See Basil Liddell Hart on Ludendorff in *Strategy,* pp. 225 ff.

35 William Stevenson, *A Man Called Intrepid,* (New York: Ballantine Books, 1976), p. 32.

36 See B. Paskins and M. Dockrill, *The Ethics of War* (London: Duckworth, 1979), pp. 15–21.

37 Bernard and Fawn M. Brodie, *From Crossbow to H-Bomb,*, pp. 200–232, 271–272.

38 Basil Liddell Hart, *Strategy,* p. 328; B. Paskins and M. Dockrill, *The Ethics of War,* pp. 48–57.

39 Basil Liddell Hart, *Strategy,* p. 370.

40 Ibid., p. 366.

41 Ibid., pp. 234, 253.

42 Ibid., p. 370.

43 Ibid., p. 235.

44 Ibid., p. 17.

45 The former Prime Minister of Canada, Pierre Elliot Trudeau, has noted that " . . . as tensions build, the East-West relationship becomes particularly vulnerable to events on the periphery." ("Global Initiative to Improve the Prospect for Peace," Address by the Right Honourable Pierre Elliot Trudeau, Prime Minister of Canada, Queen Elizabeth Hotel, Montreal, Nov. 13, 1983 [Ottawa Public Affairs Branch, Department of External Affairs, 1983] p. 2).

46 See Harvard Nuclear Study Group, *Living with Nuclear Weapons,* (Toronto: Bantam Books, 1983), pp. 71–101.

47 Contrary to the suggestions of Finn ("Pacifism and Just War: Either or Neither," in Murnion, ed., *Catholics and Nuclear War. p. 143)* and Langan ("Struggling for Clarity about Nuclear Deterrence: David Hollenbach and Michael Novak," *Thought,* vol. 59 (1984), p. 97, I would argue that the just-war theory could *logically* allow the possibility that an analysis of concrete nuclear war-fighting and/or deterrence strategies could result in all alternatives being excluded as unjust. In fact, such a situation would not imply any contradiction to the basic intent of just-war theory, for its foundation rests upon a presumption against violence.

48 Robert J. Lifton, *The Broken Connection,* (New York: Simon & Schuster, 1980).

49 Bernard Lonergan, *Insight,* pp. 225–244.

Orientations in
Economics

XXII

Economic Theorizing:
in Lonergan and Keynes

MICHAEL GIBBONS

INTRODUCTION

THE key question which has to be addressed concerning the *Circulation Analysis* is, "What has to be established to identify what is distinctive in Lonergan's reflections on economics?" This is a complex question, one that points beyond the economic manuscripts themselves to the relationship of these manuscripts to both *Insight* and *Method in Theology*. The approach taken in this paper will be the relatively simpler one of trying to identify what appears to be distinctive about Lonergan's economics when it is placed alongside the theoretical work of another economist—Keynes. If this line of thought does indeed bring to light some of the essential features of Lonergan's *Circulation Analysis,* then it may be easier to show the community of economists both how Lonergan's work relates to their own theoretical approaches and why it has a normative significance for the future of democratic capitalism.

The problem of exploring the relationship of the *Circulation Analysis* to theoretical economics and to economists is not without its difficulty. When Lonergan finished the first draft of his analysis (circa. 1942), he did try to interest economists in it, but apparently without much success. In Lonergan's own words, "they didn't seem to see what I was getting at." There are a number of possible reasons for this earlier failure to penetrate the economic community: the work *is* highly theoretical and it does require a good deal of effort to master even the central elements of the argument. Secondly, and more importantly, if we can assume that economists are no more afraid of hard work than anybody else, is the fact that the work challenges some of the basic tenets of the, then, contemporary economics—the role of prices and profits, in particular. But, unlike many apparently radical economists, Lonergan does not eliminate these notions and replace them with some of his own, creating a spray of neologisms on the way. Rather, he transforms the significance of prices and profits by developing them within a dynamic framework of analysis. Thirdly, the economics profession, like any other, is a community which has the power to determine what questions will be asked, what methods will be used, and to a degree, what the general shape of the answer will be. If the intellectual leaders of this community were too preoccupied with the Keynesian revolution to notice the genuine insights of a relative insider, Michael Kalecki, what chance was there for a relatively unknown theologian with no formal training in economics? Finally, what might have been accomplished in terms of penetrating the world of economic theory if the circulation analysis had been published will always remain unknown, for Lonergan appears to have put the manuscript aside and not to have given it serious attention until *Insight* (1959) and *Method in Theology* (1972) were completed.

For the purposes of this paper, we want to return to a version of the 1942 manuscript and to dwell on the first half-dozen pages of it. In these pages, we get a glimpse of the intellectual path that will be followed throughout the analysis. For the time being, however, it will be necessary to put to one side the technical conclusions of the analysis itself and try to come to grips with the method used by Lonergan in rendering a dynamic account of a developed economy. In any systemic account of the behavior of the economy as a whole, technical conclusions will rest upon prior assumptions about what needs to be explained and the appropriate methods to handle it. From these assumptions an explanatory structure is built up and, provided there are no logical errors, conclusions follow. Recognising and removing logical errors is a relatively straightforward task, but to critically test assumptions and methods is far more difficult because it calls into question (or it can call into question) deeply ingrained habits of thought and ways of proceeding. Indeed, economics seems little different from other areas of knowledge in its tendency to form closed schools of thought (i.e., Keynesian, Monetarist, Marxist, etc). This fragmentation into schools only seems to exacerbate the task of critical reflection by placing political and other social values at the source of theoretical differences. Rather than capitulate too easily to the prevailing tendency to explain economic theory in social terms, we shall take our stance with Keynes and acknowledge that new ideas are simply hard to come by. In the preface to *The General Theory of Employment, Interest and Money* he wrote:

> The composition of this book has been for the author a long struggle of escape. . .
> from habitual modes of thought and experience. The ideas which are here expressed
> so laboriously are extremely simple and should be obvious. The difficulty lies, not
> in the new ideas, but in escaping from the old ones, which ramify, for those brought
> up as most of us have been, into every corner of our minds.[1]

The Lonergan of *Insight, Method in Theology* and the *Circulation Analysis* would surely sympathise with Keynes on this question. But for our purposes it is the self-consciousness of Keynes' attempt to create a new theory which is interesting. No doubt Keynes was an economist first and a methodologist second but he was nonetheless very articulate about his theorizing and, in particular, about the dangers of theorizing in vacuum. Lonergan, for his part, is perhaps a methodologist first and an economist second but, as we shall see, he was able to push his economic reflections further than Keynes because he had a firmer grasp of the essentials of an effective theory.

In this paper we shall attempt to "compare and contrast" Keynes' *General Theory of Employment, Interest and Money* and the early sections of the *Circulation Analysis*. We shall make only a brief reference to the work of Roy Harrod on growth models and we shall be guided throughout by the great wisdom of the Liverpool University economist G. L. S. Shackle whose insights into Keynes' *General Theory* have, at least partly, opened this great work for me.

KEYNES ON ECONOMIC THEORY

The point of juxtaposing Keynes and Lonergan is to highlight their individual searches for the "basic significant variables" of macroeconomics. The comparison has added point when it is recalled that both were writing in the 1930s during the Great Depression that spanned that decade. Both were concerned by the apparent failure of the world capitalist system: Keynes, with the persistence of unemployment which, on classical analysis at least, should not have occurred; Lonergan with the presence of booms and slumps which, despite the existence of many "sure-fire" cures such as the one proposed by the Social Credit movement in Canada, appeared to be a recurrent feature of the macroeconomic landscape. The same problem preoccupied many other economists who were to become the intellectual leaders of the subject as soon as the Second World War ended; some of these included John Robinson, Gunnar Myrdal, Michael Kalecki, Wassily Leontieff and Roy Harrod. The period 1926-1939, in particular, saw an efflorescence of creativity in economics that has not yet been repeated and, as is so often the case, the point of departure for much of this theoretical reflection was a concrete social problem. An excellent review of the major theoretical developments in this period has been given by G. L. S. Shackle in his *The Years of High Theory: Invention and Tradition in Economic Thought, 1926-1939.*[2]

Perhaps the most tempting reason to compare Keynes and Lonergan lies in the suggestion by Lonergan that he has in some measure "gone beyond" Keynes. Thus, at the outset, Lonergan observes:

> The present inquiry is concerned with relations between the productive process and the monetary circulation. It will be shown (1) that the acceleration of the process postulates modifications in the circulation, (2) that there exists "systematic", as opposed to windfall, profits, (3) that systematic profits increase in the earlier stages of long-term accelerations but revert to zero in later stages, a phenomenon underlying the

variations in the marginal efficiency of capital of Keynesian *General Theory*, (4) that the increase and the decrease of systematic profits necessitate corresponding changes in subordinate rates of spending—a correlation underlying the significance of the Keynesian propensity to consume. (Lonergan, *Circulation Analysis* (1978), p. 1)[3]

The word "underlying" in this quotation becomes provocative once one realises the nature of the Keynesian concepts of marginal efficiency of capital and the marginal propensity to consume and the role that Keynes saw for them in the *General Theory*.

Keynes, it must be remembered, was concerned with macroeconomics; that is with the large scale behavior of a developed economy. The problem before him was to explain the persistence of high unemployment, but he seemed, instinctively, to know that the answer lay not in some modification of existing theory but in a reconceptualisation of the problem. The marginal efficiency of capital, the marginal propensity to consume and liquidity preference are three of the concepts that he developed to explain how income and employment are determined and, hence, how unemployment might arise.

It will be instructive to consider briefly how these concepts operate in the Keynesian system because this will help to clarify the sorts of terms used and the types of relationships which are operative between them. In the first place it is important to keep in mind that classical macroeconomic theory was intended to provide answers to four interrelated sets of questions:

(i)   What determines the levels of output and employment?
(ii)   What determines the price level?
(iii) What causes inflation?
(iv) How much does money matter?

These questions, in fact, identify the basic significant variables of classical macro-economics—output, employment, price level and its rate of change and the amount of money in the economy. These variables are, of course, related to one another and so constitute a system; in fact, it was *the system* of economic orthodoxy at the time that Keynes was writing. The elements of this system were related as follows:

(i)   Equilibrium in the market for goods and services was established by the laws of supply and demand operating through a flexible system of prices, reflecting individual preferences and the (flexible) responses of supply to changing demand. (Although there might be temporary disturbances,—e.g., crop failure causing economic depression and unemployment—in the longer run there could not be shortage of demand because the act of supply created its own demand.)

(ii)   Wages and the level of employment were also determined by the laws of supply and demand applied to labor. If real wages were higher than the equilibrium price, employment would be lower. (Employment could always be increased by lowering the real wage, and there could, therefore, be no such thing as involuntary unemployment.)

(iii) The amount of investment in production goods (and, thus, in longer term growth of the economy) was dependent upon the technical conditions of production, new inventions and the rate of interest. (More opportunities for investment would raise the demand for capital, raise the rate of interest and thus call forth more savings. A dearth of investment opportunities would lower the rate of interest and reduce the incentive to save. An autonomous increase in saving would lower the rate of interest and thus bring more investment within the range of profitability.)

(iv) The *relative* prices of goods, services and labor were determined by supply and demand in appropriate markets. The *absolute* price, the price level, was determined by the quantity of money. (If prices were "too high" then domestic goods became relatively more expensive than foreign goods, the balance of trade deteriorated, gold flowed out and (gold being the basis of the money stock) the quantity of money fell, prices fell and the foreign balance was, in time, corrected. Conversely, if internal prices were lower than foreign competition, gold flowed in, credit expanded and (in the process sketched above) the ripples of expenditure spread throughout the economy, raising output and, after a lag, prices. (The main lever affecting the balance of trade was seen to be the *relative price* of domestic and foreign goods but some earlier economists, foreshadowing Keynes, saw *incomes* as a factor.)

Points (i) through (iv) comprise, in outline, the system of classical economic orthodoxy.

> The essential assumption underlying it was that it was a *natural* system, obeying certain natural laws (mainly the pursuit of enlightened self interest) which *always and necessarily* operated in such a way as to bring the system back into equilibrium, should it depart from that state. It followed from this, or at least it was thought to follow that any intervention to correct the system, could only make matters worse.[4]

Turning now to Keynes, we find that he is still working with the basic set of questions to which classical theory was thought to be an effective answer; but his answers are different. In particular, Keynes' answers were in terms of three variables which were new—in the sense that Keynes was the first to formulate them with the precision necessary to function in a theoretical framework. The three new variables were, of course, the marginal efficiency of capital, the marginal propensity to consume and liquidity preference. Concerning these three original formulations, there has been no shortage of discussion about their meaning and significance. Still for our purposes it will be sufficient to observe how Keynes worked them into a coherent system in which some variables are regarded as independent while others are dependent. The Keynesian system in broad outline, may be presented as follows:

(i) A given liquidity preference schedule and a given quantity of money gives the rate of interest for a given level of income;

(ii) The rate of interest, via its relationship to the marginal efficiency of capital will determine the amount of investment which, through the multiplier derived from the marginal propensity to consume, will determine income;

(iii) Thus, the rate of interest and the level of income are mutually and simultaneously determined;

(iv) So, given the real wage, the level of income (i.e. output x price index) gives the level of employment (i.e. income/wages = the number of employed).

But, as Keynes pointed out, in opposition to classical theory, there is nothing in this system to ensure that the level is, or will be, or will move towards full employment. In other words, it will be possible for an economy to be in equilibrium at less than full employment and on this point at least theory and experience appear to be in accord.

It is not possible here to do anything like full justice to the revolutionary dimensions of Keynes' work. It will have to suffice, for the moment, to point out that in trying to deal with the questions set by the classical theorists, Keynes produced a theory in which income, employment and the rate of interest (the dependent variables) are explained by three independent variables, the marginal efficiency of capital, the marginal propensity to consume and liquidity preference. It is also important to realise that in introducing the three independent variables Keynes had taken a decisive step away from the classical view of the economy as a natural system which was self-equilibrating; with Keynes there are no "iron laws" of economics. Instead, there is a system of interrelated variables operating in the context of several "given factors". Thus, Keynes wrote:

> We take as given the existing skill and quantity of available labor, the existing quality and quantity of available equipment, the existing technique, the degree of competition, the tastes and habits of the consumer, and the distribution of different intensities of labor and of the activities of supervision and organization, as well as the social structure including forces, other than our variables set forth below, which determine the distribution of national income. This does not mean that we assume these factors to be constant; but merely that, in this place and context, we are not considering or taking into account the effects and consequences of changes in them. Our independent variables are in the first instance, the propensity to consume, the marginal efficiency of capital and the rate of interest, though, as we have already seen, these are capable of further analysis. Our dependent variables are the volume of employment and the national income (or national dividend) measured in wage units. The factors, we have taken as given, influence our independent variables, but do not completely determine them. For example, the schedule of marginal efficiency of capital depends partly on the existing quantity of equipment which is one of the given factors, but partly on the state of long-term expectation which cannot be inferred from the given factors; whilst the rate of interest depends partly on the state of liquidity preference (i.e. on the liquidity function) and partly on the quantity of money measured in wage units. Thus we can sometimes regard our ultimate independent variables as consisting of
>
> (1)   the three fundamental psychological factors, namely the psychological propensity to consume, the psychological attitude to liquidity and the psychological expectations of future yield from capital assets;
> (2)   the wage unit as determined by the bargains reached between employers and employed; and
> (3)   the quantity of money as determined by the central bank.
>
> So that, if we take as given the factors specified above, the variables determine the national income (or dividend) and the quantity of employment. But these again would be capable of being subject to further analysis, and are not, so to speak, our ultimate, atomic, independent elements.[5]

In summary, then, Keynes distinguished between *factors as given;* independent variables rooted in the psychology of the community; and *dependent* variables, the level of employment and income. "Here", Shackle argues, "by implication is Keynes' choice and faith in the matter of *analytical* policy. Some variables are to be independent and some dependent, not merely on some equations of the system but in the system as a whole. They are to have the status of a permanent and general thing. But a variable which is in all connections and throughout the argument to be treated as independent implies by this status a whole philosophy of explanation, or at least, impels us to search for such a philosophy or outlook."[6]

In the matter of the right way to proceed in the construction of an economic theory, then, Keynes has in fact "implicitly rejected the closed dynamic model of the type invented, or borrowed from physics by Ragnar Frisch and developed with such zest by Harrod, Domar, Kalecki, Samuelson, Kaldor and Hicks."[7] Keynes' reasons for this are germane to our analysis in this paper because Keynes is rejecting those models in which each variable has in effect its own determining equation. In such a system each variable is in turn exhibited as dependent on some of the others and, in the end, one has an insulated, closed, complete set of interdependent variables which between them determine, once initial conditions are given, the future timepath of the system. For Keynes, by contrast, "there are economic wind and weather, in the form of politics, fashion and the incalculable movement of expectation, great forces quite outside of and unshaped by the economic ship whose course we seek to understand and control."[8] The concrete facts of the human situation are, for Keynes, the ultimate and truly independent variables, but the *effects* of this concrete complexity are focused and canalised in the marginal efficiency of capital, the marginal propensity to consume and the rate of interest.

According to Shackle, "the values of these variables are, we must assume, the very jetsam of the tides of history in all its depth and complexity, to seek to 'explain' them would be to trespass far beyond the technical concern which the economist sets himself, and compel him to claim competence where he, and any man, can have none. History itself varies these variables by an arcane process whose nature we shall do well. . .to leave inviolate."[9]

There is, then, an immediately evident difference in the matter of method between Keynes and the tradition launched by Frisch and Harrod. The reason for the difference is clear enough. For Keynes economic prediction is not possible so the closed dynamic models developed by Harrod and others cannot have concrete applicability (or relevance) and, consequently, these models must remain entirely abstract, unconnected with the real world of economic decision-making. Once again, Shackle sums up Keynes' intuition as regards method very succinctly:

Keynes' whole theory of employment is ultimately the simple statement that rational expectation being unattainable, we substitute for it first one and then another kind of irrational expectation: and the shift from one arbitrary basis to another gives us from time to time a moment of truth, when our analytical confidence is for the time being dissolved and we, as businessmen, are afraid to invest and so fail to provide enough demand to match our society's desire to produce.[10]

So Keynes appears to conclude that economic process, in the concrete, is governed in part by irrational fear and ignorance in the present and in part by uncertainty about the future. Hence, closed dynamic theories in their search for predictability are, in fact, chasing an unattainable goal.

II. LONERGAN ON ECONOMIC THEORY

"How does Lonergan's circulation analysis relate to these views of Keynes?" On the one hand, he would almost certainly agree with Keynes that a full explanation of economic development is a matter of historical research and as such he would be skeptical of attempts to predict the future state of an economy or, for that matter, to let developments in economic theory be determined by the promise of predictability. Yet, in trying to understand how the economy works, Lonergan claims to have identified phenomena which underlie two of the independent variables of Keynes' analysis—variables which if they do change do so only very slowly and certainly not with the cyclical regularity identified by Lonergan. On the other hand, Lonergan appears to side with Harrod in the type of explanation he is looking for. The description of the nature of closed-system models seems to be very close to Lonergan's conception of an effective theory:

> The method of circulation analysis resembles more the method of arithmetic than the method of botany. It involves a minimum of description and classification, and a maximum of inter-connections and functional relations. Perforce, some description and classification are necessary; but they are highly selective and they contain the apparent arbitrariness inherent in all analysis. For analytical thinking uses classes based upon similarity only as a spring-board to reach terms defined by the correlations in which they stand. To take the arithmetic illustration, only a few of the natural numbers in the indefinitely extended number series are classes derived from descriptive similarity; by definition, the whole series is a progression in which each successive term is a function of its predecessor. It is this procedure which gives arithmetic its endless possibilities of accurate deduction; and, as has been well argued, it is an essentially analogous procedure that underlies all effective theory.[11]

In brief, Lonergan is looking for an explanation in which the terms are defined by the relations in which they stand, that is, by a process of implicit definition. This technique (implicit definition) has been used to great effect by David Hilbert in his *Foundations of Geometry* in which, for example, the meaning of a point and a straight line is fixed by the relation that two, and only two points determine a line. "The significance of implicit definition is its complete generality. The omission of nominal definitions is the omission of a restriction to the objects which, in the first instance, one happens to be thinking about. The exclusive use of explanatory or postulational elements concentrates attention upon the set of relationships in which the whole scientific significance is contained."[12] Perhaps, then, Harrod has allowed himself, too easily, to be restricted to those objects which, "in the first instance, one happens to be thinking about", and it may be that this is the reason why his analysis is in terms of the usual macroeconomic aggregates between which he tries to establish a mathematical relationship. If this is so, Lonergan's critique would be aimed at showing that by using the technique of implicit definition, the emphasis shifts from trying to *define* the relevant variables to *searching* heuristically for the maximum extent of interconnections and interdependence; and that the variables discovered in this way might not resemble very much the objects (or the aggregates) which, in the first instance, one was thinking about. There is, then, a shift away from definitions to sets of relationships:

> On such a methodological model (i.e. implicit definition) circulation analysis raises a large super-structure of terms and theorems upon a summary classification and a few brief analyses of typical phenomena. Classes of payments quickly become rates of payment standing in the mutual conditioning of a circulation; to this mutual and, so to speak, internal conditioning there is immediately added the external conditioning that arises out of transfers of money from one circulation to another; in turn this twofold conditioning in the monetary order is correlated with the conditioning constituted by productive rhythms of goods and services and from the foregoing dynamic configuration of conditions during a limited interval of time, there is deduced a catalogue of possible types of change in the configuration over a series of intervals. There results a closely knit frame of reference that can envisage any total movement of an economy as a function of variations in rates of payment, and that can define the conditions of desirable movements as well as deduce the causes of breakdowns. Through such a frame of reference one can see and express the mechanism to which classical precepts are only partially adapted; and through it again one can infer the fuller adaptation that has to be attained.[13]

The method of implicit definition, then, is an heuristic search for a set of functionally interdependent terms defined by their relations to one another. The result of this process will be, here as it is in the case of Newtonian mechanics, a relational structure in which a set of "basic significant variables" mutually define one another.

Lonergan's search is directed towards an understanding of the dynamics of a developed economy. That is, an economy which has evolved to the point where it produces both consumer goods (in the basic stage) and capital goods (in the surplus stage), a network of financial institutions in which the laws of supply and demand operate; and where exchange takes place by means of money. In such an economy, production is for sale and the economy functions successfully to the extent that the goods and services produced are, in fact, sold. In its dynamic aspect, Lonergan sets out to discover how this type of economy expands—that is, how it accelerates its production of goods and services.

While it is not possible, here, to produce even a summary of the technical conclusions reached by Lonergan, some indication of how his conclusions relate to the conclusions obtained by Keynes in relation to the basic significant variable of macroeconomics can be given. In Lonergan's Analysis, the existence of both producer and consumer goods and services sets up two circular flows in the monetary order—a surplus circulation and a basic circulation. The fact that entrepreneurs in the basic stage have a recurrent requirement for new machinery (if only for replacements) while those employed in the surplus stage have a standard of living to maintain sets up a pair of cross-overs along which money payments are transferred from one circuit to the other. From this emerges a set of interdependent variables defined in relation to the monetary function payments for goods and services are intended to fulfill. Thus,

> Money held in reserve for a defined purpose will be said to be in a monetary function. Five such functions are distinguished: basic demand, basic supply, surplus demand, surplus supply and a fifth redistributive function. Money held in reserve for basic expenditure will be said to be in the *basic demand function.* Money held in reserve for surplus expenditure will be said to be in the *surplus demand function.* Again, money on its way from...final basic operative payments to initial basic outlay, will be said to be in the *basic supply function....* Finally, money held in reserve for any number of redistributive purposes will be said to be in the *redistributive function.*[14]

These five monetary functions define a configuration of flows which can be correlated with the production and consumption of goods and services in the basic and surplus stages of the production process respectively. The significance of this relation is that in any long term acceleration of the economy, the technical production of goods and services is intrinsically cyclical and, because of this, the flow of money payments between the monetary functions must be cyclical as well. It is the emergence of the intrinsically cyclical nature of the acceleration of the production process which accounts both for the systematic fluctuation in the rates of profit which underlies variations in the marginal efficiency of capital; and for the systematic fluctuation in the rate of savings which underlies changes in the marginal propensity to consume.

On this analysis, then, the Keynesian independent variables are seen to have their origins not in the psychological constitution of the community but in the inherent dynamics of the developed exchange economy. This is an extremely important finding because in addition to clarifying the meaning of the Keynesian notions it provides a basis from which a critique of the economy can be launched. Lonergan once observed that cars operate according to the principles of Newtonian mechanics which drivers must acknowledge if they are to avoid disaster. If, on the other hand, the laws governing the operation of motor cars included as of a piece the social psychology of drivers there would be no basis from which to provide a criticism of drivers. What Lonergan was searching for—and the technique of implicit definition provides—was the dynamic laws of an expanding exchange economy; laws which provide a basis for the criticism of human actions. Such criticism is impossible as long as the basis of the terms and relations used in theory is rooted in social psychology.

III. Discussion

Lonergan's claim, made at the outset of the circulation analysis, that he had discovered phenomena that underlie the Keynesian independent variables is grounded in the method used in his analysis; the heuristic search for a set of functionally interdependent terms using the technique of implicit definition. It is a search that breaks away from the familiar objects of economic life—income, employment, wages, prices etc. to inquire after another set of terms (basic, surplus and re-distributional supply and demand functions) which can account for *movements in income, employment, wages and prices*. The problem of developing an effective analytical framework is analogous to the problem of explaining the fact that chlorine gas is green in color. It is not a sufficient explanation to say that the gas is green because it is composed of green atoms. The full explanation is in terms of the emission and absorption of light of certain wave-lengths. Analogously, it is not sufficient to say that fluctuations in aggregate income and employment are due to booms and slumps in economic activity, because booms and slumps are identified by observing fluctuations of income and employment.

Keynes recognised very clearly the nature of a theoretical explanation, hence his identification of his three independent variables, the marginal efficiency of capital, the marginal propensity to consume and liquidity preference. But as we have seen, these variables are at root an expression of the social psychological state of the community of producers and consumers and they function in Keynes' work as *explaining* the levels of income and employment. These independent variables relate to a static situation and are defined in relation to ourselves not in relation to one another as the technique of implicit definition demanded. The problem for Keynes was the clear perception that human affairs are dominated by uncertainty and, therefore, that any dynamic theory would not be capable of predicting the future development of the economy. As a result of his profound insight into the role of expectations in economic life, Keynes' theoretical framework is a halfway house between description and explanation. His work exhibits, perhaps more clearly than any other economist, a clear grasp of the concrete functioning of the economy but precisely this knowledge appears to have prevented him from "getting beyond those objects with which he was, in the first instance, familiar." At least, he appears to have admitted as much on several occasions; see for example the quotation from the preface of *The General Theory* cited above.

There is no doubt that Lonergan did not possess as much experience of economics as Keynes but it also seems fair to say that he was more conscious than Keynes of the limitations of the general methodological breakthrough inaugurated by Galileo, Kepler and Newton and copied, somewhat slavishly, by many economists. Lonergan realised in a critically self-conscious way—*firstly* that Newtonian-type theories were a triumph of the heuristic search for systematic correlations in data, but, *secondly* (and perhaps more importantly) that the possibility of systematic correlations rests upon the occurrence (or otherwise) of sequences of concrete events whose individual occurrence is governed by probabilities. The dependence of systematic relationships upon concretely functioning schemes of recurrence is plainly operative throughout the *Circulation Analysis* as is evident in Lonergan's insistence on the inherent indeterminacy in the productive process, and *a fortiori* because they are correlated, in the rates of payment in the monetary order. Whereas Keynes when faced with the problem of seeking out the systematic in macroeconomics was forced to conclude that there could not be any factors which persisted through time from one equilibrium state to another as long as individual freedom to make decisions and the future was uncertain (enterprise is risk, risk is ignorance, and equilibrium by contrast is the effective banishment of ignorance). Lonergan has identified a set of systematic relations whose character resides in the concrete principles of operation of a developed exchange economy. These relationships are not in any sense a new set of 'iron laws' of economics. On the contrary, the systematic relations apply only as long as the schemes of recurrence of the exchange economy continue to operate and the guarantee of that rests with an intelligent grasp that it is a scheme of recurrence that depends upon a form of human collaboration and cooperation in which goods are produced for sale. Insofar as the production of goods for sale is factually successful, there is set up in the monetary order a two-fold circulation and a pair of cross-overs from one circuit to the other. One can grasp immediately that for the circulation to maintain itself the cross-overs must balance. One can investigate the circumstances under which the balance can be expected to persist and, from here, one is led immediately to the significance of the basic price spread and the concrete possibility of the business cycle and to the important conclusion that the business cycle is not primarily the result of entrepreneurial greed but of a failure to understand what is going on in an economic expansion, as well as how to act appropriately to achieve it without mishap. But this is technical economics and not the subject of the present paper.

CONCLUSIONS

We set out initially to try to identify what was distinctive in Lonergan's reflection on economics. We have attempted to indicate that the answer lies less in the technical deductions of the work—though they are considerable—and more in the practical application of a self-conscious, critically controlled method. Once the method is grasped, then it becomes clear how the theory (the *Circulation Analysis*) differs from, say, that of Keynes' *General Theory*. Further, with the frame of reference, the network of interconnections reveal the conditions for successful expansion of the economy; breakdowns arise from a failure to observe the norms of behavior implied if the network is to survive. The survival of capitalism is seen to depend less on moralising about the evils of greed and more upon the intelligent behavior appropriate to a concretely functioning exchange economy.

Towards the end of his essay, "Healing and Creating in History," Lonergan observes that if we are to escape the fate that befell the Roman Empire, we must demand that two requirements be met. "The first regards economic theorists; the second regards moral theorists. From economic theorists we have to demand, along with as many other types of analysis as they please, a new and specific type that reveals how moral precepts have both a basis in economic process and so an effective application to it. From moral theorists we have to demand, along with their other various forms of wisdom and prudence, specifically economic precepts that arise out of economic process itself and promote its proper functioning.''[15]

In the circulation analysis, we have concrete evidence of the former—moral precepts that have a basis in the economic process. Not since the classical economists enunciated the principles of thrift for consumers and enterprise for businessmen have we had an economic theory that shows not only the precise conditions under which these are valid, but also how they have to be adapted to account for the more complex state of economic development we now have. Here, as in so many other areas, Lonergan has pointed a way forward.

NOTES

1. J.M. Keynes, *The General Theory of Employment Interest and Money* (London: Macmillan, 1936), xxiii; hereafter referred to as *General Theory*.

2 G.L.S. Shackle, *The Year's of High Theory: Invention and Tradition in Economic Thought 1926–1939* (Cambridge: Cambridge University Press, 1967).

3 B. Lonergan, *Circulation Analysis* (1978), p. 1. Throughout this paper *Circulation Analysis* will refer to the essay by Bernard J.F. Lonergan, S.J., "An Essay in Circulation Analysis," Theology Department, Boston College, Chestnut Hill, MA 02167 (1978).

4 The economic system of classical theory presented in this paper is taken from Peter Browning, *Economic Images: Current Economic Controversies* (London: Longman, 1983), pp. 14–15.

5 Keynes, *General Theory*, p. 245.

6 Shackle, *High Theory*, p. 158.

7 *Ibid.*

8 Shackle, *High Theory*, p. 159.

9 *Ibid.*, p. 160.

10 *Ibid.*, p. 129.

11 Lonergan, *Circulation Analysis*, p. 3.

12 B. Lonergan, *Insight: A Study of Human Understanding* (New York: Philosophical Library, 1957), pp. 12–13.

13 B. Lonergan, *Circulation Analysis*, pp. 3–4.

14 Lonergan, *Circulation Analysis*, p. 39 (Italics mine).

15 B. Lonergan, "Healing and Creating in History" in *Bernard Lonergan: 3 Lectures* (Montreal: Thomas More Institute Papers/75, 1975), pp. 55–68 (reprinted in *A Third Collection: Papers by Bernard J.F. Lonergan, S.J.* edited by Frederick Crowe, S.J. [New York: Paulist Press, 1985], pp. 100–109.

XXIII

Economic Transformations: The Role of Conversions and Culture in the Transformation of Economics

Patrick H. Byrne

INTRODUCTION

IN one of his class lectures at Boston College on "Macroeconomics and the Dialectic of History," Rev. Bernard Lonergan, S.J. stated that his work on circulation analysis was not so much a new *theory* as a new *paradigm*.[1] To put the matter succinctly, Lonergan's circulation analysis reveals the relevance of the four conversions and of a culture controlled at the "third stage of meaning"[2] for economic thought and policy. To make "conversion a topic of discussion" in the field of economics would be to propose a radically new paradigm indeed. Contemporary economic thought has been dominated by a paradigm which had its origins in the modern political philosophies of Machiavelli, Hobbes and Locke.[3] It is a paradigm which conceives of a nature as ruled by iron laws of necessity and of human nature as irredeemably corrupt.[4] Within this paradigm, the economic problem has been taken to be the discovery and implementation of conditions under which a society can prosper, regardless of the state of its social soul.[5]

Yet Lonergan's view on these issues, as expressed in his as yet unpublished *An Essay on Circulation Analysis*,[6] entails an emphatic assertion that the most fundamental conditions for economic prosperity are in fact converted human beings. The purpose of this essay is to articulate how it is that conversions, and cultural control of meanings by converted subjects, are fundamental to Lonergan's vision of the economic problem.

To do so, the essay will be divided into four sections. In the first of these sections, "Lonergan's Circulation Analysis," there will be three sub-sections: "Accelerations in Production," "Circulation of Payments," and "Redistributive Operations." In these sections I will present an abbreviated overview of Lonergan's circulation analysis. The second section, "Economic Dysfunctions," discusses the points at which Lonergan's analysis reveals economies to be vulnerable to inattentive, unintelligent, unreasonable, irresponsible or unloving responses. In the third section some concrete examples of how conversions can transform such dysfunctions will be considered. The last section, in turn, will take up the role of culture in economic thought and economic decision.

I. LONERGAN'S CIRCULATION ANALYSIS

Lonergan's "Introduction" to the 1982 version of his *An Essay on Circulation Analysis* stressed three different sources of "fluctuations" in economic process: production, payments and finance. In a nutshell, his analysis consists in identifying the terms and relations *within* each of these sources, as well as the additional relations *among* them. His analysis further shows that this network of terms and relations establishes certain norms or exigences in economic functioning, so that to disrespect these norms or exigences is to invite dire consequences. The first three sub-sections of this article will discuss in turn each of these sources.

Accelerations in Production

First, then, let us consider the sources of fluctuation in production. Lonergan begins by citing a *functional* distinction between two levels of productive activity which he names "basic" and "surplus." In basic production, activities are producing goods and services intended for use in a culture's standard of living. Roughly speaking, this corresponds to what we descriptively refer to as "consumer goods."[7] On the other hand, surplus production produces goods and services to be used in the *producing* of goods and services, not in the standard of living itself. For example, the production of milkshake, machines, oil barges, and cement trucks is surplus production. These goods are never purchased for use in someone's standard of living; they are frequently purchased by people who will use them in the production of consumer goods. On the other hand, a great many goods—socket wrenches, micro-computers, flashlights and books, for example—cannot be *automatically* classified as either basic/consumer goods, or as surplus goods. The types of uses they are actually, concretely put to determine this classification.

Now there can be minor innovations in the kinds and types of basic goods and services that are being produced which amount to little more than shifts in output. There can also be minor innovations in which one company or another temporarily streamlines its techniques of production and momentarily increases its share of the market. But there can also be major innovations in the ways in which production is being done. When these types of innovations occur, they are not limited to one type of industry, or industry in just one area. Their impact permeates through the entire economy. The use of interchangeable parts, steam power, electrical power, the assembly line, and computer assisted design and manufacture (CAD/CAM) are but a few examples of such innovations. Typically these innovations make production in general more efficient and capable of producing far greater ranges of goods and services. These types of innovations originate in the level of surplus production and have the potential to cause "accelerations" both in surplus and basic production.

Such "long term accelerations" are the very heart of all that is admirable and advanced in "advanced countries." Yet, as it turns out, the needs associated with this last kind of innovation are at the core of economic dysfunction. In particular it is the monetary needs and the problem associated with adapting to them which are at the root of these dysfunctions. This article now turns to a consideration of these issues.

Circulation of Payments

In addition to the fluctuation in economic functioning due to accelerations in production, payments constitute a second, though related, source of fluctuations. Moreover, Lonergan's concern is not just with payments, but rather with aggregates of payments, and indeed *aggregates of rates* of payments.[8]

In any complex society, it is the general rule that producers are almost always producing for someone other than themselves. Hence goods and services which are produced are subsequently exchanged to their ultimate users. Since this usually also entails a reciprocating exchange of moneys, i.e., payments, certain payments function as a measure of transitions between levels of production. Operations in the productive process reach completion when goods or services pass from the stages when they are being produced to the stage where they are being used. A basic product reaches completion when someone begins to use it in their way of life, i.e., to sustain their standard of living. A surplus product reaches completion when it begins to be used in the production of *either* surplus *or* basic products.

In the simplest barter economies, finished products are exchanged directly for one another. But in virtually all contemporary economies money is the medium of exchange, thereby overcoming what economists refer to as the "problem of the double coincidence."[9] Hence, in most economies exchanges (payments) of moneys accompany, and are the condition for the completion of, a moment in the productive process.

Now it might seem that an investigation into the ways payments condition and measure the productive process should begin with a precise cataloguing of each and every payment. Yet in a modern economy a thorough account of each and every payment every single day would not only be a practical impossibility, but would lack theoretical relevance. The practical obstacles are evident enough. For different reasons, such an accounting would also be theoretically irrelevant. The exact order in which Smith's or Jones' payments are received, the date and hour they were received, etc., in no way contribute to an explanatory understanding of the state of a whole economy.[10] Rather, the theoretical relevance of payments in Lonergan's analysis pertains to the ways they facilitate or obtrude the productive process, and ultimately transform the potentialities of nature into a standard of living, as Lonergan wrote.

> What the analysis reveals is a mechanism . . . distinct from the price mechanism, *for it determines the channels within which the price mechanism works.* (1980, p. 3, emphasis added.)

In other words, shifting patterns in the circulation of payments are responsible for certain kinds of shifts in prices. Different stages in a long-term acceleration imply rising and falling prices insofar as they are linked with shifts in rates of payments. If these shifts are misinterpreted, the potentiality of a higher standard of living will be lost.

It should be noted that Lonergan's analysis of what are and are not the appropriate "channels" for the flows of payments solves only *one* economic problem, albeit a most important one. The analysis only removes the apparent necessity of trade cycle depressions with their resultant high rates of unemployment and failures of firms, as well as the apparent necessity for exploitation of foreign countries. A well-functioning macro-economy could still be troubled by microeconomic injustices such as arbitrary manipulation of certain markets, disproportions in salary structures, etc.

While a precise catalogue of each and every payment lacks theoretical relevance, a detailed account of classes or *aggregates* of payments *is* relevant to an explanatory account of the economy. A rise in payments in a particular company's business one day may be offset by a fall in payments the next day; in a given sector of industry, variations in one company's payments may offset those of another company; and reciprocal variations in different sectors of basic and surplus producers may result in no net variations in those levels of production. Hence it is net aggregates, rather than the catalogue of particular payments, which are of theoretical concern.

In order for any discussion of aggregates of payments to have theoretical significance, however, they must be based upon an explanatory system of terms and relations. Thus, Lonergan draws upon the explanatory terms derived in his analysis of the productive process and defines various classes or aggregates of payments in relation to them. For example, the system of classification involves distinctions between basic and surplus payments, just as the analysis of production involved a distinction between basic and surplus production. In this way Lonergan secures explanatory status for his analysis of payments.

Besides the functional correlation between classes of payments and the stages and levels of the productive process, there is the mutual conditioning which follows as a corollary upon those functional relations. On the one hand, payments depend upon the productive process for clearly there will be no payments if there is nothing to be bought. Less obviously but no less significantly, stages and levels of production depend upon payments. Producers will not undertake enterprises unless they have reason to expect receipts from which they can pay suppliers, workers and satisfactorily compensate themselves for their efforts. Workers will not work nor suppliers supply unless they, too, can expect recompense. So the assembly and maintenance of the vast network of production is conditioned by the regular flows of payments.

This interdependence of cycles of production and cycles of payments is one example of what Lonergan has referred to as a "conditioned series of schemes of recurrence."[11] He later embellished his notion of a conditioned series of schemes of recurrence with the notion of a conditioned series of "ecologies" as follows:

> An ecology is an interrelated and interconnected set of schemes of recurrence. Ecologies too have their probabilities of emergence and survival. A series of ecologies can form chains of sequential dependence, with prior ecologies grounding the probability of the emergence of the next . . . Human communities devise their own schemes of recurrence:

the commonly understood and commonly accepted ways and means of cooperating. Among them are the firms that keep producing goods and rendering services and no less the households that purchase the goods produced and the services rendered. Such is the economy which is a structure [ecology] resting on the ecologies of nature and underpinning social and cultural structures [ecologies]. (1980, p. 1)

In short, Lonergan envisions an evolving "ecology" of mutually conditioning rhythms of production and payments as the appropriate way of conceiving what we call an economy. The fact of this *dynamic* mutual conditioning of production and rates of payments requires that Lonergan's analysis include relations among aggregates of *rates* of payments. Lonergan speaks of aggregates of rates of payments because producers require ever increasing rates of payments if they are to expand or accelerate their enterprises. When rates of payments received do not increase, a business is said to have a "cash flow problem." Now some cash flow problems are a result of inadequate management; but there can also be systematic sources for a failure of cash flows, for rates of payments, to increase. When this happens, the problem has to do with the *aggregate* of rates of payments.[12] In other words, a whole sector or level of production can be stymied from expanding because something is impeding the increase of rates of payments all along the line.

The details of Lonergan's derivation of the relations between the rates of payments would occupy too much space for present purposes, and I will therefore simply state certain of his conclusions. In order to follow the statement of these conclusions, the reader may find it helpful to refer to the following diagram.[13]

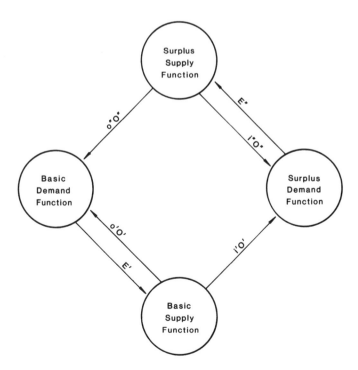

In the diagram, the circles represent what Lonergan calls "monetary functions" where money is "dynamically quiescent and. . .held in reserve for a defined purpose" (i.e., either for basic or surplus expenditures, or basic or surplus outlay). (1982, pp. 39).

Lonergan's statement of the relations among these rates of payments runs as follows:

First, there will be identifiable rates of payments which are expenditures for both basic and surplus products (for the sake of brevity, these will be abbreviated as E' and E" respectively).[14]

Second, what is an expenditure for a consumer is simultaneously a receipt for a producer. Producers, in turn, use these receipts as outlays to workers, suppliers, and themselves. In other words, the total producer receipts per month are equal to the total producer outlays per month. Hence, the rates of basic and surplus expenditures are in some way related to rates of basic and surplus outlays. (O' and O" respectively).

Third, some fraction of basic outlays, say c', eventually becomes a part of basic expenditure, insofar as basic producers' outlays are eventually spent on basic (consumer) goods and services. The remaining fraction i', of basic outlays becomes part of the expenditures of surplus producers, insofar as basic producers' outlays eventually go toward the purchase of surplus (producer) goods and services. Similarly, surplus outlays divide into fractions, c" and i."[15] Hence,

$$E' = c'O' + c''O''.$$
$$E'' = i'O' + i''O''.$$

These equations represent a pair of "crossovers" of rates of payment *from* the circuit of basic expenditures and outlays *to* the circuit of surplus expenditures and outlays (i'O') and *vice versa* (c"O").

From this analysis it follows that macroeconomic equilibrium can exist only when the crossovers balance — i.e., c"O" = i'O'.[16] In the absence of this condition, one circuit will be draining the other of the resources required to sustain its productive process.

Redistributive Operations

As long as there is nothing new under the sun, no more would need to be said about economic functioning. However, the most salient feature of modern economies is innovation and most significant are the major innovations which revolutionize ways of producing, as discussed in section I.A of this essay. Ideally, the "long-term accelerations" which issue from such major innovations as use of electrical power should consist of two stages or phases: a surplus expansion followed, after a time-lag, by a basic expansion. For example, electrical power used in the production of dynamos would be accelerating a surplus expansion. These dynamos would subsequently be used to provide electrical power both for the production and operation of consumer appliances, thus accelerating a basic expansion.

Since rates of payments and rates of production are mutually conditioning, Lonergan recognized that rates of payments must change in order to initiate and sustain long-term accelerations. In what ways might those rates change? One possibility is existing quantities of money simply change hands more rapidly, resulting in a collection of increased cash flows. In such a case, there would be no net change in the *amounts* of money circulating in either the basic or surplus circuits. Under this set of circumstances, virtually *every* producer's cash flows would have to increase together and in step. Given this kind of restriction, Lonergan concluded "there is a possibility of circuit acceleration but that possibility is quite limited." (1980 p. 48) Moreover, as his discussion shows, this "quite limited possibility" is one with an exceptionally low probability.

From these observations it follows that if major innovations in production are to issue into expansions of surplus and basic production, the circuits of aggregate rates of payments must be augmented by recurrent influxes of additional moneys. Where could such repeated supplements of amounts of moneys come from? One answer is the surplus circuit could drain money out of the basic circuit, or *vice versa*. Unfortunately, this option yields dire results.[17]

Hence, if long-term accelerations are to occur without serious economic dysfunction, a different source of the needed supplements of moneys must be sought. This source can be identified by adverting to the fact that besides outlays which go to workers, suppliers and the entrepreneur's recompense, moneys also flow into banks, bonds, stocks, insurance, taxes, and so on. These are payments which do not *directly* result in completion of a product, and thus Lonergan terms them "redistributive payments."[18] Therefore, the preceding diagram needs to be supplemented as follows:

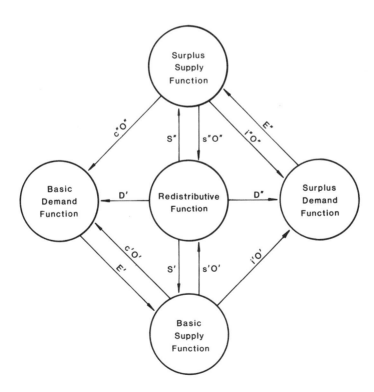

In this new diagram, basic and surplus outlays are divided into three rather than two fractions, c', i', s' and c'', i'', s'', respectively. The aggregate rates of payments, s'O' and s''O'', pertain to the operation of still another economic function in society, the "redistributive monetary function." Rates of payments received by this function enable it to "redistribute" moneys by making loans to the basic or surplus supply functions (S' and S'') enabling basic or surplus entrepreneurs to expand their operations, loans to the surplus demand function (D'') covering startup costs for new entrepreneurs , and consumer loans to the basic demand function (D').

However, insofar as the sum, S' + S'' + D'' + D', is equal to the sum, s'O + s''O'', there will be no new money added to the overall pattern of circulating moneys, and the operations of the redistributive function will merely alter paths of circulation.[19] The major contribution of the redistributive monetary function in this case is a specialization of investment. Better and more discerning criteria for loans can be developed than entrepreneurs, specializing in their fields, would be capable of.

Yet it is not necessary that S' + S'' + D'' + D' = s'O' + s''O''. Under appropriate conditions, bankers, etc., may actually loan out *more* money in a given period than they receive back in the sum, s'O' + s''O''. This is permissible, insofar as those making the loans have reasonable expectations[20] that the excess they loan out this month will be received back next month, next year, or in ten years, because the expanded process of production will make this possible. In other words, operations in the redistributive function can recurrently supplement the amounts of moneys in one or another circuit without robbing the other circuit of its economic resources. In so doing, they accelerate that circuit; and the reasonableness of their doing so consists in the amounts they will receive back in later time periods *because* of the accelerations they make possible. One can conceive of these accelerative payments, S' + S'' + D' + D'', as a second "superposed" activity of the redistributive function. The role played by s'O' + s''O'' ("savings") is *not* to finance this second level of operations but, as Lonergan puts it, "to understand" it. (1980, p. 57) Such is the normativity of redistributive operations.

II. ECONOMIC DYSFUNCTIONS

In order to introduce the relevance of conversions to economic functioning, I find it helpful to consider Lonergan's reflections on the manifold of ways this functioning can be disrupted. However, while it may be possible to outline Lonergan's functional analysis, his discussions of the dysfunctions of an economy involve a complexity of detail which defies summary. In this section, therefore, I will offer but a few illustrations of how the interdependent functioning of the cycles can be disrupted.

The analysis of the mutual conditioning of cycles of production and payments reveals a normativity, a "natural and proper" mode of economic functioning. As with Aristotle's inquiry into the "proper function" of a human being,[21] the discovery of a natural and proper economic functioning provides a basis for ethical judgments. It also provides a framework by means of which one may anticipate likely sources of aberrations in that functioning.

Lonergan's analysis reveals two related areas of economic functioning as especially vulnerable to aberrations: the balancing of crossovers, and the transition from surplus to basic expansion. Balancing of crossovers is important. Otherwise, in each period of time a quantity of money will be *permanently* removed from one circuit and transferred to the other. For example, if i'O' > c''O'', each week, month, year, there will be less money in the Basic Demand Function. Demand for basic goods will fall, not because willingness or productive capacity is lacking, but because cash flows lag ever farther behind. The most vulnerable enterprises will be forced to cut back production and lay off workers. But this will not be sufficient. Because basic demand is falling, prices for goods will drop. (Here one encounters a first example of how circulation of payments is a mechanism determining the channels within which the price mechanism works [1980, p. 3].) Soon savings of the most vulnerable firms will be depleted. Next, the credit extended to see them through hard times will be cut off because hard times have lasted too long. Finally these firms will go bankrupt; workers will be laid off; formerly successful people will be ruined; and simultaneously the supply of basic goods and services will become increasingly scarce.

The solution, on paper, is quite simple: get the crossovers balanced. If i'O' is greater than c''O'', decrease i'O' month by month until it equals c''O''. However an economy does not run on paper; it runs by a complex network of human decisions, agreements and expectations. The different rates of payments are determined by those decisions, agreements and expectations. Solutions to real concrete economic ills, therefore, must be pursued, by first discovering the constellations of human decisions, agreements and expectations which have concretely led to imbalanced crossovers. The most common and most serious mistaken decisions, agreements and expectations occur during the shift from surplus to basic expansion. Several such disturbances in the circulation of rates of payments, are discussed in the following sub-sections.

Misinterpretation of Declining Levels of Profits

The natural question is why human decisions might have a tendency to imbalance crossovers between surplus and basic cycles of payments. One answer has to do with expectations mistakenly formed by entrepreneurs during a long term acceleration of surplus production.

In such an expansion, more and more workers are employed in surplus production. In addition, sooner or later the laws of supply and demand will begin to push up the wages of these surplus level workers. These two sources will lead to a dramatic increase in the sum total, month after month, of the wages of workers involved in surplus production. Hence, the rates of payments, c''O'', will lead to dramatic growth in basic demand. Basic expenditures, E', will also grow month after month at a significant rate.

Unless the quantities of basic goods and services rise immediately and at the same pace as the increases in c''O'' (and there are good reasons to suspect they will *not*), the price mechanism will lead to growing prices for basic goods and services. This increase in prices will show up as increased profits for entrepreneurs in the basic sector. (This is another example of what Lonergan meant by the statement that his circulation analysis reveals "a mechanism . . . [which] determines the channels within which the price mechanism works." (1980, p. 3)) That is to say, the acceleration of surplus production itself induces steady increases in basic (consumer) prices.

The profits resulting from this increase in prices are proper and essential for bringing the surplus expansion to its natural term: a higher standard of living for the whole society. They are proper, for they are a measure of the increased potential productivity of the society resulting from the innovations in the means of production. They are essential for providing the initial investments for the basic expansion which will produce the higher standard of living.

Yet, while the increasing profits themselves are proper and essential, they have almost always suffered a misinterpretation which is not only illegitimate but disastrous. These increasing profits are due to a certain state of production—the surplus expansion—which *should* eventually come to an end. It *should* come to an end because it is not an end in itself, but rather a means to basic expansion. Hence, these higher levels of profits should come to an end. If, however, these higher levels of profits are interpreted as what is always expected from business, a natural downturn in those levels of profits will be mistakenly interpreted as a failure in marketing, management, etc. Firms may seek means of sustaining high levels of profits beyond their natural expiration point. The sectors in basic production which first experience such declines in profits will be the first cut back—precisely at a time when those sectors should be expanding in order to initiate the basic expansion.

In his writings Lonergan has stated that many of our economic woes have to do with a "mistaken interpretation of the significance of pure surplus income." Lonergan originally defined pure surplus income as "the fraction [H] of surplus expenditure [= surplus outlay] that goes to new fixed investment." (1944, p. 90) In other words, it is the fraction, H, of the rate of surplus outlay payments which goes strictly towards increasing rather than maintaining the means of production. In a surplus expansion, this fraction goes first towards purchase of surplus products by surplus producers, but gradually more and more towards the purchase of surplus products by basic producers. More recently Lonergan has dropped the term, "pure surplus income" and has spoken instead simply of "a failure to distinguish between normal profit, which can be constant, and a social dividend which varies." (1982, p. 68) Since the point is an important one, perhaps it would be best to quote Lonergan at length on this issue:

> By constant normal profit I mean the excess of bills receivable over bills payable in the stationary state. It is an excess that must be had if the firm is not to go bankrupt and if the persons responsible for the firm's emergence and continued existence are to have a proportionate standard of living. A profit that is normal in the stationary state is no less normal in the surplus expansion.
>
> It remains that the excess of bills receivable over bills payable during the surplus expansion is not in its entirety a contribution to personal income. The part that would be profit in the stationary state is still profit. But the excess over that part is social dividend.

It is money to be invested either directly [i'O'] or, through the redistributional area, indirectly [s'O'—D" or S"]. For it is the equivalent of the money that, if not invested, contracts surplus production, that, if invested, keeps surplus production at its attained volume and, if a further appropriate sum is added interval by interval, surplus production will not merely level off but keep accelerating. (1982, pp. 68–69)

When surplus producers begin to reach the natural completion of their acceleration, and as basic production begins to accelerate, the fraction of basic demand represented by c"O" begins to decrease and consequently the ratio of basic receipts to basic costs (i.e., c'O')[22] also decreases.

Now, if no distinction is drawn between normal profits on the one hand and pure surplus income which is a social dividend on the other, producers will interpret this shrinking of their profit margin as a sign of declining demand. When this misinterpretation is generalized, as it is in all modern economies, there will be a general cut-back in production leading to layoffs, a consequent decrease in basic demand, a further fall in prices followed by yet further layoffs. As Lonergan put it, "the egalitarian shift is achieved only through the contractions, the liquidations, the blind stresses and strains of a prolonged depression." (1944, pp. 98-99)

SQUEEZING OUT SURPLUS INVESTMENT. There is a second set of examples concerning what Lonergan has called "mistaken expectations" derived from an acceleration of the surplus level of production. In a surplus expansion, pure surplus income flows from the surplus circuit of production, along the path c"O" into the basic circuit and returns to the surplus circuit either along s'O' or i'O'. In a surplus expansion the amount flowing into the basic circuit accelerates, and consequently basic receipts as well as surplus receipts accelerate. If people fail to recognize that the natural goal of these accelerating receipts is re-investment in surplus expansion, they may come to be viewed instead as a justifiable reason for expecting producers to assume a greater proportion of society's burdens. Thus there arise programs of taxation and redistribution to basic demand. On the small scale, this need not be a problem. But if it is sustained in a major way, and especially if connected with a policy of deficit governmental spending, it can cut short the surplus (and eventually the basic) expansion. (This I take to be the real meaning of the phrase, "sluggish economy".)

UNION DEMANDS FOR HIGHER WAGES. Accelerating receipts during surplus expansion can also be misinterpreted in another fashion. Because increasing amounts of moneys are flowing into basic demand by way of c"O" (i.e., the accelerating aggregate wages of workers in surplus production) at a time when there is as yet no corresponding increase in numbers of basic goods and services, prices of basic goods and services will rise. Labor unions can argue that the increases in basic prices and the increases in producers' receipts justify increased wages. But increased wages simply flow back into basic demand in even greater quantities forcing basic prices still higher, thus generating an inflationary spiral of higher prices and wages. Those most hurt by this spiral are those who are on fixed incomes, those who are not union members, or whose unions lack the brute power of the largest unions, since their real incomes fall ever further behind.

CONTROL OF THE MONEY SUPPLY. The acceleration of money in the circuits can also be accomplished through regular addition to the money supply by means of aggregate redistributive payments [D' + D" + (S' − s'O') + (S" − s"O") > O]. This suggestion, as

Lonergan says, seems to defy the common notion that investments should equal savings. Yet that common notion requires the kind of "reorientation" Lonergan proposed in *Insight*,[23] for any significant influx of moneys into the basic or surplus circuit where crossovers are balanced and $D' + D'' + (S' - s'O') + (S'' - s''O'') = O$ has the same net effect as unbalanced crossovers. Historically means have been found to augment the amount of money in circuits, including the increase in gold coinage, governmental fiduciary issue, and policies of managed money. Clearly in any of these cases good criteria for such techniques would be needed if inflationary spirals and other disastrous consequences are to be avoided. Now there has been no lack of attempts to propose such criteria, but all have lacked one fundamental feature: namely, the kind of explanatory, functional understanding of the roles and consequences of such increases which Lonergan's analysis provides.[24] Hence, misdirected redistributive payments can be dysfunctional.[25]

Imperialism. Sometimes this traumatic readjustment has historically been averted through imperialistic foreign policies. Under such policies, various coercive means, (including imposition of quotas, control of exports, control of investments and exploitative advertising) are adopted to manipulate certain foreign markets. As a result of such manipulation, the foreign markets consume increasingly larger numbers of goods in order to sustain the surplus expansion of the imperial power beyond its natural plateau. In other words, the depression is shifted from one's own nation to someone else's.

III. Converted Constitution of the Economy

Lonergan has criticized the inadequacies of a variety of alternative techniques for avoiding these dysfunctions: socialistic central planning, manipulation of interest rates, deficit "pump-priming," warfare and multi-national corporations. What, then, is the solution?

Lonergan stated that "the exchange economy is confronted with the dilemma either of eliminating itself by suppressing the freedom of exchange or of certain classes of exchange or else of effectively augmenting the enlightenment of the enlightened self-interest that guides exchanges." (1944, p. 1) He has always insisted that the solution to this dilemma is enlightenment through *education*. When I finally got up the nerve to ask him what he meant (Educate whom and to what?) he replied, "Educate people to be attentive, intelligent, reasonable, responsible and loving."[26] In other words, Lonergan's analysis of economic functioning led him to conclude that no solution would be adequate unless it included an educational promotion of the four "conversions": intellectual, religious, moral, and psychic. These conversions reorient the aberrations at the roots of human disorientation.

In his *Philosophy of Education* lectures at Xavier University, Cincinnati, 1959, Lonergan gave prominence to "The New Learning" and the problems as well as the promises it poses for the human good. The new human science of circulation analysis poses just such a challenge. As John Quinn wrote in the Foreword to the as yet unpublished edition of those lectures, "the dominant modernist philosophies of education, whether Liberal or Marxist, take their stand on the lowest common denominator in human living."[27] The challenge posed by Circulation Analysis is to educate *all* the levels of human consciousness, not just the lowest common denominator. In this section, I would like to briefly sketch what this might mean.

Let us consider how an economy is concretely constituted. First of all, the mechanisms of an exchange economy coordinate "a vast and ever shifting manifold of otherwise independent choices from demand and of decisions from supply." (1982, p. 3) The economy is constituted by human decisions. Now we are used to thinking of the coordinating mechanisms merely as "THE MARKET" and its control of pricing. This is far too crude. Lonergan's analysis reveals a far more differentiated set of issues. *Each* of the flows of payments is constituted by an *aggregate* of human decisions. Lonergan wrote, for example, "the distinction between O' and O'' [basic and surplus outlays] is extrinsic; it is made not by the authors of outlay but by its recipients for whom it is income." (1982, p. 55) This determination of aggregates of payments by individual decisions is all the more true of how outlays are divided into fractions c', i', s' and c'', i'', and s'', and for the constitution of the aggregates of redistributive payments, S', S'', D' and D''. It is likewise true of decisions to inaugurate or curtail production rates, seek new places of employment, and so on.

Moreover, the way in which individual decisions constitute these various aggregates is complicated by the complexity of the organization of modern economies. By way of illustration Lonergan wrote:

> In the old days when the entrepreneur was also owner and manager, pure surplus income roughly coincided with what was termed profit. Today, with increasing specialization of function, pure surplus income is distributed in a variety of ways: it enters into very high salaries of general managers and top-flight executives, into the combined fees of directors when together these reach a high figure, into the undistributed profits of industry, into the secret reserves of banks, into the accumulated royalties, rents, interest receipts, fees or dividends of anyone who receives a higher income than he intends to spend at the basic final market. (1944, p. 98)

The coordination of this intricate set of decisions into a well-functioning economy is the real goal of Lonergan's analysis.

In the preceding discussion of dysfunctions, what I tried to show was that almost everyone can have (and has had) a share in bringing about a dysfunctioning economy which wreaks so much human suffering and unintelligible evil. When I first asked Lonergan what he meant by education, I expected him to reply that it was academically trained economic advisors, governmental officials and influential business executives who needed to be taught his theory. Clearly, I had missed the whole point. Such a strategy fails to go to the root of the problem, since only a massive conversion of people can allow human freedom to constitute a "good of order" by means of a highly flexible, diverse and complementary common sense. Any real good of order, because of the non-systematic aggregate of conditions inviting response, is the possession of all, not of just one dictator or oligopoly.[28] Let me, therefore, turn to a brief outline of the relevance of the conversions to the transformation of the economy.

Intellectual Conversion. By "intellectual conversion" Lonergan means the achievement of clarity and acceptance of the implications of what he calls the "positions" on knowing, objectivity and being.[29] I begin with intellectual conversion because its lack is the most persistent source of economic dysfunction, and because for most it will seem to be the least important. Lonergan has complained about this oversight in the following terms:

> Now it is true that our culture cannot be accused of mistaken ideas on pure surplus income as it has been defined in this essay; for on that precise topic it has no ideas whatsoever. . . . there exists, in the mentality of our culture, no ideas, and in the procedures of our economies, no mechanisms whatever directed to smoothly and equitably bringing about the reversal of net aggregate savings to zero as the basic expansion proceeds. (1944, p. 98–99)

Now one is likely to regard economic dysfunctions as rooted more profoundly in a lack of *moral* conversion rather than a lack of intellectual conversion. On that topic, Lonergan more recently wrote:

> The difficulty emerges in the second step, the basic expansion. In equity it should be directed to raising the standard of living of the whole society. It does not. And the reason why it does not is not the reason on which simple-minded moralists insist. They blame greed. But the prime cause is ignorance. The dynamics of surplus and basic production, surplus and basic expansions, surplus and basic incomes are not understood, not formulated, not taught. When people do not understand what is happening and why, they cannot be expected to act intelligently. When intelligence is a blank, the first law of nature takes over: self-preservation. It is not primarily greed but frantic efforts at self-preservation that turn the recession into a depression, and the depression into a crash. (1982, p. 69)

Why haven't the dynamics of basic and surplus production been heretofore understood? The answer is not simply that Lonergan had not yet arrived on the scene, but rather with the intellectual climate of our culture. Chief among the implications of the "positions" of intellectual conversion is the contention that the chief feature of the universe is its dynamism: emergent probability. For Lonergan, an economy is an "ecology" constituted by human conscious acts, and is emergent upon the recurrent schemes of nature. (1980, p. 1) Thus an economy is within the field of what Lonergan called "emergent probability." In Lonergan's characterization of the "emergent probability" of reality, the salient feature is its "upward but indeterminately directed dynamism."[30] "Upward" means that current innovations, whether natural or human, build upon earlier innovations; "indeterminately" means that the part taken by this building process is unpredictable. This means that human intelligence and decisiveness is continually challenged by this dynamism to come up with creative solutions to ever newly emerging problems.

One can attend to the data on the rhythms of the functioning of an "ecology" within such a universe, discover, verify, and embrace criteria immanent in those rhythms; but if one is inclined to regard reality as determined by iron laws of necessity, to regard the trade-off between inflation and unemployment, or the insurmountable exploitation of the working class by the capitalist class as instances of that necessity, no quest for discovery will occur. The fact is that the emergence of ideas—emergence of better methods of production—is precisely the source of the basic problem for economic adaptation. It is the failure to search for further relevant ideas which is responsible for the crisis which occurs when it becomes time for the shift to the basic expansion, the "natural goal" of the surplus expansion (1982, p. 62). If one's intellectual climate inclines one, as the modern intellectual climate does, to assume that it is unscientific to speak of a "natural goal," and to hold that contingent fact can yield no knowledge of ethical criteria, one will not seek either the general theoretical ideas Lonergan has set forth in his essay, nor the great many further practical ideas which will help the willing subject know how to responsibly dispose of his or her income. The success of Lonergan's analysis will depend in great measure upon intellectual openness to his worldview.

Hence, Lonergan's specification of the norms of an emergent scheme will be intelligible and normative only for someone whose worldview is one of emergent probability: for whom reality is intrinsically intelligible and for whom human reality is constituted by understanding. Lonergan's proposal for solution of economic problems won't be accepted by someone for whom power rather than understanding is normative; for whom an economy is governed by "iron laws of necessity"; or for whom there are no immanent norms so that conviction and social construction are all that is required.

RELIGIOUS CONVERSION. What do economics and religious conversion have to do with one another? Lonergan was frequently asked this question in the form of what economic theory had to do with theology. His answer was, "Well, the dialectic!" I think what he meant by this cryptic statement is suggested by the Parable of the Sower (Luke 8:4–15). The dysfunctions of contemporary economic structures have so trodden the spirits of human beings that the Word of God has great difficulty finding root in our hearts, let alone bearing fruit a hundredfold. Inversely, it is only those in whom the Word of God has taken substantial root who recognize the urgency for removing this impediment, not solely for the sake of justice, but for the sake of the Kingdom of God as well.

Religious conversion is unrestricted falling in love, not as an accomplished fact, but as an orientation, a new beginning. To the extent that this orientation is truly unrestricted, it will extend loving beyond the natural limitations of family, neighborhood, clan, class, and nation to the totality of participants, past, present and future, with whom one shares what Lonergan calls "the good life"[32] and beyond even this to these people as participants in the Mystical Body of Christ. This type of conversion is essential for economic transformation, for such transformation requires a habitual orientation to living and thinking which acts lovingly with regard to the generations to come. As Lonergan's analysis reveals, a failure to grasp the *future* implications in accelerations, changes in employment and price patterns, underlines most economic dysfunction.

In addition, there is the fact of sin, and the deepest sin is the sin against the Light manifested in common sense's general bias as indifference to ideas whose practicality is not immediate but long-term. The transformation of economies can occur concretely only insofar as injustice is not repaid with hatred and violence. Sacrifices and suffering accepted now for the good of those members of the human-divine community to come is the most concrete condition for the emergence of the well-adapted economy.

MORAL CONVERSION. While I have attempted to indicate that the greatest urgency is for intellectual and religious conversion, it remains that moral conversion is also essential. People *understand* how cigarette smoking destroys the functioning of the human body and still continue to smoke. Thus, intellectual openness to the dynamism of economic functioning is a necessary, but not a sufficient condition for the transformation of our economies. Moreover, insofar as modern economies operate within the paradigm of modern political thought, namely, that one needs to develop economic and legal institutions that will insure prosperity and peace among a "race of devils,"[33] the problems associated with providing values to motivate decisions which constitute flows of payments will be considered irrelevant. Hence, morally converted persons are essential to normative economic functioning.

PSYCHIC CONVERSION. Only a psychically converted subject will successfully resist the seductive rhythms of the advertising industry, the interpersonal tensions of the board room, the corrupting rhetoric of the union organizer. The psychically converted subject is the normative author of his or her own psychic rhythms. Equipped with respect for the delicacies of human psychic rhythms and understanding of economic rhythms, psychically converted subjects will be uniquely capable of creating and evaluating modes in which these two rhythms intersect in a normative fashion. They will be needed as sources and judges of the responsible and aesthetic coordination of the "vast and ever shifting manifold of otherwise independent choices" (1982, p. 3) which constitute any concrete economy. This would indeed be a radical transformation.

IV. CONCLUSION: CRITICALLY MEDIATED CULTURE

When Lonergan complained that our culture has "no ideas" concerning pure surplus profit, his emphasis was on the plural. Lonergan's own work is a beginning, but further ideas are needed. Still needed are ideas which will help the converted members of our highly specialized culture know how to gain access to the data on the current state of their economies, employ the theoretical analysis to help interpret and understand the actual data and understand how they may respond within their roles in ways which are attentive, intelligent, reasonable, responsible and loving. Such ideas can originate most flexibly and profitably with ordinary people in their economic roles, from assemblyline worker to corporate or financial executive. These ideas must subsequently be subjected to the critical control of cultural norms, values and institutions.

But are our current sets of cultural norms, values and institutions up to the task? Are the ideals of Liberalism, Marxism or classicist Christianity sufficiently liberated from biases, sufficiently nuanced, sufficiently methodical and integrative to take into account the vast array of oftentimes conflicting practical opinions, or scientific and scholarly researches about the economy? The test of time has thus far found the major contenders for cultural normativity to be wanting.

It is for this reason that Lonergan, as a theologian, found it appropriate to take up the analysis of economic functioning. In *Method in Theology,* he defined theology as follows: "A theology mediates between a cultural matrix and the significance and role of religion in that matrix."[34] He realized the enormous need for a transformation in the way theology was done, in light of developments in the modern sciences and historical methods. He realized such a transformation would have to be open to what was good and true in modern thought, but could not sacrifice the normativity of religious tradition to those aspects of modern thought which are neither good nor true. The "eight functional specialties"[35] form the heart of his solution to the problem of mediating between religion and a culture whose norms, values and institutions are saturated with modern scientific and historical thinking.

Since economic functioning determines in a most profound way the kind of life people in a given society will live, it follows that there is surprising relevance of theology to economic questions. The new ideas required to transform current patterns of economic behavior into patterns which respect and cooperate with the normativities revealed by *Circulation Analysis* must be scrutinized by sets of cultural norms, values and institutions which are not yet completely formed. There is needed a theological transformation of culture in which the four conversions are mediated by means of the eight functional specialties. In particular, new proverbs, which communicate the spirit of norms derived in a Systematics of a dynamically functioning economy will be needed to supplement those which worked well for "equilibrium" ideals (e.g., "A penny saved is a penny earned"). And as Fr. Frederick Crowe, S. J. has indicated in his book on education, *Old Things and New: A Strategy for Education,* the concrete teaching of such values begins in children's picture books and extends to the most sophisticated of journals. The task of transforming an economy becomes co-extensive with that of transforming a culture.

APPENDIX

According to Lonergan, all human creatures are beset with perennial disputes about "The Great Questions," and these disputes are a source of disorienting influences within the culture. Lonergan claims that if these persistent disorientations are to be overcome, the questions and answers must be "reoriented." He goes on to say that transforming descriptive ideas into explanatory ones plays a crucial role in this reorientation.[36] One of the most central and difficult distinctions in Lonergan's philosophical writings is that between what he calls "description" and "explanation."

> Description deals with things as related to us. Explanation deals with the same things as related among themselves. The two are not totally independent, for they deal with the same things and, as we have seen, description supplies. . . the tweezers by which we hold things while explanations are being discovered or verified, applied or revised.[37]

Lonergan clearly intended that his *Circulation Analysis* should be a work of explanation, and thereby contribute to the transformation of persistent disorientations in human living. He wrote, for example:

The procedure of circulation analysis involves a minimum of description and classification, a maximum of inter-connections and functional relations. For analytic thinking uses classes based on described similarities only as a spring-board to reach terms defined by the correlations in which they stand. . . . There results a closely knit frame of reference that can envisage any total movement of an economy as a function of a sequence of changes in rates of payment, and that define the conditions of desirable movements as well as exhibit the causes of breakdowns. . . . It follows that this analytic procedure differs notably from the procedures of the descriptive . . . economist. By the nature of his task the descriptive economist is led to use, as far as possible, the language of ordinary speech in buying and selling. He is content with resemblances that strike the eye. . . . He will take advantage of specialized terminology but, as far as he is concerned, the only justification for a terminology is a proximate possibility of measurements. (1980, pp. 4–5)

As a result, certain common and descriptive ideas—such as "consumer goods," "savings," "wages," etc., need to be oriented. Consumer goods, for example, ordinarily relate a product to the person who purchases it, rather than to the complex of operations in the productive process. Similarly, "savings" is commonly understood in relation to what a person does with his or her wages, rather than in terms of the function which that payment performs in the economy. In his *Circulation Analysis,* therefore, Lonergan uses "*basic* goods" rather than "*consumer* goods" in order to preserve explanatory meanings. Similarly, he distinguishes several meanings of "savings."

Nor does this need for reorientation pertain primarily to daily use of economic terms. As with any other science, the science of economics must begin with descriptive terms only to discover the need for explanatory ideas, explanatory relations and explanatory terms. Lonergan did not think that the terms in contemporary macroeconomic theory as yet fully embody the kind of explanatory reorientation he thought necessary. For example, the simplest diagram for the flow of payments in a standard macroeconomics textbook looks something like this:

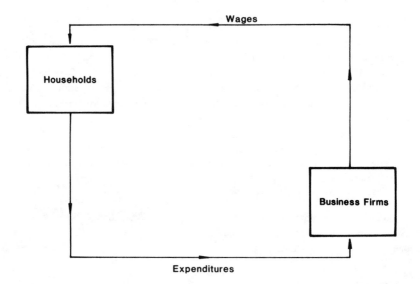

I once proposed to Fr. Lonergan a diagram resembling the above, in place of his diagram, as a means of facilitating the communication of his ideas to those of main-stream economic thought. The proposed alternative looked like this:

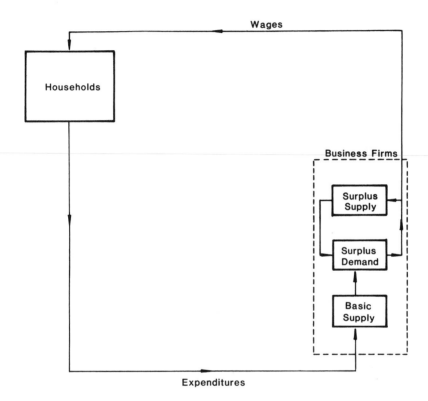

Fr. Lonergan politely looked at the diagram and returned it to me without comment. The problem was that I had missed the point. Both of the above diagrams are partly explanatory, but also partly descriptive. They distinguish and relate rates of payments, but they do so on the basis of to *whom* the payments are related, and *where* in space and time the payments are received—i.e., households and business firms. Any one with enough common sense to hold down a job or to manage a home knows the difference between where homes and firms are, and between the sums of money they receive, pay out, and have left over to put into the bank, insurance or stocks. But Lonergan's aggregates of rates of payments are distinguished by means of purely explanatory relations among stages and levels of the productive process. Measurements based upon how payments relate to our descriptive ways of thinking fail to reveal the roots of our economic problems.

NOTES

1   In using the word "paradigm," Lonergan was deliberately referring to the work of Thomas Kuhn, *The Structure of Scientific Revolutions*, (Second ed.), (Chicago: University of Chicago Press, 1970), albeit with Lonergan's typically re-oriented interpretation of the term. He has cited Brian Loasby. "Hypothesis and Paradigm in the Theory of the Firm," *Economic Journal*, 81 (1971), pp. 863–885 as having helped him understand what Kuhn was getting at.

2   On "the third stage of meaning," see Bernard Lonergan, *Method in Theology*, (N.Y.: Herder & Herder, 1972), pp. 93–96.

3   On this paradigm which Leo Strauss has called "the first wave of modernity," see his *Natural Right and History* (Chicago: University of Chicago Press, 1953), pp. 165–251 and his "The Three Waves of Modernity," *Political Philosophy: Six Essays by Leo Strauss*, H. Gilden (ed.), (Indianapolis: Pegasus, 1975).

4   The phrase, "iron laws of nature" has been attributed to James Mill, although I have been unable to locate the reference. In several lectures Lonergan suggested that this view is a development of the Cartesian method of analysing nature through solution of simultaneous equations and in the assumption that *all* scientific understanding of physical or human nature would be done within these limits. See Rene Descartes, *Geometry*, trans. D. E. Smith and M. L. Latham (New York: Dover, 1925) pp. 40–48. The notion that human nature is irredeemably corrupt is reflected in the assumptions about what is "natural" in human affairs in Machiavelli's *The Prince*, especially Chapter XVII, and in Hobbes' characterization of the "state of nature as the war of all against all."

5   "The problem of organizing a state, however hard it may seem, can be solved even for a race of devils if only they are intelligent." Immanuel Kant, "Perpetual Peace," in Lewis White Beck, ed. and trans., *On History*, (Indianapolis: Bobbs-Merrill, 1963), p. 112.

6   Lonergan's essay has undergone several revisions. I will be drawing on passages from three typescript versions, which are dated 1944, 1980 and 1982. In order to minimize footnotes, I will simply reference these passages with parentheses enclosing the date and page number.

Other essays on Lonergan's *Circulation Analysis* which were consulted in preparing this essay are Michael Gibbons, "Insight and Emergence: An Introduction to Lonergan's Circulation Analysis," in Matthew L. Lamb (ed.), *Creativity and Method*, (Milwaukee: Marquette University Press, 1981), pp. 529–541; Philip McShane, "The Actual Context of Economics," *Ibid.*, pp. 556–570; and Philip McShane, *Lonergan's Challenge to the University and the Economy*, (Washington, D.C.: University Press of America, 1980), especially pp. 92–128.

7   While the term, "consumer goods," has a perfectly legitimate usage, Lonergan refers to its mode of usage as "descriptive." As such, it is not adequate for the needs of an "explanatory" analysis, which he intends his *Circulation Analysis* to be. For a fuller discussion, see the "Appendix" to this paper.

8   The phrase, "aggregate of rates of payments" is rather cumbersome. A clarification of this awkward phrase is provided on p. 311 and requires some comment. Lonergan speaks of "aggregates," i.e., collections of groups of payments because even in a small economy, a comprehensive listing of each and every particular payment each and every day is both theoretically irrelevant and practically impossible.

9   The problem of the double coincidence is this: one has a single coincidence if I have a lecture on philosophy and bump into you who want to hear it. It is a double coincidence if you also happen to be a car mechanic, willing to receive my lecture in exchange for ministering to my ailing vehicle.

10 On the meaning of "explanatory understanding" see "Appendix" to this essay.

11 Bernard Lonergan, *Insight: A Study of Human Understanding,* (N.Y.: Philosophical Library, 1958), pp. 115–139.

Because the phrase, "aggregates of rates of payments" is awkward, I will use the simpler phrase "rates of payments" from this point onward. It should be noted, however, that Lonergan's term, though awkward, is precise.

13 The diagram has undergone many revisions. The one presented here is an adaptation of Lonergan's own in the 1982 edition of *Circulation Analysis.* Lonergan's diagram is quite different from the diagrams found in standard macroeconomics textbooks. For a discussion of the difference, see "Appendix."

14 It should be recalled that E' and E" are *aggregates* of rates of payments and hence, as with all other such aggregates, have the sense of "so and so much money per unit of time." Furthermore these aggregated rates are comprised of a multitude of distinct rates of payments.

15 The reader may wonder why these are the only two divisions of outlays. Clearly, producers do not spend all of their receipts; they save some. This fact will be taken up in the next section, "I. C., Redistributive Operations." It might be further wondered why producers' outlays for materials and components are not considered here. Lonergan does take up this issue (1982, pp. 16–20, 28–33, 42) which, for the sake of brevity, I have omitted here.

16 For Lonergan, "macroeconomic equilibrium" means that levels of aggregate rates of production and consumption remain constant, admitting only minimal, random and offsetting variations.

17 These results will be treated in Section II of this article.

18 Lonergan notes that there is another variety of redistributive payments associated with the re-sale of second-hand goods. (1944, pp. 26–27)

19 There are of course two possibilities: either these six aggregates of rates of payments contribute to macroeconomic equilibrium or they do not. Insofar as they do not, the operations of the redistributive monetary function have the same effect as unequal unbalanced cross-overs. While the net effect is the same, the complexity of the means by which such dire consequences can be effected, and the ways in which the fact that such is happening can be obscured, increase dramatically with the addition of redistributive operations. These will also be treated under the heading of "Economic Dysfunctions." Hence, let us for the moment assume the former possibility.

20 Commonly we speak of *"reasonable* expectations." However, Lonergan's exacting analyses of human consciousness incline me to prefer the more nuanced expression, *"attentive, intelligent, reasonable and responsible* expectations," in this context. However, since Lonergan's analyses are not generally familiar, I will stay with the more common but less precise phrase, "reasonable expectations." See *Method in Theology,* p. 53.

21 Aristotle, *Nichomachean Ethics,* I. 7, 1097b, 24–30.

22 It is not necessary that the *magnitudes* of c"O" and basic receipts must decrease, but rather it is their respective *ratios* to *basic* expenditures and basic costs which will. The reason for this is that as basic production begins to accelerate, the demand for workers in the basic level of production and hence c'O' accelerates.

23 *Insight.,* pp. 394, 398–399, 504–509.

24 See "Appendix" to this essay.

25 Further dysfunctions follow from investment of those making decisions concerning redistributive payments. See Bernard Lonergan, "An Essay in Circulation Analysis," Manuscript of 1944, pp. 109–112; Manuscript of 1982, pp. 67–68.

26   Also see *Method in Theology.*, p. 53.

27   P. xiv, typescript of 1979.

28   *Insight*, pp. 213–215, 223.

29   *Ibid.*, pp. 387–388.

30   *Ibid.*, pp. 444–451, 665.

31   See for example, Patrick H. Byrne, "On Taking Responsibility for the Indeterminate Future," pp. 229–238, in Stephen Skousgard (ed.), *Phenomenology and the Understanding of Human Destiny*, (Washington, D.C.: Center for Advanced Research in Phenomenology, & University Press of America, 1981).

32   "Finality, Love, Marriage," in *Collection: Papers by Bernard Lonergan, S.J.*, ed. F. E. Crowe, S. J. (New York: Herder & Herder, 1967), p. 38ff.

33   Immanuel Kant, "Perpetual Peace," in *On History*, p. 112.

34   *Method*, p. xi.

35   *Ibid.*, pp. 125–368.

36   *Insight*, pp. 394, 398–399, 504–509.

37   *Ibid.*, p. 291.

XXIV

The Possibility of a Pure Cycle of the Productive Process: The Potential for Decline in Economic Growth[1]

Eileen de Neeve

Introduction

Is there an inevitable relationship between economic fluctuations and growth? Can the dynamics of the process be captured and the "right" measurements on the dials maintained to avoid a breakdown? Does a normative view of how an economy should work imply the control of economic behavior? Would the only alternative to control be a pious hope for a millenary society expressed in different ways by Marxists and liberals? The first question will be the major concern of this paper, although the further questions lurk in the immediate background and will be briefly discussed in the conclusion.

Bernard Lonergan's elaboration of the pure cycle of the productive process addresses the first question. He sees the pure cycle of production as the process of creating a higher standard of living, which implies some quantitative or qualitative measure of increased output per man. Output per man is a commonly used definition of productivity, which is of much concern at present in the industrialized world. A frequent question is, How are we to return our economies to a path of productivity growth? To answer it we must ask, What is the process by which productivity is increased? The paradigm of the pure cycle hypothesizes the following underlying dynamic. Over a longer or shorter time period new infrastructure, equipment, or procedures are developed, or skilled workers are trained. The process is functionally the same whether one considers increasing the equipment per person or improving it. Subsequently, these new resources are put to work to produce more or better goods and services for consumers. This development delay must be financed by an increased flow of funds which goes first to investment and later to the consumption of new output. Lonergan explicitly points out that the first flow is anti-egalitarian and the second, egalitarian.[2]

In this paper, the foregoing sketch of the pure cycle will be elaborated in terms of the real production lag required by the need to expand the means of production before society can enjoy a larger output of consumer goods and services.[3] It will also discuss the channels of monetary payments that shape and match events in the real economy. These two fundamental relationships will be discussed in terms of a simple framework of equilibrium growth theories of mainstream economics.[4] The comparison suggests the explanatory power of Lonergan's analysis in drawing attention to sources of instability in the growth process, that can and do lead to negative growth rates in the total output of an economy.

The pure cycle of economic growth is a theoretical construct and is set in logical time. Nevertheless, because the construct is dynamic the analysis allows all economic variables to change, though it cannot account for random events. Output, money supply and credit, prices, investment and consumption can vary. Population, and technical changes that are available for innovation, are implicitly included because technical change enters the economy via innovating investment, and the use of output per man as a measure makes population a variable in the system. The approach is normative in that it sees the goal of the process to be the emerging standard of living and expects behavior of economic agents to conform to the requirements of achieving that goal. These requirements are defined by the technical constraint on the productive process.

I. THE ECONOMIC SYSTEM AND ITS DYNAMIC CONSTRAINTS

An economic system can grow, remain stationary or decline. In their economies people produce, distribute income, exchange and consume the goods and services which, with leisure, create their standard of living. The economic system is only one aspect of people's lives and is linked with other systems, especially the closely-related political system. The better we understand the economic system, the better we can discern the economic limits of possible political and social change. For example, Lonergan does not discuss income distribution, that is the relative levels of wages and salaries, interest and profits, except in its functional relation to the pure cycle, because it is a political or social question. He does, however, discuss the function of profits that are in excess of a normal return to risk taking and management as a social dividend, because it is an economic issue. Such profits are intended for reinvestment in the productive process either directly by businessmen or indirectly via financial intermediaries.[5]

Within a changing economic system, Lonergan defines two constraints. There is a technical constraint that relates the changes in resources available for production to changes in output which they permit. The second constraint is behavioral as it describes the distribution of income between consumption and saving needed to keep dynamic balance in the system, while using resources fully.[6] It can be called an equilibrium condition. These two limitations on the rate of production create the pure cycle of the productive process. Lonergan says of the pure cycle, "It is entirely a forward movement which, however, involves a cycle inasmuch as in successive periods of time the surplus stage of the process is accelerating more rapidly and, again later, less rapidly than the basic stage."[7]

II. A TECHNICAL CONSTRAINT ON PRODUCTION

If one considers a simplified two-sector economy, a lag in the growth of the flow of consumer goods (f_1) behind growth in the output of means of production (f_2) is given the following symbolic expression in section nine of the Essay, "A Technical Restatement":

$$K f'_2 (t-a) - B_2 = f''_1(t) - A_1$$

(a) is the time lag between the output of new producer goods and the related acceleration of output of consumer goods, so that the former takes place at time $(t-a)$.[8] B_2 is the flow of producer goods output which goes to replacement and maintenance, and A_1 is the growth of output of consumer goods that can be produced by using more fully already available production equipment. This relation, which describes a lagged technical accelerator/multiplier, or lagged marginal output-capital ratio (k), is not entirely new to economists, but Lonergan's emphasis is different.

The accelerator and the multiplier of mainstream economics are technically equivalent to each other because both are concerned with the relation between a change in output or income and the investment required to produce it. The analysis assumes that new investment is required because the system is working at capacity. New investment would also be required to produce new goods. If the economy is working below capacity and the capital equipment available could produce goods for which there is a demand, then investment would not be large and the lag between investment and output would not be significant.[9]

In the accelerator relationship of mainstream economics, because the causal relationship moves from the rise in demand for output to required investment that it induces, the lag usually considered is the one between the change in demand and the investment decision. On the other hand the multiplier discusses the change in output or income that results from a change in investment, and the lag is between investment and income in the future.[10] However, in much of the literature of economic growth, lags are ignored when stability properties are studied with the help of integral calculus. Lags would severely complicate the mathematics.[11]

Lonergan's technical accelerator/multiplier focuses on the lag between the net investment decision and the acceleration of output which raises the standard of living. By distinguishing the technical from the behavioral it has the advantage of drawing attention to the technical side of production which is largely overlooked by mainstream economists who are concerned with identifying and measuring behavioral aspects of the accelerator and multiplier in order to predict what will happen next.

From the viewpoint of behavior there is a difference between the traditional concepts of accelerator and multiplier. Each tries to capture a different aspect of the activities of economic agents. The accelerator tries to measure the behavior of entrepreneurs in their decisions to invest. It attempts to take into consideration their expectations about future demand conditions, about prices including costs and interest rates, and about the extent to which risks and uncertainty will affect their investment. The multiplier shows the effect on overall future output and income of the distribution of income between consumption and saving. In a dynamic analysis or an analysis of economic growth, the behavior effects of both accelerator and multiplier need to be taken into consideration from period to period.

Lonergan groups behavioral aspects of both accelerator and multiplier into his assertion that the crossover of payments to the sector of investment goods production (saving equal to capital investment) and the crossover of payments to the sector of consumer goods production (principally wages that are consumed) must balance. This constraint is expressed in monetary terms so that actual price changes and price expectations affect real activity and vice versa. Both investment and consumption activities and their interrelationship with output and income are considered as parts of an ongoing process. In order to maintain equilibrium not only must saving equal investment but income and expenditure flows must be synchronized with the technical lag in production and output. Then the important problem becomes how to ensure a functional distribution of income that will fully use resources as output expands. Lonergan deals with this question in his behavioral constraint or equilibrium condition.

III. Behavioral Constraint on Income and Expenditure

The customary behavioral constraint in economics is the rationality assumption, which implies behavior by consumers and producers that will maximize utility for the one and profits for the other. The rationality assumption is presently criticized by some economists, partly because it rests on the eighteenth-century philosophical view, with which they disagree, that the pursuit of personal gain would maximize the common good as well; and partly because other social sciences and psychology explain human behavior otherwise. [12] The rationality assumption of mainstream economics also requires redefinition when a static analysis is transferred to a dynamic framework; what maximization of utility or profit might mean over several time periods is not as clear as it is for a time period so short that most variables cannot be changed. [13] Lonergan's analysis is normative so that he does not assume that economic agents will behave in any particular way. Instead he explains the technical restrictions which limit the possibilities for rational action. Acting according to the limitations of the technical constraint would be rational economic behavior.

Again looking at the traditional approach, if economic agents are assumed to maximize profit and utility, one can empirically measure their behavior and obtain parameters which, barring major changes, are estimates on which to base predictions. For example, the historical proportion of an increase in income which is consumed by people once they have adjusted to the increase can be calculated for any economy. If we know this proportion, the marginal propensity to consume, we can estimate how investment will change income/output, which is the purpose of the multiplier relation. Of course this analysis omits consideration of other effects such as imports from other national economies or exports to them; and the reaction of other economic agents who might, for example, exchange work for leisure as income increased. This would mean that a larger proportion of income is consumed, if leisure is taken to be consumption.

Ignoring the government sector as well, once we know the proportion of income consumed, the balance can be said to be available for investment. The equilibrium condition is that saving must equal investment. This can happen through inflation in the prices of consumer goods, which transfers income to profits making funds available for investment; or via national and international financial intermediaries who furnish credit to entrepreneurs; or through consumer investment of savings or borrowings in residential construction. But the important step is the response of entrepreneurs to their expectations of price and other economic factors. Their reaction is described by the behavioral aspect of the accelerator, and which can lead to an acceleration of output and income. Michal Kalecki, for example, assumes that entrepreneurs' behavior is such that they re-invest less than a hundred percent of profits, and from that excess saving assumption he derives a mechanical business cycle.[14] Whether or not this assumption is correct can be explored by looking at historical data on profits and investment, which is a way of reaching some estimate of future behavior.

Lonergan's behavioral constraint on income and expenditure, however, is not empirical; that is, it does not try to measure the historical propensities to consume and invest out of change in income. Rather, it responds to the question, What behavior on the part of producers and consumers is required to maintain equilibrium; that is, what behavior is needed to adjust sectoral expenditure flows to match output flows in the two sectors of producer and consumer goods and services? In terms of Lonergan's paradigm, the behavioral constraint is expressed by the statement that crossovers of monetary payments between the surplus and basic circuits must balance.[15] What this means can be illustrated by the circulation diagram, Figure 1.

If the crossovers do not balance, the positive or zero acceleration of output that characterizes the pure cycle changes to negative acceleration and the economy declines. The balance between the growth of supply and demand in each circuit is upset and the economy slides into the familiar world of recession with consequent efforts to remedy income imbalances by transfer payments, tax policies and monetary policies. What the crossovers represent and why they may tend not to balance will be discussed below in the section on the saving function. Lonergan's diagram also illustrates the system's potential for self-adjustment through indirect flows from the redistributive function to the supply or outlay functions.[16] It would be interesting to explore whether the redistributive function could include government as an economic agent as well as financial markets, when a mixed economy is considered.

In both equilibrium growth theory and Lonergan's pure cycle, saving equals investment. This equality is extended by Lonergan to include an equality of flows between circuits. When these are in balance, saving is growing as a proportion of total output to

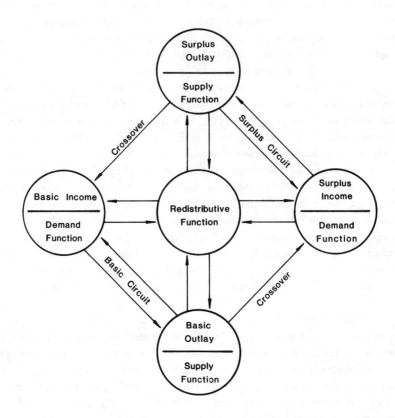

match the growth of employment and basic income in the surplus expansion. Similarly, as the surplus expansion comes to an end saving must fall, both to balance the levelling off of employment in the surplus circuit and so that consumption can rise to meet the growth in output of final goods and services. The acceleration of crossover flows in the surplus expansion, and the need for an eventual deceleration of these flows in the basic expansion, create situations with potential for explosive growth or decline of the economic system.

The problem can be illustrated by the fact that actual saving and investment behavior of economic agents will reflect profits and sales, and expectations about the future. Uncertainty about the future will tend to shorten the period over which business managers would like investment costs to be covered, and thus long-term investments are discouraged. Attitudes to risk and uncertainty or, as Lonergan suggests, concern for self-preservation, bias the system toward excess saving so that savings are greater than investment and the economy moves away from the rhythm of the pure cycle.[17] Lonergan notes another behavior which is not appropriate to a pure cycle, namely that some economic agents are sheltered and can protect the income levels proper to the surplus expansion when demand exceeds supply. Weaker economic units in the economy are unable to do so and the burden of the aggregate profit decline falls on them. The possibility of changing such behavior may depend on some institutional framework to compensate losses due to unforseeable events as suggested by Lester C. Thurow in his book *Dangerous Currents*. [18] In addition, policies can attempt to modify expectations in order to encourage behavior that will permit the pure cycle to occur. For example, government investment financed by bonds would take up investment slack in the surplus expansion, or production of public consumer goods and services, such as health care and some education, could encourage the basic expansion. Here coordination between the government and private sectors would be essential. [19]

IV. THE PURE CYCLE AS A MOVEMENT FROM ONE LONG-TERM EQUILIBRIUM GROWTH PATH TO ANOTHER

The pure cycle can be discussed using a simple framework of neoclassical growth theory. Following William H. Branson's analysis of economic growth in Part IV of his *Macroeconomic Theory and Policy*, we can distinguish four kinds of growth illustrated in his Figure 22–4. [20] (See Figure 2.) These four kinds of growth are a) from under-employment levels of output to full-employment equilibrium, b) growth toward a long-run equilibrium growth path, c) growth along an equilibrium growth path defined by the rate of population growth and technical change, and d) growth from one such path to another. Branson notes the similarity between b) and d) types of growth, and Lonergan's analysis is related to both of these. Type a) growth is usually considered to be short-term, related to business cycles, stabilization policy and, for Lonergan, to the revival that follows a collapse of the pure cycle. Types b) and d) growth take place in the medium term and concern the growth of output per man or growth in the standard of living, and are usually associated with a higher saving rate and higher investment, and larger stock of capital per worker.

While mainstream economic growth theory generally considers growth along an equilibrium trend path, Lonergan looks at how the economy moves from one equilibrium growth path to another either as a process of development in economies operating at low levels of output per man, or as a process of integrating technical change, in its broadest sense, into economies already technically advanced. For Lonergan the time curve of real output per man is not a rising straight line but an S-curve. The underlying reason for this is the functioning of innovative investment, which view Lonergan shares with Schumpeter. [21] New investment, for them, is bunched because different sectors are joint in production, or because the concrete conditions, and the expectations of economic actors, that encourage investment, tend not to be restricted to a few sectors once they occur. This grouping of investment decisions in a short time span means that the technical lags in production discussed above are significant and behavior must adjust accordingly.

FIGURE 2

Illustration of Possible Economic Growth Paths

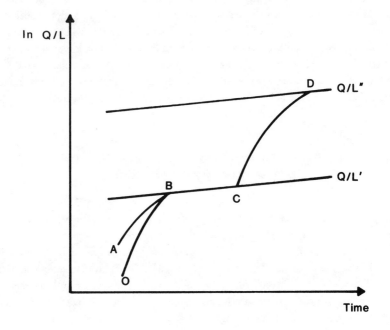

Q/L = output per man, which is measured on a log scale, and is shown as growing at a trend rate along an equilibrium growth path, as from B to C

OA = Type a) growth; AB = Type b) growth; BC = Type c) growth; CD = Type d) growth.

Source: Adapted from William H. Branson, *Macroeconomic Theory and Policy*, op. cit., p. 432.

In neoclassical growth theory the achievement of a new equilibrium is discussed in relation to the comparative statics of production and saving functions. The question considered is, If the system moves out of its equilibrium position, in which direction will it continue to move? If it moves toward equilibrium the system is stable. If it moves away from equilibrium, the system is unstable in that range.

Analogously, Lonergan is considering the movement of an economy from one stationary state to another, and he discusses how to maneuver the change successfully. In recent drafts of his essay, Lonergan distinguishes two phases of economic growth: the surplus and the basic expansions. An initial phase of proportional expansion mentioned in earlier drafts refers to type a) growth, when employment and capacity utilization of plants are increasing toward full employment of resources.[22] His production and saving functions will be discussed only with reference to the surplus and basic expansions.

Figure 3 shows different possible relationships between output per man and capital per man. For a given ratio of output per man to capital per man, the saving function shows the proportion of income that will be saved, and whether the saving rate rises or falls as capital per man increases.[23] The production function shows the relation between output per man and capital per man as the latter is increased.

FIGURE 3

*Production and Saving Functions Showing the Potential
for Decline in the Pure Cycle of Economic Growth*

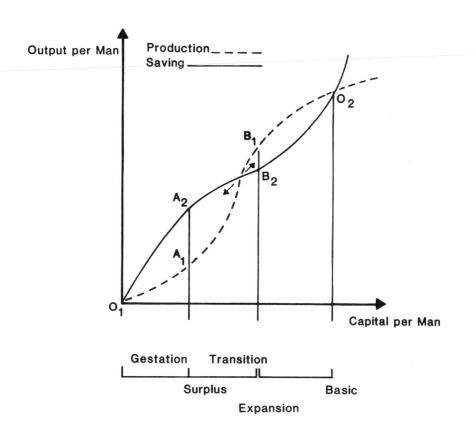

Source: Adapted from Branson, *Macroeconomic Theory,* op. cit., pp. 395–6, 412.

V. LONERGAN'S PRODUCTION FUNCTION

Constrained by the technical accelerator/multiplier discussed above, in the surplus expansion the production function shows output per man rising little as investment increases capital per man. Following Figure 3, 0_1 is the level of output per man and capital per man at the beginning of the surplus expansion. The economy is in equilibrium with resources fully employed. How economic growth increases productivity, that is output per man, through new investment per man over a pure cycle is shown by the dashed line $0_1 0_2$. The $0_1 A_1$ section of the curve shows the relationship in the gestation period of the surplus expansion. Productive capacity in capital goods industries is increasing and new skills are being acquired, but output per man is rising little. This could be so for the supply-side reasons described and also because of the slowness of new market demand to develop. In the transition period, output per man begins to increase more rapidly until the output rise is more than proportional to investment of resources, as shown in Figure 3 on the production curve between A_1 and B_1. This period of increasing returns continues into the early part of the basic expansion. As the basic expansion progresses, decreasing returns is more typical because markets are eventually limited by population growth and innovations become fully implemented in the productive processes of an economy. Growth then continues at the rate of population growth without changing output per man or standard of living. Output per man as a function of capital per man in the basic expansion is reflected in the shape of the production curve between B_1 and 0_2. At 0_2 the economy enters a stationary phase. Output per man levels off until new innovations are implemented through a new cycle of investment.

This view of growth is not entirely new, but Lonergan synthesizes into a general explanation of economic dynamics various views that are not rejected by economists, but which do not fit into the generally accepted paradigm of growth theory. For example, Branson also notes the possibility of increasing returns occurring during growth prior to decreasing returns.[24] Such is the case when investment in infrastructure creates, for example, a new highway system, with the result that output per man accelerates because much other investment is thereby made more productive. Furthermore, Lonergan's production function is shaped like the S-curve of growth, which has been viewed as a production curve as well as a product cycle curve in a marketing context.[25]

VI. LONERGAN'S SAVING FUNCTION

Just as Lonergan's production function in a pure cycle would reflect his lagged technical accelerator/multiplier, his saving function reflects the need to balance crossovers of monetary flows between the surplus and basic circuits. The proportion of saving in income will depend on the behavioral constraint discussed above and will vary over the pure cycle. This saving ratio can be seen as a function of profits, following Nicholas Kaldor, Ricardo, Marx and other classical economists, and Kalecki.[26]

Simpler neoclassical growth models usually assume that saving is a fixed proportion of income, which would result in a straight line saving function. A presentation of Lonergan's pure cycle can be made with a fixed saving ratio because the saving function would still cut the S-shaped production function from above creating an unstable equilibrium. In cases where a constant saving ratio is not assumed the saving rate declines in a well-behaved neoclassical saving function as the stock of capital per man increases. Such a view does not consider the period of gestation of capital stock during which saving rises as investment decisions are being made and capital goods produced. The need to reverse the situation so that the saving function in fact becomes well-behaved creates the potential for cyclic decline. Lonergan's surplus expansion, and the rising saving rate it requires, draws attention to the gestation lag.

At the beginning of the surplus phase of the pure cycle, increasing turnover magnitudes in the system require a growing monetary circulation in the surplus circuit.[27] In other words growth requires credit expansion to increase outlays of producers of capital goods. A part of these surplus outlays will hire labor and augment the crossover to the basic circuit in Figure 1 of their income that is to be consumed. The first effect of such increased demand in the basic circuit is on prices, because the circuit is assumed to have reached capacity output already in the proportional expansion mentioned above. Profits increase in the basic sector as demand for consumer goods rises proportionately with expanding employment and activity in the surplus sector, while output of consumables in the basic sector, having reached a maximum in the proportional expansion cannot be increased further before capacity is expanded. So that crossovers will balance, the profits of the basic sector ought to flow into orders for investment goods that are required to expand the productive capacity for consumer goods to meet the expanding demand for the latter. It is through this flow of income to the surplus circuit, and any indirect flows through the redistributive function, that saving keeps pace with investment.[28]

The saving function in Figure 3 shows the relation between increases in capital or investment, and the proportion of income saved. The curve $O_1 A_2$ rises more sharply than a $45°$ line would because the rise in saving is more than proportional to the rise in income. In other words saving will rise with profits at a faster rate of growth than output in the surplus phase. The variation in saving required by the pure cycle of economic growth is hard to achieve because economic agents tend to behave defensively when the profit rate declines and risk and uncertainty increase in the transition as the surplus expansion ends. Such tendencies to excess saving or under-consumption will lead to a cutting back in investment orders, that is to negative growth in investment per man or disinvestment, indicated by the arrow to the left of X, the unstable equilibrium point. Disinvestment occurs because excess saving prevents the consumption of output, leading to a build-up of unsold inventories and a consequent reduction of future output and of the investment required to produce it. If instead the system lowers its saving growth along with the decline in profits, the transition to the basic expansion can continue. When income begins to rise sharply as output increases in the transition to the basic expansion, the proportion of saving in income must decline along with the profit share. The productive capacity of the capital goods industries has been enlarged and output flows to increase productive capacity of the consumer goods industries.

Consequently the final output of those industries accelerates and becomes available for consumption. A new functional distribution of income is needed. As the basic expansion progresses, output per man can continue to accelerate though at a declining rate, showing diminishing returns to increased capital investment per man. Demand for and output of capital equipment will be prevented from falling as replacement investment increases to a higher equilibrium level. In terms of Figure 3, this occurs when the system moves beyond X toward a stable equilibrium at O_2. The ratio of saving to income is less than the ratio of capital investment in income as investment increases the capital stock per man, so that capital investment moves to the equilibrium replacement level and the economy moves toward an equilibrium stationary state where saving equals replacement investment.

In terms of Lonergan's circulation diagram, Figure 1, as the surplus expansion comes to an end, both crossovers stop growing because production in the surplus sector stabilizes at higher levels of output. The crossover from surplus to basic circuit stabilizes and profits level off as the basic sector's excess demand, which comes from the surplus sector, subsides. On the production side the rate of growth of capital per man slows and there is an acceleration of growth in productivity or output per man as the economy makes the transition to the basic expansion by putting to work the new tools of production.

Lonergan's saving function, as seen in Figure 3, shows how rising output/income creates more than proportional growth in saving and profits reinforcing the incentive to increase investment per man. Such investment will increase capital per man, which will produce more output. In the surplus expansion the demand is rising in both surplus and basic sectors. But as the surplus expansion ends the acceleration of demand subsides in both sectors, just as output potential reaches a maximum. How the boom ends and a recession begins has been variously described in cycle theory. For example, Kalecki explains the decline by assuming entrepreneurs do not fully re-invest profits.[29] Lonergan looks to the balancing of crossover flows to prevent decline and maintain the pure cycle. This requires a deceleration of saving (the crossover from basic to surplus circuit) to match the deceleration of demand (the crossover from surplus to basic circuit) so that the system can move into the basic expansion.

Given the present climate of business, it is unlikely that saving by entrepreneurs and consumers will decelerate just as output climbs sharply in the changeover from the surplus to the basic expansion. This is so for several reasons:

- Surplus circuit producers will tend to reduce credit demands as their expectations stabilize. This may squeeze the volume of monetary circulation just as volume of output is accelerating thus leading to monetary constraints on output and employment in the surplus circuit, which will affect demand in the basic circuit. In this case there will be an absolute fall in both crossovers, rather than a deceleration as would occur in the pure cycle and the system contracts.

- There is a tendency to protect profit rates by keeping prices high and reducing output where competition between firms is weak.[30] In such cases the deceleration in the crossover flow of payments to the surplus circuit, that is surplus income, is less than that to the basic circuit where deceleration reflects the falling rate of job creation in capital goods-related industries. The basic circuit will be drained and the surplus circuit will remain too large.

- The increase in real income of consumers as the basic expansion gets underway may also be saved rather than consumed or taken in leisure. This behavior implies excess income available for investment and inadequate growth of demand for the output of the basic sector.

- Cost reductions owing to more efficient machines may not be passed on to consumers so that profit rates and saving will remain high. Such behavior would have the same effects on crossovers as those discussed under the second point above.

- The likelihood of structural unemployment increases as production growth in the surplus sector levels off and output accelerates in the basic sector. The increased risk of job loss could lead to defensive saving, and consequently reduced consumption. Again the effects on crossovers would be as discussed under point two above.

When the adjustment of income needed for the basic expansion does not occur, the economy continues to move away from X, the unstable equilibrium in Figure 3, toward a low-level equilibrium such as O_1. Saving as a share of income continues to remain excessive with respect to a falling investment rate during this process.

CONCLUSION

Lonergan's pure cycle is a possible explanation of factors leading to a breakdown in the economic growth process. It shows explicitly the behavioral criteria for preventing such a breakdown. Not only must saving equal investment but the flows of expenditure between the investment goods and consumer goods circulation of payments must be matched, or adjusted through redistribution. Lonergan's approach is linked closely to Schumpeter's view of economic development in which periods of implementation of innovations are followed by periods when few changes occur. The approach appears to be applicable to various time frames in which investment can be considered; business cycles of inventory investment, cycles of machinery investment, longer building cycles and very long waves as described by Kondratieff.[31]

There are many points of comparison between the economic ideas of Bernard Lonergan and the history of economic thought. This paper has made a preliminary linking of the pure cycle to a simple equilibrium growth framework. Among other economists, Harry G. Johnson discussed the possibility of unstable equilibria.[32] In the present paper Lonergan's explanation of the possibility of breakdown of the pure cycle is discussed with respect to instability in economic growth.

Readers may have been bothered by the fact that Lonergan uses a two-sector model while a simple one-sector model of equilibrium growth is matched with it in this paper. This procedure simplified the discussion of an unstable equilibrium, but does require readers to keep in mind the difference between production equipment and consumer goods, and the production lag between them in economic growth.

Mainstream equilibrium growth theory is interested, as Lonergan is, in behavioral criteria for maintaining a rising standard of living. Explorations also led to considerations of how welfare was affected by national policies to encourage economic growth. For example, the Stalin period in the Soviet Union was felt to be too growth oriented by some, and in the 1970's groups found economic growth undesirable for environmental reasons which pointed to the existence of physical and social limits to growth.[33] Economic theory, including "Circulation Analysis," attempts to explain interrelationships within the economy such as lags in production, and links between consumption, saving and investment; that is, between supply and demand. Economic theory asks questions about how the economic process works, and such questions are prior to development of policies to improve the operation of the system. However, social problems usually cannot wait and action must be taken in the light of the best knowledge economic theory makes available.

Beyond understanding what the pure cycle means, there is the problem of finding out how history fits such a view. Economists do not agree, for example, about where we are in the present Kondratieff cycle, if they believe in it at all. Lonergan's work would provide a fruitful policy framework once better empirical criteria for identifying phases could be established. While the presentation points to the kind of data that might be studied to obtain support for Lonergan's view of economic growth, some difficulties remain. Historical data that are used in empirical work reflect aberrations from the pure cycle. Measures of potential output that might be used as proxies for what the economy could produce, and which might indicate the possibility of a pure cycle, are not regarded as satisfactory.

Finally, the questions raised in the introduction can be asked again. As this paper has attempted to show, Lonergan sees the pure cycle of the productive process as the way in which economic growth or dynamics occurs. Negative output growth rates imply that there has been a collapse of the pure cycle into the fluctuations of varying lengths and severity with which we are familiar.[34]

A response to question two—Can the dynamics of the process be captured and the "right" measurements on the dials maintained to avoid a breakdown?—was not attempted in this paper. The answer to this question will depend a great deal on the development of appropriate data sources to measure significant variables, and the development of appropriate institutions to deal with disruptions of economic change.

On question three—Does a normative view of how an economy should work imply the control of economic behavior? The fact that Lonergan's cycle is a normative view does not need to imply control of economic behavior because it is based on a technical constraint. Rather it is a matter of understanding the paradigm, developing hypotheses on the basis of it, presenting historical evidence for hypotheses, persuading colleagues of the greater explanatory power of the paradigm, and developing policies based on a such a view.

The last question—Would the only alternative to control be a pious hope for a millenary society expressed in different ways by Marxists and liberals?—raises the issue of whether an economic role for government can be fitted into Lonergan's explanation. Lonergan developed the circulation of payments analysis for a closed national economy without government. This is a frequent procedure in the presentation of economic analysis. Furthermore, the role of government in the economy grew mainly after "Circulation Analysis" was written in the early 1940's. Perhaps it can be suggested that while Keynesian government policies propose moving an economy out of the doldrums of an unemployment equilibrium or slump by supplementing income and demand, Lonerganian policies could attempt to balance the crossovers not only by increasing demand, but by monetary and tax policies, and legal and institutional changes aimed at easing the start of new production and trade. Such policies would need to take into consideration the constraints of the pure cycle. The "laissez-faire" approach to the economy implied by a liberal view of the state, and the centralized control of the economy used by communist states as they, presumably, guide their societies to the stateless millenium, are both inappropriate to the operation of the pure cycle. Rational behavior, that is behavior appropriate to the pure cycle of the productive process is both spontaneous, when the cycle is understood, and encouraged by the redistributive function. I suggest this function can be seen to include both credit institutions and government.

NOTES

1   This paper was prepared for the 1984 Santa Clara International Lonergan Symposium. It is based on an unpublished economics manuscript of Bernard Lonergan. I am very grateful to him for the opportunity of using it, and to Nicholas Graham and Therese Mason who drew my attention to it. In the course of writing, I have been helped by comments from Stanislas Machnik, the editorial expertise of Helene Loiselle; and the frank and lively discussions with other members of the panel on economics, and with participants at the symposium.

2   *An Essay on Circulation Analysis* (Unpublished). Copyright by Bernard Lonergan 1944, 1978, 1980, 1982. 1944 typescript, p. 98.

3   "Real" is a term used by economists to refer to quantity measures of goods and services. Real is distinguished from monetary. For example, the value of shoe production could rise twenty percent, with ten percent of the rise coming from price increases and the other ten percent from a quantity, or real, increase in the output of shoes.

4   Mainstream economics refers to the economics generally learned from undergraduate textbooks.

5   See Patrick H. Byrne, "Economic Transformations." (Paper prepared for the Santa Clara International Lonergan Symposium, March 1984), section on "Misinterpretation of profits".

6   Saving will equal investment when the system is in equilibrium.

7   Lonergan, *Circulation Analysis*, p. 19. The surplus stage of production is roughly equivalent to output of producer goods, but includes services such as transport and power. The basic stage production refers to the output of consumer goods and services and, again, it includes production of power and transport related to consumer goods' production. (Lonergan, *Circulation Analysis*, p. 32)

8   Lonergan, *op. cit.*, 1982 typescript, p. 34.

9   In such a case f_2 would be for working capital and thus not much larger than B_2. Furthermore, the acceleration in output of consumer goods (f_1) would be accounted for by A_1, the increase in output that could be achieved with existing production facilities.

10   Output equals income as in the national accounting identities. See for example Wynne Godley & Francis Cripps, *Macroeconomics*, (Oxford: The University Press, 1983) (Fontana Masterguides).

11   Giancarlo Gandolfo, *Mathematical Methods and Models in Economic Dynamics* (New York: American Elsevier Publishing Co., Inc., 1970).

12   Daniel Bell and Irving Kristol eds., *The Crisis in Economic Theory*, (New York: Basic Books, 1981).

13   A short period is one in which supply can be varied by employing more labor and materials, but not by renewing or increasing capital equipment. Capital is, therefore, a fixed value or given parameter for the analysis.

14   Michal Kalecki, *Selected Essays on the Dynamics of the Capitalist Economy*, (Cambridge, England: The University Press, 1971), p. 128.

15   The *surplus circuit* is the round of outlays of entrepreneurs to factors of production and to suppliers, and the expenditure of other producer goods firms and households, on the output of producer goods and services. The *basic circuit* is the flow of outlays to factors in consumer goods industries and the expenditures of all consumers for such goods. These circuits are linked by the flow of wage and other income to be consumed from the surplus circuit to buy consumer goods in the basic circuit, and the flow in the other direction of replacement investment and the social dividend, or abnormal profits, in consumer goods industries to purchase the output of producer goods in the surplus circuit. See flows on the perimeter of Figure 1.

16   Lonergan, *op. cit.*, 1982 typescript, p. 58.

17   Ibid., p. 7.

18   Lester C. Thurow, *Dangerous Currents—The State of Economics* (New York: Random House, 1983) p. 235.

19   See, for example, the conclusion in Garry J. Schinasi, "A Nonlinear Dynamic Model of Short Run Fluctuations", *Review of Economic Studies* XLVIII, (1981) pp. 649–656.

20   William H. Branson, *Macroeconomic Theory and Policy* (New York: Harper & Row, 1972).

21 · Joseph A. Schumpeter, *The Theory of Economic Development* (New York: Oxford University Press, 1961) p. 66.

22   Lonergan, *op. cit.* (1944 typescript).

23   In the pure cycle as in equilibrium growth analysis, saving will equal investment.

24   Branson, *op. cit.*, p. 395.

25   J. J. van Duijn, *The Long Wave in Economic Life* (London: George Allen & Unwin Ltd., 1983).

26   N. Kaldor and J. A. Mirrlees, "A New Model of Economic Growth", in F. H. Hahn ed., *Readings in the Theory of Growth*, (London: MacMillan, 1971) p. 406.

27   Turnover magnitude is the volume of production in a period. A turnover period is the time it takes to produce a good, taking into consideration the goods that are joint in production.

28   Cf. J. E. Meade, "The Adjustment of Savings to Investment in a Growing Economy", in Hahn, *op. cit.*, p. 203.

29   Kalecki, *op. cit.*, p. 129.

30   Lonergan, *op. cit.*, 1982 typescript, p. 78.

31   Using the framework mentioned in van Duijn, *op. cit.*, p. 6.

32   Harry G. Johnson, "The Two-Sector Model of General Equilibrium", Yrjo Jahnsson Lectures, (London: George Allen & Unwin, 1971).

33   For further discussion of these views see Eileen de Neeve, *Economic Growth and Investment Cycles in Eastern European Socialist Economies*, (Unpublished M.A. Thesis, Concordia University, Montreal, 1979); and Herman E. Daly, ed., *Economics, Ecology, Ethics, — Essays Toward a Steady-State Economy* (San Francisco: W.H. Freeman and Company, 1973).

34   Trade cycles, business cycles, investment cycles, or Kondratieff cycles or long waves.

List of Contributors

Patrick E. Byrne, Associate Professor of Philosophy at Boston College, Chestnut Hill, Massachusetts

Walter E. Conn, Associate Professor of Religious Ethics at Villanova University, Villanova, Pennsylvania

Frederick E. Crowe, S.J., Professor Emeritus at Regis College, Toronto, Ontario

Eileen de Neeve, Vice-President, Thomas More Institute for Research in Adult Liberal Studies, Montreal; formerly research economist with the C. D. Howe Institute for Economic Policy Analysis

Tad Dunne, S.J., Director of Novices for the Detroit and Chicago Provinces of the Society of Jesus and formerly Assistant Professor of Systematic Theology at Regis College, Toronto

Michael Gibbons, Professor of Interdisciplinary Studies, Department of Liberal Studies in Science at the University of Manchester, Manchester, England

Stephen Happel, Associate Professor of Hermeneutics and Culture, Department of Religion and Religious Education, School of Religious Studies at the Catholic University of America, Washington, D.C.

Charles C. Hefling, Assistant Professor of Theology at Boston College, Chestnut Hill, Massachusetts

Thomas E. Hosinski, C.S.C., Assistant Professor of Theology at the University of Portland, Portland, Oregon

William Johnston, S.J., Professor of Theology at the Jesuit Scholasticate, Tokyo, Japan; formerly Professor of Religious Studies at Sophia University, Japan

William P. Loewe, Associate Professor of Theology, Department of Religion and Religious Education, School of Religious Studies at the Catholic University of America, Washington, D.C.

William Matthews, S.J., Professor of Philosophy and Dean at Milltown Institute of Philosophy and Theology, Dublin, Ireland

Sean McEvenue, Associate Professor of Theological Studies at Concordia University, Montreal, Quebec

Thomas J. McPartland, Lecturer of History at Bellevue Community College, Washington and at the University of Washington, Seattle, Washington

Kenneth Melchin, Assistant Professor of Theology at Saint Paul University/Université Saint-Paul, Ottawa, Ontario

Sebastian Moore, a monk of Downside Abbey in England, currently in Campus Ministry and the Theology Department at Boston College, Chestnut Hill, Massachusetts

Elizabeth Morelli, Lecturer in Philosophy at Loyola Marymount University, Los Angeles, California

Michael O'Callaghan, Associate Professor of Religious Studies at Marist College, Poughkeepsie, New York

Geoffrey Price, Lecturer in Liberal Studies in Science at the University of Manchester, Manchester, England

James R. Price, Associate Professor of Theology, Department of Religion and Religious Education, School of Religious Studies at the Catholic University of America, Washington, D.C.

Quentin Quesnell, Professor of Religion and Biblical Literature at Smith College, Northampton, Massachusetts

William F. Ryan, S.J., Associate Professor of Philosophy at Gonzaga University, Spokane, Washington

Stephen Toulmin, Professor in the Committee on Social Thought at the University of Chicago, Chicago, Illinois

Michael Vertin, Associate Professor of Philosophy and Religious Studies at St. Michael's College, University of Toronto, Toronto, Ontario

Index